THE

AFRICAN SLAVE TRADE

AND

ITS REMEDY

BUXTON, Thomas Fowell. **The African Slave Trade and Its Remedy.**
2nd ed. Cass (dist. by Barnes & Noble), 1968 (orig. pub. by Murray,
1840). 582p map (Cass Library of African Studies/Slavery Series,
1) 68-90658. 14.50
A double volume (the first part was originally printed in 1839) that generated widespread controversy when it was published. Part I is a compi-
lation of information on the slave trade zealously amassed by Buxton
and his associates. The British public was appalled to learn that slaving
was flourishing as never before. Part II is addressed to "the remedy."
Buxton advocated anti-slave trade treaties with African rulers and renewed naval efforts to suppress the Atlantic traffic combined with encouragement of African agriculture and legitimate commerce. ("The
desert shall rejoice and blossom as the rose" reads the prefatory in-
scription.) Buxton was the prime mover behind an ambitious expedition dispatched in 1841 to found a "model farm" at the juncture of
the Niger and Benue rivers, a project that had to be aborted after
disease exacted a heavy toll among the Europeans who participated.
Index; six appendices. Buxton's work remains a valuable source for the
slave trade and a starting point for new research. With the renewal of
interest in the slave trade in recent years this reprint will find many
readers.

CHOICE   *DEC. '68*

History, Geography &
Travel

Africa

CASS LIBRARY OF AFRICAN STUDIES

SLAVERY SERIES

No. 1

General Editor: DUNCAN RICE
Department of History, University of Aberdeen

THE
AFRICAN SLAVE TRADE
AND
ITS REMEDY

THOMAS FOWELL BUXTON

FRANK CASS & CO. LTD.
1967

Published by
FRANK CASS AND COMPANY LIMITED
67 Great Russell Street, London WC1

First edition	1839
Second edition	1840
New impression	1967

210446

Printed in Great Britain by
Stephen Austin and Sons Ltd., Hertford.

PROSPECTUS

OF THE

SOCIETY FOR THE EXTINCTION OF THE SLAVE TRADE

AND FOR THE

CIVILIZATION OF AFRICA,

INSTITUTED JUNE, 1839.

IN the year 1807, Great Britain prohibited all her subjects from engaging in the Slave Trade, and the Legislature of this country, in accordance with the voice of the people, repudiated a commerce which had produced more crime and misery, than perhaps any other single course of guilt and iniquity ; but neither the Government nor the Legislature, nor the subjects of this realm, were satisfied with a mere cessation from crime.

Remembering how deeply, in times of comparative ignorance, we had sustained and augmented this trade, so repugnant to every Christian principle and feeling, the nation determined to use its utmost influence, and expend its resources, in the noble attempt to extinguish it for ever.

The compass of this address will not allow even of the most compendious statement of the measures resorted to, of the treaties concluded with foreign powers, of the monies expended, and the various other efforts made to effect this object; suffice it to say, that since the year 1807, all the great powers of Europe have been induced by Great Britain to unite in expressing their abhorrence of this traffic; and with all, treaties more or less stringent have been made for its extinction.

The United States of America, though from political reasons they have declined any actual co-operation, have not the less denounced and prohibited all traffic in Slaves from Africa. Great Britain has expended, in bounties alone, upwards of £940,000, and in the maintenance of the courts established for the adjudication of captured slaves, above £330,000 : besides a very large sum annually in supporting a considerable force of cruizers in various parts of the globe, to intercept and destroy the traffic.* An infinitely more important sacrifice has been made in the loss of British life, which has been necessarily incurred in pursuing this object. The result, the melancholy result, remains to be stated. The traffic has not been extinguished, has ot been diminished, but, by the latest accounts from which any estimate can be correctly formed, the numbers exported have increased —the destruction of human life, and all the guilt and misery consequent thereon, have been fearfully aug-

* This Expenditure, together with that caused by the payments to foreign powers on account of the Slave Trade, for the support of liberated Africans, and for other incidental expenses, may be shown, from official documents, to have amounted to upwards of fifteen millions sterling.

mented; and at the same time it may be stated, that
the numbers exported from Africa, are, as compared
with the year 1807, as two to one, and that the annual
loss of life has risen from seventeen to twenty-five
per cent.

Let no man, however, say that these efforts have
been thrown away. Who can tell how fearful might
not have been the amount of enormity, if those exertions had not been made? Who would presume to
say that the very assertion of the great principles of
justice and truth has not accelerated the final extir-
pation of those detested practices? Who would
venture to assert that a criminal inaction on the part
of Great Britain might not have caused an indefinite
continuance of the guilt on the part of other nations?

But the people of England have not succeeded to
the extent of their wishes:—Assuming it to be so,
what remains to be done?—but led on by the same
Christian principles, the same devotion to truth,
justice, and humanity, to continue our efforts, and to
apply, if possible, other and more efficient remedies
in accordance with these great principles.

Animated by these feelings, a number of noblemen
and gentlemen of all political opinions, and of
Christian persuasions of divers kinds, have formed
themselves into a Society for the purpose of effecting
the extinction of the Slave Trade; and they now call
on the public to unite their exertions for the accomplishment of this great end.

That the British public, apprized of the extent of

the enormity, and deeply feeling the guilt and misery now prevailing, will receive with favour the announcement of the formation of this Society, no doubt is entertained; but various opinions do and will exist as to the most fitting means to be adopted for the establishment of peace and tranquillity in Africa.

It is expedient, therefore, to state the leading principles on which this Society is formed, and the measures intended to be pursued.

It is the unanimous opinion of this Society, that the only complete cure of all these evils, is the introduction of Christianity into Africa. They do not believe that any less powerful remedy will entirely extinguish the present inducements to trade in human beings, or will afford to the inhabitants of those extensive regions a sure foundation for repose and happiness.

But they are aware that a great variety of views may exist as to the manner in which religious instruction should be introduced. Distinctly avowing, therefore, that the substitution of our pure and holy faith for the false religion, idolatry and superstitions of Africa, is, in their firm conviction, the true ultimate remedy for the calamities that afflict her, they are most anxious to adopt every measure which may eventually lead to the establishment of Christianity throughout that Continent; and hoping to secure the cordial co-operation of all, they proceed to declare that the grand object of their association is—the extinction of the Slave Trade.

The primary object of this Society will be constantly kept in view under all circumstances of difficulty or discouragement, as the grand end to which their efforts, of whatever character, should be resolutely and unchangeably directed.

As one of the principal means, they have cordially co-operated with Mr. Buxton in inducing Her Majesty's Government to undertake an expedition to the river Niger, with the view of obtaining the most accurate information as to the state of the countries bordering on its mighty waters.

The immense importance of this object alone, as opening a highway into the interior of Africa, and bringing the efforts of British philanthropy into immediate contact with the numerous and populous nations it contains, will be at once perceived and acknowledged.

It will be one of the first duties then of this Society to watch over the proceedings of this expedition, to record its progress, and to digest and circulate the valuable information which it may be confidently expected to communicate.

When this leading step has been taken, it is anticipated that a large field for exertions of a different description will then be opened; but desirable as such exertions may be, it must be clearly understood that this Society, associated solely for benevolent purposes, can bear no part whatever in them: still, in order that a comprehensive view may be taken of the whole, though each part must be accomplished by agencies entirely distinct, it may be expedient to state some of the expectations which are entertained.

One most important department must entirely rest with Her Majesty's Government,—the formation of Treaties with the native rulers of Africa for the suppression of the Slave Trade. Such Treaties, however, will not be carried into execution, unless those wants which have hitherto been supplied from the profits arising from the sale of the natives, should be satisfied through the means of legitimate commerce. It may appear expedient to the Government to obtain from the Chiefs the possession of some convenient districts which may be best adapted to carrying on trade with safety and success, and when this is effected, another and wholly distinct Society may perhaps be formed, for the purpose of aiding in the cultivation of those districts, and of promoting the growth of those valuable products for which the soil of those Countries is peculiarly fitted.

The present Society can take part in no plan of Colonization or of Trade. Its objects are, and must be, exclusively pacific and benevolent; but it may by encouragement, and by the diffusion of information, most materially aid in the civilization of Africa, and so pave the way for the successful exertions of others, whether they be directed to colonization and the cultivation of the soil or to commercial intercourse, or to that which is immeasurably superior to them all, the establishment of the Christian faith on the Continent of Africa.

At home this Society will direct its vigilant attention to all which may arise with respect to the traffic in Slaves, and give publicity to whatever may be deemed most essential to produce its suppression.

In Africa there are various means whereby it may effectually work to the same end. One of the great impediments at present existing to the advancement of knowledge, is the state of the native languages of Western and Central Africa.

Amongst the many nations which inhabit those regions, there are certainly many different dialects, and not improbably several leading languages. A few only of those languages have yet been reduced into writing, and consequently the difficulty of holding intercourse with the natives and imparting knowledge to them is greatly increased. By the adoption of effectual measures for reducing the principal languages of Western and Central Africa into writing, a great obstacle to the diffusion of information will be removed, and facility afforded for the introduction of the truths of Christianity.

There is another subject of no light importance which would legitimately fall within the views of this Institution. In Africa, medical science can scarcely be said to exist, yet in no part of the world is it more profoundly respected. As at present understood by the natives, it is intimately connected with the most inveterate and barbarous superstitions; and its artful practitioners, owing their superiority to this popular ignorance, may be expected to interpose the most powerful obstacles to the diffusion of Christianity and of science.

To encourage therefore the introduction of more enlightened views on this subject;—to prevent or mitigate the prevalence of disease and suffering among the people of Africa,—and to secure the aid of medical science generally to the beneficent objects of African civilization, must be considered of immense importance; nor would its benefits be confined to the native population. It is equally applicable to the investigation of the climate and localities of that Country. To render Africa a salubrious residence for European constitutions may be a hopeless task; but to diminish the danger, to point out the means whereby persons proceeding thither may most effectually guard against its perils, may perhaps be effected; nor must it be forgotten that in however humble a degree this advantage can be attained, its value cannot be too highly appreciated.

Various other measures may come within the legitimate scope of this Institution. It may be sufficient to recapitulate a few;—the encouragement of practical science in all its various branches,—the system of drainage best calculated to success in a climate so humid and so hot, would be an invaluable boon to all who frequent that great Continent, whatever might be their purpose. Though this Society would not embark in agriculture, it might afford essential assistance to the natives, by furnishing them with useful information as to the best mode of cultivation; as to the productions which command a steady market, and by introducing the most approved agricultural implements and seeds. The time may come when the knowledge and practice of the mighty powers of steam might contribute rapidly to promote the improvement and prosperity of that Country.

Even matters of comparatively less moment may engage the attention of the Society. It may assist in promoting the formation of Roads and Canals. The manufacture of Paper, and the use of the Printing Press, if once established in Africa, will be amongst the most powerful auxiliaries in the dispersion of ignorance, and the destruction of barbarism.

It is hoped that enough has now been stated to justify the Society in calling for the aid and co-operation of all who hold in just abhorrence the iniquitous traffic in human beings—of all who deeply deplore the awful crimes which have so long afflicted, and still continue to devastate Africa—of all who remember with deep sorrow and contrition that share which Great Britain so long continued to have, in producing those scenes of bloodshed and of guilt. A variety of collateral means has thus been suggested sufficiently important and interesting to demonstrate the necessity of a distinct Society, and to entitle it to the best wishes and firmest support of every sincere friend of Africa.

To its success, cordial and united co-operation is indispensable. It proposes to act by means in which the whole community, without regard to religious or political opinions, may concur; and though it does not embrace the establishment by its own agency of schools for the spread of Religious Instruction, it abstains from such an undertaking, not because it does not value the introduction of Christian knowledge as the greatest blessing which can be bestowed on that idolatrous land, but because a diversity of opinion as to the mode of proceeding, must of necessity interfere with the unity of action so essential for the common prosecution of such an important object, and thus impede instead of facilitate the objects of this Institution.

It is impossible, however, to close this address without again expressing, in the most emphatic terms, the conviction and earnest hope of all who have already attached themselves as members of this Institution, that the measures to be adopted by them for the suppression of the traffic in Slaves—for securing the peace and tranquillity of Africa—for the encouragement of agriculture and commerce, will facilitate the propagation and triumph of that faith which one and all feel to be indispensable for the happiness of the inhabitants of that Continent. Howsoever the extension of the Christian religion may be attempted, it is far more likely to take root and flourish where peace prevails, and crime is diminished, than where murder and bloodshed, and the violation of every righteous principle, continue to pollute the land.

OFFICE OF THE SOCIETY,
15, Parliament Street,
14th *February*, 1840.

THE PROVISIONAL COMMITTEE.

Chairman.

THOMAS FOWELL BUXTON, ESQ.

Deputy Chairmen.

The Right Hon. STEPHEN LUSHINGTON, D.C.L. M. P.

Sir ROBERT HARRY INGLIS, BART., M. P.

The Earl of Euston, M. P.
The Earl of Chichester
The Lord Charles Fitz Roy, M. P.
The Lord Nugent.
The Lord Viscount Sandon, M. P.
The Lord Ashley, M. P.
The Lord Eliot, M. P.
The Lord Worsley, M. P.
The Lord Bishop of London.
The Lord Calthorpe.
The Lord Seaford.
The Lord Wharncliffe.
The Lord Teignmouth, M. P.
The Hon. C. P. Villiers, M. P.
The Hon. F. G. Calthorpe.
The Right Hon. T. B. Macaulay, M. P.

Sir Thomas Dyke Acland, Bart., M. P.

Sir George Stephen.

Thomas Dyke Acland, Esq., M. P.

William Allen, Esq.

Captain W. Allen, R. N.

Captain Bird Allen, R. N.

George Babington, Esq.

Edward Baines, Esq., M. P.

John J. Briscoe, Esq., M. P.

E. N. Buxton, Esq.

Edmund Buxton, Esq.

Robert Barclay, Jun., Esq.

Jos. Gurney Barclay, Esq.

Arthur Kett Barclay, Esq.

Jos. Beldam, Esq.

John Bandinel, Esq.

The Rev. Dr. Bunting.

The Rev. John Beecham.

Frederick Bell, Esq.

James Bell, Esq.

Captain Bosanquet, R. N.

William Brackenbury, Esq.

James Cook, Esq.

Captain Cook.

Emanuel Cooper, Esq.

Dandeson Coates, Esq.

William Ewart, Esq,. M. P.

William Evans, Esq., M. P.

William Storrs Fry, Esq.

J. Gurney Fry, Esq.

W. E. Forster, Esq.

H. Goulburn, Jun., Esq.

Charles Grant, Esq.

Dr. Gregory.

Samuel Gurney, Esq.

Samuel Gurney, Jun., Esq.

John Henry Gurney, Esq.

Samuel Hoare, Esq.

John Gurney Hoare, Esq.

William Hamilton, Esq.

The Rev. R. E. Hankinson, Jun.

Benjamin Hawes, Jun., Esq., M. P.

Dr. Hodgkin.

John Irving, Esq., M. P.

Andrew Johnston, Esq.

Captain Kelly, R. N.

J. J. Lister, Esq.

L. C. Lecesne, Esq.

Charles Lushington, Esq., M. P.

James M'Queen, Esq.

Richard Matthews, Esq.

The Hon. Captain Maude, R. N.

Colonel Nicholls.

Robert Pryor, Esq.

C. L. Phillips, Esq.

G. R. Porter, Esq.

W. Foster Reynolds, Esq.

William Rothery, Esq.

Thomas Sturge, Esq.

W. C. Stretfield, Esq.

Benjamin Smith, Esq., M. P.

William Taylor, Esq.

Colonel Torrens.

Captain Trotter, R. N.

H. R. Upcher, Esq.

Captain Washington, R. N.

Henry Waymouth, Esq.

Treasurer.

J. GURNEY HOARE, ESQ.

Secretary.

The REV. J. M. TREW.

Receiving Bankers :—Messrs. BARNETTS, HOARE, and Co., 62, Lombard-street ; Messrs. BARCLAY, BEVAN, and Co., 54, Lombard-street ; Messrs. COUTTS and Co., 59, Strand ; Messrs. DRUMMONDS, Charing-cross ; Messrs. HANBURY, TAYLOR, and Co., 60, Lombard-street ; Messrs. HANKEYS, 7, Fenchurch-street ; Messrs. HOARES, 37, Fleet-street ; Messrs. WILLIAMS, DEACON, and Co., 20, Birchin-lane.

THE

AFRICAN SLAVE TRADE

AND

ITS REMEDY.

BY

THOMAS FOWELL BUXTON, Esq.

" This is a people robbed and spoiled; they are all of them snared in holes, and they are hid in prison houses; th ey are for a prey, and none delivereth; for a spoil, and none saith, Restore."—*Isaiah*, xiii. 21.

" The desert shall rejoice and blossom as the rose."—*Isaiah*, xxxv. 1.

LONDON:
JOHN MURRAY, ALBEMARLE-STREET.

MDCCCXL.

ADVERTISEMENT

TO THE

PRESENT EDITION.

THE first part of this work, delineating the extent and the horrors of the African Slave Trade, was published early in 1839; it was then my intention to add the other part, containing " The Remedy" in the form of a second volume, but for reasons not necessary to detail, I found myself obliged to defer its publication for a longer period than I had at first proposed. Meanwhile, fresh sources of information opened themselves to me, and I have thus been furnished with so much new matter, that I have found it necessary (another edition being also required) to republish the first volume in its present shape.

Those even who have fully possessed themselves of the case as it then stood will not I hope refuse it some further examination now; I have added to every part the results of the most recent information; have, in some respects, revised and perfected the calculations, and have subjoined a chapter on a topic which strictly belongs to the State of Africa, and is in every sense closely allied to the Slave Trade,—the Superstitions and Cruelties existing in that country. A " Remedy" is almost as urgently demanded for these as for the Traffic itself. This Remedy, as it presents itself to my mind, is unfolded in Part II. of this volume.

I have judged it expedient, in order to condense into one view all the facts appertaining to this part of my subject, to incorporate the substance of the chapter, entitled " Commercial Intercourse with Africa," into this latter portion of the work, and I submit my views to the consideration and correction of all who are interested in the cause, with the trust that, if accepted in Theory, they will obtain a cordial and persevering co-operation in Practice.

CONTENTS.

PART I.

THE SLAVE TRADE.

PART II.

THE REMEDY.

PART I.

THE SLAVE TRADE.

" This is a people robbed and spoiled ; they are all of them snared in holes, and they are hid in prison houses; they are for a prey, and none delivereth ; for a spoil, and none saith, Restore."— *Isaiah*, xiii. 21.

INTRODUCTION.

TO THE

SECOND EDITION.

No one possessing any knowledge of, or anxiety on the subject of the Negro race can fail to deplore the present state of Africa.

Desirous to ascertain why it is that all our gigantic efforts and costly sacrifices for the suppression of the Slave Trade have proved unavailing, I have employed some leisure time in surveying this whole subject, and in tracing out, as far as I have been able, the true cause of our failure. My original impression was, that, in increased efforts at sea, and in reducing Portugal to the necessity of executing her engagements with us, the effective remedy was to be found, and that little more than these would be required for the gratification of the ardent desire felt by the British nation for the abolition of the Slave Trade. But a closer scrutiny into the facts of the case has conducted me to a different conclusion.

There are, I now think, reasonable grounds for believing, that we should still be disappointed, although we were to double our naval force engaged in that branch of service, and although it were resolved to take the most peremptory measures with Portugal.

I do not underrate the value of our maritime exertions. I think it may be good policy, and, in the long run, true economy, to multiply the number of our vessels, to do at once and by a blow, all that can be done in this way; to increase our expenses for a few years, in order to escape the necessity of incurring cost, not materially less, for an indefinite period. Neither do I wish that our government should address Portugal in any terms short of a declaration that our cruisers will have orders to seize, after a fixed and an early day, every vessel under Portuguese colours engaged in the slave traffic, to bring the crew to trial as pirates, and inflict upon them the severest secondary punishment which our law allows. Decisive measures of this kind would, there is no doubt, facilitate our success, by removing some of the great impediments which stand in the way of other remedial measures; nevertheless, I am compelled, by the various evidence which it has been my province to examine, to place my main reliance, not on the employment of force, but on the encouragement which we may be able to give to the legitimate commerce and the agricultural cultivation of Africa.

We attempt to put down the Slave Trade " by the

strong hand" alone; and this is, I apprehend, the
cause of our failure. Our system, in many respects
too feeble, is, in one sense, too bold. The African
has acquired a taste for the productions of the civilized world. They have become essential to him.
The parent—debased and brutalised as he is—bar-
ters his child; the chief his subject; each individual
looks with an evil eye on his neighbour, and lays
snares to catch him,—because the sale of children,
subjects, and neighbours, is the only means as yet
afforded, by European commerce, for the supply of
those wants which that commerce has created. To
say that the African, under present circumstances,
shall not deal in man, is to say that he shall long in
vain for his accustomed gratifications. The tide, thus
pent up, will break its way over every barrier. In
order effectually to divert the stream from the direction which it has hitherto taken, we must open
another, a safer, and a more convenient channel.
When we shall have experimentally convinced the
African, that it is in his power to obtain his supplies, in more than their usual abundance, by honest
means, then, and not till then, we may expect that
he will be reconciled to the Abolition of the Slave
Trade.

To a description of the extent and horrors of the
Slave Trade, the failure of our efforts for its suppression, and an account of African superstitions and
cruelties, I have added some practical suggestions for

calling forth the latent energies of that quarter of the globe, and for exhibiting to its inhabitants where their true interest lies.

The principles of my suggestions are comprised in the following propositions :—

1. That the present staple export of Africa renders to her inhabitants, at infinite cost, a miserable return of profit.

2. That the cultivation of her soil, and the barter of its productions, would yield an abundant harvest, and a copious supply of those articles which Africa requires.

3. That it is practicable to convince the African, experimentally, of the truth of these propositions, and thus to make him our confederate in the suppression of the Slave Trade.

I despair of being able to put down a traffic, in which a vast continent is engaged, by the few ships we can afford to employ: as auxiliaries they are of great value, but alone they are insufficient. I do not dream of attempting to persuade the African, by appealing merely to his reason or his conscience, to renounce gainful guilt, and to forego those inhuman pursuits which gratify his cupidity, and supply his wants. But when the appeal we make is to his interest, and when his passions are enlisted on our side, there is nothing chimerical in the hope that he may be brought to exchange slender profits, with danger, for abundant gain, with security and peace.

If these views can be carried into effect, they have at least thus much to recommend them.

They will not plunge this country into hostility with any portion of the civilized world ; for they involve no violation of international law. We may cultivate intercourse and innocent commerce with the natives of Africa, without abridging the rights or damaging the honest interests of any rival power.

They require no monopoly of trade ; if other nations choose to send their merchantmen to carry on legitimate traffic in Africa, they will but advance our object, and lend their aid in extinguishing that which we are resolved to put down.

They involve no schemes of conquest ; our ambition is of another order. Africa is now torn to pieces. She is the victim of the most iron despotism that the world ever saw : inveterate cruelty reigns over her broad territory. We desire to usurp nothing,—and to conquer nothing,—but the Slave Trade.

Finally, we ask of the Government only that which subjects have a right to expect from their rulers, namely, *protection to person and property* in their lawful pursuits.

Here I must pause ; for I feel bound to confess, much as it may tend to shake the whole fabric of my views, that there is a great danger to which we shall be exposed, unless it be most carefully guarded against at the outset : the discovery of the fact that man as a labourer on the soil, is superior in value to man as an article of merchandise, may induce the continuance, if not the increase, of that internal slavery which now exists in Africa.

I hope we shall never be so deluded as to give the slightest toleration to anything like constrained labour. We must not put down one iniquity by abetting another. I believe implicitly that free labour will beat all other labour; that slavery, besides being a great crime, is a gross blunder; and that the most refined and sagacious policy we can pursue is, common honesty and undeviating justice. Let it then be held as a most sacred principle, that, wherever our authority prevails, slavery shall cease; and that whatever influence we may obtain shall be employed in the same direction.

I have thus noticed several of the negative advantages which attach to these views, and I have frankly stated the danger which, as I conceive, attends them. I shall now briefly allude to one point, which, I own, weighs with me beyond all the other considerations, mighty as they are, which this great question involves.

Grievous, and this almost beyond expression, as are the physical evils endured by Africa, there is yet a more lamentable feature in her present condition. Bound in the chains of the grossest ignorance, she is a prey to the most savage superstition. Christianity has made but feeble inroads on this kingdom of darkness, nor can she hope to gain an entrance where the traffic in man pre-occupies the ground. But, were this obstacle removed, Africa would present the finest field for the labours of Christian missionaries which the world has yet seen opened to them. I have no hesitation in stating my belief, that there is in the negro race a capacity for receiving the truths of the Gospel beyond most other heathen nations; while, on the other hand, there is this remarkable, if not unique, circumstance in their case—that a race of teachers of their own blood is already in course of rapid preparation for them; that the providence of God has overruled even slavery and the Slave Trade for this end; and that from among the settlers of Sierra Leone, the peasantry of the West Indies, and the thousands of their children now receiving Christian education., may be expected to arise a body of men who will return to the land of their fathers, carrying Divine truth and all its concomitant blessings into the heart of Africa.

One noble sacrifice in behalf of the negro race has already been made. In the words of the most eloquent citizen of another nation—" Great Britain, loaded with an unprecedented debt, and with a grinding taxation, contracted a new debt of a hundred million dollars, to give freedom, not to Englishmen, but to the degraded African. I know not that history records an act so disinterested, so sublime. In the progress of ages England's naval triumphs will shrink into a more and more narrow space in the records of our race. This moral triumph will fill a broader, brighter page."*

Another, it may be a more inveterate evil, remains, —an evil which for magnitude and malignity stands without a parallel. One thousand human victims† (if my facts will bear sifting) are daily required to feed this vast and devouring consumer of mankind. In vain has Nature given to Africa noble rivers; man is the only merchandise they carry. In vain a fertile land, lavish in wild and spontaneous productions,—no cultivating hand calls forth its riches. In vain has she placed it in the vicinity of civilisation and Christianity; within a few weeks' voyage of the Thames there is a people who worship the shark and the snake, and a prince who imagines the agency of an evil spirit in the common properties of the loadstone.‡ Africa is, indeed, encircled by an effectual barrier against the entrance of commerce, cultivation, and Christianity. That barrier is the Slave Trade.

It may be thought wild extravagance to indulge the hope that evils so rank are capable of cure. I do not deny that it is, of all tasks, the most arduous, or that it will require the whole energy of Great Britain; but if it shall be made a capital object of British policy, for the accomplishment of which our whole strength, if necessary, shall be put forward, and if it shall be, as I am sure it is, a cause in which we may look for Divine countenance and help, I see

* Dr. Channing.   † See page 220.
‡ Laird, vol. i. p. 219.

no reason for despair. What has been done, may be done again; and it is matter of history, that from superstitions as bloody, from a state of intellect as rude, and from the Slave Trade itself, a nation has been reclaimed, and now enjoys, in comparison with Africa, a blaze of light, liberty, religion, and happiness. That nation is Great Britain. What we find the African, the Romans found us;* and it is not unreasonable to hope that, in the language of Mr. Pitt, " even Africa will enjoy, at length, in the evening of

* By the concurrent testimony of the best ancient historians, our forefathers were nothing better than " painted savages," the votaries of a sanguinary superstition which consumed its hecatombs of human victims: " Alii immani magnitudine simulacra habent; quorum ' contexta viminibus membra vivis hominibus complent; quibus succensis, circumventi flammâ exanimantur homines." (Cæsar, Bell. Gall., l. vi. c. 16.) And, if we may credit the testimony of Diodorus Siculus, they were also addicted to cannibalism; " for," says he, " the Gauls are such savages that they devour human flesh; as do also those British nations which inhabit Ireland." (l. v. c. 32.) Cicero, in one of his letters, speaking of the success of an expedition against Britain, says, the only plunder to be found, consisted " ex mancipiis: ex quibus nullos puto te literis aut musicis eruditos expectare;" thus, in the same sentence, proving the existence of the Slave Trade, and intimating that it was impossible that any Briton should be intelligent enough to be worthy to serve the accomplished Atticus. Ad Att. l. iv. 16. Henry, in his History of England, gives us also the authority of Strabo for the prevalence of the Slave Trade amongst us, and tells us that slaves were once an established article of our exports. " Great numbers," says he, " were exported from Britain, and were to be seen exposed for sale, like cattle, in the Roman market."—Henry, vol. ii. p. 225.

her days, those blessings which have descended so
plentifully upon us in a much earlier period of the
world."

To raise Africa from the dust is an object worthy
of the efforts of the highest order of ambition. It is
calculated that Napoleon, in the course of his career,
occasioned the sacrifice of three millions of the
human race. The suppression of the Slave Trade
would, in a very few years, save as many lives as he
was permitted to destroy. The most patriotic and
loyal amongst us cannot frame a loftier wish for
our country and its sovereign, than that her reign,
which, in its dawn, witnessed the deliverance of our
colonies from slavery, may be prolonged, till, through
British agency, Africa shall also be released from a
still greater curse :—not, however, for the honour's
sake, though it would give imperishable renown;
nor for the profit's sake, though it promises to open
boundless fields for capital, industry, and enterprise;
but in pity to Africa, and for His favour who has
said—" Undo the heavy burdens, let the oppressed
go free, and break every yoke." " Then shall thy
light break forth as the morning;" " and the glory
of the Lord shall be thy rereward."*

* Isaiah lviii. 6, 8.

THE SLAVE TRADE.

"You will perceive that this horrid traffic has been carried on to an extent that almost staggers belief."

Commodore Sir Robert Mends, Sierra Leone.

In preparing this work, my chief purpose has been to offer some views which I entertain of the most effectual mode of suppressing the Slave Trade; but before I enter upon these, I must state the extent to which that traffic is now carried on, and the sacrifice of human life which it occasions.

EXTENT.

My *first* proposition is, that upwards of 150,000 human beings are annually conveyed from Africa, across the Atlantic, and sold as slaves.

It is almost impossible to arrive at the exact extent to which any contraband trade, much more a trade so revolting, is carried on. It is the interest of those concerned in it to conceal all evidence of their guilt; and the Governor of a Portuguese colony is not very likely, at once to connive at the crime, and to confess that it is extensively practised. By the mode of calculation I propose to adopt, it is very possible I may err; but the error must be on the right side; I may underrate, it is almost impossible

that I can exaggerate, the extent of the traffic.
With every disposition on the part of those who are
engaged in it to veil the truth, certain facts have,
from time to time, transpired, sufficient to show, if
not the full amount of the evil, at least that it is one
of prodigious magnitude.

I commence with what appears to be the most
considerable slave market, viz.—that of

BRAZIL.

In the papers on the subject of the Slave Trade
annually presented to Parliament by royal authority,
(and entitled " Class A" and " Class B"), the following official information is given by the British
Vice-Consul at Rio de Janeiro, as to the number of
slaves imported there :—

From 1 July to 31 Dec. 1827 . . .	15,481*
From 1 Jan. to 31 March, 1828 . . .	15,483†
From 1 April to 30 June, 1828, say . .	11,532‡
From 1 July to 31 Dec. 1828 . . .	24,488§
From 1 Jan. to 30 June, 1829 . . .	25,179‖
From 1 July to 31 Dec. 1829 . . .	22,813¶
From 1 Jan. to 30 June, 1830 . . .	33,964**
	148,940

* Class B, 1828, p. 105.   † Class B, 1828, p. 107.
  ‡ No returns.   These numbers are given on the average of the
three months previous to, and three months subsequent to, the
dates here mentioned.
  § Class B, 1829, pp. 80, 81.   ‖ Class B, 1829, p. 89.
  ¶ Ditto, 1830, p. 71.   ** Ditto, 1830, p. 78.

That is, in the twelve months

preceding the 30th June,	1828	.	.	.	42,496
,,	,,	1829	.	.	.	49,667
,,	,,	1830	.	.	.	56,777

148,940

Thus it stands confessed, upon authority which cannot be disputed, that from the 1st of July, 1827, to the 30th of June, 1830 (three years), there were brought into the single port of Rio de Janeiro, 148,940 negroes, or, an average of 49,643 annually. It appears also, that, in the last year, the number was swelled to 56,777 per annum.*

Caldcleugh, in his Travels in South America, speaking of the Slave Trade at Rio, (which, however, was not then so extensive as it now is,) states, " that there are *three* other ports in Brazil trading *to the same extent.*"† If this be correct, the number of negroes annually imported vastly exceeds any estimate I have formed; but it is more safe to rely on the authority of the British Commissioners,‡ scanty as

---

* I see in the *Patriot* newspaper of 25th June last (1838), the following statement:—" A Brazil mail has brought advices from Rio to the 22nd April. That fine country appears ˌto be making rapid strides in civilization and improvement; the only drawback is the inveterate and continued encouragement of the slave-trade. The Rover corvette had just captured two slavers, having 494 negroes on board ; and the traffic is said to amount to 60,000 annually, into Rio alone, almost entirely carried on under Portuguese colours.

† Caldcleugh's Travels, London, 1825, vol. ii. p. 56.

‡ By the treaties with foreign powers for the suppression of the

it necessarily is. They reside in the capital; and
their distance from the three outports of itself might
render it difficult for them to obtain full information.
But when to the distance is added the still greater
difficulty arising from the anxiety on the part of
almost all the Brazilian functionaries to suppress
information on the subject, it is clearly to be inferred that the number stated by the Commissioners
must fall materially below the truth. They tell us,
however, that in a year and a half, from 1st of
January, 1829, to 30th of June, 1830, the numbers
imported were, into

Bahia	22,202
Pernambuco	8,079
Maranham	1,252
	31,533
To these we must also add those imported into the port of Para .	799
Total in eighteen months . .	32,332*
Or annually	21,554
To which add Rio, as before stated†	56,777
And we have for the annual number landed in Brazil . . .	78,331

Slave Trade, Commissioners are appointed to act as Judges, in a
Court of Mixed Commission, for the adjudication of captured
slave-vessels.

So many, *at least*, were landed. That number is undisputed. The amount, however, great as it is, probably falls short of the reality. If the question were put to me, what is the number which I believe to be annually landed in Brazil, I should rate it considerably higher. I conceive that the truth lies between the maximum as taken from Caldcleugh, and the minimum as stated in the Official Returns ; and I should conjecture that the real amount would be moderately rated at 100,000, brought annually into these five Brazilian ports. But as the question is, not how many I suppose, but how many I can show to be landed, I must confine myself to what I can prove ; and I have proved that 78,331 were landed at five ports in Brazil, in the course of twelve months, ending at the 30th June, 1830.

But is it easy to believe, while Brazil receives so vast a number into five of her principal ports, that the trade is confined to them, and that none are introduced along the remaining line of her coast, extending over 38 degrees of latitude, or about 2,600 miles, and abounding in harbours, rivers, and creeks, where disembarkation can easily be effected ?

It may safely be assumed, that the slave-trader would desire to avoid notoriety, and to escape the duty which is paid upon all imports ; either of these motives may induce him to smuggle his negroes ashore. That numbers are so smuggled is established by the fact, that most vessels from the coast of Africa report themselves " in ballast" on arriving at Bahia. In the last Parliamentary Papers,* more than half the vessels are found to have thus reported themselves, and the remainder to have come from Prince's Island, Ajuda (Wydah), and Angola,—the very places where the Slave Trade most prevails.† The Commissioners interpret these returns in ballast thus:—" In the six months ending 30th June, 1836, twenty vessels entered this port (Rio) from the coast of Africa; they came in ballast, and, upon the usual declaration, that the master or pilot had died on the voyage, were stopped, with scarcely an exception, by the police, on suspicion of having landed slaves on the coast; but as usual also, were, after a few days' detention, released."‡ The Juiz de Direito, of Ilha Grande, (one of the few functionaries who appears to have done his duty with respect to the Slave Trade, and whose activity has been rewarded, on the part of the populace, by attempts on his life, and on the part of the Brazilian Government, as I have been informed, by dismission from his office,) confirms this view of the Commissioners in a Report, dated 12th November, 1834, in which he says :—" I see that in the trade in Africans brought to this district, are committed almost the whole population of this place, and of the neighbouring district." "Here, since I have been in the district, there have been twenty-two disembarkations, which I can remember ; and I can assure your Excellency, that an equal or even a greater

* Class B, 1837, and Class B, Further Series, 1837.

† Class B, 1837, p. 83.   ‡ Class A, 1836, p. 251.

number have called off this port; and it is certain that they did not return to Africa.''*

It is then clear that, over and above the number annually introduced into the five ports, negroes are landed along the line of the Brazilian coast; but, as we have no facts to guide us to the precise number, I will assume that the trading in slaves is confined to these five places, and that not a single negro was landed in Brazil beyond the 78,331 negroes in twelve months, ending in June, 1830.

I admit that this proves little as to the Slave Trade at the present time. It is very possible that it raged at a former period, but that it has now ceased; and it may be argued that the facts stated were prior to the treaty with Great Britain, and that the operation of that treaty has considerably reduced the number. If we are to believe the official reports made to our Government, it is just the reverse. The Slave Trade has increased since that time. The Brazilian Minister of Marine recommends to his government the formation of a " *cordon sanitaire,* which may prevent the access to our shores of those swarms of Africans that are continually poured forth from vessels engaged in so abominable a traffic.''†
This, be it observed, was on the 17th of June, 1833, three years after the treaty had come into operation.

The Ministers of Foreign Affairs and of Justice, in their report to the Chamber of Deputies, in 1835, speak " of the continuance of the traffic, to an extent

* Class B, 1834, p. 233.   † Class A, 1833, p. 58.

at once frightful to humanity, and alarming to the
best interests of the country." " The fury of this
barbarous traffic continues every day to increase with
a constantly progressing force." " Sixteen hundred
new blacks are openly maintained on an estate in
the neighbourhood of Ilha Grande." " The continued—we might almost say the uninterrupted—traffic
in slaves is carrying on, on these coasts."* On the
17th June, 1836, Mr. Gore Ouseley, British resident at Rio Janeiro, states in his despatch, that "The
Slave Trade is carried on in Brazil with more activity than ever."† In the preceding May, in a despatch to Viscount Palmerston, he speaks of " an
association of respectable persons who were going to
use steam-boats for the importation of Africans."‡
Mr. Ouseley, of date 15th Jan., 1839, states that in
1838, 84 slave-vessels had entered Rio almost openly,
going through the formality, become almost ridicu-
lous, of being examined by " Juiz de Paz," and had
imported 36,974 negroes with impunity. But the
real number imported into this province is probably
40,000 or upwards.

In March, 1836, the President of Bahia observed,
in a speech to the Assembly of that province, " That
the contraband in slaves continues with the same
scandal."§ In the following September the British

* Class A, 1835, p. 265.   † Class B, 1836, p. 68.
‡ Class B, 1836, p. 67.   § Class A, 1836, p. 231.
The British Consul reports from Bahia, that from 1st June to
31st July, 1838, there arrived from Africa seven vessels, 1028

Commissioners say, " At no period, perhaps, has the trade been ever carried on with more activity or daring."* And again, in November, 1836, " The traffic in slaves is every day becoming more active and notorious on this coast."† And Mr. Ouseley, of date 10th August, 1838, reports that the number of vessels fitted out at Rio for the coast of Africa continues to increase : and of date 1st Sept., 1838, he says, " The traders are more animated than formerly, being under the belief that, as no cruizers have appeared to enforce the instructions, Great Britain is unable to interrupt the traffic. Several Portuguese-built vessels lately arrived from Europe have been fitted out for slave voyages. These are of larger tonnage than those hitherto employed. Thus the trade is decidedly on the increase."‡

Thus, then, not only by the reports of our Commissioners and our Resident, but, by the admission of the Brazilians themselves, it appears, that the Slave Trade has increased since the treaty was formed. It seems hardly necessary to add, that I have received letters to the same effect from gentlemen on whom I have entire reliance. A naval officer, in a letter dated 16th September, 1835, says, " For the last six months the importation of new slaves is greater than ever remembered." A gentleman writes

tons, and sailed for Africa 5 vessels, 876 tons, all reputed to be engaged in slave trading. Class B, 1838, p. 406-7.

* Class A, 1836, p. 250.   † Class A, 1836, p. 260.

‡ Class B, 1839, pp. 394—406.

to me, of date 7th April, 1837, " It may be well to acquaint you, that the Slave Trade has now got to an unprecedented pitch." Lieut. Armitage, who is lately returned from that coast, where he has been actively engaged in the suppression of the traffic, states, in a letter dated March 5, 1839, " I have from good authority that 90,000 is about the number annually imported into Brazil."

The Parliamentary Papers presented in 1838, remarkably confirm the two positions which I have laid down; first, that the Slave Trade is enormous; and, secondly, that so far from abating, it has increased since the period when the treaty was formed.

By a private letter from a highly respectable quarter, I learn that in the month of December, 1836, the importation of slaves into the province of Rio alone was not less than . . 4,831

Our Minister at Rio states that there
    arrived in the following month of

January, 1837 . . .	4,870*
February . . .	1,992†
March . . .	7,395‡
April	5,596§
May	2,753‖

27,437

Thus, within six months, in the province of Rio, or the vicinity, there were known to have been landed

---

* Class B, 1837, p. 58.   § Class B, 1837, p. 65.
† Ibid. —— 60.   ‖ Ibid. —— 71.
‡ Ibid. —— 64.

this vast number.* This is hardly disputed by the Brazilian authorities. Our Minister at Rio, in a letter to Lord Palmerston, dated 18th April, 1837, speaking of 7,395 negroes landed in the preceding month, says :—" As a satisfactory proof of the general accuracy of these reports, it may be observed here, that the Government has excepted to two only of the numerous items they comprehend."†

It would be an error to suppose that these reported numbers comprehend anything like the whole amount of the importations : conclusive evidence to the contrary appears in a variety of passages of the same reports. I shall take but one as an instance. Mr. Hamilton, in his enclosure of 1st March, 1837, states as follows :—" Brig *Johovah* from Angola. This vessel, since she left this port, thirteen months ago, has made three voyages without entering any port. The first voyage she landed 700 slaves, very sickly, at Ponta Negra, about half way betwixt this port and Cape Frio ; on the second voyage, 600

* Lord Howard de Walden, in a note to the Portuguese Minister, of date 2d April, 1838, says that in 1837, 92 vessels laden with slaves had landed their cargoes in or near Rio ; and that the numbers amounted to upwards of 41,600. Mr. Gordon writes, of date Jan. 27th, 1838, to the Brazilian Minister, that, from all the information he is able to collect, the trade appears to be rather on the increase than otherwise ; that during the year which had just elapsed, 92 vessels imported into this province, within a very limited extent of coast, 46,000 unhappy Africans destined to bear the degrading yoke of slavery. Class B, 1839, p. 141 and 358.

† Class, B.. 1837, p. 63.

slaves at the island of St. Sebastian ; and on the present voyage, 520 slaves at Tapier, close to the entrance of this port. The greater number of these last were put into boats and fishing canoes, and brought to town."* The last number, namely 520, only, are reported in the return for the month of February preceding ; but the remaining 1300 have not appeared in any returns. It is evident from this, as well as many other passages, that vessels land their negroes on the coast, and return direct to Africa, and all who do so, escape notice, and are not included in the account. If these 1300 are added to the returns for the first six months in the year 1837, the importations into Rio alone for this year will exceed those of 1830. Mr. Ouseley says, of date 23d March, 1839, " There are at this moment in Rio harbour between 30 and 40 vessels, bought and equipped by a notorious slave trader, provided with Portuguese papers by H. M. F. M. Consul-general.†

So much for the province of Rio. I would next observe as to Pernambuco.‡ In a letter from Mr.

---

* Class B, 1837, p. 60. † Class B, 1839, F. S. p. 142.

‡ It appears from the papers taken on board the Portuguese brig Veloz, captured 18th Sept., 1837, by the " Fair Rosamond," that a joint stock company had been formed at Pernambuco for the importation of slaves. They had purchased the right of establishing factories in the river Benin, and had stipulated that the King of Benin and Ocry should expel from the river those who did not favour the Slave Trade.

The agent of the company, Joao Baptista Cezar, writes to his employers that, being in want of irons, the Queen of Benin gave

Watts, the British Consul, to Lord Palmerston, of date 5th May, 1837, he says, " I have just received directions to furnish Mr. Hamilton with a monthly return of vessels arriving from the coast of Africa, at any port within my consulate," &c.; and he adds, " the supineness, not to say connivance, of the Government of Brazil in general, on the subject in reference, the gross venality of subordinate officers, the increasing demand of hands for the purposes of husbandry, the enormous profits derivable from this inhuman traffic, which is rapidly increasing at this port in the most undisguised manner, combined with the almost insuperable difficulty of procuring authentic information through private channels *from the dread of the assassin's knife or bullet, even in the* OPEN *day, and in the public gaze ;* and the dark and artful combinations of the dealers in slaves, their agents, and the agriculturists, to mask and facilitate the disembarkation of imported slaves;—all these glaring and obstructive facts combine to render the

him 48 pairs; that he had " bought a very pretty girl for two rolls of tobacco, two fathoms of flannel, and one piece of calico." He adds, " There are plenty of slaves for goods; had I more articles I should to-day have had 200 slaves, for there are many more here waiting." He writes to his wife Josephina :

DEAR SPOUSE OF MY HEART,

I send you three fine mats and two parrots, one ram goat for my little son John to play with, and three sea-horse teeth for our little daughter Henrietta ; also a little girl, very pretty, and a little black boy for Johnny. They have the mark O on the left arm, &c. &c.

attainment of authentic data, on which to ground
effective official representation on the subject of the
unprecedented increase of the Slave Trade all along
the coast of Brazil, an almost insurmountable obstacle."*

I am not sure that we have by any means reached
the extent of the importation. The British Consul
at Pernambuco, of date 29th March, 1838, repeats
some of the arguments used by the Brazilians in favour of the traffic. They say that the population of
African slaves in Brazil is estimated at two millions,
and that the yearly casualties of life being ascertained
to be in the ratio of five per cent. beyond the annual
births, the population would suffer a decrease in the
short space of ten years, of half its numbers, unless
supplied by a yearly importation without restraint.†

This in itself, supposing the population to be stationary, would require an importation of 100,000 annually; but we have reason to believe that, although the
deaths so much exceed the births, the slave population is
rapidly increasing. According to Sir George Staun-
ton, the number of slaves in the then territory of
Brazil was in 1792 nearly 600,000. According to
the official census of 1835, it was 2,100,000. It is
impossible to account for this actual increase on a
decreasing population, except through the Slave
Trade carried on to a prodigious extent.

The case, however, may be stated thus : prior to
the treaty the annual importation of negroes into *five*

* Class B, 1837, p. 84.   † Class B, 1839, p. 428, 429.

ports of Brazil was 78,331, to which might be added the indefinite but considerable number smuggled into other places in Brazil. Since that time the trade has, by general testimony, increased. Notwithstanding the difficulty thrown in the way of obtaining information, the facts which we have been enabled to glean demonstrate what the Marquis of Barbacena stated in the Senate of Brazil on the 30th of June, 1837, namely, *That it may be safely asserted, without fear of exaggeration, that, during the last three years, the importation has been much more considerable than it had ever before been when the commerce was unfettered and legal.*"* On these grounds we might be entitled to make a considerable addition. It is enough for us to know, that, at the *very least*, 78,331 human beings are annually torn from Africa, and are imported into Braizl.

Cuba.

It is scarcely practicable to ascertain the number of slaves imported into Cuba: it can only be a calculation on, at best, doubtful data. We are continually told by the Commissioners, that difficulties are thrown in the way of obtaining correct information in regard to the Slave Trade in that island. Everything that artifice, violence, intimidation, popular countenance, and official connivance can do, is done, to conceal the extent of the traffic. Our ambassador at Madrid, Mr. Villiers, April, 1837, says,

* Class B, 1837, p. 69.

" That a privilege (that of entering the harbour after
dark), denied to all other vessels, is granted to the
slave-trader ; and, in short, that with the servants of
the Government, the misconduct of the persons concerned in this trade finds favour and protection.   The
crews of captured vessels are permitted to purchase
their liberation ; and it would seem that the persons
concerned in this trade have resolved upon setting
the Government of the mother country at defiance."*
Almost the only specific fact which I can collect
from the reports of the Commissioners, is the statement, "that 1835 presents a number of slave vessels
(arriving at the Havana), by which there must have
been landed, at the very least, 15,000 negroes."† But
in an official letter, dated 28th May, 1836, there is
the following remarkable passage :—" I wish I could
add, that this list contains even one-fourth of the
number of those which have entered after having
landed cargoes, or sailed, after having refitted in this
harbour."‡   This would give an amount of 60,000 for
the Havana alone ; but is Havana the only port in
Cuba in which negroes are landed ?   The reverse is
notoriously true.   The Commissioner says, " I have
every reason to believe that several of the other ports
of Cuba,§ more particularly the distant city of St.

* Class B, 1837, p. 2.   † Class A, 1835, p. 206.
‡ Class A, 1836, p. 153.
§ Mr. Hardy also reports that in the year 1838 there were
landed at Juragua 2803 slaves, being the cargoes of nine vessels.
And Mr. Consul Tolmè, of date March 20, 1839, writes to Lord

Jago de Cuba, carry on the traffic to a considerable extent." Indeed, it is stated by Mr. Hardy, the consul at St. Jago, in a letter to Lord Palmerston, of the 18th February, 1837, " That the Portuguese brig *Boca Negra* landed on the 6th instant at Juragua, a little to windward of this port (St. Jago), 400 Africans of all ages, and subsequently entered this port."* Further confirmation of this has recently arrived:—in a note given to the commander of Her Majesty's cruizer, on the coast of Cuba, by consul Tolmè, it is stated that, though the owners dislike their vessels discharging on the south side of the island, which is much exposed, yet many cargoes are landed there, as will be seen by the following list of the places at which, during the last six months, vessels have put their negroes on shore. Of 25 cargoes, nine were landed at Guanima, four near Trinidad, three at Manil, two at Camarisca, one at Puente de Guano, one at Cabanos, one at Banes, one at Cogimar, one at Santa Cruz, one at Canimar, one near St. Jago di Cuba.

But in order that we may be assuredly within the mark, no claim shall be made on account of

Palmerston, that " the trade of late years, in spite of the Spanish treaty, has materially increased ;" and he adds, " I hesitate not to say that, so long as the increasing prosperity of this island creates a demand for slaves, the traffic will be carried on to the same and even a greater extent than at present, unless Great Britain adopt much more efficient measures than heretofore for putting a stop to it." Class B., F. S., 1839, pp. 32—35.

* Class B., 1837, p. 29.

these distant ports. Confining ourselves to the
Havana, it would seem probable, if it be not demonstrated, that the number for that port, *à for-
tiori* for the whole island, may fairly be estimated
at 60,000.* I have many strong grounds for believing that this is no exaggeration, some of which I will
mention. In the first place, I observe that the great
majority of slaves, captured by our cruisers on the
coast of Africa, are bound to the island of Cuba; out
of 30 vessels which were adjudicated at Sierra
Leone during the years 1834 and 1835, 21 are
described as having that destination. Again, it is an
acknowledged fact† that there is in that island an

* " THE SLAVE TRADE.—It has occurred to us, now that
the Spaniards and Portuguese are pushing the inhuman traffic
with so much zeal and energy, whether it would not be preferable
to employ steamers than sailing-vessels in cruizing about that grand
receptacle of stolen Africans, the island of Cuba. *We have heard
it stated that upwards of sixty vessels per month arrive in Cuba
from the coast of Africa with slaves.* Supposing that each vessel
on an average carries two hundred of these, and that the number
of arrivals continue the same for one year certain, we should have
the incredible number of one hundred and forty-four thousand
slaves imported into that colony in twelve months! Although
we cannot believe that the trade is carried on to this extent, still
we think the Government is called upon to resort to prompt and
vigorous measures to repress, if not put a stop to it. Whether
steamers would be preferable to schooners, such as were previously
employed, we are not seamen enough to decide; certainly the
slavers would have less chance of escape from the former than
the latter."—*Watchman, February* 21, 1838.

† This fact has been admitted to me by a gentleman resident at
Havana, who at the same time suspects that I have considerably

annual decrease of 10 per cent. among the slaves employed in the cultivation of sugar, the chief produce of Cuba, and of 5 per cent. in the coffee-plantations. The slave population, as I learn from statistical accounts,* amounted, in the year 1828, to 301,000 ; therefore, with an average annual decrease of at least $8\frac{1}{2}$ per cent., it ought, in the year 1830, to have amounted to 252,006, or nearly that, whereas, on the same authority, I find it increased to 479,000, leaving an excess, which nothing but the Slave Trade can account for, of 226,994. Lastly, the produce of sugar, in 1829, amounted to 164,710,700 lbs. ; in 1836 it was increased to 369,600,000 lbs. ; and I have learnt, on good authority, that there were exported in 1828, 40,000,000 lbs. more than in any preceding year. These undoubted facts would warrant a much higher estimate than that which I have adopted ; but let the number deduced from the re-

over-estimated the numbers imported into Cuba. This, however, is the only case in which an objection has been raised to my calculation on the ground of exaggeration. I have cancelled this sheet since the work went to press, that I might extend this note to say that Dr. Madden, the gentleman here referred to, has again written to me in very decided terms to express his dissent from the calculation I have here made of the annual decrease of the slaves, and consequently from the result, so far as it depends on that fact; his estimate of the annual importation into Cuba is materially short of mine, but the data on which it is founded are not sufficiently clear to induce me to alter the text, though I feel it right thus pointedly to mention the difference between us.

* Statistical Account of Cuba, by Don Ramon de Sagra, Havana,

ports of the Commissioners be taken, and the account
will stand thus :—

Cuba	60,000
Brazil	78,331
	138,331

To this number of slaves actually landed
must be added those who have been
captured, which, on the average of
the years 1836 and 1837, was at
Sierra Leone   7,852

146,183

And at Havana in 1837 . . .   442

I cannot find that any have been adjudicated at Rio.

Further than this I cannot go by actual
proof; but there can be no doubt that
the Slave Trade has other victims than
those included in this calculation. For example, we know that several slave vessels
are annually wrecked or founder at sea;*
though it is impossible to arrive at anything
like exact numbers. Many negroes also
are thrown overboard, either during a chase,
or from dearth of provisions and water.†

For these, I will assume . .   3,375

Total . . 150,000

* See Wrecks, &c., page 166, &c.

† See p. 157, Captain Wauchope, R.N. See also the Paris
petition at p. 118.

I have no authority for this assumption of 3,375, it is merely a guess; it may be excessive. I only take this number to make a round sum. And if in this trivial point I have gone beyond the mark, I shall give abundant compensation for it hereafter.

I will next take the case of the Island of

PORTO RICO.

In regard to Porto Rico, I learn from the valuable work of Colonel Flinter, entitled " Present State of the Island of Porto Rico," some important facts: the exports from that island amounted to—

in 1814 . . . 500,840 dollars.

1830 . . 3,411,845

The amount of sugar produced has increased

from 37,969 arrobas in 1810

to 414,663 ,, in 1830.

He calculates that there are only 45,000 slaves in the island; but he tells us that the landed proprietors conceal the real number of their slaves in order to escape a tax.*

From the Parliamentary Papers of 1837, it appears, as stated by Mr. Courtenay, the British Consul at Port-au-Prince, Haiti, "that a slaving schooner, under the Brazilian flag, called Paquete de Capo Verde,

* From statistical accounts as furnished by Mr. M'Queen it appears that the slave population

in 1820 amounted to . . . 20,191

1831 41,819

1836 from the best accounts 60,000

was wrecked on the Folle reefs near Aux Cayes on the 28th February, 1837, having previously landed his cargo at Ponces, in the Island of Porto Rico."* It appears also, that one-ninth part of all the vessels condemned at Sierra Leone in 1837 were bound for Porto Rico, and that one of them at least, the Descubierta, belonged to the island and was built there.†

In a Report by the Commissioners at Sierra Leone, of date 20th March, 1837, it is stated that the Temerario had been captured with 352 slaves on board, bound for the island of Porto Rico ;‡ the Commissioners, on the 25th of April following, report the case of the Cinco Amigos, "belonging to the Spanish Island of Porto Rico, where slaving adventures have latterly been fitted out, with increased activity."§

A gentleman on whom I can rely, has informed me that in November, 1836, he saw two slave-vessels fitting out in the harbour of Porto Rico, and on his return in March, 1837, he saw a slaver entering the harbour, and he learned on the spot, from good authority, that about 7,000 negroes had been landed in the space of the preceding year.

From the above facts, especially from the increased production of sugar; from the constant smuggling communication which is known to exist with the slave-mart of St. Thomas; from the circumstance

* Class B., 1837, p. 140.
† Class A., (Further Series,) 1837, pp. 5, 13.
‡ Class A., 1837, p. 50.
§ Class A., 1837, p. 28.

that apprentices have been kidnapped by their masters in the British settlement of Anguilla,* for the purpose of being carried to Porto Rico,—and from the fact, that there is some Slave Trade with that island, it is not difficult to come to the conclusion, that there has been a traffic in slaves to a considerable amount. Upon the same principle, however, which has led me to waive all additions to which any shade of doubt may attach, I will not claim any increase on the sum of slaves exported from Africa, in respect of Porto Rico.

BUENOS AYRES, ETC.

I am afraid that some addition might too justly be claimed with regard to the countries in the vicinity of the rivers Plata and Uruguay.

In a letter from Mr. Hood to Lord Palmerston, dated from Buenos Ayres, the capital of the provinces of Rio de la Plata, 1833, it is stated, " that the dormant spirit of slave trading has been awakened;" that the Aguila Primera, a schooner belonging to this place, and under this flag, was fitting, and in a forward state, to proceed to the coast of Congo for a cargo of slaves; and that other fast-sailing vessels were in request for the same service." The Uruguese minister did not deny that the Government were cognizant of the proceedings, and confessed that " they had given their concurrence to import 2000 colonists from the coast of Africa, which he considered a fair and legitimate trade." Nor is it to be

* Class B., 1837, p. 10.

wondered at that he had arrived at so extraordinary
a conclusion; for it appears by the same letter that
the same " minister had received a bribe of 30,000
dollars to permit a company of merchants to import
2000 slaves, under the denomination of colonists."*

In September, 1834, Lord Palmerston, in a letter
to Mr. Hamilton, states that the Slave Trade is now
increasing in the river Plata, supported by the capital
of Monte Video† citizens, and covered by the flag of
the United Provinces of the Uruguay," and that the
Abolition Law is wholly without effect.‡

How unavailing were the remonstrances then made,
appears by the fact of the seizure, on the 10th November, 1834, of the Rio da Prata, a slave-brig of
202 tons, under the flag of Monte Video, with licence
from the authorities to import 650 colonists, with 521
slaves on board, men, women, and children."§

" We may form some idea," says Mr. M'Queen,
" of the numbers imported into the Argentine Republic, or provinces of Rio de la Plata, from the fact
that, in 1835 (see Porter's Tables), twenty Portuguese
vessels departed for Africa, and as many arrived from
it in the port of Monte Video, after landing their cargoes of slaves from Africa on the adjacent coasts." ‖

* Class B., 1833, pp. 55 and 56.

† Monte Video is the capital of the United Provinces of the
Uruguay, otherwise called the Oriental Republic, or Banda
Oriental.

‡ Class B., 1834, p. 81.   § Class B., 1835, p. 141.

‖ Mr. Mandeville, of date 24th January, 1839, writes from

It is most disheartening to find, that, in spite of all our efforts, the Slave Trade, instead of ceasing where it has long prevailed, is spreading over these new and petty states ; and that the first use they make of their flag (which but for us they never would have possessed) is to thwart Great Britain, and to cover the Slave Trade : and, further, to learn that their slave-traffic is attended with even more than the usual horrors. It must not be forgotten that, as we have just seen, for a voyage from the southern coast of Africa to Monte Video, (a voyage of some thousands of miles,) the space allowed is less than one ton for three slaves.

Lists are given in the Parliamentary Papers of many vessels employed in the Slave Trade, which are

Buenos Ayres that the Consul at Monte Video had acquainted him with a new method of smuggling slaves into the republic of the Uruguay. A Brazilian becomes owner of a vessel under Monte Videan colours ; he sends a cargo to Rio, where the vessel receives Brazilian produce. With a regular clearance, she then sails for Monte Video : having got outside the harbour, little sail is made, and at night a boat comes off from the shore with 20 or 40 negroes. These are landed at Maldonado, or in the neighbourhood, and then the vessel makes her entry to Monte Video in the usual manner ; and no questions are asked. By a systematic repetition of this fraud a great number of slaves are introduced into the "Banda Oriental." I do not quote this to prove that the Slave Trade from Africa is increased by this practice, for this is obviously not the case; but it shows an appetite for Slave Trading on the part of the Monte Videans, and the shifts to which they resort in order to satisfy it. Class D., F. S., 1839, p. 16.

continually arriving at, or sailing from, Monte Video ;*
but it seems hardly necessary to pursue the subject
further.   We know there is a Slave Trade with these
states; but as we have no data to compute the extent
of it, I cannot avail myself of the fact, however certain it may be.   I must, therefore, in regard to these
countries, as I have done in the case of Porto Rico,
wave extending my calculations.   I will next advert
to

THE UNITED STATES.

In the Report of the Commissioners at Havana,
for 1836, dated 25th Oct., 1836, I find these words :—
" During the months of August and September
(1836) there arrived here for sale, from the United
States, several new schooners, some of which were
already expressly fitted for the Slave Trade.

" The Emanuel and Dolores were purchased, and
have since left the port (we believe with other names)
on slaving expeditions, under the Spanish flag.

" But, to our astonishment and regret, we have
ascertained that the Anaconda and Viper, the one on
the 6th, and the other on the 10th current, cleared
out and sailed from hence for the Cape de Verde
Islands, under the American flag.†

* Class B, 1835, pp. 141—143.

† Mr. Barker, the British Consul at the Cape de Verde Islands,
of date 31st December, 1838, states that the American Consul at
Havana, Mr. Trist, had granted more than ten false bills of sale
of vessels, and passes to these islands.   Class B, 1839, F. S.,
p. 110.

" These two vessels *arrived in the Havana, fitted in every particular for the Slave Trade ;* and took on board a cargo which would at once have condemned, *as a slaver,* any vessel belonging to the nations that are parties to the equipment article."*

The Commissioners further observe, that the declaration of the American President " not to make the United States a party to any convention on the subject of the Slave Trade, has been the means of inducing American citizens to build and fit, in their own ports, vessels, only calculated for piracy or the Slave Trade, to enter this harbour, and, in concert with the Havana slave-traders, to take on board a prohibited cargo, manacles, &c. ; and proceed openly to that notorious depôt for this iniquitous traffic, the Cape de Verde Islands, under the shelter of their national flag :" and " we may add, that, while these American slavers were making their final arrangements for departure, the Havana was visited more than once by American ships of war, as well as British and French."

The Commissioners also state, that " two American vessels, the Fanny Butler and Rosanna, have proceeded to the Cape de Verde Islands and the coast of Africa, under the American flag, upon the same inhuman speculation."† A few months afterwards they report that—" We cannot conceal our deep re-

* Class A, 1836, p. 191.
† Class A, 1836, pp. 191, 192.

gret at the *new and dreadful impetus* imparted to the Slave Trade of this island (Cuba), by the manner in which some American citizens impunably violate every law, by embarking openly for the coast of Africa under their national flag, with the avowed purpose of bringing slaves to this market.* Consul Tolmè¦ of date 11th April, 1839, says, " In fact there appears, more than I ever knew it before, an eagerness on the part of the Slave Traders to purchase fast-sailing American built vessels, and to send them out to Africa under the flag of the United States."† We are likewise assured that it is intended, by means of this flag, to supply slaves for the vast province of Texas ; agents from thence being in constant communication with the Havana slave merchants."‡

This " new and dreadful impetus" to the Slave Trade, predicted by our commissioners, has already come to pass. In the recent Parliamentary papers, the number of American vessels employed in the

* Class A, 1836, p. 218, and Class B, 1836, pp. 123 and 129.
† Class B., F. S., 1839, p. 36.
‡ While preparing this work for the press, I received a communication from Major M'Gregor, late Special Magistrate at the Bahamas, in which he notices the wreck of the schooner Invincible, on the 28th October, 1837, on one of these islands ; and he adds, " the captain's name was Potts, a native of Florida. The vessel was fitted out at Baltimore in America, and three-fourths of the crew were natives of the United States, although they pretended to be only passengers."

trade in 1837 is stated to be 11, and, in 1838, 19.*
In a list of the departure of vessels for the coast of
Africa from the Havana, up to a recent date, I find
that, " in the last four months," no other flags than
those of Portugal and the United States have been
used to cover slavers.†

The list states that vessels, fitted for the Slave
Trade, sailed from Havana for the coast of Africa,
bearing the American flag, as follows :—

* Class A, F. S., 1838-9, p. 104.

† The Venus, said to be the sharpest clipper-built vessel ever
constructed at Baltimore, left that place in July, 1838, and
arrived at Havana on the 4th of August following. She sailed
from thence, in September, for Mozambique ; there she took in a
cargo of slaves, being all this time under the flag of the United
States. On the 7th of January, 1839, she landed 860 negroes
near Havana, under Portuguese colours ; and on the 9th these
blacks, with 1200 more, were seen at one of the Barracoons, within
two miles of that city, " exposed for sale, and presenting a most
humiliating and melancholy spectacle."—PRIVATE LETTERS.

Lieut. Reeve, of date 2d April, 1839, writes to the Secretary of
the Admiralty, that unless immediate steps be taken to check the
protection of the American flag to the slaver, it will be useless for
Her Majesty's cruizers to be employed for the suppression of the
traffic ; and he adds, " No other flag will be seen on the coast in
a short time, for it affords all the protection a slaver can require
under the existing laws."

Admiral Elliot, of date 6th Feb., 1839, says, " Several of the
slave dealers have declared their intention to have an American
sailing master and American colours in each vessel, and some
have had the impudence to assert that the government of the
United States would not discountenance such practices." Class
D, F. S., 1839, p. 31.

		American.
During the month of June, 1838,		2
,,	July	2
,,	August	5
,,	September	1
		──
		10

The Commissioners at Havana, of date 1st January, 1839, say, " It appears that the American flag will be at the command of whoever chooses to embark in such inhuman speculations."*

No symptom in the case is so alarming as this. It remains to be seen, whether America will endure that her flag shall be the refuge of these dealers in human blood.

I confidently hope better things for the peace of Africa and for the honour of the United States.†

This leads me to the province of

TEXAS.

I have been informed, upon high authority, that " within the last twelve months ‡ 15,000 negroes were imported from Africa into Texas." I have the

---

* Class A, F. S., 1838-9, p. 104.

† I am glad to find that, in the course of 1838, an American sloop of war was stationed at Havana for the special purpose of putting down abuses of the American flag; and that the commander of this vessel had seized a brig, pretending to be American, from the coast of Africa, and delivered her up to the Spanish authorities. Class A, F. S., 1838-9, p. 102.

‡ Referring to 1837 and 1838.

greatest reliance on the veracity of the gentleman from whom this intelligence comes; but I would fain hope that he is in error. I can conceive no calamity to Africa greater than that Texas should be added to the number of the slave-trading states. It is a gulf which will absorb millions of the human race. I have proof, quite independent of any statements in this work, that not less than four millions of negroes have in the last half century been torn from Africa for the supply of Brazil. Texas, once polluted with the Slave Trade, will require a number still more appalling.

In the case of Texas, as I have not sufficient proof to adduce in support of the numbers which it is reported have been carried into that country, I shall, as I have already done in similar instances, wave my claim for increasing my general estimate.

SUMMARY.

I have then brought the case to this point. There is Slave Trading, although to an unknown and indefinite amount, to Porto Rico; to Texas; and to some of the South American republics.

There is the strongest presumptive evidence, that the Slave Trade into the five ports of Brazil which have been noticed, is " much more considerable " than my estimate makes it; and that I have also underrated the importation of negroes into Cuba. There are even grounds for suspicion that there are other places (besides Porto Rico, Texas, Cuba,

Monte Video, &c., and Brazil), where slaves are introduced. But for all these presumptions I reckon nothing—I take no account of them ; I limit myself to the facts which I have established ; viz., that there are, at the present time, imported annually into

Brazil	78,331
That the annual importations into Cuba amount to	60,000
That there have been captured . .	8,294
And I assume that the casualties* amount to	3,375
Making together .	150,000

CORROBORATIVE PROOFS OF THE EXTENT OF THE SLAVE TRADE.

I confess there is something startling in the assertion, that so vast a number are annually carried from Africa to various parts of the New World.

Such a statement may well be received with some degree of doubt, and even suspicion. I have not been wholly free from these feelings myself; and I have again and again gone over the public documents, on which I have alone relied, in order to detect any inaccuracy which might lurk in them, or in the inferences deduced from them. No such mistake can I discover; but my conviction that the calculation is not excessive, has been fortified by finding that other persons, who have had access to

* See p. 34.

other sources of information, and who rest their estimates on other data than those on which I have relied, make the number of human beings torn from Africa still greater than I do.

For example:—Captain M'Lean, Governor of Cape Coast Castle for many years, who estimates the extent of the Slave Trade by the vessels which he has seen passing along the coast, rates the number of slaves annually taken from the Bights of Benin and Biafra alone, at 140,000.

In a letter from that gentleman, dated June 11, 1838, he says :—

SIR,

    In compliance with your wishes, I beg leave to state to you, in this form, what I have already mentioned to you verbally; namely, that " in the year 1834, I have every reason to believe that the number of slaves carried off from the Bights of Benin and Biafra amounted to 140,000."* I have not beside me the *particular data* whereon I grounded this calculation; but I can state generally, that I founded it upon the number of slave-vessels which actually passed the forts on the Gold Coast during that year, and of those others, of whose presence on the coast I had certain information from Her Majesty's cruisers or otherwise. When I say that I have rather under than over-stated the number, I ought at the same time to state that, in the years 1834-5, more slavers appeared on the coast than in any previous year within

---

* This fact, taken in connexion with an opinion expressed to me by Governor M'Lean, and confirmed by several merchants and captains trading to the coast of Africa, that *three* out of five of all the slave-vessels from the Bight of Benin are bound to Cuba, gives 84,000 as the extent of the Slave Trade of that island; an amount far exceeding my estimate.

my observation; and this was partially, at least, accounted for (by those engaged in the traffic) by the fact of the cholera having swept off a large number of the slaves in the island of Cuba. The ports of Bahia, also, were opened for the introduction of slaves, after having been shut for some time previous, on account of an insurrection among the negro population in that country.

Governor M'Lean returned to Cape Coast Castle in 1838, and found, it appears, that the Slave Trade had by no means decreased during his absence. In a letter, dated 16th October of that year, he says, " Slavers have continued to pass the forts; some of them, as usual, stopping here. From various inquiries that I have made, and by collating my information, as received from several sources, I can state as a *fact*, that there are at this moment on the coast 200 slave-vessels, all under Portuguese colours." He was assured, by the master of one of the slave-ships which stopped at the fort, that " the trade was on the increase, the prices given for slaves in Cuba being higher than ever."

This does not include the slaves embarked from the many notorious slave-ports to the northward of Cape Coast, nor those carried from the eastern shores of Africa, nor those who are shipped at Loango and the rest of the south-western coast. I confess that I have not any very clear grounds for calculating or estimating the numbers shipped from these three quarters. Along the south-eastern coast, we know that there are a great many ports from whence slaves are taken. With respect to the majority of these, we are left in the dark as to the extent to which the Slave Trade is carried on; but, in a few cases, we have specific information. For example:—in the letters found on board the Soleil, which was captured by Commodore Owen, H. M. S. Leven, we have the following statement:—" From the port of Mozambique are exported every year upwards of 10,000 blacks."* Commodore Owen, in the account of his voyage to the eastern coast, informs us that from eleven to fourteen slave-vessels come annually from Rio Janeiro to Quilimane, and return with from 400 to 500 slaves each, on an average, which would amount to about 5,500.†

Captain Cook‡ has informed me that, during the year 1837, twenty-one slave-vessels sailed from Mozambique, with an average cargo of 400 slaves each, making 8,400. These, added to 7,200 exported from Quilimane in eighteen vessels, also in 1837, according to Captain Cook, give a total of 15,600 slaves conveyed to Brazil and Cuba from these two ports alone. Of all the vessels, in number about thirty-eight, which sailed from the eastern coast in that year, Captain Cook believes that only one was captured. He adds,—" Some slaves are shipped from Inhambane, and other places along the coast;" but, having

* Class B, 1828, p. 84.

† Owen's Voyage, &c., London, 1833, vol. i., p. 293.

‡ Captain Cook commanded a trading vessel, employed on the east coast of Africa, in 1836, 7, and 8.

no accurate information, he has altogether omitted them.

Lieutenant Bosanquet, of H. M. S. Leveret, in a letter addressed to Admiral Sir P. Campbell, dated 29th September, 1837, says:—" From my observations last year, and from the information I have since been able to obtain, I conceive that upwards of 12,000 slaves must have left the east coast of Africa in 1836 for the Brazils and Cuba; and I think, from the number of vessels already arrived,* and there being many more expected, that that number will not be much decreased this year."†

I will now turn to the south-western coast:—

In 1826, the Governor of Benguela informed Commodore Owen that, " Some years back, that place had enjoyed greater trade than St. Paul de Loando, having then an annual averaged export of 20,000 slaves."‡   Owen also informs us that, " From St. Paul de Loando, 18,000 to 20,000 slaves are said to be annually exported, in great part to Brazil; but that the supply had considerably decreased, on account of the dishonesty of the black agents in the country."

Commodore Owen shortly afterwards (in 1827) visited Kassenda, near the river Congo, which place, he says, " is principally resorted to by slavers, of whom

* The letter is dated at the close of the rainy season on the eastern coast.

† Class B, Further Series, 1837, p. 25.

‡ Owen's Voyage, &c., vol. ii., p. 272.

five were at anchor in the harbour on our arrival,
'one French, and the rest under the Brazilian flag."*

On looking over the Slave Trade papers presented
to Parliament in 1838,† I find it stated, in monthly
lists, that, in the course of the year 1837, seventy
vessels were reported by the British authorities to
have imported into the vicinity of Rio Janeiro
29,929 slaves, from Angola, Benguela, and Loando.
All these vessels came in ballast to the port of Rio
Janeiro, after having landed their slaves on the coast.

The reader will see (vide p.18, &c.) that there are
other points in Brazil at which slaves are disem-
barked.   To say nothing of these, though the consul
at one of them reports the arrival of the Portuguese
brig Aleide, from Angola, on the 10th July, 1837,
having previously landed 460 slaves in the neighbourhood; though the consul at another states that
" the frequent disembarkation of negroes imported
from the coast of Africa in the vicinities of this port,
is the common public talk of the day;" and though
the vice-consul at a third notices the arrival of three
vessels from Angola, in the months of November and
December, 1836, I only claim from Angola 29,929
negroes landed in Brazil in 1837.

Then, as to the ports and rivers to the north of
Cape Palmas, I find that General Turner, late
Governor of Sierra Leone, in a despatch dated the
20th December, 1825, states that the exports of

* Owen's Voyage, &c., vol. ii. p. 292.
† Class B, 1837, and Class B, Further Series, 1837.

slaves from that part of the coast amount·annually to 30,000.*

From these extracts it appears that we have satis-factory evidence that the export of slaves from the south-eastern coast of Africa to America amounts annually to, say, ...   15,000
From Angola, &c. to America .   .   .   29,929
From the ports to the northward of Cape
      Coast to America   30,000
                                        _____
      Amounting in all to .   .   .   74,929

Thus then stands the case.   We have information that the Slave Trade prevails in a variety of ports and rivers besides those in the Bights of Benin and Biafra.   This information, though conclusive as to the fact that the Slave Trade prevails, is vague as to the extent to which it is carried on; but we have specific authority to this extent, that from a limited number of these ports there is an annual draft of about   75,000
To these we must confine ourselves, and
      these, added to   140,000
      given by Mr. M'Lean for the exports

* Extracted from the Records of the Colonial Office for 1825.

The Sierra Leone Commissioners, of date 8th March, 1838, notice " the increasing activity of the Slave Trade in this neigh-bourhood.   In confirmation of this opinion, we may remark," they add, " that the two cargoes of slaves shipped by the Isabelita in the space of about five months, were drawn from the Sherbro' and Galenas."

from the Bights of Benin and Biafra,
make the total annual Slave Trade ————————
between Africa and America amount to   215,000

If we deduct from this number the usual amount of mortality, it will leave a remainder not very different from, though somewhat exceeding, the estimate of 150,000 landed annually in America.

With another gentleman, Mr. M'Queen, whose authority I have already quoted, I did not become acquainted until after the time that I had completed my own estimate. His channels of information are totally distinct from mine. Besides being conversant with all the information which is to be found in this country, he has recently returned from a visit to Cuba and Porto Rico, where he went on the business of the Colonial Bank, and where he availed himself of opportunities of collecting information relative to the Slave Trade.

He rates the Slave Trade of Brazil at   90,000
    Cuba and Porto Rico   .   .   100,000
    Captured in the year 1837 .   .   6,146
                            ——————
                            196,146

Besides Texas, Buenos Ayres, and the Argentine Republic, into which he believes there are large importations, though to what extent he has no means of judging.

I now resort to a mode of proof totally different from all the foregoing. I have had much communication with African merchants, engaged in legitimate trade; and it was suggested by one of them that a very fair estimate of numbers might be formed, from the amount of goods prepared for the Slave Trade, (and absolutely inapplicable to any other purpose except the Slave Trade,) manufactured in this country.*   At my request, they furnished me with the following very intelligent summary of the argument, prepared, as I understood, by Captain M'Lean :—

It is necessarily impossible, from the very nature of the Slave Trade, to ascertain directly, or with any degree of precision, the number of slaves actually exported from the coast of Africa for the Transatlantic slave-markets, in any given year or space of time.   But it is very possible, by instituting careful and minute inquiries into the several ramifications into which that traffic branches, to obtain results, by the combination of which we may arrive at an approximation to the truth, sufficiently accurate for all the purposes of the main inquiry.   And if we find that the *data* thus obtained from the most opposite sources, and from parties upon whose judgment and veracity the most implicit reliance may be placed, bring us to the same general result, it may, we think, be fairly taken for granted that the result is substantially correct.

Among the various sources to which we have applied ourselves, in order to ascertain the present actual extent of the Slave Trade, not the least important or satisfactory in its results has been a careful inquiry as to the quantity and value of goods, manufactured expressly and exclusively for the purchase of slaves.   The grounds

---

* I have just heard from a highly respectable correspondent, who has long resided in Brazil, that " the manufacture of goods exclusively for Africa and the Slave Trade, and exported to Rio de Janeiro, for the support of that trade, is generally admitted by the English merchants in that city.   They neither disguise nor deny that the traffic is chiefly upheld by means of English capital."

upon which we instituted and carried on this investigation were these:—

1. We ascertained, by the concurrent testimony of competent and unimpeachable authority, that the merchandise chiefly, if not exclusively, given in exchange for slaves, consists of cowries, Brazilian tobacco in rolls, spirits, and Manchester piece-goods.

2. That the *proportions* of the goods thus paid, might be taken generally to be,—one-third cowries, a third tobacco and spirits, and a third Manchester cotton goods.

3. We ascertained that the *average* sum paid for each slave (taking the goods at cost prices) was about £4 sterling.

Lastly, we ascertained that all, or nearly all, the cotton goods purchased for the Slave Trade, were manufactured in Lancashire ; and that the description of goods so manufactured were altogethe unsuitable for any other market save that traffic alone.

Assuming these premises to be correct, and we verified them with much care, and by the most strict investigation, it of course followed that, if, by any means, we could ascertain, even proxi-mately, the value and quantity of the cotton goods manufactured in and exported from Lancashire, for the Slave Trade, during any one of the few last years, we should arrive at a proximate (but, in the main, correct) estimate of the number of slaves actually purchased on the coast of Africa.*

To some this indirect *modus probandi*, as to an important fact, may appear far-fetched ; but we are assured by those who are most conversant with the African trade generally, as well as with the Slave Trade and its operations in particular, that it is much more

---

* The commissioners at Rio Janeiro, of date 14th July, 1838, make the following remark :—"We have been assured that it is no uncommon practice (which, however, we do not undertake to vouch for as a fact) with some of the commission houses here of Liverpool, Leeds, Manchester, and Birmingham, to sell their goods intended for the African market on conditional terms ; the debt to be acquitted in part or in whole, according as the adventure may ultimately prove successful or otherwise."—Class A, 1838—9, p. 171.

Mr. Gordon, of date 21st April, 1838, speaking of the Slave

conclusive than, to those unacquainted with that peculiar trade, it would appear.   As corroborative of other proofs, at least, it must certainly be regarded as very valuable.

From returns with which we have been furnished by parties whose names, were we at liberty to mention them, would be a sufficient guarantee for their correctness, we have ascertained that the entire quantity of cotton goods manufactured in Lancashire, for the African trade (including the legitimate as well as the Slave Trade), was, in the year 1836, as follows :—

Value of Manchester goods manufactured exclusively for the African legitimate trade .   .   £150,000

Value of goods manufactured in Lancashire, and
shipped to Brazil, Cuba, United States, and
elsewhere, intended for the Slave Trade, and
adapted *only* for that trade   .   .   .   £250,000

Trade at Rio de Janeiro, says:—" It appears probable that much British capital is engaged therein, even directly.   Indirectly many British houses in this city have for some time past greatly assisted enterprises for the nefarious end."   He adds, "That when there was a risk from the British cruizers, these merchants sold only for ready money, but now they give the slave-dealers credit."— Class B, 1839, p. 369.

It is satisfactory to observe that this painful intimation has not been unnoticed by the Home Government.

Viscount Palmerston to Her Majesty's Commissioners at Rio de Janeiro.

Gentlemen,   Foreign Office, Feb. 20, 1839.

With reference to that part of your despatch of the 14th July, 1838, in which you state that British merchants are concerned, and British capital is employed, in Brazil, in Slave Trade ; I have to desire that you will collect and transmit to me all the information you can obtain, with a view to facilitate the identification and prosecution of such persons as may be concerned in these transactions.

I am, &c.,

(Signed)   PALMERSTON.

Class A, F. S., 1838—9, p. 131.

Thus showing an excess in the quantity of goods manufactured for the Slave Trade, over that intended for legitimate trade, during the year 1836, of £100,000, or two-fifths of the whole amount.

Calculating by the *data* already given, we shall find that the number of slaves to the purchase of which the above amount of goods (manufactured and exported in one year, 1836) was adequate, would amount to the large number of 187,500,*—a number which we have strong reason to believe, according to information derived from other sources, to be substantially correct.

Assuming the data on which the merchants calculate to be correct, some considerable addition must be made to the number of 187,500, for

1. Goods only suited for the Slave Trade are manufactured at Glasgow as well as in Lancashire.

2. Specie to a very considerable extent finds its way through Cuba and Brazil to Africa, and is there employed in the purchase of Slaves. To the number then purchased by goods must be added the number purchased by money.

3. Ammunition and fire-arms to a large amount, and, like the goods, of a quality only fit for the Slave Trade, are sent from this country to Africa. The annual amount of such exports is stated in the Official Tables,† No. 6, of 1836, to be 137,698*l.* This item alone would give an increase of 34,424.

---

* Each slave averaging £4 for his cost price, £250,000 will purchase 62,500 slaves, and as only one-third of the whole number purchased are bought with manufactured goods, 62,500 multiplied by three will give 187,500 for the annual number imported.

† Tables of Revenue, &c., published by authority of Parliament.

4. The Americans also furnish Cuba and Brazil with arms, ammunition, and goods.

5. East Indian goods also are employed in the Slave Trade.

It is superfluous to quote authority for the facts just enumerated, as they are notorious to commercial men. Thus, by the aid of this circumstantial evidence, of scarcely inferior value to direct and immediate proof, we show that the Slave Trade between Africa and the West cannot be less than 200,000, and probably reaches 250,000, annually exported.

There is also another mode of looking at the same question, though under an aspect quite distinct.

From an examination of the number of slave-ships which left Brazil, Cuba, &c., in the year 1829,* as compared with the number captured in the same year, it appears that on the average one in thirty only is taken: now, on the average of the years 1836 and 1837, we have 7,538 negroes as the number captured, which, being multiplied by 30, gives a total, 226,140.

Thus, then, the estimate of 150,000, at which, on the authority, principally, of the British Commissioners, I have myself arrived, with the number which perish on the passage,† make together an amount, which corresponds with, and is confirmed, 1st, by the actual observation of the—

---

* Mr. M'Queen communicated this to me last year.

† See Summary—Mortality, Middle Passage, p. 144.

Governor of Cape Coast Castle, coupled
with other authorities, by which the
number must amount to .   .   .   200,000

2ndly, by Mr. M'Queen's researches,
by which the number must amount to   196,000

3rdly, by the estimates founded on the
quantity of goods exported for the
Slave Trade, by which it must amount
to, from   .   .   .   200,000 to 250,000

4thly, by a comparison between the proportion captured with those who es-
cape, by which it must amount to   .   226,000

I have now to consider the

MOHAMMEDAN SLAVE TRADE.

Hitherto, I have confined my observations to the
traffic across the Atlantic, from the east and west
coasts of Africa; there is yet another drain upon this
unhappy country, in the immense trade which is carried on for the supply of the Mohammedan markets
of Morocco, Tunis, Tripoli, Egypt, Turkey, Persia,
Arabia, and the borders of Asia.

This commerce comprises two distinct divisions,
1st, the maritime, the victims of which are shipped
from the north-east coast, in Arab vessels; and 2nd,
the Desert, which is carried on, by means of caravans, to Barbary, Egypt, &c.

The maritime trade is principally conducted by
the subjects of the Imaum of Muskat; and as this is
a branch of our subject, heretofore but little known,

I will make a few remarks as to its extent, the countries which it supplies, and the amount of its annual export.

Captain Cogan, of the Indian Navy, who, from his frequent intercourse with the Imaum, and, from having been his accredited agent in England, had the best opportunities of becoming acquainted with this Prince and his subjects, has informed me that the Imaum's African dominions extend from Cape Delgado, about 10° S. lat., to the Rio dos Fuegos, under the line; and that formerly this coast was notorious for its traffic in slaves with Christians as well as Mohammedans; the River Lindy, and the Island of Zanzebar, being the principal marts for the supply of the Christian market.

In 1822, a treaty was concluded by Captain Moresby, R.N., on behalf of the British Government, with the Imaum, by which the trade with Christian countries was declared abolished for ever, throughout his dominions and dependencies; but this arrangement, it must be remembered, does not in any way touch upon the Slave Trade carried on by the Imaum's subjects with those of their own faith.

By means of this reserved trade, slaves are exported to Zanzebar; to the ports on both sides of the Arabian Gulf; to the markets of Egypt, Cairo, and Alexandria; to the south part of Arabia; to both sides of the Persian Gulf; to the north-west coasts of India; to the island of Java, and to most of the Eastern islands. The vessels which convey these negroes are in general the property of Arabs, or other Mohammedan traders.

Both Sir Alexander Johnston, who was long resident at Ceylon in a judicial situation, and Captain Cogan, have heard the number thus exported reckoned at 50,000 per annum; but Captain Cogan admits 20,000 to be the number legally exported from Africa, upon which the Imaum derives a revenue of so much per head; and he also admits that there is, besides, an illicit trade, by which 10,000 more may be smuggled every year.*

All travellers who have recently visited the chief seats of this traffic agree in describing it as very considerable.

"At Muskat," says Lieutenant Wellsted,† "about 4000 slaves of both sexes, and all ages, are disposed of annually."

Captain Cook, (to whom I have already referred,) who returned, in 1838, from a trading voyage to the eastern coast of Africa, informs me, that he was at Zanzebar at several different periods, and that he always "found the slave-market, held there daily, fully supplied. He could not ascertain the number annually sold, but slaves were constantly arriving in droves, of

---

* In a despatch dated Zanzebar, May 6th, 1839, Captain Cogan writes,—" The trade in slaves on this island is much greater than I had previously understood, as there appears from good authority to be not less than 50,000 sold annually in the market of Zanzebar."

† Wellsted's Travels in Arabia, &c. vol. i. p. 388.

from 50 to 100 each, and found a ready sale; they were chiefly," he understood, "purchased by Arab merchants, for the supply of Egypt, Abyssinia, Arabia, and the ports along the Arabian Gulf, to the markets of which countries hundreds were carried off and sold daily."

Many, however, are kept in Zanzebar, where there are sugar and spice plantations, and where, according to Ruschenberger,* the population amounts to 150,000, of which about two-thirds are slaves.

I also find, from Lieutenant Wellsted,† that there is a Slave Trade carried on with the opposite coast of Arabia by the Somaulys, who inhabit the coast of Berbera, between Cape Guardafui and the Straits of Babel Mandel.

I am therefore warranted in taking Captain Cogan's estimate, viz., 30,000 per annum, as the number of negroes annually drained off by the Mohammedan Slave Trade from the east coast of Africa.‡

---

* Ruschenberger's Voyage, 1835, 6, 7, vol. i. p. 40.

† Wellsted's Travels in Arabia, &c. vol. ii. p. 363.

‡ There seems also to be an export of slaves from the Portuguese settlements on the east coast of Africa to their possessions in Hindustan, which, as appears from the accounts of travellers, commenced towards the close of the seventeenth century, and has continued to the present time. In a despatch to the Court of Directors from the Bombay Government, dated 12th May, 1838, Mr. Erskine, resident at Kattywar, (in the province of Guzerat,) states, that " a considerable importation of slaves takes place, at Diu, both directly from the Arabian Gulf, and from Goa, and

I now come to the other division, that of the Desert, or caravan Slave Trade; and here I shall briefly notice the countries which furnish its victims, so that we may see how vast a region lies under its withering influence.

By the laws of the Koran, no Mohammedan is allowed to enslave one of his own faith. The powerful Negro Moslem kingdoms, south of the desert, are thus, in a great measure, freed from the evils of this commerce; and the countries from which it is supplied are almost entirely Pagan, or only partially Mohammedan, and comprehend, in addition to the Pagan tribes (chiefly Tibboos), which are scattered over parts of the Desert, and lie intermixed among the Moslem kingdoms, all the northern part of Pagan Negroland, reaching, in a continuous line, from the banks of the Senegal to the mountains of Abyssinia and the sources of the Nile. The Negro Mohammedans, though not themselves sufferers from this Slave Trade, are active agents in carrying it on.

The Mohammedan towns of Jenné, Timbuctoo; Kano and Sackatoo, in Houssa; Kouka and Angornou, in Bornou; Wawa, or Ware, the capital of Waday; and Cobbe, the capital of Darfour,—are so many large warehouses, where the stores of human

Dumaun, from whence they are brought into the province. For this I may confidently say, I see no remedy whatever, as it rests entirely with the British Government to say how far they consider it politic to interfere with their allies, the Portuguese, on this important question."

merchandise are kept for the supply of the Arab carriers or traders, who convey them in caravans across the Desert. The Soudan* negroes, so conveyed, and by many different routes,† are not only intended for the supply of Barbary and Egypt, and the banks of the Nile, from its mouth to the southern frontiers of Abyssinia, but, as I have learnt from a variety of authorities, are exported to Turkey, Arabia, Syria, Persia, and Bokhara.‡

With regard to the number thus annually exported, the absence of official documents, the imperfect evidence afforded by the statements of African travellers, and the immense extent of the subject itself, in its geographical relations, render it extremely difficult to obtain anything approaching to a correct estimate.

For these reasons, and as I have no wish to go beyond the bounds of producible proofs, I shall not estimate the Mohammedan Slave Trade at a greater extent than that which I am fairly entitled to assume, from the observations of African travellers.

* The term " Soudan" is chiefly applied to the countries lying to the south of the Sahara, or Great Desert.

† The great posts on the northern side of the Desert, where the traders collect, appear to be Wednoon, Tafilet, Fez, and Ghadanies; Mourzouk, the capital of Fezzan; and Siout and Shendy, on the Nile.

‡ The Hon. Mountstuart Elphinstone, in his account of Caubul (London, 1839, vol. i. p. 318,) says, " There are slaves in Afghanistan: Abyssinians and Negroes are sometimes brought from Arabia."

Jackson, in his Travels in Africa,* speaks of a caravan from Timbuctoo to Tafilet, in 1805, consisting of " 2,000 persons, and 1,800 camels."

Riley tells us,† that the Moor, Sidi Hamet, informed him, that in a caravan, with which he travelled in 1807, formed by the merchants who remained in Timbuctoo after the departure of the annual caravans to the north, there were 2,000 slaves.

Captain Lyon‡ gives 5,000 or 5,500, as the annual import into Fezzan; and Ritchie,§ who travelled with him, says, that, in 1819, 5,000 slaves arrived at Mourzouk from Soudan.

Ritter,‖ in his observations on the Slave Trade, tells us, that the Darfour caravans arrive yearly at Cairo, from the interior, varying in their numbers according to time and circumstances; the smaller caravans, consisting of from 5,000 to 6,000 (according to Browne,¶ only 1,000); the larger, which however do not often arrive, of about 12,000.** Far fewer come down the Nile with the Sennaar caravan, and only a few, from Bornou through Fezzan, by the Maugraby caravan, although hunting-parties are

* Jackson's Travels, 1809, p. 239.

† Riley's Narrative, p. 382.

‡ Lyon's Narrative, London, 1821, pp. 188, 189.

§ Ritchie, quoted in the Quart. Review, 1820, No. xlv. p. 228.

‖ A German, who published a geographical work in 1820, p. 380.

¶ Browne's Travels, 1793, p. 246.

** Mémoires sur L'Egypte, tom. iii. p. 303. Lapanouse, iv. p. 77.

fitted out in Bornou, against the negroes, in the adjoining highlands.

Browne, who resided in Darfour three years, about the end of the last century, says, that in the caravan with which he travelled through the Desert to Cairo, there were 5,000 slaves.[*]

Burckhardt, who travelled in Nubia, &c., in 1814, informs us,[†] that 5,000 slaves are annually sold in the market of Shendy, " of whom 2,500 are carried off by the Souakin merchants, and 1,500 by those of Egypt ; the remainder go to Dongola and the Bedouins, who live to the east of Shendy, towards Akbara and the Red Sea ;" and he afterwards says,[‡] " Souakin, upon the whole, may be considered as one of the first Slave Trade markets in eastern Africa ; it imports annually, from Shendy and Sennaar, from 2,000 to 3,000 slaves, equalling nearly, in this respect, Esne and Es Siout, in Egypt, and Massouah in Abyssinia, where, as I afterwards learnt at Djidda, there is an annual transit from the interior of about 3,500 slaves. From these four points, from the southern harbours of Abyssinia, and from the Somauly and Mozambique coast, it may be computed, that Egypt and Arabia draw an annual supply of 15,000 or 20,000 slaves, brought from the interior of Africa."[§]

* Pinkerton's Voyages, &c., vol. xv. p. 155.

† Burckhardt's Travels, p. 324.　　　　‡ Ib. p. 442.

§ In the ' Times ' newspaper of the 14th February, 1839, I find that on the evening of the 11th, at the meeting of the Royal

Colonel Leake, who was in Egypt a few years ago, has informed me, that besides the supply from Shendy, noticed by Burckhardt, Cairo derives an additional number of 5,000 annually, who are brought to the market there, from Soudan, by other routes.

Dr. Ruppell, in describing the expedition undertaken by the Pasha of Egypt against the provinces south of his dominions, in the years of 1820 and 1821, states that "above 40,000 negroes were torn away from their country."*

Dr. Holroyd, who has lately returned from travelling in Nubia and Kordofan, has stated that Mehemet Ali's troops bring into Kordofan captives from his northern frontiers to the amount of 7,000 or 8,000 annually; that about one-half so introduced are retained for the use of the army and the inhabitants, while the other half are sold to the merchants of Shendy and Es Siout : that 5,000 negroes, annually, reach Cairo by Es Souan, but that others also are brought there from Abyssinia by the Red Sea, and from Darfour, by the Desert; and that slaves

Geographical Society, " the paper read was, an account of the survey of the south-east coast of Arabia by Captain Haines of the Indian navy." After describing Aden, he says, " The next town of importance is Mokhara, containing about 4,500 inhabitants, with a very considerable trade, particularly in slaves. The writer has seen exposed for sale· in the market, at one time, no less than 700 Nubian girls, subject to all the brutality and insults of their masters; the prices which they fetch varying from 7*l.* to 25*l.*

* Ruppell's Travels in Abyssinia, vol. i. p. 25.

are conveyed from Sennaar, by three separate routes, in daily caravans, varying in extent from 5 to 200. Dr. Holroyd visited the governor of Kordofan in 1837; he had then just returned from a " gazzua " (slave-hunt) at Gebel Nooba, the product of which was 2,187 negroes. From these, "the physician to the forces was selecting able-bodied men for the army; but so repeatedly has the Pasha waged war against this chain of mountains, that the population has been completely drained, and from the above number, only 250 men were deemed fit for military service."*

Dr. Bowring, who visited Egypt in 1837, has informed me, that he estimates the annual importation of slaves into Egypt at from 10,000 to 12,000; that the arrivals in Kordofan amount to about the same number : that in 1827, a single caravan brought 2,820 slaves to Es Siout;' but that, in general, the annual arrivals there fluctuate between 500 and 5,000; and that such is the facility of introducing slaves, that they " now filtrate into Egypt by almost daily arrivals."

* Statement by Dr. Holroyd, yet unpublished.

† The Allgemeine Zeiting, Oct. 19, 1838, states that " a few days ago a great caravan, the first for three years past, arrived from Darfour. It was 50 days in travelling in a straight line across the Desert from Darfour to Essiout. There it left the camels, and embarked with the slaves, that it brought, on the Nile for Cairo. This caravan consists of 18,000 camels, and, besides a vast quantity of the productions of the interior of Africa, brings nearly 8,000 slaves, who are sold in the slave-market at Cairo."

From the authorities which I have now given, I think I may fairly estimate the northern or Desert portion of the Mohammedan Slave Trade at 20,000 per annum.

I am aware that this amount is far below the numbers given by others who are well acquainted with the subject; for example, the eminent eastern traveller, Count de Laborde, estimates the number that are annually carried into slavery from East Soudan, Abyssinia, &c., at 30,000. He also tells us that in the kingdom of Darfour an independent Slave Trade is carried on;* and Burckhardt states, that Egypt and Arabia together draw an annual supply of from 15,000 to 20,000 from the same countries; but having no desire to depart from the rule I have laid down, of stating nothing upon conjecture, however reasonable that conjecture may be, I shall not take more than

For the Desert trade . . . . . . 20,000†
which, added to the annual export from
the eastern coast, proved to be . . . 30,000
_____
gives the number of 50,000

* Chasse aux Nègres. Leon de Laborde. Paris, Dupont et Cie., 1838, pp. 14 and 17.

† The following are some of these authorities :—
1st. For the number exported annually from Soudan to
      Morocco, &c., I take Jackson and Riley at . . 2000
2nd. From Soudan to Mourzouk, Lyon and Ritter give . 5000
3rd. From Abyssinia to Arabia, &c., Burckhardt, says about 3500

as the annual amount of the Mohammedan Slave
Trade.*

4th. From Abyssinia, Kordofan, and Darfour, to Egypt
     Arabia, &c., I take Browne, Burckhardt, Col. Leake,
     Count de Laborde, Dr. Holroyd, and Dr. Bowring, at 12,000

                 Total for Desert trade 22,500

   * It ought to be borne in mind, that I have not taken into the
account the number of slaves which are required for the home
slavery of the Mohammedan provinces and kingdoms in Central
Africa. These are very extensive and populous, and travellers
inform us that the bulk of their population is composed of slaves.
We have, therefore, the powerful nations of Houssa (including the
Felatahs), Bornou, Begarmi, and Darfour, all draining off from
Soudan annual supplies of negroes, for domestic and agricultural
purposes, besides those procured for the foreign trade. On this
head, Burckhardt says,† " I have reason to believe, however, that
the numbers exported from Soudan to Egypt and Arabia bear
only a small proportion to those kept by the Mussulmen of the
southern countries themselves, or, in other words, to the whole
number yearly derived by purchase or by force from the nations
in the interior of Africa. At Berber and Shendy there is scarcely
a house which does not possess one or two slaves, and five or six
are frequently seen in the same family ; the great people and
chiefs keep them by dozens. As high up the Nile as Sennaar, the
same system prevails, as well as westwards to Kordofan, Darfour,
and thence towards Bornou. All the Bedouin tribes, also, who
surround those countries, are well stocked with slaves. If we may
judge of their numbers by those kept on the borders of the Nile,
(and I was assured by the traders that slaves were more numerous
in those distant countries than even at Shendy,) it is evident that
the number exported towards Egypt, Arabia, and Barbary, is very
greatly below what remains within the limits of Soudan." He
then states that, from his own observation, the slaves betwixt

             † Burckhardt, p. 340.

SUMMARY.

Such, then, is the arithmetic of the case; and I earnestly solicit my reader, before he proceeds further, to come to a verdict in his own mind, upon the fairness and accuracy of these figures. I am aware that it requires far more than ordinary patience to wade through this mass of calculation; I have, however, resolved to present this part of the subject in its dry and uninviting form, partly from utter despair of being able, by any language I could use, to give an adequate image of the extent, variety, and intensity of human suffering, which must exist if these figures be true; and partly from the belief that a bare arithmetical detail, free from whatever could excite the imagination or distress the feelings, is best fitted to carry conviction along with it. I then ask, is the calculation a fair one? Some may think that there is exaggeration in the result, and others may complain that I have been too rigorous in striking off every equivocal item, and have made my estimate as if it were my object and desire, as far as possible, to reduce the sum total. It signifies little to the argument, whether the error be on the one side or the other; but

Berber and Shendy amount to not less than 12,000, and that, probably, there are 20,000 slaves in Darfour; "and every account agrees in proving that, as we proceed further westward, into the populous countries of Dar Saley, Bornou, Bagarmè, and the kingdoms of Afnou and Houssa, the proportion of the slave population does not diminish."

it is of material importance that the reader, for the purpose of following the argument, should now fix and ascertain the number which seems to him the reasonable and moderate result from the facts and figures which have been produced. To me, it seems just to take, annually,

For the Christian Slave Trade . . 150,000
For the Mohammedan 50,000

Making a total of . . 200,000

CHAPTER II.

MORTALITY.

HITHERTO, I have stated less than the half of this dreadful case. I am now going to show that, besides the 200,000 annually carried into captivity, there are claims on our compassion for almost countless cruelties and murders growing out of the Slave Trade. I am about to prove that this multitude of our enslaved fellow men is but the remnant of numbers vastly greater, the survivors of a still larger multitude, over whom the Slave Trade spreads its devastating hand, and that for every ten who reach Cuba or Brazil, and become available as slaves, fourteen, at least, are destroyed.

This mortality arises from the following causes :—

1. The original seizure of the slaves.

2. The march to the coast, and detention there.

3. The middle passage.

4. The sufferings after capture and after landing. And

5. The initiation into slavery, or the " seasoning," as it is termed by the planters.

It will be necessary for me to make a few remarks on each of these heads; and 1st, As to the mortality incident to the period of

Seizure.

" The whole, or the greater part, of that immense continent is a field of warfare and desolation ; a wilderness, in which the inhabitants are wolves to each other."—*Speech of Bryan Edwards.*

On the authority of public documents, parliamentary evidence, and the works of African travellers, it appears that the principal and almost the only cause of war in the interior of Africa, is the desire to procure slaves for traffic ; and that every species of violence, from the invasion of an army to that of robbery by a single individual, is had recourse to, for the attainment of this object.

Lord Muncaster, in his able historical sketches of the Slave Trade,* in which he gives us an analysis of the evidence taken before the Privy Council and the House of Commons about the year 1790, clearly demonstrates the truth of my assertion, at the period when he published his work (1792) ; and the authorities from that time, down to the present day, as clearly show, that the most revolting features of the Slave Trade, in this respect, (at least, as regards the native chiefs and slave-traders of Africa,) have continued to exist, and do now exist.

Bruce, who travelled in Abyssinia in 1770, in describing the slave-hunting expeditions there, says : " The grown-up men are all killed, and are then mutilated, parts of their bodies being always carried away as trophies ; several of the old mothers are

* Lord Muncaster's Historical Sketches. London, 1792.

also killed, while others, frantic with fear and despair, kill themselves. The boys and girls of a more tender age are then carried off in brutal triumph."*

Mr. Wilberforce, in his letter to his constituents in 1807,† has described the mode in which slaves are usually obtained in Africa, and he quotes several passages from the work of the enterprising traveller, Mungo Park, bearing particularly on this subject. Park says, " The king of Bambarra having declared war against Kaarta, and dividing his army into small detachments, overran the country, and seized on the inhabitants before they had time to escape; and in a few days the whole kingdom of Kaarta became a scene of desolation. This attack was soon retaliated; Daisy, the king of Kaarta, took with him 800 of his best men, and surprised, in the night, three large villages near Kooniakary, in which many of his traitorous subjects had taken up their residence; all these, and indeed all the able men who fell into Daisy's hands, were immediately put to death."‡ Mr. Wilberforce afterwards says : ." In another part of the country, we learn from the most respectable testimony, that a practice prevails, called ' village breaking.' It is precisely the ' tegria' of Mr. Park, with this difference, that, though often termed

* Bruce's Travels in Abyssinia.

† Wilberforce's Letter on the Abolition of the Slave Trade. London, 1807, p. 392.

‡ Park's Travels, London, 1817, vol. i. p. 164.

making war, it is acknowledged to be practised for the express purpose of obtaining victims for the slave-market. The village is attacked in the night; if deemed needful, to increase the confusion, it is set on fire, and the wretched inhabitants, as they are flying naked from the flames, are seized and carried into slavery." "These depredations are far more commonly perpetrated by the natives on each other, and on a larger or smaller scale, according to the power and number of the assailants, and the resort of ships to the coast; it prevails so generally, as throughout the whole extent of Africa, to render person and property utterly insecure."* And in another place, "Every man who has acquired any considerable property, or who has a large family, the sale of which will produce a considerable profit, excites in the chieftain near whom he resides the same longings which are called forth in the wild beast by the exhibition of his proper prey; and he himself lives in a continual state of suspicion and terror."†

The statements of Mr. Wilberforce have been corroborated by Mr. Bryan Edwards, (from whom I have already quoted,) himself a dealer in slaves, and an able and persevering advocate for the continuance of the traffic. In a speech delivered in the Jamaica Assembly, he says, "I am persuaded that Mr. Wilberforce has been very rightly informed as to the manner in which slaves are very generally

* Wilberforce's Letter, &c., p. 23. † Ibid. p. 28.

procured. The intelligence I have collected from my own negroes abundantly confirms his account; and I have not the smallest doubt that in Africa the effects of this trade are precisely such as he represents them to be."

But it may be said, admitting these statements to be true, they refer to a state of things in Africa which does not *now* exist. A considerable period of time has indeed elapsed since these statements were made; but it clearly appears, that the same system has obtained, throughout the interior of Africa, down to the present time; nor is it to be expected that any favourable change will take place during the continuance of the slave-traffic.

Professor Smith, who accompanied Captain Tuckey in the expedition to the Congo in 1816, says, " Every man I have conversed with acknowledges that, if white men did not come for slaves, the wars, which nine times out of ten result from the European Slave Trade, would be proportionally less frequent."[*]

Captain Lyon states that, when he was at Fezzan in 1819, Mukni, the reigning Sultan, was continually engaged in these slave-hunts, in one of which 1,800 were captured, all of whom, excepting a very few, either perished on their march before they reached Fezzan, or were killed by their captor.[†]

Major Gray, who travelled in the vicinity of the River Gambia, and Dupuis, who was British Consul

[*] Tuckey's Expedition, &c., p. 187.
[†] Lyon's Travels, p. 129.

at Ashantee about the same period, 1820, both agree in attributing the wars, which they knew to be frequent in the countries where they travelled, to the desire of procuring slaves for traffic.* Dupuis narrates a speech of the king of Ashantee. " Then my fetische made me strong, like my ancestors, and I killed Dinkera, and took his gold, and brought more than 20,000 slaves to Coomassie. Some of these people being bad men, I washed my stool in their blood for the fetische. But, then, some were good people, and these I sold or gave to my captains; many, moreover, died, because this country does not grow too much corn, like Sarem, and what can I do? Unless I kill or sell them, they will grow strong and kill my people. Now, you must tell my master (the King of England) that these slaves can work for him, and if he wants 10,000 he can have them."†

Captain Moresby, a naval officer, who was stationed on the eastern coast in 1821, and who had peculiar opportunities of learning the mode in which slaves were obtained, informed me that "The Arab traders, from the coast of Zanzebar, go up the country, provided with trinkets and beads, strung in various forms; thus they arrive at a point where little intercourse has taken place, and where the inhabitants are in a state of barbarism; here they display their beads and trinkets to the natives, according to the number of slaves they want. A certain

---

* Gray's Travels in Western Africa. London, 1825, p. 97.
† Dupuis' Residence in Ashantee. London, 1824, p. 164.

village is doomed to be surprised; in a short time
the Arabs have their choice of its inhabitants—
the old and infirm are either left to perish, or be
slaughtered."

In 1822, our Minister at Paris thus addressed
Count de Villele : "There seems to be scarcely a spot
on that coast (from Sierra Leone to Cape Mount)
which does not show traces of the Slave Trade,
with all its attendant horrors; for the arrival of a
ship, in any of the rivers on the windward coast,
being the signal for war between the natives, the
hamlets of the weaker party are burnt, and the
miserable survivors carried off and sold to the slave-
traders."

We have obtained most valuable information as to
the interior of Africa from the laborious exertions o
Denham and Clapperton. They reached Soudan, or
Nigritia, by the land-route through Fezzan and
Bornou, in 1823, and the narrative of their journey
furnishes many melancholy proofs of the miseries to
which Africa is exposed through the demands for the
Slave Trade. Major Denham says : " On attacking a
place, it is the custom of the country instantly to fire
it; and, as they (the villages) are all composed of
straw huts only, the whole is shortly devoured by the
flames. The unfortunate inhabitants fly quickly
from the devouring element, and fall immediately
into the hands of their no less merciless enemies,
who surround the place; the men are quickly mas-
sacred, and the women and children lashed together

and made slaves."* Denham then tells us that the Begharmi nation had been discomfited by the Sheik of Bornou, " in five different expeditions, when at least 20,000 poor creatures were slaughtered, and three-fourths of that number, at least, driven into slavery."† And, in speaking of these wars, he uses this remarkable expression—" The season of the year had arrived (25th November) when the sovereigns of these countries go out to battle." He also narrates the terms of an alliance betwixt the Sheik of Bornou and the Sultan of Mandara. " This treaty of alliance was confirmed by the Sheik's receiving in marriage the daughter of the Sultan, and the marriage-portion was to be the produce of an immediate expedition into the Kerdy country, by the united forces of these allies. The results were as favourable as the most savage confederacy could have anticipated. Three thousand unfortunate wretches were dragged from their native wilds, and sold to perpetual slavery, while probably *double that number were sacrificed to obtain them.*"‡

Denham, himself, accompanied an expedition against Mandara, one of the results of which was, that the town, " Darkalla, was quickly burnt, and another smaller town near it, and the few inhabitants who were found in them, chiefly infants and aged persons, were put to death without mercy, and thrown into the flames."§

* Denham and Clapperton's Travels, &c. in Africa. London, 1826, p. 164.　† Ib. p. 214.　‡ Ib. p. 116.　§ Ib. p. 131.

Commodore Owen, who was employed in the survey of the eastern coast of Africa about the years 1823 and 1824, says, "The riches of Quilimane consisted, in a trifling degree, of gold and silver, but principally of grain, which was produced in such quantities as to supply Mozambique. But the introduction of the Slave Trade stopped the pursuits of industry, and changed those places, where peace and agriculture had formerly reigned, into the seat of war and bloodshed. Contending tribes are now constantly striving to obtain, by mutual conflict, prisoners as slaves for sale to the Portuguese, who excite these wars, and fatten on the blood and wretchedness they produce."

In speaking of Inhambane, he says, "The slaves they do obtain are the spoils of war among the petty tribes, who, were it not for the market they thus find for their prisoners, would in all likelihood remain in peace with each other, and probably be connected by bonds of mutual interest."

Mr. Ashmun, agent of the American Colonial Society, in writing to the Board of Directors, from Liberia, in 1823, says, "The following incident I relate, not for its singularity, for similar events take place, perhaps, every month in the year, but it has fallen under my own observation, and I can vouch for its authenticity:—King Boatswain, our most powerful supporter, and steady friend among the natives, (so he has uniformly shown himself,) received

* Owen's Voyage, &c., vol. i. p. 287.

a quantity of goods on trust from a French slaver, for which he stipulated to pay young slaves—he makes it a point of honour to be punctual to his engagements. The time was at hand when he expected the return of the slaver, and he had not the slaves. Looking around on the peaceable tribes about him for his victims, he singled out the Queahs, a small agricultural and trading people of most inoffensive character. His warriors were skilfully distributed to the different hamlets, and making a simultaneous assault on the sleeping occupants in the dead of the night, accomplished, without difficulty or resistance, in one hour, the annihilation of the whole tribe ;— every adult, man and woman, was murdered—every hut fired! Very young children, generally, shared the fate of their parents ; the boys and girls alone were reserved to pay the Frenchman."*

The Colonization Herald of April 29, 1837, gives the following extract from a number of the Liberia Herald recently received :—" The wars among the natives contiguous to us continue to rage with increasing fury· The whole line of coast from the Gallinas to Grand Sesters is in a state of fearful commotion."

" Wars increase with the demand for slaves, and the demand is urgent in proportion to the scarcity. And that slaves in these belligerent tribes are becoming scarce there can be no doubt. The requisite number being made up of the free, every method of kidnapping and violence is resorted to at the instigation of

* Ashmun's Life.   New York, 1835, p. 160.

these fiends. They are always to be found near the scenes of warfare, ready to purchase with merchandise the unhappy victims of wars that they themselves excite for the purpose.

" Immediately on the breaking out of the war between the Dey tribes and that of the Gorah, a slave factory was established in the capital town of each tribe. Both of these factories, we believe, belonged to one concern. Thus, while a powerful temptation was continually presented to the cupidity of both parties, a ready market was always at hand, in which they could dispose of the victims of their avarice. Both of these towns have been sacked, each tribe prevailing in its turn ; and it is with feelings far from painful, that we add, the slavers were also taken."

The Commissioners at Sierra Leone, in a despatch of April 10, 1825, speaking of a great increase in the Slave Trade, which had then lately taken place on the coast between that colony and the Gallinas, state that the increased demand for slaves consequent thereon was "the cause of the destructive war which had raged in the Sherbro' for the last eighteen months, between the 'Cassoos,' a powerful nation living in the interior, and the Fi people, and Sherbro' Bulloms, who live near the water-side, and are completely under the influence of the slaving chiefs and factors settled in the neighbourhood."* The Cassoos are represented as having carried fire, rapine, and murder, throughout the different villages through which they

* Class A, 1826, p. 7.

passed, most of the women and children of which, together with the prisoners, were immediately sold to the slave-factors, who were at hand to receive them.

We have also, on this head, the more recent testimony of Lander and Laird. Lander accompanied Clapperton from Badagry to Sockatoo, and on the death of Clapperton he returned to Badagry, with little variation, by the same route. In 1830 he was sent out by the British Government to Africa, and succeeded in navigating the Niger from Boossa, where Park was drowned, to the sea, in the Bight of Benin. In his journal, he observes that slavery has " produced the most baleful effects, causing anarchy, injustice, and oppression to reign in Africa, and exciting nation to rise up against nation, and man against man ; it has covered the face of the country with desolation. All these evils, and many others, has slavery accomplished ; in return for which the Europeans, for whose benefit, and by whose connivance and encouragement it has flourished so extensively, have given to the artless natives ardent spirits, tawdry silk dresses, and paltry necklaces of beads."*

Laird ascended the Niger, and its tributary the Tschadda, in 1832, and was an eye-witness of the cruelties consequent on the Slave Trade, while in the river near to the confluence of the two streams. He says, speaking of the incursions of the Felatahs, " Scarcely a night passed, but we heard the screams of some unfortunate beings that were carried off into

* Lander's Records. London, 1830, vol. i. p. 38.

slavery by these villanous depredators. The inhabitants of the towns in the route of the Felatahs fled
across the river on the approach of the enemy." " A
few days after the arrival of the fugitives, a column
fsmoke rising in the air, about five miles above the
confluence, marked the advance of the Felatahs; and
in two days afterwards the whole of the towns, including Addah Cuddah, and five or six others, were in a
blaze. The shrieks of the unfortunate wretches that
had not escaped, answered by the loud wailings and
lamentations of their friends and relations (encamped
on the opposite bank of the river), at seeing them
carried off into slavery, and their habitations destroyed, produced a scene, which, though *common
enough in the country*, had seldom, if ever before,
been witnessed by European eyes, and showed to me,
in a more striking light than I had hitherto beheld it,
the horrors attendant upon slavery."*

Rankin, in the narrative of his visit to Sierra
Leone in 1833, says, the warlike Sherbros had recently invaded the territories of the Timmanees, and
had fallen on the unguarded Rokel, which became a
prey to the flames. " The inhabitants who could not
escape across the river to Magbelly perished, or were
made slaves, and the town was reduced to ashes."†

Colonel Nicolls, late Governor at Fernando Po,
has informed me, that when he visited the town of

* Laird and Oldfield's Narrative. London, 1837, vol. i. pp. 149,
247.

† Rankin's Sierra Leone.   London, 1836, vol. ii. p. 259.

Old Calebar in 1834, he found the natives boasting of a predatory excursion, in which they had recently been engaged, in which they had surprised a village, killed those who resisted, and carried off the remainder as slaves. In alluding to this excursion, Colonel Nicolls heard an African boy, who had formed one of the party, declare that he had killed three himself!

The Rev. Mr. Fox, a Wesleyan missionary at the Gambia, in a letter dated 13th March, 1837, addressed to the Secretary of the Wesleyan Missionary Society, says,—" I visited Jamalli a few weeks ago, and also Laming, another small Mandingo town, on the way : at the latter place I counted twelve huts that had been destroyed by fire, and at the former about forty. Proceeding to the Foulah town, about half a mile eastward, I found it was not in the least injured, but, like the other two, was without inhabitants; not a soul was to be seen."

" Foolokolong, a large Foulah town in Kimmington's dominions, has lately been attacked by Wooli, and, I believe, nearly the whole of it destroyed, the cattle driven away, many of the inhabitants killed, and many others taken prisoners. On Wednesday evening last I returned from a hasty visit to the upper river. I went as far as Fattatenda. At Bannatenda, not quite half the way, I found a poor aged Foulah woman in irons, who, upon inquiry, I found was from Foolokolong, one of the many who were captured in the recent war, and that she was sent on the south side of the river to be sold, for a

horse. I immediately rescued the half-famished and
three-parts-naked female from the horrors of slavery
by giving a good horse, broke off her chains, and
brought her to this settlement, where, by a singular
but happy coincidence, she met with her own brother
(who lives upon Hattaba's land), who, hearing that
she, her daughter, and daughter's children, had been
taken in the war, had been a considerable way up
the river to inquire after them, but heard nothing of
them, and had consequently returned. I, of course,
gave the woman up to her brother, from whom, as
well as herself, and several Foulahs who came to see
her, I received a number of blessings."

In another part of the same letter he writes,—
" From the king himself I learned that they brought
350 Foulahs from Foolokolong (Kimmington's
largest Foulah town), besides 100 whom they killed
on the spot."

In another letter, dated 5th January, 1838, Mr.
Fox says, " The Bambarras have proceeded a considerable distance down the north bank of the river
(Gambia), have pillaged and destroyed several small
towns, taken some of the inhabitants into slavery,
and a few people have been killed."

" The neighbourhood of M'Carthy's Island is
again in a very disturbed state. Scarcely are the
rains over, and the produce of a plentiful harvest
gathered in, ere the noise of battle and the din of
warfare is heard at a distance, with all its attendant
horrors ; mothers, snatching up their children with a

few necessary articles, flee for their lives ; towns, after being pillaged of as much cattle, &c. as the banditti require, are immediately set on fire ; columns of smoke ascend the heavens ; the cries of those who are being butchered may be more easily conceived than expressed; and those who escape destruction are carried into the miseries of hopeless slavery. A number of Bambarras are again on the north bank of the river, not far from this place, and the poor Foulahs at Jamalli have consequently fled to this island for protection, bringing with them as many of their cattle, and other things, as they could."

The Rev. Mr. M'Brair, another Wesleyan missionary, who has seen much of the interior of Africa, in the vicinity of the Gambia, from which he has recently returned to this country, makes the following observations, in a letter also to the Secretary of the Wesleyan Missionary Society :

" On other occasions a party of men-hunters associate together, and, falling suddenly upon a small town or village during the night, they massacre all the men that offer any resistance, and carry away the rest of the inhabitants as the best parts of their spoil. Or, when a chieftain thinks himself sufficiently powerful, he makes the most frivolous excuses for waging war upon his neighbour, so that he may spoil his country of its inhabitants. Having been in close connexion with many of the liberated Africans in M'Carthy's Island, 250 miles up the Gambia, and also in St. Mary's, at the mouth of that river, we had many opportunities of learning the various modes in which they had been captured; from which it appeared that the wholesale method of seizure is by far the most frequent, and that, without this plan, a sufficient number of victims could not be procured for the market; so that it may be called the prevailing way of obtaining slaves."

" Whilst I was in M'Carthy's Island, a capture took place at the distance of half a day's journey from my abode. The king of Woolli, on a very slight pretence, fell upon a village during the night, slew six men, and carried off forty captives. The inhabitants also of a neighbouring place were destined to the same fate, but having had timely notice of his approach, they saved themselves by a precipitous flight, and M'Carthy's Island was filled for a time with refugees from all the country round about."

The Rev. Mr. Morgan, another Wesleyan missionary, lately from the Gambia, writes to the Secretary as follows :—" I feel confident that the Slave Trade has established feuds among them (the African tribes around the Gambia), by which they will be embroiled in war for generations to come, unless the disposition be destroyed by the Christian religion, or their circumstances be changed by civilization."

A private letter, dated Rio Nunez, 26th June, 1839, states, "There are now at this present moment five slavers in the Rio Pongas : the whole are under American colours, and it is likely, before two months are over, the natives of that river will be at war again, as they were but a few months ago; all on account of these slavers, who are the instigators of all the disturbances and war on the coast."

I must not leave this part of my subject without calling attention to the extraordinary facts which have recently been made public, regarding the practices of the Pasha of Egypt, and the chiefs in Nubia and Darfour. There has been revealed to us a new feature in the mode of procuring negroes for slaves; and we find that troops regularly disciplined are, at stated seasons, led forth to hunt down and harry the defenceless inhabitants of Eastern Nigritia.

In a despatch from Lieutenant-Colonel Campbell, Her Majesty's Consul at Cairo, of date 1st December 1837,* we are informed that the Consul waited on Mahommed Ali, and communicated to him " that statements had gone home to the Government and people of England, from eye-witnesses, that slave-hunts (*gazzua*) had been carried on by the officers and the troops of the Pasha; that large numbers of negroes had been taken, and had been distributed among the soldiers, in liquidation of the arrears of their pay; that on one occasion the gazzua had collected 2,700 slaves, of whom 250 had been forced among the ranks of his army, and the remainder had been divided among the officers and soldiers at fixed prices, according to the state of their arrears."

The Pasha professed not to know that his army had been employed in slave-hunts for the purpose of

* Class B, Further Series, 1837, p. 69.

discharging arrears of pay ; but he admitted that he was aware that his officers had carried on the Slave Trade for their own account, "a conduct of which he by no means approved." We have no further particulars in this important despatch : but the enterprise of a traveller, Count de Laborde, who has lately returned from Nubia and Egypt, will enable me to introduce those of my readers who have not seen his work,* to the scenes of cruelty and devastation perpetrated by the pasha's troops, which he has graphically described.

The narrative, of which I can only give a brie outline, was communicated to him by a French officer, who went to Cairo in 1828, and resided ten years in Egypt.

M. —— there learnt that four expeditions, called gaswahs, annually set out from Obeid, the capital of Kordofan, towards the south, to the mountains inhabited by the Nubas negroes. The manner and object of their departure are thus described : " One day he heard a great noise ; the whole village appeared in confusion ; the cavalry were mounted, and the infantry discharging their guns in the air, and increasing the uproar with their still more noisy hurras. M. ——, on inquiring the cause of the rejoicing, was exultingly told by a follower of the troop, " It is the gaswah." " The gaswah ! for what—gazelles ?" " Yes, gazelles ; here are the nets, ropes, and chains ; they are to be brought home

* Chasse aux Nègres, Leon de Laborde, Paris, 1838.

alive." On the return of the expedition, all the
people went out, singing and dancing, to meet the
hunters. M. ——— went out also, wishing to join in
the rejoicing. He told Count Laborde he never could
forget the scene presented to his eyes. What did he
see ? What spoil did these intrepid hunters, after
twenty days of toil, drag after them ? Men in chains ;
old men carried on litters, because unable to walk ;
the wounded dragging their weakened limbs with
pain, and a multitude of children following their
mothers, who carried the younger ones in their
arms. Fifteen hundred negroes, corded, naked, and
wretched, escorted by 400 soldiers in full array. This
was the gaswah. These the poor gazelles taken
in the Desert. He himself afterwards accompanied
one of these gaswahs. The expedition consisted of
400 Egyptian soldiers, 100 Bedouin cavalry, and
twelve village chiefs, with peasants carrying provisions. On arriving at their destination, which
they generally contrive to do before dawn, the cavalry
wheel round the mountain, and by a skilful movement form themselves into a semicircle on one side,
whilst the infantry enclose it on the other. The negroes, whose sleep is so profound that they seldom
have time to provide for their safety, are thus completely entrapped. At sunrise the troops commence
operations by opening a fire on the mountain with
musketry and cannon ; immediately the heads of the
wretched mountaineers may be seen in all directions,
among the rocks and trees, as they gradually retreat,

dragging after them the young and infirm. Four
detachments armed with bayonets are then despatched up the mountain in pursuit of the fugitives,
whilst a continual fire is kept up from the musketry
and cannon below, which are loaded only with
powder, as their object is rather to dismay than to
murder the inhabitants. The more courageous natives,
however, make a stand by the mouths of the caves,
dug for security against their enemies. They throw
their long poisoned javelins, covering themselves
with their shields, while their wives and children
stand by them and encourage them with their voices ;
but when the head of the family is killed, they surrender without a murmur. When struck by a ball,
the negro, ignorant of the nature of the wound, may
generally be seen rubbing it with earth till he falls
through loss of blood. The less courageous fly with
their families to the caves, whence the hunters expel
them by firing pepper into the hole. The negroes,
almost blinded and suffocated, run into the snares
previously prepared, and are put in irons. If after
the firing no one makes his appearance, the hunters
conclude that the mothers have killed their children,
and the husbands their wives and themselves. When
the negroes are taken, their strong attachment to
their families and lands is apparent. They refuse
to stir, some clinging to the trees with all their
strength, while others embrace their wives and
children so closely, that it is necessary to separate
them with the sword ; or they are bound to a horse,

and are dragged over brambles and rocks until they reach the foot of the mountain, bruised, bloody, and disfigured. If they still continue obstinate, they are put to death.

Each detachment, having captured its share of the spoil, returns to the main body, and is succeeded by others, until the mountain, " de battue en battue," is depopulated. If from the strength of the position, or the obstinacy of the resistance, the first assault is unsuccessful, the General adopts the inhuman expedient of reducing them by thirst ; this is easily effected by encamping above the springs at the foot of the mountain, and thus cutting off their only supply of water. The miserable negroes often endure this siege for a week ; and may be seen gnawing the bark of trees to extract a little moisture, till at length they are compelled to exchange their country, liberty, and families, for a drop of water. They every day approach nearer, and retreat on seeing the soldiers, until the temptation of the water shown them becomes too strong to be resisted. At length they submit to have the manacles fastened on their hands, and a heavy fork suspended to their necks, which they are obliged to lift at every step.

The march from the Nuba mountains to Obeid is short. From thence they are sent to Cairo. There the pasha distributes them as he thinks proper ; the aged, infirm, and wounded, are given to the Bedouins, who are the most merciless of masters, and exact their due of hard labour with a severity proportioned to the probable short duration of the lives of their unhappy victims.

At Obeid alone 6000 human beings are annually dragged into slavery, and that at the cost of 2000 more, who are killed in the capture. The king of Darfour also imports for sale yearly 8000 or 9000 slaves, a fourth of whom usually die during the fatigues of a forced march : they are compelled, by the scarcity of provisions, to hurry forward with all speed. In vain the exhausted wretches supplicate for one day's rest; they have no alternative but to push on, or be left behind a prey to the hungry jackals and hyænas. "On one occasion," says the narrator, "when, a few days after the march of a cara- van, I rapidly crossed the same desert, mounted on a fleet dromedary, I found my way by the newly- mangled human carcases, and by them I was guided to the nightly halt."

Dr. Holroyd, whom I have already mentioned, in a letter to me of date 14th January, 1839, says, in re- ference to these " gazouas," of the Egyptian troops, " I should think, if my information be correct, that, in addition to 7000 or 8000 taken captive, at least 1500 were killed in defence or by suffocation at the time of being taken ; for I learnt that, when the blacks saw the troops advancing, they took refuge in caves ; the soldiers then fired into the caverns, and, if this did not induce them to quit their places of concealment, they made fires at the entrances, and either stifled the negroes, or compelled them to surrender. Where this latter method of taking them was adopted, it was not an uncommon circumstance to see a female with a child at her breast, who had been wounded by a musket-ball, staggering from her hiding-place, and dying immediately after her exit."*

* In the same letter, dated January 14, 1839, Dr. Holroyd having mentioned that he had "brought from Kordofan, at his own request, a negro (an intelligent boy) about twelve years of age, who had been seized by Mahomed Ali's troops from Gebel Noobah, and from whom all particulars can be obtained in reference to that inhuman method of taking the blacks," I asked that the boy might be questioned as to what he had seen of the slave-hunts. Dr. Holroyd has favoured me with the following "Statement of Almas, a negro boy taken in the gazoua of Gebel Noobah, three years ago, by the troops of Mahomed Ali Pasha. Almas is a native of Korgo, a very considerable district on the south side of Gebel Noobah; it is governed by a sheik, who is under the command of a local sultan. He was living at Korgo at the time of his capture, and says, that the pasha's troops made the attack during the night, whilst the negroes were sleeping; that they fired repeatedly upon the district with cannon and muskets, both loaded with shot; and that they burnt the straw huts of the negroes. As they escaped from their burning huts they were seized by the troops: many, especially the children, were burnt to death, and many were killed. Those who ran away, and were pursued by the soldiers, defended themselves with stones, spears, and trombashes; the latter, an iron weapon in common use among the natives of these mountains.

" The negroes retreated to the caves in the sides of the mountains, from whence they were eventually obliged to come forth, from fear of suffocation from the fires made at the entrances, or from want of food and water. He never heard of pepper, mentioned by Laborde, as having been used in loading the guns, or of firing it into the caves to blind or stifle the negroes. Pronged stakes were fastened round the throats of the men, and their hands were fixed in blocks of wood nailed together. Boys, of twelve or fourteen years, had their hands only manacled, and the

I could add, were it necessary, a thousand other instances of the scenes of cruelty and bloodshed which are exhibited in Africa, having their origin in the Slave Trade; but enough has been said to prove the assertion with which I set out, that the principal and almost the only cause of war in the interior of Africa is the desire to procure slaves for traffic; and that the only difference betwixt the former times and the present day is this—that the mortality consequent on the cruelties of the system has increased in proportion to the increase of the traffic, which, it appears, has doubled in amount, as compared with the period antecedent to 1790.

I shall now estimate, as nearly as I can, the probable extent of mortality peculiarly incident to the period of seizure; but the difficulty of this is great, because our authorities on this point are not numerous.   Lord Muncaster notices a statement of an African Governor to the Committee of

young children and women were without any incumbrance.   Two or three times Almas saw a stubborn slave drawn (to use his expression) like a carriage, by a horse across the rocks, until he was dead.   He cannot say how many were killed in the attack; he thinks 500 were taken along with him from Korgo, but many of these died of thirst, hunger, and fatigue, on their march to Kordofan.   Almas's father and brother were captured along with him, and the former was compelled to wear the pronged stick from Gebel Noobah to Kordofan.   They are both soldiers at Sobeyet. His mother was seized by the sultan of Baggarah, who makes expeditions continually against the inhabitants of Gebel Noobah."

1790 :—" Mr. Miles said, he will not admit it to be'
war, only skirmish-fighting ; and yet," Lord Muncaster adds, " Villault, who was on the Gold Coast
in 1663, tells us, that in one of these ' skirmishes'
above 60,000 men were destroyed ; and Bosman says
that in two of these ' skirmishes ' the outrage was so
great, that above 100,000 men were killed upon the
spot. Mr. Devaynes also informs us that, while he
was in the country, one of these ' skirmishes ' happened between the kings of Dahorney and Eyo, in
which 60,000 lost their lives."*

The Rev. John Newton, rector of St. Mary's
Woolnooth (who at one period of his life was engaged in slave-traffic on the coast of Africa), observes,
" I verily believe that the far greater part of the
wars in Africa would cease, if the Europeans would
cease to tempt them by offering goods for slaves ;
and, though they do not bring legions into the field,
their wars are bloody. I believe the *captives reserved
for sale* are FEWER than *the slain*. I have not sufficient data to warrant calculation, but I suppose that
not less than 100,000 slaves are exported annually
from all parts of Africa. *If but an equal number* are
killed in war, and if many of these wars are kindled
by the incentive of selling their prisoners, what an
annual accumulation of blood must there be crying
against the nations of Europe concerned in this
trade !"†

* Lord Muncaster on the Slave Trade, p. 42.
† Newton on the Slave Trade. London, 1788, p. 30.

I have no *modern* authority to support the specific statements of Newton and Lord Muncaster, excepting that of Denham, who says, " That in one instance *twenty thousand* were *killed*, for *sixteen thousand* carried away into slavery ;"* and in another case, that " probably *more than double* " the number of those captured for slaves fell a sacrifice in the onset of the captors.†

The second head of mortality, arising from the March, and Detention before being embarked, must now be considered ; and first as to the

March.

" The Begarmese," says Browne, in his journey to Darfour in 1793, " attack on horseback the Kardee, Serrowa, Showa, Battah, and Mulgui tribes, and seizing as many captives as possible, drive them like cattle to Begarmi."‡   Mungo Park informs us that " by far the greater number of slaves purchased by Europeans on the coast, are brought down in large caravans from the inland countries, of which many are unknown even by name to the Europeans.

" I was met," he says, " by a coffle (caravan) of slaves, about seventy in number, coming from Sego. They were tied together by their necks, with thongs of bullocks' hide twisted like a rope, seven slaves upon a thong, and a man with a musket between

* Denham's Narrative, p. 214.   † Ibid., p. 116.
‡ See Leyden's Discoveries, vol. i. p. 413.

every seven. Many of the slaves were ill-conditioned, and a great number of them women; they were going to Morocco by the way of Ludamar and the Great Desert."*

In another part of his journal, Park says that, on his route to Pisania, (a distance of 500 miles,) he joined a coffle, under a slattee (slave-merchant), Kaarfa, who was particularly kind to him, and whom he describes as " a worthy negro, with a mind above his condition—a good creature," and therefore not likely to be among the most cruel, in the treatment of his slaves. While this slattee was collecting the coffle, Park arrived at his house. Kaarfa liberally offered to keep him there till the country should be fit for travelling. On the third day after his arrival Park fell ill with the fever, and he bestows great praise on his " benevolent landlord," for his kindness and attention.† We are afterwards informed of the treatment of the slaves during the journey, which, be it remembered, was performed under the direction of this " worthy, good, and benevolent negro." It appears that " The slaves are commonly secured by putting the right leg of one and the left of another into the same pair of fetters. By supporting the fetters with a string, they can walk, though very slowly. Every four slaves are likewise fastened together by the neck, with a strong pair of twisted thongs; and in the night an additional pair of fetters

* Park's Travels, vol. i. pp. 438, 290.
† Ibid., vol. i. p. 388, &c.

is put on their hands, and sometimes a light iron chain passed around their necks."

" Such of them as evince marks of discontent are secured in a different manner; a thick billet of wood is cut about three feet long, and, a smooth notch being made upon one side of it, the ancle of the slave is bolted to the smooth part by means of a strong iron staple, one prong of which passes on each side of the ancle. All these fetters and bolts are made from native iron. In the present case they were put on by the blacksmith, as soon as the slaves arrived from Kancaba, and were not taken off until the morning when the coffle departed for Gambia."

He goes on to say, " Even to those who accompanied the caravan as a matter of choice, the toil was immense; and they travelled sometimes from morning till night without tasting a morsel of food." And afterwards, " During this day's travel, two slaves, a woman and a girl, were so much fatigued that they could not keep up with the coffle. They were severely whipped and dragged along, until about three o'clock in the afternoon, when they were both affected with vomiting, by which it was discovered that they had eaten clay." He then narrates a case of great cruelty: one of the female slaves had become quite exhausted, and every exertion was made with the whip to cause her to keep up with the coffle. When every effort failed, " the general cry of the coffle was kangtegi" (cut her throat). I had not walked forward a mile, when one of Kaarfa's domestic slaves came up to me with poor Nealee's garment upon the end of

his bow, and exclaimed, ' Nealee is lost ;' he afterwards said, he had left her on the road."* A few
days after this took place, a party of Serawoole traders
joined the coffle, and one of their male slaves became
also completely exhausted ; he was whipped and
tortured to no purpose, and then left in charge of
another slave, who, it was generally believed, put
him to death.

It appears that there is also great suffering when
these poor victims are conveyed to the coast, by the
rivers. Falconbridge says, " While I was on the
coast, during one of the voyages I made, the black
traders brought down in different canoes from 1200
to 1500 negroes, which had been purchased at one
fair." They consisted of all ages. Women sometimes form a part of them, who happen to be so far
advanced in their pregnancy, as to be delivered
during their journey from the fairs to the coast.
And there is not the least room to doubt, but that,
even before they can reach the fairs, great numbers
perish from cruel usage, want of food, travelling
through inhospitable deserts, &c. They are brought
in canoes, at the bottom of which they lie, having
their hands tied, and a strict watch being kept over
them. Their usage, in other respects, during the
passage, is equally cruel. Their allowance of food
is so scanty as barely to support nature. They are,
besides, much exposed to the violent rains which frequently fall here, being covered only with mats that
afford but a slight defence ; and, as there is usually

* Park's Travels, vol. i. p. 507, &c.

water at the bottom of the canoes from leaking, they
are scarcely ever dry."*

Here, again, it may be rejoined, " But these were
the practices of the last century."   Riley informs us
that Sidi Hamet, the Moor, narrated to him, as an
instance of the sufferings consequent on the route by
the Desert, that the caravan which he accompanied
from Wednoon to Timbuctoo, in 1807, consisted, on
its setting out, of 1000 men and 4000 camels; but
only twelve camels and twenty-one men escaped alive
from the Desert.†   Let us examine whether these
cruel sufferings have been mitigated in our own
times; and whether we may flatter ourselves that
Africa is no longer the scene of such atrocities.
Burckhardt, in 1814, accompanied a caravan from
Shendy in Nubia, across the Desert, to Suakin on the
Red Sea.   There were slaves with the caravan on
their way to Arabia.   In the middle of the journey
the caravan was alarmed by a threatened attack of
robbers ; they " moved on," we are told, " in silence ;
nothing was heard but the groans of a few infirm
female slaves, and the whips of their cruel masters."‡
He also says that the females are almost universally
the victims of the brutal lusts of their drivers.

Major Gray, while travelling in the country of
Galam in 1821, fell in with a part of the Kaartan

* Falconbridge on the Slave Trade, London, 1788, pp. 12, 13,
19, &c.

† Riley's Narrative, p. 361.

‡ Burckhardt's Travels, pp. 381, 336.

force, which he said had taken 107 prisoners, chiefly women and children. " The men were tied in pairs by the necks, their hands secured behind their backs ; the women by their necks only, but their hands were not left free from any sense of feeling for them, but in order to enable them to balance the immense loads of pang, corn, or rice, which they were forced to carry on their heads, and the children (who were unable to walk, or sit on horseback) behind their backs. They were hurried along at a pace little short of running, to enable them to keep up with the horsemen, who drove them on as Smithfield drovers do fatigued bullocks. Many of the women were old, and by no means able to endure such treatment." On a subsequent day he says, " The sufferings of the poor slaves during a march of nearly eight hours, partly under an excessively hot sun and east wind, heavily laden with water, of which they were allowed to drink but very sparingly, and travelling barefoot on a hard and broken soil, covered with long dried reeds, and thorny underwood, may be more easily conceived than described."

In the course of his journey Major Gray fell in with another detachment of slaves, and he says, " The women and children (all nearly naked, and carrying heavy loads) were tied together by the neck, and hurried along over a rough stony path, that cut their feet in a dreadful manner. There were a great number of children, who, from their tender years, were unable to walk ; and were carried, some

on the prisoners' backs, and others on horseback behind the captors, who, to prevent their falling off,
tied them to the back part of the saddle with a rope
made from the bark of the baoball, which was so
hard and rough that it cut the back and sides of the
poor little innocent babes, so as to draw the blood.
This, however, was only a secondary state of the sufferings endured by those children, when compared
to the dreadfully blistered and chafed state of their
seats, from constant jolting on the bare back of the
horse, seldom going slower than a trot, or smart
amble, and not unfrequently driven at full speed for
a few yards, and pulled up short."*

In speaking of the route by the Desert, Lyon
says :†—" Children are thrown with the baggage on
the camels, if unable to walk ; but, if five or six years
of age, the poor little creatures are obliged to trot on
all day, even should no stop be made for fourteen or
fifteen hours, as I have sometimes witnessed." " The
daily allowance of food is a quart of dates in the
morning, and half a pint of flour, made into bazeen,
at night.   Some masters never allow their slaves to
drink after a meal, except at a watering-place."
" None of the owners ever moved without their
whips, which were in constant use. Drinking too
much water, bringing too little wood, or falling
asleep before the cooking was finished, were considered nearly capital crimes ; and it was in vain for

* Gray's Travels in Africa, pp. 290, 295, and 323.
† Lyon, p. 297.

these poor creatures to plead the excuse of being tired,—nothing could avert the application of the whip." "No slave dares to be ill or unable to walk ; but, when the poor sufferer dies, the master suspects there must have been something ' wrong inside,' and regrets not having liberally applied the *usual* remedy of burning the belly with a red-hot iron ; thus re-conciling themselves to their cruel treatment of these unfortunate wretches."

This description is confirmed by Caillie, who, in his account of his journey from Timbuctoo through the Desert, gives the following case of barbarity, which he says he had the misfortune to see too often repeated :—"A poor Bambara slave, of twenty-five years, was cruelly treated by some Moors, who com-pelled him to walk, without allowing him to halt for a moment, or to quench his burning thirst. The complaints of this unfortunate creature might have moved the hardest heart. Sometimes he would beg to rest himself against the crupper of a camel, and at others he threw himself down on the sand in despair. In vain did he implore, with uplifted hands, a drop of water : his cruel masters answered his prayers and his tears only with stripes." *

In another part of his work Caillie says :—

" Our situation was still the same ; the east wind blew with violence ; and, far from affording us any refreshment, it only threatened to bury us under the mountains of sand which it raised ; and, what was still

* Caillie's Travels, vol. ii. p. 89.

more alarming, our water diminished rapidly from
the extreme drought which it occasioned. Nobody
suffered more intensely from thirst than the poor
little slaves, who were crying for water. Exhausted
by their sufferings and their lamentations, these unhappy creatures fell on the ground, and seemed to
have no power to rise; but the Moors did not suffer
them to continue there long when travelling. Insensible to the sufferings which childhood is so little
fitted to support, these barbarians dragged them
along with violence, beating them incessantly till
they had overtaken the camels, which were already
at a distance."[*]

In 1824 Denham and Clapperton penetrated to
Nigritia, by the Desert from Fezzan, the route usually
taken by slave-caravans going to the north of Africa.
In narrating his excursion to Munga, Major Denham
speaks of a caravan which he met at Kouka, consisting of ten merchants from Soudan, with nearly 100
slaves; and he observes, "If the hundreds, nay thousands, of skeletons that whiten in the blast between
this place and Mourzouk, did not of themselves tell
a tale replete with woe, the difference of appearance
in all slaves here, where they are fed tolerably, and
the state in which they usually arrive in Fezzan,
would but too clearly prove the acuteness of the
sufferings which commence on their leaving the
negro country. Going, as they do, poor creatures,
nearly naked, the cold of Fezzan, in the winter sea-

* Caillie's Travels, vol. ii. p. 114.

son, kills them by hundreds."* This fact, as to the change of climate, is also noticed by Captain Lyon, who, speaking of the passage across the mountains of Fezzan, says, " Feb. 12th. Ther. 30° below 0°.—Water freezes, and the poor negroes in great distress from the cold."†

When the travellers arrived at the well of Meshroo, Denham says :—" Round this spot were lying more than 100 skeletons. Our camels did not come up till dark, and we bivouacked in the midst of those unearthed remains of the victims of persecution and avarice, after a long day's journey of twenty-six miles, in the course of which one of our party counted 107 of these skeletons." Shortly afterwards, he adds :—" During the last two days we had passed on an average from sixty to eighty or ninety skeletons each day; but the numbers that lay about the wells at El Hammar were countless."‡ Jackson informs us§ that, in 1805, " a caravan from Timbuctoo to Tafilet was disappointed at not finding water at the usual watering-place, and entirely perished : 2,000 persons and 1,800 camels."

Dr. Holroyd, in the letter to me which I have already quoted, in speaking of the " gazoua" in Kordofan, says :—" These slave-hunts have produced a great depopulation in the districts where they are practised : there is not only a terrible waste of life

* Denham, pp. 172, 280.   † Lyon, p. 298.
‡ Denham, p. 12.
§ Jackson's Travels in Africa, 1809, p. 239.

in the attempts to capture the negroes, but after they are seized there is so much of ill-usage and brutality, that I have been assured that *no less than thirty per cent. perish* in the first ten days after their seizure."

This account is confirmed by Dr. Ruppell, who says that " in Mehemet Ali's expedition, in 1820 and 1821, above 40,000 were torn from their country, not a third of whom reached Egypt; and even of those who did, a great part soon died off." He goes on to state that, as they were apt to desert on their passage from Kordofan or Shendy, through the Desert, and return to Dongola, each of them was branded by a hot iron on the arm, and a pole, nine feet long, fastened to their necks. The escort was obliged to deliver as many slaves as they had received, or the ears of those who might die on the road. " Many of the unhappy victims, who could be no longer urged, by the whips of their drivers, to further exertions on the march, had their ears cut off while yet alive, and were then left to await the agonies of the last moment in the Desert. I myself, in my journey to Ambukol, in the year 1824, passed many of the bodies of these miserable creatures, on whose necks the dreadful poles were still fastened : the bar-barous drivers had not relieved the wretches from their fetters, even in the hour of death."*

Dr. Bowring says,—" In conversations which I have had with the domestic slaves in the towns of Egypt, they talk with the greatest horror of the suf-

* Ruppell's Travels in Abyssinia, vol. ii. pp. 25, 27.

ferings connected with their first experience of the
bitterness of slavery. And these are but the beginning of sorrows. In the progress across the Desert,
many perish from thirst and from fatigue. I have
often heard their miseries described on their way,
from the poverty of the fellahs and insufficiency of
the caravans, which are often charged with an excessive number of slaves. An estimate being made
of the greatest number which it is possible to preserve
with the supply of water that remains, all the rest
are abandoned, and die of starvation in the sandy
wilderness.

" I will give you, from the mouth, and nearly in
the words, of a female slave at Cairo, her account of
the journey across the Desert to Siout. ' We had a
long, long journey, and we suffered very much. We
had not food enough to eat; and sometimes we had
no drink at all, and our thirst was terrible. When
we stopped, almost dying for want of water, they
killed a camel, and gave us his blood to drink. But
the camels themselves could not get on, and then
they were killed, and we had their flesh for meat and
their blood for water. Some of the people were too
weak to get on, and so they were left in the Desert
to die. The fellahs were some of them good people,
and when we were tired allowed us to ride upon the
camels; but there were many who would never let the
negroes ride, but forced them always to walk, always
over the sand. But when we had been days without
water, many dropped down, and were left upon the

sand ; so that, when we got to the end of our journey, numbers of those that had been with us were with us no longer.' "

Dr. Holroyd also states that " These unfortunate individuals (those selected for the army) were marched down to Kartoom, fourteen days' journey, completely naked ; and, to add to their misery, a wooden stake six or seven feet long, and forked at one extremity, was attached to the neck of one, by means of a cross bar retained in its position by stripes of bull's hide ; to the other end of the stake an iron ring was fastened, which encircled the throat of another of these poor harmless creatures.   They were then un-mercifully driven to Kartoom, with scarcely anything to eat on the way, and compelled to traverse a burn-ing desert with a very sparing and scanty supply of water.   They were despatched in companies of fifties ; and so great were their privations and fatigue on the journey, that a letter arrived at Kordofan, addressed to Mustapha Bey, from Khourshid Pasha, of Kartoom, Governor General of Soudan, and which was read during a visit I made to the divan of the former, in which the latter stated, that of fifty slaves who left Kordofan some days before, only thirty-five were living on the arrival of the caravan at Kartoom.

Richard Lander, in his account of Captain Clap-perton's last journey in 1826, in which he attended that traveller, speaking of the state of the slaves whom he saw on their journeys, observes : " In their toil-some journeyings from one part of the country to

another, it must be admitted that the captured slaves
undergo incredible hardships." He left Socatoo, with
a party of traders, and the " king of Jacoba," who
had fifty slaves, whom he was conducting (with heavy
loads on their heads) to his own country. Two days
afterwards Lander was informed that the whole of
these slaves were missing ; and, on search being made,
it was ascertained that they *had all perished from
excessive fatigue and want of water.*"*

Mr. Oldfield, who accompanied Laird in the expedition up the Niger in 1833, in giving a description
of Bocqua market, says : " Under the tmas and in the
enclosures are to be seen male and female slaves
from the age of five up to thirty. Some of these
children of misfortune, more intelligent than others,
are to be seen sitting pensive and melancholy, apparently in deep thought, while their poor legs are
swelled from confinement in irons, or being closely
stowed at the bottom of a canoe ; and he adds, " It is
painful to contemplate the number of slaves annually
sold at this market, most of whom are forwarded to
the sea-side."†

Many more extracts might have been taken from
the remarks of modern travellers on this branch of
the subject ; but enough has been adduced to prove
that the cruelties and consequent mortality arising
from *the march after seizure* have not *decreased* since
the time of Falconbridge and Park.

* Lander's Records, vol. i. p. 301 ; and vol. ii. p. 95.
† Laird and Oldfield, vol. i. p. 409.

I shall only further add, on the authority of Dr. Meyen, (a German who, a few years ago, published an account of a Voyage round the World,) that " M. Mendez, the author of a very learned treatise on the causes of the great mortality of the Negro Slaves, estimates the number of those who die, merely on the journey from the interior to the coast, *at five-twelfths of the whole.*"*

DETENTION.

The next cause of mortality arises from the detention of the slaves on the coast before they are embarked, and this occurs, for the most part, when the vessel for which they may be destined has not arrived, or is not ready to sail, or may be in dread of capture after sailing.

A gentleman resident at Senegal in 1818 stated to his correspondent at Paris, that, " No one in the town is ignorant that there are here 600 wretched creatures shut up in the slave-yards, waiting for embarkation. The delay which has occurred causing a serious expense, they receive only what is sufficient to keep them alive, and they are made to go out for a short space of time, morning and evening, loaded with irons."†

When Commodore Owen visited Benguela in 1825, he says, " We had here an opportunity of seeing bond-slaves of both sexes chained together in

* Dr. Meyen, German edition, vol. i. p. 77.
† 13th Report of the African Institution, Ap. G. p. 99.

pairs. About 100 of these unhappy beings had just arrived from a great distance in the interior. Many were mere skeletons labouring under every misery that want and fatigue could produce. In some, the fetters had, by their constant action, worn through the lacerated flesh to the bare bone, the ulcerated wound having become the resort of myriads of flies, which had deposited their eggs in the gangrenous cavities."*

Oiseau, commanding the brig Le Louis, on completing his cargo of slaves at the Old Calebar, thrust the whole of the unfortunate beings between decks, a height of nearly three feet, and closed the hatches for the night. When morning made its appearance, fifty of the poor sufferers had paid the debt of nature. The wretch coolly ordered the bodies of his victims to be thrown into the river, and immediately proceeded on shore to complete his execrable cargo.†

Richard Lander tells us that the Brazen, in which he went to Africa in 1825, captured a Spanish brigantine which was waiting off Accra, for a cargo of slaves. A few days after this capture, the commander of the Brazen landed at Papoe, and demanded the slaves which were to have been embarked in the brigantine. They were ultimately given up, and Lander says, " The slaves at length made their appearance, and exhibited a long line of melancholy faces and emaciated frames, wasted by disease and close confinement, and by their having suffered dread-

* Owen, vol, ii. p. 234.   † Class B, 1825, p. 123.

fully from scantiness of food, and the impure air of their prison-house. They were in a complete state of nudity, and heavily manacled; several of them were lamed by the weight of their irons, and their skin sadly excoriated from the same cause."*

At the close of this journey, Lander says:—" I saw 400 slaves at Badagry in the Bight of Benin, crammed into a small schooner of eighty tons. The appearance of these unhappy human beings was squalid and miserable in the extreme; they were fastened by the neck in pairs, only one-fourth of a yard of chain being allowed for each, and driven to the beach by a parcel of hired scoundrels, whilst their associates in cruelty were in front of the party pulling them along by a narrow band, their only apparel, which encircled the waist." " Badagry being a general mart for the sale of slaves to European merchants, it not unfrequently happens that the market is either overstocked with human beings, or no buyers are to be found; in which case the maintenance of the unhappy slaves devolves solely on the Government. The king then causes an examination to be made, when the sickly, as well as the old and infirm, are carefully selected and chained by themselves in one of the factories (five of which, containing upwards of one thousand slaves of both sexes, were at Badagry during my residence there); and next day the majority of these poor wretches are pinioned

* Lander's Records, vol. i. p. 31.

and conveyed to the banks of the river, where having arrived, a weight of some sort is appended to their necks, and, being rowed in canoes to the middle of the stream, they are flung into the water, and left to perish by the pitiless Badagrians. Slaves who for other reasons are rejected by the merchants undergo the same punishment, or are left to endure more lively torture at the sacrifices, by which means hundreds of human beings are annually destroyed."*

Mr. Leonard informs us, " that about 1830 the king of Loango told the officers of the Primrose that he could load eight slave-vessels in one week, and give each 400 or 500 ; but that, having now no means of disposing of the greater part of his prisoners, he was obliged to kill them. And, shortly before the Primrose arrived, a great number of unfortunate wretches, who had been taken in a predatory incursion, after having been made use of to carry loads of the plundered ivory, &c., to the coast, on their arrival there, as there was no market for them, and as the trouble and expense of their support would be considerable, were taken to the side of a hill, a little beyond the town, and coolly knocked on the head."†

In 1833 Mr. Oldfield found several dozen human skulls lining the bank of the river Nunn, (one of the mouths of the Niger,) at a barracoon or slave-house,

* Lander's Records, vol. ii. pp. 241, 250.
† Leonard's Voyage to Western Africa, p. 147.

which he discovered were the remains of slaves who had died there.*

An intelligent master of a merchant-vessel, who, for many years past, has been engaged in the African trade, informs me that, after the slave-dealing captains have made their selection of the slaves brought on board for sale, the unfortunate creatures who may be rejected " are sent · immediately on shore, and marched down to the barracoon, chained together, a distance of five miles. I have seen the most piteous entreaties made by the poor rejected creatures to the captain to take them, for they knew that to be returned on shore was only to encounter a worse fate by starvation." He is speaking of the River Bonny, and he goes on to say, " Ju Ju town contains about twelve barracoons : they are built to contain from 300 to 700 slaves each. I have seen from 1500 to 2000 slaves at a time, belonging to the several vessels then in the river."

" I have known disease to make dreadful havoc in these places, more especially in the year 1831, when the small-pox carried off 200 in one barracoon. Great numbers are carried off annually by diarrhœa and other diseases."

Colonel Nicolls has stated to me, that during his residence at Fernando Po he visited the River Cameroons, where he saw a number of slaves in a barracoon ; " they were confined in irons two and two, and many

* Laird and Oldfield's Journal, vol. i. p. 339.

of them had the irons literally grating against their bones through the raw flesh."

It is stated by a naval officer serving in the Preventive Squadron, in a letter to a relative, dated about a year ago, and communicated to me, that in 1837, having been employed in blockading a Portuguese brig up one of the rivers in the Bight of Biafra, " On arriving at my station, I had positive information that the Portuguese had bought upwards of 400 slaves, and was about to sail. By some means or other she got information that a British boat was blockading her, consequently she postponed her sailing for several weeks. Shortly afterwards, on my inquiring into her state, I found 300 of her slaves had died, chiefly of starvation, and a few were shot by the Portuguese whilst attempting to escape. A few days afterwards the brig sailed without any slaves, all, with the exception of about a score, having fallen victims to the system pursued."

Captain Cook has informed me that he saw many blind negroes in Quilimane (1837), who subsisted by begging ; they were the remains, he was informed, of a cargo landed from a Monte Videan vessel, which had been attacked by ophthalmia. If they lived, they were left to starve.

He also says that, in September, 1837, a number of slaves were suffocated on board the brig Generous at Quilimane.   " The boatswain had, it appeared, shut the hatches close down after the slaves had been put below in the evening; it was his duty to have kept the hatch uncovered, and to have placed guards over them; but this would have required his own vigilance, and he considered a sound sleep was to him worth all the slaves on board, especially as they cost him nothing." This case came to Captain Cook's knowledge in consequence of a quarrel between the captain and the boatswain. " The pecuniary loss was all that was regretted by the captain."

Captain Cook adds, that slaves who " die on board, in port, are never interred on shore, but are invariably thrown overboard, when they sometimes float backward and forward with the tide for a week, should the sharks and alligators not devour them. Should a corpse chance to be washed on shore at the top of high-water, it is permitted to remain until the vultures dispose of it." " I have known one to be near the Custom-house upwards of a week, during which time the stench was intolerable."

In a letter addressed by Captain Cook to the editor of the Standard, dated 16th July, 1838, he says that instances have been known of slaves having been buried alive in Quilimane for some trifling offence, and that the consequent punishment (if there was any at all) was a mere trifle, as imprisonment for a month; and he adds,—

" The fact, however, which I am now about to state occurred in August, 1837, and came under my own observation, and to all of which I am ready to bear testimony on oath, if required. Slaves to the number of 250, or thereabouts, male and female,

adults and children, were brought in canoes from
Senna, a Portuguese settlement at some distance in
the interior of Africa, to be sold at Quilimane, there
being at that time several slavers lying in the river.
These unfortunate beings were consigned to a
person holding a high civil appointment under the
Portuguese Government (the collector of customs) :
these poor creatures were from a part of the country
where it is said that the natives make bad slaves;
consequently, and as there was abundance of human
flesh in the market, they did not meet with a ready
sale. The wretch to whom they were consigned
actually refused them sustenance of any kind. Often
have I been compelled to witness the melancholy
spectacle of from twelve to twenty of my fellow-
creatures, without distinction of age or sex, chained
together, with a heavy iron chain round the neck,
wandering about the town in quest of food to satisfy
the cravings of nature, picking up bones and garbage
of every description from the dung-heaps, snails from
the fields, and frogs from the ditches, and, when the
tide receded, collecting the shell-fish that were left
on the bank of the river, or sitting round a fire roast-
ing and eagerly devouring the sea-weed.

" Again and again have I seen one or more of
these poor creatures, when unable from sickness to
walk, crawling on their hands and knees, accom-
panying the gang to which they were chained when
they went in search of their daily food .... for one
could not move without the whole. In consequence

of this treatment, they soon became so emaciated that the slave-dealers would not purchase them on any terms ; in this state, horrid as it must appear, the greater part were left to perish, without food, medicine, or clothing, for the little piece of coarse cotton cloth, worn by a few of the females, did not deserve the name, and could answer no other purpose than to lodge the vermin with which they were covered ; their bones protruding through the skin, they presented the appearance of living skeletons, lingering amidst hunger and disease, till death, their best friend, released most of them at once from suffering and bondage."*

From these extracts it is evident that this branch of the case furnishes an item of no small magnitude in the black catalogue of negro destruction.

I now proceed to the

MIDDLE PASSAGE—

* Through the haste with which the embarkation is usually conducted, some of the boats are, it is said, frequently swamped amidst the breakers, and many slaves are thus lost.—Col. Herald, 1st July, 1837.

MIDDLE PASSAGE.

" The stings of a wounded conscience, man cannot inflict; but nearly all which man can do to make his fellow-creatures miserable, without defeating his purpose by putting a speedy end to their existence, will still be here effected; and it will still continue true, that never can so much misery be found condensed into so small a space as in a slave-ship during the middle passage."—Wilberforce, Letter, 1807.

It was well observed by Mr. Fox, in a debate on the Slave Trade, that " True humanity consists not in a squeamish ear; it consists not in starting or shrinking at such tales as these, but in a disposition of heart to relieve misery. True humanity appertains rather to the mind than to the nerves, and prompts men to use real and active endeavours to execute the actions which it suggests."

In the spirit of this observation, I now go on to remark, that the first feature of this deadly passage, which attracts our attention, is the evident insufficiency, in point of tonnage, of the vessels employed, for the cargoes of human beings which they are made to contain.

In 1788 a law passed the British legislature, by which it was provided that vessels under 150 tons should not carry more than five men to every three tons; that vessels above 150 tons should not carry more than three men to every two tons; and that the height of slave-vessels between decks should not be less than five feet. In 1813 it was decreed by the government of Portugal and Brazil that two tons should be allowed for every five men ; and the Spanish " Cedula," of 1817, adopted the same scale. It is understood that the Spanish and Portuguese ton bears the proportion of one and a half to the British ton. The allowance in British transports is three men to every two tons.

	Men.		Tons.
The lowest rate, then, allowed by the British was	5	to	3
And by Spain, Portugal, and Brazil, it should be	5	to	3
But for British soldiers the regulation is .	3	to	2

and, although this allowance in the transport of troops seems to be liberal, when compared with the space afforded for slaves, even here complaints have often been made of the insufficiency.

Let us, then, keep in view these rates of tonnage, as we proceed to ascertain the accommodation which has been, and is now, afforded to the negroes on the middle passage ;* and here, at least, one reason will be apparent for the increase of suffering and mortality which has recently occurred, viz. that the extent of accommodation, limited as it was, has been *greatly curtailed.*

* I am informed that the slavers which have been brought to this country and remeasured have been found to be of much less tonnage than that stated in their papers : for instance, the " Napoleon," said to be 71 tons, was found to be only 31. The " William Allen," said to be 350 tons, was found to be only 134 tons.

We have a faithful description of the miseries of the middle passage, from the pen of an eye-witness, Mr. Falconbridge. His account refers to a period antecedent to 1790. He tells us that " The men negroes, on being brought aboard ship, are immediately fastened together two and two, by handcuffs on their wrists, and by irons riveted on their legs . . . . They are frequently stowed so close as to admit of no other posture than lying on their sides. Neither will the height between decks, unless directly under the grating, permit them the indulgence of an erect posture, especially where there are platforms, which is generally the case. These platforms are a kind of shelf, about eight or nine feet in breadth, extending from the side of the ship towards the centre. They are placed nearly midway between the decks, at the distance of two or three feet from each deck. Upon these the negroes are stowed in the same manner as they are on the deck underneath." After mentioning some other arrangements, he goes on to say, " It often happens that those who are placed at a distance from the buckets, in endeavouring to get to them, tumble over their companions, in consequence of their being shackled. These accidents, although unavoidable, are productive of continual quarrels, in which some of them are always bruised. In this distressed situation they desist from the attempt, and . . . . . . this becomes a fresh source of broils and disturbances, and tends to render the situation of the poor captive wretches still more uncomfortable.

" In favourable weather they are fed upon deck,
but in bad weather their food is given to them below.
Numberless quarrels take place among them during
their meals; more especially when they are put upon
short allowance, which frequently happens. In that
case, the weak are obliged to be content with a very
scanty portion. Their allowance of water is about
half a pint each, at every meal.

" Upon the negroes refusing to take sustenance, I
have seen coals of fire, glowing hot, put on a shovel,
and placed so near their lips as to scorch and burn
them, and this has been accompanied with threats of
forcing them to swallow the coals, if they any longer
persisted in refusing to eat. These means have generally the desired effect. I have also been credibly
informed that a certain captain in the Slave Trade
poured melted lead on such of the negroes as obsti-
nately refused their food." Falconbridge then tells
us that the negroes are sometimes compelled to
dance and to sing, and that, if any reluctance is exhibited, the cat-o'-nine-tails is employed to enforce
obedience. He goes on to mention the unbounded licence given to the officers and crew of the slavers, as
regards the women; and, speaking of the officers, he
says, they " are sometimes guilty of such brutal ex-
cesses as disgrace human nature . . . . But, ' he continues, " the hardships and inconveniences suffered by
the negroes during the passage are scarcely to be enumerated or conceived. They are far more violently

affected by the sea-sickness than the Europeans. It frequently terminates in death, especially among the women. The exclusion of the fresh air is among the most intolerable. Most ships have air-ports; but, whenever the sea is rough and the rain heavy, it becomes necessary to shut these and every other conveyance by which air is admitted. The fresh air being thus excluded, the negroes' rooms very soon grow intolerably hot. The confined air, rendered noxious by the effluvia exhaled from their bodies, and by being repeatedly breathed, soon produces fevers and fluxes, which generally carry off great numbers of them. During the voyages I made, I was frequently a witness to the fatal effects of this exclusion of the fresh air. I will give one instance, as it serves to convey some idea, though a very faint one,* of the state of these unhappy beings. Some wet and blowing weather having occasioned the portholes to be shut, and the gratings to be covered, fluxes

* One circumstance has struck me very forcibly. I have received communications, both by letter and in conversation, from many naval officers who have boarded slave-ships, and I have observed that, without an exception, they all make this observation : —" No words can describe the horrors of the scene, or the sufferings of the negroes." I have recently shown these pages to a naval officer, now a captain in the service, who had long been employed in the preventive squadron, requesting him to point out any error into which I might have fallen. He replied, " Your statement is true, as far as it goes; but it is, after all, only a faint picture of the reality."

and fevers among the negroes ensued. My profession requiring it, I frequently went down among them, till at length their apartments became so extremely hot as to be only sufferable for a very short time. But the excessive heat was not the only thing that rendered their situation intolerable. The deck, that is, the floor of their rooms, was so covered with the blood and mucus which had proceeded from them in consequence of the flux, that it resembled a slaughter-house. It is not in the power of human imagination to picture to itself a situation more dreadful or more disgusting.

" Numbers of the slaves having fainted, they were carried on deck, where several of them died ; and the rest were with great difficulty restored. It had nearly proved fatal to me also : the climate was too warm to admit the wearing of any clothing but a shirt, and that I had pulled off before I went down : notwithstanding which, by only continuing among them for about a quarter of an hour, I was so overcome by the heat, stench, and foul air, that I had nearly fainted ; and it was not without assistance that I could get upon deck. The consequence was, that I soon after fell sick of the same disorder, from which I did not recover for several months. A circumstance of this kind sometimes repeatedly happens in the course of a voyage, and often to a greater degree than what has just been described : particularly when the slaves are much crowded, which was not the case at that time, the ship having

more than 100 short of the number she was to
have taken in : yet, out of 380, 105 died on the passage,—a proportion seemingly very great, but by no
means uncommon."

He proceeds to notice the case of a Liverpool
vessel which took on board at the Bonny River
nearly 700 slaves (more than three to each ton!) ;
and Falconbridge says,—" By purchasing so great
a number, the slaves were so crowded, that they
were even obliged to lie one upon another. This
occasioned such a mortality among them, that, without meeting with unusual bad weather, or having a
longer voyage than common, nearly one-half of them
died before the ship arrived in the West Indies."
He then describes the treatment of the sick as
follows :—" The place allotted for the sick negroes
is under the half-deck, where they lie on the bare
plank. By this means, those who are emaciated
frequently have their skin, and even their flesh, entirely rubbed off, by the motion of the ship, from the
prominent parts of the shoulders, elbows, and hips,
so as to render the bones in those parts quite bare.
The excruciating pain which the poor sufferers feel
from being obliged to continue in so dreadful a situation, frequently for several weeks, in case they
happen to live so long, is not to be conceived or
described. Few indeed are ever able to withstand
the fatal effects of it. The surgeon, upon going
between decks in the morning, frequently finds several of the slaves dead, and, among the men, some-

times a dead and a living negro fastened by their irons together."

He then states that surgeons are driven to engage in the " Guinea Trade" by the confined state of their finances ; and that, at most, the only way in which a surgeon can render himself useful, is by seeing that the food is properly cooked and distributed to the slaves : " When once the fever and dysentery get to any height at sea, a cure is scarcely ever effected." " One-half, sometimes two-thirds, and even beyond that, have been known to perish. Before we left Bonny River no less than fifteen died of fevers, and dysenteries, occasioned by their confinement."* Falconbridge also told the Committee of 1790, that, " in stowing the slaves, they wedge them in, so that they had not as much room as a man in his coffin : that, when going from one side of their rooms to the other, he always took off his shoes, but could not avoid pinching them ; and that he had the marks on his feet where they bit and scratched him. Their confinement in this situation was so injurious, that he has known them to go down apparently in good health at night, and be found dead in the morning."

Any comment on the statement of Falconbridge must be superfluous : he had been a surgeon in slave-ships, he was a respectable witness before the Committee of Inquiry in 1790, and gave the substance of this statement in evidence. And it ought to be borne in mind that he was an eye-witness of the scenes which he has described. His evidence

* Falconbridge, p. 19, &c.

is the more valuable, when it is considered that we
have long been debarred from testimony equally cre-
dible and direct: as, since 1807, Britain has taken
no part in the slave-traffic; and it has been the
policy of the foreign nations who have continued the
trade to conceal, as far as they could, the horrors and
miseries which are its attendants.

Mr. Granville Sharpe (the zealous advocate of
the negro) brought forward a case which aroused
public attention to the horrors of this passage. In
his Memoirs we have the following account taken
from his private memoranda :—

" March 19, 1783. Gustavus Vasa called on
me with an account of 132 negroes being thrown
alive into the sea, from on board an English slave-
ship.

" The circumstances of this case could not fail to
excite a deep interest. The master of a slave-ship
trading from Africa to Jamaica, and having 440 slaves
on board, had thought fit, on a pretext that he might
be distressed on his voyage for want of water, to
lessen the consumption of it in the vessel, by throwing overboard 132 of the most sickly among the
slaves. On his return to England, the owners of the
ship claimed from the insurers the full value of those
drowned slaves, on the ground that there was an
absolute necessity for throwing them into the sea, in
order to save the remaining crew, and the ship itself.
The underwriters contested the existence of the alleged necessity; or, if it had existed, attributed it to the
ignorance and improper conduct of the master of the

vessel. This contest of pecuniary interest brought to light a scene of horrid brutality which had been acted during the execution of a detestable plot. From the trial it appeared that the ship Zong, Luke Collingwood master, sailed from the island of St. Thomas, on the coast of Africa, September 6, 1781, with 440 slaves and fourteen whites on board, for Jamaica, and that in the November following she fell in with that island; but, instead of proceeding to some port, the master, mistaking, as he alleges, Jamaica for Hispaniola, ran her to leeward. Sickness and mortality had by this time taken place on board the crowded vessel: so that, between the time of leaving the coast of Africa and the 29th of November, sixty slaves and seven white people had died; and a great number of the surviving slaves were then sick and not likely to live. On that day the master of the ship called together a few of the officers, and stated to them that, if the sick slaves died a natural death, the loss would fall on the owners of the ship; but, if they were thrown alive into the sea, on any sufficient pretext of necessity for the safety of the ship, it would be the loss of the underwriters, alleging, at the same time, that it would be less cruel to throw sick wretches into the sea, than to suffer them to linger out a few days under the disorder with which they were afflicted.

"To this inhuman proposal the mate, James Kelsal, at first objected; but Collingwood at length prevailed on the crew to listen to it. He then chose out from the cargo 132 slaves, and brought them on deck, all or most of whom were sickly, and not likely to recover, and he ordered the crew by turns to throw them into the sea. ' A parcel' of them were accordingly thrown overboard, and, on counting over the remainder the next morning, it appeared that the number so drowned had been fifty-four. He then ordered another parcel to be thrown over, which, on a second counting on the succeeding day, was proved to have amounted to forty-two.

" On the third day the remaining thirty-six were brought on deck, and, as these now resisted the cruel purpose of their masters, the arms of twenty-six were fettered with irons, and the savage crew proceeded with the diabolical work, casting them down to join their comrades of the former days. Outraged misery could endure no longer; the ten last victims sprang disdainfully from the grasp of their tyrants, defied their power, and, leaping into the sea, felt a momentary triumph in the embrace of death." *

The evidence taken before the Parliamentary Committees of 1790 and 1791 abounds with similar cases of enormity. I should be entitled, if it were necessary, to quote every one of them, because the middle passage, at that time, when the traffic was legal, was less horrible than now, when it is contraband. But I have limited myself to two extracts: the one, because it is the narrative of a surgeon,† a class of

---

* " Memoirs of Granville Sharpe," edited by Prince Hoare. London, 1820, pp. 236—238.

† Captain Cook, from whose communication to me I have already given extracts, narrating some of the cruelties of the middle pas-

officers now scarcely to be met with in a slave-ship, and because it gives, in a brief and continuous narrative, the chief features of the voyage across the Atlantic: the other, because every fact was proved in a court of justice.

Such were some of the cruelties of the middle passage towards the end of the last century; and it might have been expected that, since that time, some improvement should have taken place; but it is not so : the treatment of slaves by the British, subsequent to the Slave Regulation Act, and down to 1808, was mildness itself, when compared with the miseries consequent on the trade, and the system which has been pursued in the vain attempt to put it down, since that period to the present time.

Mr. Wilberforce, in his letter to his constituents in 1807, observes, "Many of the sufferings of these wretched beings are of a sort for which no legislative regulations can provide a remedy. Several of them, indeed, arise necessarily out of their peculiar circumstances, as connected with their condition on shipboard. It is necessary to the safety of the vessel to secure the men by chains and fetters. It is necessary to confine them below during the night, and in very stormy weather during the day also. Often it happens, that with the numbers still allowed to be taken, especially when some of those epidemic diseases pre-

sage, says, "With all this probability, or rather certainty, of disease, I never knew but one slaver that carried a surgeon."

vail, which, though less frequent than formerly, will yet occasionally happen; and when men of different countries and languages, or of opposite tempers, are linked together, that such scenes take place as are too nauseous for description. Still in rough weather their limbs must be excoriated by lying on the boards; still they will often be wounded by the fetters; still food and exercise will be deemed necessary to present the animal in good condition at the place of sale; still some of them will loathe their food, and be averse to exercise, from the joint effect perhaps of sea-sickness and mental uneasiness; and still, while in this state, they will probably be charged with sulkiness; and eating and dancing in their fetters will be enforced by stripes; still the high netting will be necessary, that standing precaution of an African ship against acts of suicide; but more than all, still must the diseases of the mind remain entire, nay, they may perhaps increase in force, from the attention being less called off by the urgency of bodily suffering; the anguish of husbands torn from their wives,—wives from their husbands, and parents from their children; the pangs arising from the consideration that they are separated for ever from their country, their friends, their relations, and connexions, remain the same."*

Such is the statement of Wilberforce as to the middle passage in its mildest form. This truly great

* Wilberforce's Letter, p. 99, &c.

man had the satisfaction shortly afterwards to witness
the abolition of the traffic on the part of Britain,—a
triumph on the side of humanity which his unceasing
and strenuous efforts were mainly instrumental in
obtaining.

Since 1808 the English Government has, with
various success, been indefatigably engaged in endeavouring to procure the co-operation of foreign
powers for the suppression of the Slave Trade.   In
virtue of the treaties which have been entered into,
many vessels engaged in the traffic have been captured; and much information has been obtained,
which has been regularly laid before Parliament.   A
few of the cases which have been detailed will now
be noticed, for the purpose of ascertaining whether
the miseries which have been narrated have ceased to
exist; or whether they do not *now* exist in a more
intense degree than at any former period.

The first case I notice is that of the Spanish brig
Carlos, captured in 1814.   In this vessel of 200
tons, 512 negroes had been put on board (nearly
180 *more* than the complement allowed on the proportion of five slaves to three tons).   The captor
reported that " they were so miserably fed, clothed,
&c., that any idea of the horrors of the Slave Trade
would fall short of what I saw.   Eighty were thrown
overboard before we captured her.   In many instances I saw the bones coming through the skin
from starvation."*

In the same year (1814) the schooner Aglae, of

* African Institution Report, 1815, p. 17.

40 tons, was captured with a cargo of 152 negroes
(nearly four to each ton). "The only care seemed
to have been to pack them as close as possible, and
tarpaulin was placed over tarpaulin, in order to give
the vessel the appearance of being laden with a well-
stowed cargo of cotton and rice."*

In 1815 a lieutenant of the navy thus describes
the state of a Portuguese slaver, the St. Joaquim: he
says, "That within twenty-two days after the vessel
had left Mozambique thirteen of the slaves had died:
that between the capture and their arrival at Simon's
Bay, the survivors of them were all sickly and weak,
and ninety-two of them afflicted with the flux; that
the slaves were all stowed together, perfectly naked,
and nothing but rough, unplaned planks to crouch
down upon, in a hold situated over their water and
provisions, the place being little more than two feet
in height, and the space allowed for each slave so
small, that it was impossible for them to avoid touching and pressing upon those immediately surrounding. The greater part of them were fastened, some
three together, by one leg, each in heavy iron shackles,
a very large proportion of them having the flux.
Thus they were compelled," &c. (here a scene of
disgusting wretchedness is described.) "The pilot
being asked by Captain Baker how many he supposed would have reached their destination, replied,
' About half the number that were embarked.' " †

We have next the case of the Rodeur, as stated in

* African Inst. Report, Appendix, p. 86.
† Afr. Inst. Report, 1818, p. 27.

a periodical work, devoted to medical subjects, and published at Paris. This vessel, it appears, was of 200 tons burden. She took on board a cargo of 160 negroes, and after having been fifteen days on her voyage, it was remarked that the slaves had contracted a considerable redness of the eyes, which spread with singular rapidity. At this time they were limited to eight ounces of water a-day for each person, which quantity was afterwards reduced to the half of a wine-glass. By the advice of the surgeon, the slaves who were in the hold were brought upon deck for the advantage of fresh air ; but it became necessary to abandon this expedient, as many of them who were affected with nostalgia threw themselves into the sea, locked in each other's arms. The ophthalmia, which had spread so rapidly and frightfully among the Africans, soon began to infect all on board, and to create alarm for the crew. The danger of infection, and perhaps the cause which produced the disease, were increased by a violent dysentery, attributed to the use of rain-water. The number of the blind augmented every day. The vessel reached Guadaloupe on June 21, 1819, her crew being in a most deplorable condition. Three days after her arrival, the only man who during the voyage had withstood the influence of the contagion, and whom Providence appeared to have preserved as a guide to his unfortunate companions, was seized with the same malady. Of the negroes, thirty-nine had become perfectly blind, twelve had lost one eye, and fourteen were affected with blemishes more or less considerable.

This case excited great interest, and several additional circumstances connected with it were given to the public. It was stated that the captain caused several of the negroes who were prevented in the attempt to throw themselves overboard, to be shot and hung, in the hope that the example might deter the rest from a similar conduct. It is further stated, that upwards of thirty of the slaves who became blind were thrown into the sea and drowned; upon the principle that had they been landed at Guadaloupe, no one would have bought them, while by throwing them overboard the expense of maintaining them was avoided, and a ground was laid for a claim on the underwriters by whom the cargo had been insured, who are said to have allowed the claim, and made good the value of the slaves thus destroyed.

What more need be said in illustration of the extremity of suffering induced by the middle passage, as demonstrated by the case of the Rodeur? But the supplement must not be omitted. At the time when only one man could see to steer that vessel, a large ship approached, "which appeared to be totally at the mercy of the wind and the waves. The crew of this vessel, hearing the voices of the crew of the Rodeur, cried out most vehemently for help. They told the melancholy tale as they passed along,—that their ship was a Spanish slave-ship, the St. Leon; and that a contagion had seized the eyes of all on board, so that there was not one individual sailor or slave who could see. But alas! this pitiable narrative was in vain; for no help could be given. The St. Leon passed on, and was never more heard of!"*

In the African Institution Report for 1820, I find the following case stated. Captain Kelly, of H.M.S. Pheasant, captured on July 30, 1819, a Portuguese schooner, called the Nova Felicidade, belonging to Prince's Island, having on board seventy-one slaves, and a crew, consisting of one master and ten sailors. This vessel measured only eleven tons. She was carried by Captain Kelly to Sierra Leone for adjudication, and his judicial declaration contains the following statement:—

"I do further declare, that the state in which these unfortunate creatures were found is shocking to every principle of humanity;—seventeen men shackled together in pairs by the legs, and twenty boys, one on the other, in the main hold,—a space measuring eighteen feet in length, seven feet eight inches main breadth, and one foot eight inches in height; and under them the yams for their support."

The appearance of the slaves, when released from their irons, was most distressing; scarcely any of them could stand on their legs, from cramp and evident starvation. The space allowed for the females, thirty-four in number, was even more con-

* Afr. Inst. Report, 1820, p. 7.

tracted than that for the men, measuring only nine feet four inches in length, four feet eight inches main breadth, and two feet seven inches in height, but not being confined in irons, and perhaps allowed during the day to come on deck, they did not present so distressing an appearance as the men."*

We have next another instance of the varied cruelties of this part of the subject—La Jeune Estelle, captured by Admiral Collier in 1820, after a chase of some hours, during which several casks were observed to be floating in the sea; but no person could be spared at the time to examine them. On boarding the Estelle, the captain denied that he had any slaves on board; but from the very suspicious appearances around, the officer ordered a strict search to be made. An English sailor, on striking a cask, heard a faint voice issue from it, as if of some creature expiring. The cask was immediately opened, when two slave girls, about twelve or fourteen years of age, were found packed up in it;†

* Afr. Inst. Report, 1820, p. 11.

† I have great satisfaction in being able to trace the sequel to this tale of horror. Mr. Kilham thus writes in 1824: " The wives of the missionaries find no insurmountable difficulty in teaching the African girls to be clever cooks, housemaids, and laundresses. I had the gratification last week to see one of the poor girls who was rescued from the iron-hearted slave-dealer, who had confined his two remaining victims in a cask on board. One of the girls is now married: the other is chief monitor in the Church Missionary School at Leopold."

a prisoner on board the captor's ship recognized the girls as two out of fourteen, whom the slaver had carried off from a village on the coast. Admiral Collier, on this, ordered another search to be made, in hopes of discovering the other twelve; but they were nowhere to be found. The painful suspicion then arose that the slaver had packed up the twelve girls in casks, and had thrown them overboard during the chase; but it was too late to ascertain the truth of this conjecture, as the chase had led the English frigate many leagues to leeward of the place where they had observed casks floating in the sea.*

Some of the following extracts are also taken from the Reports of the African Institution:—

A Spanish schooner, the Vicua, when taken possession of, in 1822, had a lighted match hanging over the open magazine hatch. The match had been placed there by the crew before they escaped. It was seen by one of the British seamen, who boldly put his hat under the burning wick, and removed it. The magazine contained a large quantity of powder. One spark would have blown up 325 unfortunate victims, lying in irons in the hold. These monsters in iniquity expressed their deep regret, after the action, that their diabolical plan had failed. Thumbscrews were also found in this vessel. From confinement and suffering the slaves often injured themselves by beating, and venting their grief upon

* Afr. Inst. Report, 1821, p. 15.

such as were next them, by biting and tearing their flesh.*

Les Deux Sœurs was a vessel of forty-one tons; the Eleanor of about sixty; the first had crammed 132 negroes, the last 135, into a space capable of containing about thirty, at full length.†

In the Report of 1823, we have an account of a gallant feat achieved by the boats of a man-of-war, commanded by Lieutenant Mildmay, on the 15th of April, 1822. The action took place in the river Bonny. On the one side were six sail of slavers, three of which opened a heavy fire upon " the English boats as they advanced. When the latter were near enough for their shots to take effect, the firing was returned. They advanced, and in a short time took possession of all the vessels.

" Many of the slaves jumped overboard during the engagement, and were devoured by the sharks. On board the Yeanam the slaves suffered much ; four were killed, and ten wounded. Of the wounded, three were females; one girl, of about ten years old, lost both her legs, another her right arm, and a third was shot in the side. Even after the vessel had been surrendered, a number of the Spanish sailors skulked below, and, arming the slaves with muskets, made them fire upwards on the British. On board this ship Lieutenant Mildmay observed a slave girl, about twelve or thirteen years of age, in irons, to which

* Afr. Inst. Report, 1823, p. 29.
† Ib., 1826, p. 55.

was fastened a thick iron chain, ten feet in length, that was dragged along as she moved."*

Commodore Bullen writes, of date September 5, 1825, that the Brazen, last October, overtook L'Eclair. " She belongs to Nantz. The master stated that he had lost a third of his cargo in embarking them. She measured three feet one inch between decks; the men chained; many of them unable to sit upright."†

A resident at Freetown thus writes in the Sierra Leone Gazette of the 11th of December, 1823 :— " Having gone off to the slave-vessels lately sent into this harbour, I was struck by the appearance of some very fierce dogs, of the bloodhound species, natives of Brazil; and, on inquiry, found that they had been taken on board for the purpose of assisting their inhuman masters in coercing the unfortunate victims of their lawless cupidity. They had been trained, it appears, to sit watch over the hatches during the night, or whenever the wretched beings were confined below, and thus effectually precluded them from coming up. This abominable system is, I understand, pretty generally practised on board the slavers from Bahia and Cuba."

In the Sierra Leone Advertiser of November 20, 1824, we have some striking instances of the frauds practised by the Portuguese slavers in carrying on their trade. Of three vessels captured, it appeared that the Diana had a royal licence to carry 300

* Afr. Inst. Report, 1823, p. 28. † Ib., 1826, p. 60.

slaves, as being a vessel of 120 tons; and this in accordance with the law allowing five slaves to every two tons (equal to three tons British); but in fact she admeasured only sixty-six tons, which would give a rate of five slaves to *one* ton. She had shipped at Badagry, for Brazil, 156 slaves, besides her crew, eighteen in number.

The Two Brazilian Friends, licensed to carry 365 slaves, as being of 146 tons, proved to be of only 95 tons; and the platform for the men only two feet six inches in height: yet she had on board 260 slaves, besides a crew of eighteen persons.

The Aviso, asserted to be 231, found to be only 165 tons: 465 slaves were stowed in this vessel, with a crew thirty-three in number.

A great many deaths had occurred in these vessels, and the survivors were in a very emaciated state.*

* " 'Of all the vessels I was on board of,' says Captain Wool- combe, ' this (the Diana) was in the most deplorable condition; the stench from the accumulation of dirt, joined to that of so many human beings packed together in a small space (the men all ironed in pairs) was intolerable. To add to the scene of misery, the small-pox had broken out among them.'

" Commodore Bullen, who visited the Two Brazilian Friends, says, ' Its filthy and horrid state beggars all description. Many females were far advanced in pregnancy, and several had infants from four to twelve months of age; all were crowded together in one mass of living corruption; and yet this vessel had not her prescribed complement by near 100.'

" Commodore Bullen found the Aviso in a most crowded and wretched condition, although she had on board 120 less than directed in her passport. Such were the filth and crowd, that not

The Paris petition of — February, 1825, states, " That it is established, by authentic documents, that the slave captains throw into the sea, every year, about 3000 negroes, men, women, and children ; of whom more than half are thus sacrificed, whilst yet alive, either to escape from the visits of cruisers, or because, worn down by their sufferings, they could not be sold to advantage."*

In the Appendix (G.) to the Report of the African Institution for 1827, we have the case of the schooner L'Espoir, as narrated by General Milius, governor of Bourbon. "In the month of September, 1826, the schooner left the Mauritius under English colours, shaping its course towards the coasts of Madagascar. The Sieur Lemoine was the master ; he fell in with a Portuguese vessel laden with negroes and gold-dust. An eagerness and thirst of gain seized upon his soul ; he ran alongside of the Portuguese vessel, and immediately killed the mate by a musket-shot ; having boarded her, he soon obtained possession of the vessel attacked, and his first questions were addressed to a Portuguese colonel, aged fifty, of whom he inquired where the money and gold-dust were

one-half could have reached the Brazils alive. At the date of her capture she had scarcely 20 days' provisions for the slaves, and less water. ' How they intended to subsist them till their arrival at Bahia,' says the Captain, ' is to me a problem, unless they could have calculated on a great decrease from death.' "—Afr. Inst. Report for 1825, pp. 27, 28.

* Afr. Inst. Report for 1826, pp. 62, 63.

deposited. After this short interrogatory, Lemoine purposely stepped aside, and a man named Reineur, who was behind him, with a pistol blew out the unfortunate colonel's brains. The master of the captured vessel, alarmed by the rapid succession of these massacres, threw himself overboard, in order to escape a more immediate death. Vain hope! the fury of Lemoine and his accomplices was not yet allayed. They pursued him in a boat, and having soon overtaken him, they cut him on the head with a sabre. The unfortunate man, feeling himself wounded, caught hold, in order to support himself, of the boat in which his murderers were, who, profiting by this last effort of despair, had the dastard cruelty to run a sword into his throat, the point of which came out at his side: the body disappeared, and they returned on board, fatigued but not satiated with murder. They shut up in the hold the remaining Portuguese sailors, and, after taking off the rich cargo, they scuttled the ship, and sunk her with the crew they had thus shut up.

" This is one of many proofs of the piratical habits and cruelty produced by the Slave Trade."*

In the evidence before the committee on Sierra Leone, &c., in 1830, we find it stated by Lieutenant Tringham, that, about 1825, the vessel in which he sailed captured a slave-schooner of seventy or eighty tons, bound for Brazil, with 280 slaves on board. There were about 100 on deck and 180 below. They

* Afr. Inst. Report, 1827. App. G., p. 144.

were so crowded on deck, that (as the witness says) " We were not able to work the vessel without treading on them." As to their provisions, he remarked that the " jerked beef" was very salt, and that there was always a scarcity of water ; " the allowance was about a pint a-day ; they had two meals in the day, and about half a pint at each meal was their full allowance."*

In the despatches of Sir Charles M'Carthy, dated the 3rd of August, 1822, I find the case of the San José Hallaxa, a schooner under seven tons burden, which was captured by H.M.B. Thistle, in the river Calabar ; and it appears, by the acknowledgment of the master, that he shipped at Duke Ephraim's Town, on that river, thirty slaves ; that he had gone to sea with that number on board, intending to proceed to Princes Island, but, not having been able to make that port, he had returned to Calabar, having his provisions and water nearly expended, after having been at sea five or six weeks.

During this voyage, ten unfortunate objects of his avarice, not being able to procure sufficient nourishment to satisfy the cravings of nature, had been released from further sufferings by starvation ! One poor female, in the absence of food, had existed on salt water until her faculties were destroyed, and she became raving mad ; but even the deplorable and affecting state of insanity did not shield her from the

---

* Parl. Report. Sierra Leone, &c., 1830, p. 33.

brutal outrage of her oppressors, who, with a view
of stifling her cries by frequent repetitions of the lash,
literally flogged her to death. The owner of this
vessel, and the purchaser of these human beings, is
a woman!—Doña Maria de Cruz, daughter of the
notorious Gomez, formerly governor of Princes Island,
and now holding the appointment of fiscal, and member of council. This woman is known to the Mixed
Commission Court, having been under their cognizance some time since as proprietor of the ' Concei-
çao,' condemned by the British and Portuguese
judges.*

Sir John Barrow, in his able observations on the
Slave Trade in 1826, says :—" We have also discovered among the papers before us (those laid before Parliament), that the amiable Donna Maria de
Cruz, daughter of the governor of Princes Island, of
whom we had occasion once before to make honourable mention, is still engaged in carrying on the
traffic, though in a small way. The Victor sloop-
of-war fell in with and captured a schooner-boat belonging to this paragon of her sex, called the Maria
Pequeña. Her burden was five tons. She had taken
on board in the river Gaboon, besides her crew, water,
and provisions, twenty-three slaves, six of whom had
already died : they were stowed in a space between
the water-casks and the deck, of eighteen inches in
height ; and Lieutenant Scott reports that, when he

* Parl. Paper, 11th July, 1823, p. 9.

seized her, the remaining negroes were in a state of actual starvation."*

Commodore Bullen, in his despatch of 26th November, 1826, describing the capture of *Le Daniel*, says, " in consequence of the heavy rain which commenced shortly after I brought him to, the slaves quarrelled among themselves regarding the right of precedence of those below to get on deck for fresh air, and those who had already the possession of it, when, shocking to relate, 19 fell victims."† The Commissioners at Havana, in their despatch of the 28th August, 1828, mention the case of the " Intrepido," which, out of a cargo of 343, lost 190 in her passage, and 18 after capture, making a total of 208.   They attribute a certain portion of this mortality to two insurrections of the negroes on board, but principally to the horrible confinement of so great a number on board so small a vessel.‡

" The Invincible had on board a cargo of 440 negroes, a number, it seems, sixty-three short of her full complement; but these so crowded together, that it became absolutely impossible to separate the sick from the healthy; and dysentery, ophthalmia, and scurvy breaking out among them, the provisions and water being of the worst kind, and the filth and stench beyond all description, 186 of the number had perished in less than sixty days."§

* Edinburgh Review, No. 44, 1826.
† Class A. 1829, p. 138.   ‡ Class A. 1829, p. 153.
§ Afr. Inst. Report, 1827, pp. 4, 5.

The Maria, 133 Spanish tons burden, captured by H.M.B. Plumper, 26th December, 1830, was found to contain 545 persons, including the crew,—thus allowing only the unprecedented small space of one ton for the accommodation of four persons; the consequence was, that though she was out only eleven days, the small-pox, dysentery, and other diseases had broken out with great virulence.*

Captain Wauchope, R.N., late of H.M.S. Thalia, has stated to me, that Commander Castle, R.N., while on service with the preventive squadron in 1828, in command of H.M.S. Medina, captured the Spanish brig El Juan, with 407 slaves on board. It appeared that, owing to a press of sail during the chase, the El Juan had heeled so much, as to alarm the negroes, who made a rush to the grating. The crew thought they were attempting to rise, and getting out their arms, they fired upon the wretched slaves through the grating, till all was quiet in the hold. When Captain Castle went on board, the negroes were brought up, one living and one dead shackled together; " it was an awful scene of carnage and blood; one mass of human gore : Captain Castle said he never saw anything so horrible in his life."

Dr. Walsh, in his " Notices of Brazil," gives a most animated picture of the state of a Spanish slaver, detained by the vessel of war in which he returned from Brazil, in May, 1829. He says, " When we mounted her decks we found her full of slaves : she

* Class A. 1832, p. 13.

had taken on board 562, and had been out seventeen days, during which she lost fifty-five. The slaves were all enclosed under grated hatchways between decks. The space was so low that they sat between each other's legs, and stowed so close together that there was no possibility of their lying down, or at all changing their position by night or day. As they belonged to, and were shipped on account of different individuals, they were all branded like sheep, with the owners' marks of different forms. These were impressed under their breasts, or on their arms ; and, as the mate informed me with perfect indifference, ' burned with the red-hot iron.' "

After many other particulars, the detail of which my limits will not admit, Dr. Walsh continues : —" The poor beings were all turned up together. They came swarming up like bees from the aperture of a hive, till the whole deck was crowded to suffocation from stem to stern. On looking into the places where they had been crammed, there were found some children next the sides of the ship. The little creatures seemed indifferent as to life or death, and when they were carried on deck many of them could not stand. Some water was brought : it was then that the extent of their sufferings was exposed in a fearful manner. They all rushed like maniacs towards it. No entreaties, or threats, or blows could restrain them ; they shrieked, and struggled, and fought with one another for a drop of the precious liquid, as if they grew rabid at the sight of it. There is nothing which slaves, during the middle passage, suffer from so much as want of water. It is sometimes usual to take out casks filled with sea-water, as ballast; and when the slaves are received on board, to start the casks, and refill them with fresh. On one occasion, a ship from Bahia neglected to change the contents of the casks, and, on the mid-passage, found to their horror that they were filled with nothing but salt water. All the slaves on board perished! We could judge of the extent of their sufferings from the sight we now saw. When the poor creatures were ordered down again, several of them came and pressed their heads against our knees, with looks of the greatest anguish at the prospect of returning to the horrid place of suffering below. It was not surprising that they had lost fifty-five in the space of seventeen days. Indeed, many of the survivors were seen lying about the decks, in the last stage of emaciation, and in a state of filth and misery not to be looked at.

" While expressing my horror at what I saw, and exclaiming against the state of this vessel, I was informed by my friends, who had passed so long a time on the coast of Africa, and visited so many ships, that this was one of the best they had seen. The height sometimes, between decks, was only eighteen inches; so that the unfortunate beings could not turn round, or even on their sides, the elevation being less than the breadth of their shoulders; and here they are usually chained to the decks by the neck and legs.

After much deliberation, this wretched vessel was allowed to proceed on her voyage.

" It was dark when we separated; and the last parting sounds we heard from the unhallowed ship were the cries and shrieks of the slaves, suffering under some bodily infliction.*

In the same year (1829), the Commissioners at Havana reported that " The Fama de Cadiz came into port, having previously landed 300 slaves at Santa Cruz. It is said that this notorious slave-trader and pirate had plundered other slave-vessels on the coast of Africa of about 980 slaves, and had scarcely sailed for Cuba, when the small-pox and other contagious diseases broke out, which reduced the crew of 157 to 66, and her slaves to about 300; of whom the greatest part are in so wretched a state that her owners have been selling them as low as 100 dollars."

They also report the arrival of the schooner Constantia, in ballast, after having landed 70 slaves on the coast. She is said to have left Africa with 438 negroes, who have been reduced, by the small-pox, to the above small number. And they add,— " The mortality on board the slave-vessels, this year, has been truly shocking."†

In 1829 we have the case of the Midas. This vessel left the Bonny with a cargo of 560 slaves,

* Walsh's Notices of Brazil. London, 1830. Vol. ii. p. 475, &c.

† Class A. 1829, p. 156.

and had only 400 on board at the time of detention.
Of these, after the surrender, about thirty threw
themselves into the sea.   Before she arrived at Havana, nine other negroes had thrown themselves
overboard : sixty-nine had died of the small-pox and
other diseases.   After their arrival, ten more died.
The remainder (282) were then in a most dreadful
state ; so ill and so emaciated, that " it has hitherto
been impossible," says the medical officer, " to make
out the descriptions of their persons and marks that
are inserted in their certificates of emancipation."*

In 1831, Captain Hamilton thus writes to the
Commissioners :—" On our getting into Bahia, in
the afternoon of the same day, I sent two officers on
board the Destimida, to search.   They, after some
time, and with much difficulty, discovered fifty male
negro slaves concealed in the bottom of the vessel."†
" Five young men were extricated from one water-
butt ; but the greater part had been stowed or
forced into the small or close spaces between the
water-casks under the false decks."‡

Captain Hayes, R.N., mentions the case of a
slaver having a large cargo of human beings chained
together.   " The master of the vessel, with more
humanity than his fellows, permitted some of them
to come on deck (but still chained together) for the
benefit of the air, when they immediately commenced jumping overboard, hand in hand, and

* Class A. 1829, p. 148.   † Class A. 1831, p. 127.
‡ Class B. 1831, p. 117.

drowning in couples." He explains the cause of this circumstance by saying, " they were just brought from a situation between decks, and to which they knew they must return, where the scalding perspiration was running from one to the other, covered also with their own filth, and where it is no uncommon occurrence for women to be bringing forth children, and men dying by their side, with, full in their view, living and dead bodies chained together; and the living, in addition to all their other torments, labouring under the most famishing thirst, being in very few instances allowed more than a pint of water a-day. He goes on to say:—" I have now an officer on board the Dryad, who, on examining one of these slave-vessels, found, not only living men chained to dead bodies, but the latter in a putrid state; and we have now a case which, if true, is too horrible and disgusting to be described."*

In the same year (1831), the Black Joke and Fair Rosamond fell in with the Rapido and Regulo, two slave-vessels, off the Bonny river. On perceiving the cruisers, they attempted to make their escape up the river; but, finding it impracticable, they ran into a creek, and commenced pitching the negroes overboard. The Fair Rosamond came up in time to save 212 slaves out of the Regulo; but, before she could secure the other, she had discharged her whole human cargo into the sea. Captain

* Class B. p. 70.

Huntley, who was then in command of the Rosamond, in a letter to me, remarks,—" The scene
occasioned by the horrid conduct of the Rapido
I am unable to describe ; but the dreadful extent to
which the human mind is capable of falling was
never shown in a more painfully humiliating manner
than on this occasion, when, for the mere chance of
averting condemnation of property amounting to
perhaps £3,000, not less than 250 human beings
were hurled into eternity with utter remorselessness."

The master of an English merchant-vessel, who
happened to be in the Bonny at the time, witnessed
the whole affair. He lately told me that " the chase
was so vigorous, and the slavers so anxious to escape,
that they came flying into the creek, and ran aground
in the mud. They then threw overboard what remained of the negroes ; but very few, from their
being shackled together, reached the shore ; and that
he and his crew helped to get the vessels again afloat,
which was accomplished with much difficulty. He
afterwards met the captain of one of the slavers, who
justified what he had done as an act which necessity
compelled him to adopt for the preservation of his
property."

Captain Ramsay, who at the time commanded the
Black Joke, has stated to me that, during the chase,
he and his men distinctly saw the sharks tearing the
bodies of the negroes who were thrown overboard
by the slavers ; and that, had it not been for the fortunate rescue of two of the slaves of the Rapido, who

had been flung into the sea, shackled together, and
who were brought up from under water by a boat-
hook, that vessel would have escaped condemnation,
as all her slaves had been thrown overboard, or
landed in canoes before they came up with her.*

In a letter which I received from Captain Wauchope, of date 13th August, 1838, he says,—" In
February, 1836, I was informed by Commander
Puget, that the Spanish slaver, Argus, three months
before this date, was chased by the Charybdis, Lieutenant Mercer; that, during the chase, ninety-seven
slaves had been thrown overboard, and that a Spanish
captain he had captured declared he would never
hesitate to throw the slaves overboard to prevent
being taken."

Were it not that the evidence on these cases is
unexceptionable, we could not believe that there did
exist human beings capable of uttering such sentiments, or of performing such infamous deeds.

Captain Wauchope, in the same letter, informs
me, that on the 18th September, 1836, the Thalia
captured the Portuguese brig Felix, 590 slaves on
board. "After capture," he says, " I went on board,
and such a scene of horror it is not easy to describe :
the long-boat on the booms, and the deck aft, were
crowded with little children, sickly, poor little unhappy things, some of them rather pretty, and some
much marked and tattooed : much pains must have

* See an account of this case in the United Service Journal for
1833, part i., p. 505, &c.

been taken by their miserable parents to ornament and beautify them.

"The women lay between decks aft, much crowded, and perfectly naked : they were not barred down, the hatchway, a small one, being off; but the place for the men was too horrible: the wretches, chained two and two, gasping and striving to get at the bars of the hatchways, and such a steam and stench as to make it intolerable even to look down. It requires much caution at first, in allowing them to go on deck, as it is a common practice for them to jump overboard to get quit of their misery.

" The slave-deck was not more than three feet six in height, and the human beings stowed, or rather crushed as close as possible ; many appeared very sickly. There was no way of getting into the slave-room but by the hatchway. I was told, when they were all on deck to be counted, that it was impossible for any of our people to go into the slave-room for a single minute, so intolerable was the stench. The colour of these poor creatures was of a dark squalid yellow, so different from the fine glossy black of our liberated Africans and Kroomen. I was shown a man much bit and bruised : it was done in a struggle at the gratings of their hatchways for a mouthful of fresh air."

It is fearful to contemplate the increase of late years, in the mortality during the middle passage. The chief reason, as it appears, is well given by Laird in his journal of the recent expedition to the

Niger. He says :—"Instead of the large and commodious vessels which it would be to the interest of the slave-trader to employ, we have, by our interference, forced him to use a class of vessels, (well known to naval men as *American clippers*,) of the very worst description that could have been imagined for the purpose, every quality being sacrificed for speed. In the holds of these vessels the unhappy victims of European cupidity are stowed literally in bulk."*

It ought also to be kept in view, that there is this material difference betwixt these "clippers" and other merchant-vessels : that while the latter usually carry far more than their registered tonnage would seem to permit, the former invariably exhibit a capacity for a cargo greatly below the tonnage by registration.

As a proof of the increase in the mortality on the middle passage, I may adduce the evidence of Mr. Jackson (who had been a judge in the Mixed Commission Court at Sierra Leone) before the Committee on Sierra Leone, &c., in 1830. In answer to a question, he said, "I think the sufferings of those poor slaves are greatly aggravated by the course now adopted ; for the trade is now illegal, and therefore whatever is done, is done clandestinely : they are packed more like bales of goods on board than human beings, and the general calculation is, that if

* Laird, vol. ii. p. 369.

in three adventures one succeeds, the owners are well paid."*

Were it not that I feel bound to substantiate my case up to the present time, I would gladly pass over the numberless instances of cruelty and mortality connected with this branch of the subject, which are made known to us by the papers laid before Parliament within the last few years. But I shall notice some of these instances, as briefly as can be done, without suppressing the main facts which are established by them.

The Carolina, captured in 1834, off Wydah.† "This vessel was only seventy-five tons burden, yet she had 350 negroes crammed on board of her, 180 of whom were literally so stowed as to have barely sufficient height to hold themselves up, when in a sitting posture. The poor creatures crowded round their deliverers, with their mouths open and their tongues parched for want of water, presenting a perfect spectacle of human misery."

The Patacho, reported by the Commissioners at Rio de Janeiro in 1835:—This "vessel was in the first instance detained only on suspicion, and the capturing party had had possession forty-eight hours, and had made every possible search, as they supposed, before it was discovered that there were any slaves concealed on board. What the state of these wretched beings, to the number of forty-seven, must have been,

* Sierra Leone Report, 1830, pp. 55.
† Class A. 1834, p. 17.

deprived for so long a time of air and food, and packed in the smallest possible compass, like so many bales of goods, we need not pain your Lordship by describing."*

In a letter from the Cape of Good Hope, of date 20th January, 1837, we find it stated that Her Majesty's brig Dolphin had lately captured the corvette Incomprehensible; and that, on taking possession of her, "the scene presented on board was harrowing in the extreme. One hundred had died from sickness, out of the 800 embarked; another 100 were lying nearly lifeless on her decks, in wretchedness and misery, and all the agony of despair; the remaining 600 were so cramped from the close manner in which they were packed (like herrings in a barrel), and the length of time they had been on their voyage, and the cold they had endured in rounding the Cape, in a state of nudity, that it took the utmost exertions of the English sailors, favoured by a hot sun, to straighten them."†

In the Shipping and Mercantile Gazette of 2d June, 1838, is the following paragraph :—" A letter from the 'Snake' sloop of war, dated 31st March, 1838, says, 'We have captured a very fine schooner, called the Arogan, off Cape Antonio, having 350 slaves of both sexes, under the age of 20, and have sent her into the Havana for adjudication. She cleared out from Gallinas, and lost 50 on her pas-

* Class A. 1835, p. 286.

† From a correspondent of the 'Times' newspaper.

sage by death, owing to the crowded manner in which they were packed, resembling goods in a draper's shop.'"

I know of no more striking case of excessive crowding than that of the Spanish Felucca *Si*, of only 71 British tons, which was captured in May, 1839, by Her Majesty's brig Waterwitch, with 360 slaves on board, making an average of more than *five* to one ton, with which she was about to proceed across the Atlantic.

In the parliamentary papers printed in 1838 by the House of Commons, I observe the following cases reported:—"The brig Don Manuel de Portugal, from Angola, embarked 600 slaves; of these 73 died on the voyage."

"Brig Adamastor, from Quilimane, embarked 800 slaves; of these 304 died on the voyage!"

"Brig *Leão*, from Quilimane, embarked 855 slaves; of these 283 died, or were thrown overboard alive, during the voyage. The small-pox having appeared among the slaves, 30 of them were immediately thrown overboard alive; afterwards the measles made its appearance, of which 253 died. The remaining slaves, 572 in number, were landed on the coast of Brazil at Mozambayo, near to Ilha Grande, but in so miserable a state that, the greater part could not walk, but were carried on shore."*

"The brig Flor de Quilimane, from Quilimane, embarked 850 slaves; of these 163 died on the pas-

* Class B. 1837, p. 58.

sage, and 697 were landed at Campos in a very sickly state."*

In a letter from a member of the Society of Friends, dated Havana, July 14th, 1836, and published in the Colonization Herald, Philadelphia, Aug. 15th, 1838, I find the following passage :—"In company with an English naval officer, I made a visit across the bay to several of these slave-vessels. We were permitted to walk over them, but no particular attention was paid to us; on the contrary, we were looked upon with suspicion, and received short and unsatisfactory answers to our questions in general; all attempts to enter into conversation with those on board appeared useless. With one, however, we were more successful : an old weather-beaten Spaniard was walking the deck ;

* Class B. 1837, p. 60.

In the Commissioners' Report for 1838-9, I find the loss on the passage thus stated :—

	Shipped.	Died on Voyage.
Cintra . .	970	214
Brillante . .	621	214
Commodore . .	685	300
Esplorador . .	560	360
	2,836	1,088

These vessels had sailed from the eastern coast of Africa, and arrived at Rio ; excepting the Esplorador, which arrived at Havana. The report contains the names of many other vessels, but of these four only the numbers are stated. It is impossible not to believe that the deaths in the remainder have been at least equal in proportion. Class A. 1838-9, *passim.*

although an old pirate, his expression of countenance was fine : taking a seat under the awning on the quarter-deck, offering him a bundle of cigaritas, and lighting one ourselves, by degrees induced him to enter into conversation, and, in the course of one hour or more, I learned from him some horrid truths. He told us that, in four voyages, he had brought in the vessel in which we were 1,600 human beings ; his was a fortunate vessel, and seldom lost more than half a dozen a voyage : once, however, he told us, he was not so lucky ; a malignant disease broke out on board soon after leaving the coast, and, of 300 taken in in Africa, but ninety-five were landed, more dead than alive, on the island.

"The materiel, such as handcuffs, chains, and even the lower-decks, are taken out and are fitted up on the coast of Africa. We saw the apertures in the decks to admit the air, and, as we were leaving the brig in our boat alongside, the captain exultingly told us that he knew we were officers of the British sloop-of-war, pointing to the Champion, which was riding at anchor at a little distance from us ; ' but,' added he, ' you are welcome. I yesterday showed your captain (meaning of the Champion) all over my trim vessel. I have nothing to conceal—you dare not touch me here ; and, once outside (with an expressive shrug of the shoulders), you may catch me if you can.' "

We have little authentic information as to the transport of the slaves from one part of the coast to another in south-east Africa, or from that coast to

Arabia, and the other countries northwards, to which they are conveyed. But Captain Moresby, to whom I have alread alluded, described to me the passage coastways, in the following terms:—" The Arab dows, or vessels, are large, unwieldy, open boats, without a deck. In these vessels temporary platforms of bamboos are erected, leaving a narrow passage in the centre. The negroes are then stowed, in the literal sense of the word, in bulk ; the first along the floor of the vessel, two adults, side by side, with a boy or girl resting between or on them, until the tier is complete. Over them the first platform is laid, supported an inch or two clear of their bodies, when a second tier is stowed, and so on until they reach the gunwale of the vessel.

" The voyage, they expect, will not exceed twenty-four or forty-eight hours : it often happens that a calm, or unexpected land-breeze, delays their progress : in this case a few hours are sufficient to decide the fate of the cargo ; those of the lower portion of the cargo, that die, cannot be removed. They remain until the upper part are dead, and thrown over, and, from a cargo of from 200 to 400 stowed in this way, it has been known that not a dozen, at the expiration of ten days, have reached Zanzebar. On the arrival of the vessels at Zanzebar the cargo are landed ; those that can walk up the beach are arranged for the inspection of the Imaum's officer, and the payment of duties—those that are weak or maimed by the voyage are left for the coming tide to relieve their miseries. An examination then takes place, which for brutality has never been exceeded in Smithfield."

In immediate connexion with the mortality incident to the middle passage, I come now to the subject of

WRECKS, ETC.

In Appendix D, of the African Institution Report for 1820, we are told that a " Spanish brig, on arriving at Point à Petre, experienced a severe squall, and, on the captain opening the hatches (which were let down during the squall), he found fifty of the poor Africans dead."

In Appendix B. of the same report, we find, in a statement of Sir G. Collier, Dec. 27, 1821, that the schooner Carlotta embarked, off Cape Palmas, " 269 slaves; and the very next day, in a tornado off St. Ann's, for want of timely precaution, upset, and, dreadful to relate, the whole of these wretched people, confined in irons, sank with her."

In the parliamentary papers for 1822 we find, " The schooner Yeanam was separated from the other vessels in a dreadful storm, as they were proceeding to Havana, and sank, with 380 slaves on board."[*]

The Accession, an English brig, brought into Bahia thirty-nine negroes, whom she rescued from a wreck abandoned by its crew. Thirty-one were found holding by the top of a mast. On cutting the side of the vessel open, they took out ten more from an almost pestilential atmosphere, and saw a number

* Parl. Papers, 11th July, 1823, p. 7.

lying dead. The crew, and 138 of the slaves, had been previously taken out by the Viajante ; but, as that vessel was herself carrying 622 negroes, she had left these others to perish in the waves.*

I find, by an extract from the Sierra Leone Gazette of the 12th June, 1824, that, " on the appearance of H.M.S. Victor, a boat full of men was seen to leave the lugger (l'Henriette Aimée), after which she got under weigh, but, instead of attempting to escape, run on shore in a heavy surf, where she immediately went to pieces ; and, from the number of blacks observed on her decks, there can be no doubt she had her cargo of slaves on board, all of whom perished."

By the despatch of the Commissioners at Havana, of 26th February, 1826, it appears that " the Magico was fallen in with and chased by H.M.S. Union, and, having been brought to action in the course of the 21st January, she was finally run on shore on the morning of the 22nd, and shortly after taken possession of. The crew had previously escaped to land with (it is supposed) about 200 negroes ; many, however, were left behind, severely wounded, some were hanging on at different parts of the vessel, and from twenty to thirty of their dead bodies were seen in the sea, evidently the consequence of the endeavours made to force them to jump overboard and swim to the shore. The crew even carried their barbarity so far as to leave a lighted match in the powder-magazine."†

* Afr. Inst. Report, 1826, pp. 37, 38.   † Class A. 1827, p. 99.

In the parliamentary papers of 1827 I find the case of the " Teresa," a Spanish schooner, which was suddenly laid on her beam-ends by a tornado, and almost immediately went down, with 186 slaves on board.*

We have also the account of a wreck of a Portuguese slave-schooner, the Piombeter, at the Bahamas, on the 20th of January, 1837, communicated to me by Major M'Gregor, a special justice. He states that the vessel was under fifty tons burden, and that 180 slaves had been embarked in her : " they were chiefly fine young lads under fifteen years of age." About twenty had died before the wreck took place.

In another letter, dated Nov. 1, 1837, he states that several wrecks of slavers had taken place in his vicinity. As to one of these he says, " Last Friday, the 27th ult., a schooner vessel, under the Portuguese flag, was totally wrecked on the shore of Harbour Island, where I now reside in my official capacity, having upwards of 200 African slaves on board at the time, only fifty-three of whom were saved ; the greater part of the ablest men, being chained together below at the time, were consequently drowned in the hold of the vessel. Sixty bodies have since been washed ashore, which I got interred ; upwards of twenty were drifted yesterday to the mouth of the harbour, who seem to have been fettered upon the deck, and grouped together in one heap. It is

* Class A. 1827, p. 30.

supposed that from fifty to sixty bodies are still remaining in the hold of the hull, now almost imbedded
in the sand. Attempts have been made to dive for
the bodies, but without success, they being found so
fast chained and crowded together, it was found impossible to remove them.

" I shall not shock your feelings by entering into
the details of the abominable conduct of the captain
and crew of this vessel during the passage towards
some of the most youthful and best-looking on board :
this was brought to my knowledge by two of the
Africans, who speak Portuguese, and one who speaks
a little broken English. They appear to have conducted themselves more like demons than human
beings.

"The slaver, named the Invincible, took in the
Africans at Port Prague, Cape de Verde Islands, and
was bound for Matanzas in the island of Cuba."

In a letter from Colonel Nicolls, at the Bahamas,
of date 1st August, 1837,* it is stated that " the Es-
peranza, a Spanish slave-schooner, had been wrecked
on one of these islands during the preceding month.
It was ascertained that this vessel had embarked
320 negroes on the coast of Africa ; of these only
220 were landed at the time of the wreck. It
appears that between sixty and seventy murders had
been committed during the voyage on the helpless
Africans ; and in this manner :—When any of the

* Communicated to me by his brother, Col. Nicolls, R.M.

slaves refused their food or became sick, the boat-swain's mate, with a weighty club, struck them on the back of the neck, when they fell, and were thrown overboard."

I make the following extract from the Jamaica Watchman, of 29th May, 1838 :—A report having reached Port Royal, that a Spanish schooner,* hav-ing on board upwards of 300 Africans, had been stranded off the Pedro shoals, H. M. ship Nimrod, and the Hornet schooner, sailed yesterday morning for the purpose of taking her cargo, and bringing them into port. The vessels of war, humanely sent to seek the unfortunate Africans on board the slaver lately wrecked on the Pedro reefs, have returned, bringing the melancholy information that no traces of them could be found. The vessel had gone to pieces, and 300 human beings consigned to a watery grave. The crew had taken to their boats and landed at Black River."†

* Since this was written, the official account of the wreck of this vessel, the Estella, has reached us, in which it is stated that " the crew escaped on shore, leaving the unfortunate Africans on the shoal, and had been landed some days before they made known the fatal circumstances of the wreck ; so that when the fact transpired and search was made, it was found their victims had all perished."—Class A. 1838-9, p. 111.

† Her Majesty's judge at Havana writes to Lord Palmerston, of date 17th July, 1838 :—" The vessel which came in here under the name of the Esplorador, sailed hence on 13th June, 1837, to Madagascar and Mozambique, and not finding any negroes on the coast to be bought, forcibly and piratically took from the other

Lieut. Wilson, of H. M. S. Excellent, who was on the coast of Africa in 1824, in a letter dated 9th January, 1839, says:—" I have overhauled many slave-ships, and freely confess that it is impossible to exaggerate the horrors they exhibit : they are all very much alike, the greater or less misery depending, usually, upon the size of the vessel, and the time they might have been embarked, as every day brings with it a fearful increase of disease, desperation, imbecility, and death."

Passing over hundreds of cases of a description similar to those which I have noticed, I have now done with these heart-sickening details; and the melancholy truth is forced upon us, that, notwithstanding all that has been accomplished, the cruelties and horrors of the passage across the Atlantic have increased ; nay, more, they have been aggravated by the very efforts which we have made for the abolition of the traffic.

" Facts, too, like these just mentioned, are not extraordinary incidents, selected and remembered as such. They are hourly occurrences of the trade ; and as they

vessels there the cargoes they had collected. Having thus got together about 500 negroes, before they got out of the range of the monsoons they encountered very violent weather, which lasted two days, and compelled them to shut down the hatches, without being able to give the negroes, during that time, air or food. The consequence was that, when the storm abated, and they went to examine their condition, they found that about 300 negroes had perished ! With the ordinary mortality attending such voyages, they arrived here with only about 200 surviving."

are found in every instance where detection affords an opportunity of inquiry, it is absurd to suppose that the undetected slave-vessel is exempted from scenes of similar cruelty. It may fairly be assumed that greater cruelty does not obtain in the one vessel which is captured, than in the one hundred which escape. Some of these have made eleven, some thirteen, successful voyages, and there is little doubt that similar acts of atrocity have been perpetrated in all—that all have been marked by the same accumulation of human agony, and the same waste of human life."*

I will endeavour to give a

SUMMARY

of the extent of the mortality incident to the middle passage. Newton states, that in his time it amounted to one-fourth, on the average, of the number embarked.†

From papers presented to the House of Lords, in 1799, it appears that, in the year 1791, (three years after the passing of the Slave Carrying Regulation Act,) of 15,754 negroes embarked for the West Indies, &c., 1378 died during the passage, the average length of which was fifty-one days, showing a mortality of $8\frac{3}{4}$ per cent.

The amount of the mortality in 1792 was still greater. Of 31,554 slaves carried from Africa, no

* Afr. Inst. Report for 1825, p. 31.　　　† Newton, p. 36.

fewer than 5,413 died on the passage, making somewhat more than 17 per cent. in fifty-one days.*

Captain Owen, in a communication to the Admiralty, on the Slave Trade with the eastern coast of
Africa, in 1823, states—" That the ships which use
this traffic consider they make an excellent voyage
if they save one-third of the number embarked:"
" some vessels are so fortunate as to save one-half of
their cargo alive."†

Captain Cook says, in the communication to which
I have before alluded, as to the East coast traffic, " If
they meet with bad weather, in rounding the Cape,
their sufferings are beyond description; and in some
instances one-half of the lives on board are sacrificed.
In the case of the ' Napoleon,' from Quilimane, the
loss amounted to two-thirds.   It was stated to me by
Captains and Supercargoes of other slavers, that they
made a profitable voyage if they lost fifty per cent.;
and that this was not uncommon."

Caldcleugh says, " scarcely two-thirds live to be
landed."‡

Governor Maclean, of Cape Coast, who has had
many opportunities of acquiring information on the
subject, has stated to me, that he considers the average of deaths on the passage to amount to one-third.

Captain Ramsay, R. N., who was a long time on
service with the Preventive Squadron, also stated to
me, that the mortality on the passage across the

* Debates in Parliament, 1806, Ap. p. 191.
† Class B. 1825, p. 41.   ‡ Vol. i. p. 56.

Atlantic must be greater than the loss on the passage to Sierra Leone, from the greater liberty allowed after capture, and from the removal of the shackles. He believes the average loss to be one-third.

Rear-Admiral Sir Graham Eden Hamond, Commander-in-Chief on the South American station, in 1834, thus writes to the British Consul at Monte Video:—" A slave-brig of 202 tons was brought into this port with 521 slaves on board. The vessel is said to have cleared from Monte Video in August last, under a licence to import 650 African colonists.

" The licence to proceed to the coast of Africa is accompanied by a curious document, purporting to be an application from two Spaniards at Monte Video, named Villaca and Barquez, for permission to import 650 colonists, and 250 *more—to cover the deaths on the voyage.*"*

Here we have nearly one-third given apparently for the average loss on the passage, and this estimated by the slave-dealers themselves on the American side of the Atlantic.

I come next to consider the loss after capture.

* Class B. 1835, p. 141.

MORTALITY AFTER CAPTURE.

I HAVE just adverted to the painful reflection that the efforts which we have so long and so perseveringly made for the abolition of the Slave Trade should not only have been attended with complete failure, but with an increase of negro mortality. A striking example of the truth of this remark is afforded, when we consider the great loss of negro life which annually takes place subsequently to the capture of the slave-vessels, on their passage to South America and the West Indies.

I do not intend, in this part of my subject, to discuss the merits of the construction of the Mixed Commission Courts, or their forms of proceeding; nor do I propose, here, to say anything as to the preference which, it appears to me, ought to be given to Fernando Po, over Sierra Leone, as a station for a Commission Court, and a depôt for liberated Africans: my purpose for the present is, merely to state the facts which have come to my knowledge, with the requisite evidence, bearing on the mortality after capture.

Admiral Hamond, in a despatch to the Admiralty on this subject, in the year 1834, puts the case of a

slaver overloaded with negroes, many of them in a
sickly or dying state, captured and brought into Rio
Janeiro, (as in the case of the " Rio de la Plata,")
where the miserable slaves, confined to the vessel, in
a hot and close port, must await the tardy process of
the Mixed Commission Court; and he goes on to say,
that, in such a case, " the stopping of the slave-vessel
is only exposing the blacks to greater misery, and a
much greater chance of speedy death, than if they
were left to their original destination of slavery."*

In the 21st Report of the African Institution, we
have the case of the Pauleta, captured off Cape Formosa, in Ferbuary, 1826, by " Lieutenant Tucker,
H. M. Ship Maidstone, with 221 slaves on board.
Her burden was only 69 tons, and into this space
were thrust 82 men, 56 women, 39 boys, and 44
girls. The only provision found on board for their
subsistence was yams of the worst quality, and fetid
water. When captured, both small-pox and dysentery had commenced their ravages; 30 died on the
passage to Sierra Leone, and the remainder were
landed in an extreme state of wretchedness and emaciation."†

In 1830, a Committee of the House of Commons
was appointed to consider the relative merits of Sierra
Leone and Fernando Po. Captain Bullen stated in
evidence before the Committee, that the Aviso, captured near Fernando Po, took five weeks to reach
Sierra Leone, during which time forty-five of the

* Class B. 1835, p. 66.   † Afr. Inst. Report for 1827, p. 9.

slaves died; and that in the case of the Segunda Rosalia, the passage occupied eleven weeks, during which more than 120 of the slaves were lost.*

Lieutenant Tringham informed the Committee that he carried a Spanish schooner up to Sierra Leone as prize-master. She had 480 slaves on board at the time of capture. The voyage to Sierra Leone occupied six weeks, and 110 slaves died on the passage. In answer to the question, " If you had had to have taken the vessel to Fernando Po for adjudication, instead of Sierra Leone, the lives of those persons would have been saved?" he replied, " I think so." He afterwards said, that the average voyage of the vessels he had taken from the Bights of Benin and Biafra to Sierra Leone, was five weeks.†

Mr. Jackson stated to the Committee, that the condition of the slaves, at the time of capture, was " most deplorable, as to disease, and as to the mortality which has ensued: in one instance, 179 out of 448 slaves, on board of one vessel, died in their passage up; in another, 115 out of 271. In all, with only one exception, the numbers have been considerable."‡

Mr. John M'Cormack, in his evidence, said, that on going aboard slave-vessels after capture and the passage to Sierra Leone, he generally found the slaves who had been any length of time on the voyage " in a most miserable state of debility." And he

* Sierra Leone Report, 1830, p. 8.   † Ib. p. 32.
‡ Ib. p. 52.

adds, " They unavoidably must, from the description
of the vessels, suffer very greatly: many of these vessels have not more than three feet between decks, and
no air can get to them except what comes down the
hatchways.   They are so low in the water, no air-
ports can be cut in their sides."*

In the Appendix to the Report of this Committee,
a return is given for the period between 10th August,
1819, and 11th October, 1829,—

Of slaves captured   25,212
Landed at Sierra Leone, or Fernando Po   21,563
                                           ————
          Loss on the passage   .   3,649†

Being nearly one-seventh, or about 14 per cent.; and
this almost entirely on the passage to Sierra Leone.

Mr. Rankin, in his visit to Sierra Leone, tells
us of a Portuguese schooner, the Donna Maria
da Gloria, which he saw there, with a cargo of
slaves on board.   She had embarked them at
Loando, in August, 1833, and was captured by
H. M. B. Snake.   The captor took the vessel to Rio,
but the Brazilian Mixed Commission Court would
not entertain the case: he was therefore obliged to
send her to Sierra Leone, where she arrived on February 4, 1834.   On her arrival, it was ascertained that
she had lost 95 out of 430 slaves.   A long process ensued before the Mixed Commission Court, the result
of which was the liberation of the vessel; and at this

* Sierra Leone Report, p. 66.   † Ib. Ap. p. 122.

period her state is thus described : " Notwithstanding the exertions of Mr. Thomas Frazer, assistant-surgeon of the capturing ship, who continued to administer to them while himself in a state of extreme suffering and danger, before reaching Sierra Leone, 104 had died, and 64 more (in a state that moved the heart even of the slave-crew) were voluntarily landed by the master, and taken charge of by the liberated African department. The miserable remnant, in a state impossible to describe, afflicted with ophthalmia, dysentery, and frightful ulcers, and showing, also, some symptoms of small-pox, left the harbour of Sierra Leone, the slaves having been then on board 165 days, 137 having elapsed since her capture ; and of her original cargo of 430, 240 alone remained."*

Dr. Cullen, of Edinburgh, who lately returned from Rio de Janeiro, after a five years' residence there, thus writes to Lord Glenelg, of date 28th February, 1838, in reference to the Donna Maria having been released at Sierra Leone : " Some months after this, they were met by a Brazilian ship of war, near Bahia, in distress ; and their numbers reduced to 170."†

Mr. Rankin visited La Pantica, another vessel which had been brought into Sierra Leone. "The ship," he says, " was thronged with men, women, and children, all entirely naked, and disgusting with

* Rankin's Visit, &c., vol. ii. p. 96.
† Class A. (Further Series), 1837, p. 91.

disease : 274 were at this moment in the little schooner. When captured, 315 had been found on board ; 40 had died during the voyage from Old Calebar. Of the remainder, 8 or 10 died in the first week after liberation. The majority of the survivors were miserably persecuted by ophthalmia and dysentery, and 50 were sent to the hospital, for fever, at Kissey." *

In a report of the Sierra Leone Commissioners, dated 4th February, 1835,† it is stated that "the Sutil arrived in this harbour on the 23rd ult. with 228 slaves on board, 79 having died on the passage to this port, whilst the vessel was in charge of the captors ; in addition to a frightful loss of life which had previously occurred on the first night of the voyage, owing to a ferocious scramble for room, amongst the densely-crowded negroes, and by which many were suffocated and killed. The surgeon to the courts immediately visited the slaves, and reported that there were 21 men and boys, and 8 girls, sick with dysentery, many of them being in an advanced stage of the disease."

The case of the Flor de Loando is one which deserves considerable attention, as it affords an instance, and that a modern one, of dreadful suffering and mortality, and shows the disposition of the Brazilian authorities to thwart, as far as possible, the intentions of the British Government.

* Rankin, vol. ii. p. 1.   † Class A. 1835, p. 48.

This slaver was captured on the 11th April, 1838, by H. M. corvette, Rover, with 289 negroes on board, and taken to Rio de Janeiro. The Mixed Commission Court at that port refused to condemn her, on the ground of her having been seized in Portuguese colours, although both the vessel and slaves were known to be Brazilian property. The Brazilian Government having afterwards received an application to condemn her as a smuggler, or a vessel with false papers, refused to take cognizance of her, or to render any assistance to the slaves, who were now in a dreadful state of disease, having been kept confined in the hold of the slave ship more than three months from the time of her capture. With considerable difficulty the authorities were induced to allow the worst cases to be transferred to the hospital, on being guaranteed their expenses; but persisted in refusing any means for conveying the wretched negroes to a more wholesome situation, though such a change was pronounced absolutely necessary for the preservation of their lives. The deaths up to this period amounted to 80. On the 23rd August, Lieutenant Armitage, the officer in command, was ordered to proceed to Sierra Leone, with the slaver and her cargo, then reduced to 140; but on the 27th instant she sprung a leak, and was compelled to return to Rio in a sinking condition. On examination, her timbers were found to be rotten, and she was pronounced totally unfit for sea. The deaths at this time amounted to 119; notwithstanding, permission was still denied by the Brazilian Government to land the negroes till the 15th September, *five months* after their capture ; during which time expenses were incurred by the British Government to the amount of £812. In order to form an idea of the sufferings of the miserable victims, we must conceive them lying for so many months in the state thus described by Lieutenant Armitage .—" They were stowed so close, till thinned by death, as necessarily to press one against another, and there was barely room for them to sit upright. He used to visit them of a morning, accompanied by a sailor, in a crouching position, and draw out those who had died, by the legs, there not being room to go between them to take up their bodies." The stench he represents to have been most horrible.

The following list of seventeen vessels, most of which were captured in the Bights of Benin and Biafra, and brought for adjudication to Sierra Leone, will serve to exhibit the loss after capture in a forcible manner :—

Where con-demned.	Vessel's Name.	Nation.	Number on Board.	Died before Adjudi-cation.	Reference. Class A.	Page.
Sierra Leone.	Emelia	Spanish	282	107	1828	39
	Invincivel	Portuguese	440	190	,,	59
	Clementina	Brazilian	471	115	1829	82
	Ceres	do.	279	151	1830	64
	Arcinia	do.	448	179	,,	38
	Mensageira	do.	353	109	,,	58
Havana.	Midas	Spanish	562	281	,,	148
	Constancia *	do.	438	368*	,,	162
	Fama de Cadiz †	do.	980	680†	,,	156
Sierra Leone.	Christina	do.	348	132	1831	21
	Tentadora	Brazilian	432	112	,,	54
	Umbellina	do.	377	214	,,	65
	Formidable	Spanish	712	304	1835	50
	Sutil	do.	335	124	,,	48
	Minerva	do.	725	208	,,	56
Havana.	Marte	do.	600	197	,,	163
	Diligencia	do.	210	90	,,	200
			7992	3561		

* This vessel was not brought before the Court. The numbers are given on the authority of Mr. Commissary Judge Macleay.
† The same of the Fama de Cadiz.

Showing a loss on these selected cases of 44 per cent. !

In 1830, the Committee of the House of Commons came to the following resolution: that captured vessels are, " on an average, upwards of five weeks on their passage from the place of capture to Sierra Leone, occasioning a loss of the captured slaves amounting to from *one-sixth to one-half* of the whole number, while the survivors are generally landed in a miserable state of weakness and debility." *

* Sierra Leone Report, 1830, p. 4.

I have not adverted to Rio de Janeiro, or the Havana, on this head, because there are very few captures on the American side of the Atlantic, and when captures do occur, the time consumed in the passage to either of these ports is little, if at all, more than what would have been required for completing the voyage.

But it appears to be demonstrated, by evidence which cannot be impugned, that the loss *after capture* on the African side of the Atlantic varies from *one-sixth to one-half of the whole number*.

Loss after Landing and in the Seasoning.

The last head of mortality is that which occurs after landing from the slave-vessel, and in the seasoning.

We are here again obliged to go back for information to the evidence at the end of the last century : but in this branch of the subject, so far as can be ascertained, there has been no improvement; on the contrary, the slaves are now subjected to greater hardships, in their being landed and concealed as smuggled goods, than they were in former times, when a slave-vessel entered the ports of Rio Janeiro and Havana as a fair trader, and openly disposed of her cargo.

Mr. Falconbridge, whose evidence has already been largely quoted, tells us, that, on being landed, the negroes are sold, sometimes by what is termed a *scramble ;* " but previous thereto," he adds, " the sick or refuse slaves, of which there are frequently many, are usually conveyed on shore, and sold at a tavern by public auction. These, in general, are purchased by the Jews and surgeons, but chiefly upon speculation, at so low a price as five or six dollars a-head.

" I was informed," he says, " by a Mulatto woman, that she purchased a sick slave at Grenada upon speculation, for the small sum of one dollar, as the poor wretch was apparently dying of the flux. It seldom happens that any who are carried ashore in the emaciated state to which they are generally reduced by that disorder long survive their landing. I once saw sixteen conveyed on shore, and sold in the foregoing manner, the whole of whom died before I left the island, which was within a short time after." Various are the deceptions made use of in the disposal of the sick slaves, and many of these such as must excite in every humane mind the liveliest sensations of horror. I have been well informed that a Liverpool captain boasted of his having cheated some Jews by the following stratagem : " A lot of slaves afflicted with the flux, being about to be landed for sale, he directed the surgeon to . . . . .
. . . Thus prepared, they were landed, and taken to the accustomed place of sale, where, being unable to stand, unless for a very short time, they are usually permitted to sit. The Jews, when they examine them, oblige them to stand up . . . .

. . . . and when they do not perceive this appearance, they consider it as a symptom of recovery. In the present instance, such an appearance being prevented, the bargain was struck, and they were accordingly sold. But it was not long before a discovery ensued. The excruciating pain, which the prevention occasioned, not being to be borne by the poor wretches, was removed, and the deluded purchasers were speedily convinced of the imposition." *

In the report of the African Institution for 1818, the case of the Joaquim, a Portuguese slave-vessel, is noticed; and Lieutenant Eicke, after stating the wretched condition of the slaves at and subsequent to the time of capture, says, " That between the nineteenth and twenty-fourth day of their being landed, *thirteen* more died, notwithstanding good provisions, medical aid, and kind treatment, and *thirty more* died between the 24th of February and 16th instant; all occasioned, as he in his conscience is firmly persuaded, by the cruel and inhuman treatment of the Portuguese owners; that more than 100 of them were at the time of their landing just like skeletons covered with skin, and moving by slow machinery, hardly maintaining the appearance of animated human beings. That the remainder of them were all enervated, and in a sickly state." *

In a report from the Sierra Leone Commissioners,

* Falconbridge, p. 33.
† Afr. Inst. Report, 1818, p. 28.

I find the following passage :—Unfortunately their
sufferings do not terminate here, for the ill effects of
their privations and hardships, during their detention
on board the slave vessels, continue to be felt long
after the cause that produced them has ceased.

In proof of this, we beg to refer to the returns of
the Mixed Courts, which show in the case of the
Portuguese vessel " Uniao," that besides 112 out of
361 slaves having died prior to, 35 died after emancipation (but before it was possible to have them registered), owing to the wretched state to which they
had been reduced by dysentery and small-pox.

In the General Return of Liberated Africans (Appendix), it is stated of the same slaves, that the total
number which died of small-pox after landing was
55, of whom 40 were men, five women, eight boys,
and two girls.   That this is not an isolated fact is
shown by the returns from the villages of Leopold
and Waterloo (Appendix A. 6 and 7).   By the first
of these it appears, that of 73 children received at
Leopold in 1822, 54 died during the year ; and that
of 243 children received in 1825, 58 died in that
year, which mortality is accounted for in the return
as arising " from the debilitated state in which they
were received from the slave vessels."

By the return from the village of Waterloo, it appears that of 221 of different ages, who were received
in 1822, 72 died in the same year, of whom 26 were
men, 6 women, and 40 children ; and the explanatory remark is, " that the deaths are not to be ascribed

to local circumstance, but to the deplorably emaciated state in which the men, women, and children were when sent to the village, having been afflicted with a dysentery which proved incurable."

In addition to these facts, it is stated by Mr. Reffell, chief superintendent, in his reply to the queries which were addressed to him, as well as by Mr. Cole, assistant chief superintendent, in his evidence (Appendix B. 9 and 10), as their opinion, that even in vessels where there has been no infectious disease, full one-half, on an average, arrive "in a sick or debilitated and weak state."

In an official medical report as to the health of the liberated Africans at the Gambia, of date 31st of December, 1833, and drawn up by Mr. Foulis, Assistant-Surgeon of the Royal African Corps, and Dr. James Donovan, Acting Colonial Surgeon, it is stated that the greater part of those who are weak and emaciated on arrival soon afterwards die ; many, after a longer or shorter residence, fall into the same state, linger, and also perish from causes not very dissimilar. For this mortality, the medical board assigned, as probable causes, the long confinement in slave-houses previous to embarkation, want of cleanliness and ventilation while on board the slave-ships, alterations in dress, food, and habits, and, not the least, change of climate. These act directly, simultaneously, and banefully on the system in a very great number of instances. But when the sad recollection of perpetual expatriation, the lacerated feelings of kindred and friendship, the rude violation of all the sacred and social endearments of country and relationship, the degrading anticipation of endless unmitigated bondage are added to these, they act still more injuriously on the constitution, although exerted through the medium of mind. The moral and physical combination of such extraordinary circumstances, concentrated with such fearful intensity, conjointly creates disease in such a redoubtable shape, as to induce a belief that nothing similar has yet appeared in the annals of physic."*

Mr. Rankin, in his work on Sierra Leone, says,† " To the King's Yards I paid frequent visits, and found an interest awakened on behalf of the people. Of the women, many were despatched to the hospital at Kissey, victims to raging fevers. Others had become insane. I was informed that insanity is the frequent fate of the women captives, and that it chiefly comes upon such as at first exhibit most intellectual development, and greatest liveliness of disposition. Instances were pointed out to me. The women sustain their bodily sufferings with more silent fortitude than the men, and seldom destroy themselves; but they brood more over their misfortunes, until the sense of them is lost in madness."‡

* Records of the Colonial Office for 1833.
† Vol. ii. p. 124.   ‡ Ibid.

Dr. Cullen,* in his letter to Lord Glenelg, mentions the following case : " About the beginning of 1834, a small schooner (I think the name was the Duqueza de Braganza) was captured by one of Her British Majesty's cruisers, and brought into Rio de Janeiro, having on board between 300 and 400 Africans, mostly children ; these poor creatures had suffered much from their long confinement in such a small vessel, and it is believed a great many had died on the passage. By the humanity of the late Admiral Sir Michael Seymour they were taken on shore, and properly cared for, otherwise the mortality amongst them after landing must have been greater than it was." He then says, that they were adjudged to be free. At the time of the sentence of the Court " they were reduced by deaths to 288, all of whom were sent to the house of correction, to work for the Brazilian government.   I called at this house of correction eight days after their arrival there, when seven more had died, and there were then thirty-five sick, confined in a small room, lying on the floor,

* Dr. Cullen also writes. that, about the same time, a British cruiser, the Raleigh, Captain Quin, brought in a slaver, the Rio da Plata, with about 400 Africans on board, who were landed, and a guard placed over them ; and that, " a few nights after they were put ashore, the guard was surprised in the middle of the night by a band of fellows pretending to be justices of the peace, who carried off 200 of the negroes, and next day no traces of them could be found.   Those that remained were taken to the house of correction, and disposed of in the Brazilian fashion.'"

[1]   Class A (Further Series), 1837, p. 91.

without bed or covering of any kind, with their heads to the wall and their feet towards the centre, leaving a narrow passage between the rows. The same day I saw about 100 of these children in an apartment on the ground-floor, sitting all round on their heels, after the fashion of the country, and looking most miserable. On the November following I again visited the house of correction, and learned that out of the 288, sent there in June, 107 had died, and a great many more were sick."[*]

In the letter from Havana, dated in 1838, from which I have already quoted, the following account is given : " In the cool of the evening we made a visit to the bazaar. A newly imported cargo of 220 human beings was here exposed for sale. They were crouched down upon their forms around a large room : during a visit of more than an hour that we were there not a word was uttered by one of them. On entering the room the eyes of all were turned towards us, as if to read in our countenances their fate ; they were all nearly naked, being but slightly clad in a light check shirt, upon which was a mark upon the breast ; with a few exceptions they were but skin and bone, too weak to support their languid forms ; they were reclining on the floor, their backs resting against the wall. When a purchaser came they were motioned to stand, which they obeyed, though with apparent pain ; a few were old and grey ; but the greater proportion were mere children, of from

* Class A (Further Series), 1837, p. 91.

ten to thirteen or fifteen years of age; when they
stood their legs looked as thin as reeds, and hardly
capable of supporting the skeletons of their wasted
forms. The keeper informed us they were of several
distinct tribes, and that they did not understand one
another : this was apparent from the formation of the
head. While we were there, five little boys and
girls were selected and bought to go into the interior:
no regard is paid to relationship, and, once separated, they never meet again! We left the tienda,
and, turning through the gateway, we saw some who
were lying under the shade of the plantain, whose
appearance told that they, at least, would be liberated from bondage by death. They were those who
had suffered most during the voyage,—their situation
was most melancholy. I offered to one the un-
tasted bowl of cocoa-nut milk I was about drinking,
—she motioned it away with a look which, even
from a negress, was expressive of thankfulness, and
which seemed to say how unused she was to such
kindness."

The Quarterly Review (vol. xxx.) contains an
article on Mengin's ' Histoire de l'Egypte,'* in
which the reviewer, speaking of Ismael Pacha's
expedition to the south, says, " The hopes of the
Pacha, however, were greatly disappointed in these
black troops (captured in Soudan.) They were

* Histoire de l'Egypte par Felix Mengin, 1823.—Quarterly
Review, vol. xxx. p. 491.

strong, able-bodied men, and not averse from being taught; but when attacked by disease, which soon broke out in the camp, they died like sheep infected with the rot. The medical men ascribe the mortality to moral rather than physical causes; it appeared in numerous instances, that having been snatched away from their homes and families they were even anxious to get rid of life, and such was the dreadful mortality that ensued, that, out of 20,000 of these unfortunate men, 3,000 did not remain alive at the end of two years."

Dr. Bowring has stated to me, that the negroes which have been conveyed into Egypt " suffer much from nostalgia, and, when they have been gathered together into regiments, the passionate desire to return home frequently produced a languishing malady, of which they die in large numbers. The mortality among the slaves in Egypt is frightful,—when the epidemical plague visits the country, they are swept away in immense multitudes, and they are the earliest victims of almost every other domineering disease. I have heard it estimated that five or six years are sufficient to carry off a generation of slaves, at the end of which time the whole has to be replenished. This is one of the causes of their low market-value. When they marry, their descendants seldom live; in fact, the laws of nature seem to repel the establishment of hereditary slavery."

But it is needless to multiply instances on this head; and I shall only further notice a few of the authorities for the amount of the mortality after landing, and in the seasoning.

Mr. Pitt, in the debate on the Slave Trade, in 1791, made the following observation—" The evidence before the House, as to this point (the mortality,) was perfectly clear; for it would be found in that dreadful catalogue of deaths in consequence of the seasoning and the middle passage, which the House had been condemned to look into, that *one-half* die."

Mr. Wilberforce, in his letter of 1807, (page 98,) says, " The survivors were landed in such a diseased state, that $4\frac{1}{2}$ per cent. of the whole number imported were estimated to die in the short interval between the arrival of the ship and the sale of the cargo, probably not more than a fortnight ; and, after the slaves had passed into the hands of the planters, the numbers which perished from the effects of the voyage were allowed to be very considerable." It ought not to be forgotten, that Pitt and Wilberforce are speaking of a period when the Slave Trade was legal, and the Slave Carrying Act in operation. What then may be the *increase* of this mortality, now that the trade is clandestine, and the slaves packed on board of the " clippers," like " bales of goods ?"

The Duc de Broglie, when addressing the Chamber of Peers on this subject, in March 1822, made the following remark—" And it is a well-known fact, that a *fourth*, or even a *third*, of the cargo generally perishes either on ship-board, or soon after the landing, from the diseases incident to the voyage."*

In the debate of 1791, Mr. Stanley (then agent for the islands, and advocating the continuance of the Slave Trade) said, speaking of the negroes—" As to their treatment in the West Indies, he was himself witness that it was in general highly indulgent and humane," and yet " he confessed that ONE-HALF, very frequently, died in the SEASONING."

I have now, in the discharge of a most painful duty, brought under review a complication of human misery and suffering, which I may venture to say has no parallel ; but, before concluding this branch of the case, it may be proper to exhibit, in a summary manner, the amount of negro mortality, consequent on the Slave Trade.

SUMMARY.

1st. The loss incident to the seizure, march to the coast, and detention there.

Newton (p. 98) is of opinion, that the captives reserved for sale, are fewer than the slain.

Mr. Miles (p. 98) stated to the Committee in 1790, that in one of the " Skirmishes" for slaves, " above 60,000 men" were destroyed.

Bosman narrates, that in two of these skirmishes " above 100,000 men were killed ;" and Mr. Devaynes has said, that in one of these skirmishes

* Afr. Inst. Report, Ap. 2, No. 16, 1823.

" 60,000 lost their lives."*   And Denham (p. 80)
narrates, that in five marauding excursions, " 20,000,
at least," were slaughtered, and 16,000 sent into
slavery ; and he gives another instance, where " probably 6,000" were slaughtered, in procuring 3,000
slaves.

On the route to the coast, we may cite the authority of Park, Denham, &c. ; and M. Mendez (p. 113)
estimates the loss on this head to amount to five-
twelfths of the whole.

For the mortality occasioned by detention before
embarkation, we have the authority of Frazer, Park,
Leonard, Landers, and Bailey.

From these authorities, we are fairly entitled to
assume that from the sources—seizure, march, and
detention, *for every slave embarked, one life is sacrificed.*

2ndly.   The loss from the middle passage appears to be *not less than 25 per cent., or one fourth
of the number embarked.*   For this there is conclusive evidence.   The witnesses have no assignable
motive for exaggeration ; they are men holding
public situations, of unimpeachable veracity, and
with the best opportunities of forming a correct estimate.

The Rev. John Newton had, himself, been for
many years a Slave Trader, and speaks of what he

---

* It is obvious that these very large numbers must be received
with considerable qualification.   There can be no doubt, however,
that the slaughter was great.

saw.   The Slave Trade was then legal, and the vessels employed were usually large and commodious,
and very different from the American clippers now in
use.   He rates the loss during the middle passage at
25 per cent.   Captain Ramsay had commanded one
of Her Majesty's cruisers, employed in suppressing
the Slave Trade, had taken many slavers, and could
not be ignorant of the state of the captured cargoes.
His estimate is 33 per cent.

Slave-trading vessels are continually passing under
the eye of the Governor of Cape Coast Castle.   His
attention has been constantly kept alive to the subject, and few men have had such opportunities of
arriving at the real truth.   Mr. Maclean's estimate
is 33 per cent.

Commodore Owen reports that which came to his
knowledge while he was employed by Government
in surveying the eastern coast of Africa.   His estimate is 50 per cent.   This excess, as compared with
the others, is accounted for by the additional length
of the voyage round the Cape of Good Hope.

If, after such testimony, there were room for hesitation, it must be removed by witnesses of a very
different kind.   The Spanish slave-merchants of
Monte Video, it is fair to presume, are well acquainted with the usual rate of mortality in their
slave-vessels; and we may give them credit for not
acting contrary to their own interests; so confident
are they that, at least, one-third will perish, that they
providently incur the expense of sending out that

amount of surplus, for the purpose (in their own words) " of covering the deaths on the voyage."

I should be justified in taking the average of these authorities, which would be 34 per cent; but, as it is my wish to be assuredly within the mark, I will state the mortality from the middle passage at *twenty-five per cent.*

In the same spirit I will take no notice of the mortality after capture, which, says the report of the Parliamentary Committee, amounts to from one-sixth to one-half.

3dly. As to the loss after landing, and in the seasoning.

Under this head, we have, among others, two authorities which require particular attention; one of them referring to the time when the Slave Trade was legal, the other to a recent date, and both of them of unexceptionable character. Mr. Stanley, a West India Agent, arguing for the continuance of the Slave Trade, and lauding the treatment of the negroes, confesses that *one-half* frequently die in the seasoning. The other, the report of the Medical Officers appointed to investigate the state of the liberated Africans at the Gambia, describes a large proportion of them as labouring under disease, " nothing equal to which has been known hitherto in the annals of physic." If such be their state when they fall into the hands of the British, are treated by them with kindness, and are relieved from their most frightful apprehensions, may we not suppose that their state is still more miserable, and the mortality still greater, when they are landed clandestinely at Cuba, and know that they are doomed to interminable bondage?

Upon the strength and authority of these facts, I might fairly estimate the loss under this head at one-third; but I think I cannot err, on the side of exaggeration, in setting it down at *twenty per cent, or one-fifth of the number landed.*

Nor does the mortality stop here. In slave countries, but more especially where the Slave Trade prevails, there is, invariably, a great diminution of human life; the numbers annually born fall greatly below the numbers which perish. It would not be difficult to prove, that in the last fifty years there has been, in this way, a waste of millions of lives; but as this view of the subject would involve the horrors of slavery, as well as of the Slave Trade, I shall abstain from adding anything on this head to the catalogue of mortality which I have already given.

Our calculation may thus be brought into a narrow compass:—

Of 1000 victims to the Slave Trade,
One-half perish in the seizure, march,
   and detention   500
Of 500 consequently embarked,—
One-fourth, or 25 per cent, perish in the
   Middle Passage   125

Of the remaining 375 landed, *one-fifth*,
     or 20 per cent., perish in the seasoning   75

             Total loss   700

So that 300 negroes only, or *three-tenths* of the whole number of victims, remain alive at the end of a year after their deportation; and the number of lives sacrificed by the system, bears to the number of slaves available to the planter, the proportion of *seven* to *three*.

Then applying this calculation to the number annually landed at Brazil, Cuba, &c., which I have rated at   150,000
     Of these *one-fifth* die in the seasoning   30,000

     Leaving available to the Planter .   120,000
The number of lives annually sacrificed,
     being in the proportion of seven to
         three*   280,000

---

* This amount may be verified in the following manner:—

Taking the annual victims at . . .	400,000
One-half perish before embarkation . .	200,000
Embarked	200,000
One-fourth in the Middle Passage . .	50,000
Landed	150,000
One-fifth in the Seasoning . . .	30,000
Available	120,000

Annual victims of Christian Slave

    Trade   400,000

Proceeding in like manner with the Mohammedan Slave Trade, we find the numbers to be

Exported by the Imaum of Muscat   30,000

Carried across the Desert . .   20,000

                                50,000

Loss by seizure, march, and detention* 50,000

Annual victims of Mohammedan Slave

    Trade   100,000

    ,,   ,,   Christian .   400,000

        Annual loss to Africa   500,000

It is impossible for any one to reach this result,
without suspecting, as well as hoping, that it must
be an exaggeration; and yet there are those who
think that this is too low an estimate.†

I have not, however, assumed any fact, without

* It may be objected, that the loss arising from detention at
the Mohammedan Slave markets is not so great as that which
takes place in the barracoons in the Transatlantic trade, but, on
the other hand, the march is much more destructive to human
life; we may therefore fairly calculate that in the three items of
seizure, march, and *detention,* the average mortality is equal to
that in the former case, which we estimated at "*one life sacrificed for every slave embarked.*"

† Mr. Rankin says:—
"The old and new Calebar, the Bonney, Whydah, and the Gallinas, contribute an inexhaustible supply for the French islands of
the West Indies, Rio Janeiro, Havana, and the Brazils, where,

giving the data on which it rests; neither have I extracted from those data any immoderate inference. I think that the reader, on going over the calculation, will perceive that I have, in almost every instance, abated the deduction which might with justice have been made. If, then, we are to put confidence in the authorities which I have quoted, (most of them official,) we cannot avoid the conclusion,—terrible as it is,—that the Slave Trade annually dooms

to the horrors of slavery (Christian)		120,000
(Mohammedan)	.	50,000
		170,000
And murders (Christian)	280,000	
(Mohammedan)	50,000	
		330,000
		*500,000

notwithstanding every opposition and hinderance from the British cruisers, one hundred thousand are supposed to arrive in safety annually; five times that number having been lost by capture or death. Death thins the cargoes in various modes; suicide destroys many; and many are thrown overboard at the close of the voyage; for, as a duty of ten dollars is set by the Brazilian Government upon each slave upon landing, such as seem unlikely to survive, or to bring a price sufficiently high to cover this custom-house tax, are purposely drowned before entering port. Those only escape these wholesale murders, who will probably recover health and flesh when removed to the fattening pens of the slave-farmer, a man who contracts to feed up the skeletons to a marketable appearance." Vol. ii. p. 71.

* It may perhaps be observed that this result disagrees with

CHAPTER III.

FAILURE OF EFFORTS ALREADY MADE FOR SUPPRESSION OF THE SLAVE TRADE.

It is then but too manifest that the efforts already made for the suppression of the Slave Trade have not accomplished their benevolent object.

The people of England take a more lively and intense interest in this than perhaps in any other foreign subject. The Government, whether in the hands of the one party or the other, cannot be accused of having, for a long series of years, been wanting either in zeal or exertion for its suppression. Millions of money and multitudes of lives have been sacrificed; and, in return for all, we have only the afflicting conviction, that the Slave Trade is as far as ever from being suppressed. Nay, I am afraid the fact is not to be disputed, that while we have thus been endea-

that given in the former editions of this work. The fact is, on revising my calculation, I found I had adopted an erroneous method of computing the per-centage, which made my result fal considerably short of the reality: this estimate, enormous as it is, I might have still further augmented, for I find (as stated in note, page 61) that the annual Mohammedan export from the Eastern coast is now ascertained to amount to 50,000, being 20,000 more than I had rated it; and as we assume an equal number perish in the seizure, march, and detention, 40,000 might fairly be added to the amount above fixed. But enough, and more than enough, has been proved to establish my argument.

vouring to extinguish the traffic, it has actually doubled in amount.

In the debate of 2d April, 1792, Mr. Fox rated the Slave Trade at 80,000 annually: he says, " I think the least disreputable way of accounting for the supply of slaves, is to represent them as having been convicted of crimes by legal authority. What does the House think is the whole number of these convicts exported annually from Africa ?   80,000." In the same debate Mr. Pitt observed, " I know of no evil that ever has existed, nor can imagine any evil to exist, worse than the tearing of 80,000 persons annually from their native land, by a combination of the most civilised nations in the most enlightened quarter of the globe." The late Zachary Macaulay, than whom the African has had no better friend, told me a few days before his death, that upon the most accurate investigation he was able to make as to the extent of the Slave Trade, he had come to the conclusion that it was 70,000 annually, fifty years ago. Twenty years ago the African Institution reported to the Duke of Wellington that it was 70,000. We will assume, then, that the number at the commencement of the discussion was 70,000 negroes annually transported from Africa. There is evidence before the Parliamentary Committees to show that about one-third was for the British islands, and one-third for St. Domingo: so that, strictly speaking, if the Slave Trade of other countries had been stationary, they ought only at the utmost to import 25,000 ; but I have already proved that the number annually landed in Cuba and Brazil, &c., is 150,000, being more than double the whole draught upon Africa, including the countries where it had ceased when the Slave Trade controversy began. Twice as many human beings are now its victims as when Wilberforce and Clarkson entered upon their noble task ; and each individual of this increased number, in addition to the horrors which were endured in former times, has to suffer from being cribbed up in a narrower space, and on board a vessel, where accommodation is sacrificed to speed. Painful as this is, it becomes still more distressing if it shall appear that our present system has not failed by mischance, from want of energy, or from want of expenditure, but that the system itself is erroneous, and must necessarily be attended with disappointment.

Hitherto we have effected no other change than a change in the flag under which the trade is carried on. It was stated by our ambassador at Paris, to the French minister, in 1824 (I speak from memory), that the French flag covered the villains of all nations. For some years afterwards the Spanish flag was generally used. Now, Portugal sells her flag, and the greater part of the trade is carried on under it. Her governors openly sell, at a fixed price, the use of Portuguese papers and flags.

So grave an accusation ought not to be made without stating some of the authorities on which it is grounded. In a Parliamentary paper on the subject of the Slave Trade, presented in 1823, Sir Charles M'Carthy states in his letter of the 19th June 1822,* that "the case of the ' Conde de Villa Flor,' seized near Bissao, fully establishes that Signor Andrade, the governor, had shipped a number of slaves on his own account." Sir Charles further states that " he received repeated reports of the governors of Bissao and Cacheo having full cargoes of slaves in irons ready for all purchasers ; and that the traffic is carried on openly at the Cape de Verd Islands, St. Thomas, and Prince's." This statement is confirmed by " Lieutenant Hagan, of Her Majesty's brig Thistle, who informed him that the traffic in slaves was carried on at Bissao and Cacheo in the most open manner, under the sanction of the governor, the latter of whom is the principal dealer in slaves."

The practice of 1822 has continued to the present time. On the 3d March, 1838, Lord Palmerston, in a spirited note, states to the Portuguese Minister, " that the Portuguese flag is lent, with the connivance of Portuguese authorities, to serve as a protection for all the miscreants of every other nation in the world, who may choose to engage in such base pursuits."†

The charge thus made extends only to the *lending* of the flag of Portugal : it might have gone farther. In an enclosure in a letter from Lord Palmerston to

---

* Papers, Slave Trade, 11th July, 1823.

† Class B. (Further Series), 1837, p. 29, presented 1838.

our Ambassador at Lisbon, dated 30th April, 1838, it appears that " the Governor of Angola has established an impost or fee of 700,000 reis to be paid to him for every vessel which embarks slaves from thence, it being understood that upon payment of the above-mentioned sum, no impediment to the illicit trade shall be interposed by the governor, nor any further risk be incurred by the persons engaged in the trade."* Nor is this all. In the same document we find that the governor, not content with lending and letting out the flag of Portugal, has set up as a slave-trader himself; " sending from Angola, for his own account, a shipment of slaves, sixty in number, which he has consigned to a notorious slave-dealer of the name of Vicente, at Rio de Janeiro."†

It is very truly added, that these violations of the treaties " form but a small portion of the offences of this kind constantly committed by Portuguese subjects, both in and out of authority."‡

When Portugal shall have been persuaded or compelled to desist from this insulting violation of treaty, it is but too probable that Brazil will step into her place. We find it stated in a despatch from

---

* Class B. (Further Series), 1837, p. 35. † Ibid.

‡ It appears from the last Parliamentary papers, that " the Diligente was captured by the Brisk while under Portuguese colours, and furnished with Portuguese papers, from the Portuguese Consul-General at Cadiz, who, in this instance, seems to have been at no pains to conceal the disgraceful part which he took."— Class A. (Further Series), 1838-9, p. 11.

Her Majesty's Commissioners at Rio de Janeiro to Lord Palmerston, of date the 17th November, 1837,* that "The change in the Brazilian Government which took place on the 19th September has had this important consequence in respect to the Slave Trade, that while the late Government appeared to wish to put down the traffic, as matter of principle, and of compact with Great Britain, the present Government, as far as it is represented by Señor Vasconcellos (Minister of Justice, and provisionally Minister for the empire), has proclaimed the traffic to be indispensable to the country; has released those concerned in it who were under prosecution; and set at nought the engagement with Great Britain on this head." And the British Consul at Pernambuco writes to Lord Palmerston, of date 15th February, 1838, "The editor of the Jornal do Commercio declares, that this important subject has already passed the Senate, and that there is every probability it will be made law in the next Session of the Legislature, to annul the enactment of 17th November, 1831, which prohibits the Slave Trade in Brazil under severe penalties."† When Brazil shall be induced to surrender the traffic, it is not improbable that it will be transferred to Buenos Ayres, or one of the many remaining flags of South America: then to Texas; and when we shall have dealt with all these, and shall have wrung from them a reluctant

* Class A. (Further Series), 1837, p. 80.
† Class B. (Further Series), 1837, p. 54.

engagement to renounce the iniquity, we shall still have to deal with the United States of North America.

How long, it may be asked, will it take before we have succeeded in gaining from the whole world a concurrence in the provisions of the existing treaty with Spain?   We began our negotiations with Portugal about thirty years ago; and in what state are they now?   By a despatch from Lord Howard de Walden, our ambassador at Lisbon, to Lord Palmerston, of date 25th February, 1838, we are informed that Viscount de Sa da Bandeira, the Portuguese minister, having been urged to proceed with the negotiations, replied, " That he would do so as soon as he had settled a treaty with Spain for the navigation of the Douro, the negotiation of which occupied his whole time."*

To touch upon one only of the many difficulties which lie in the way of a universal confederacy for putting down the Slave Trade, I ask, how shall we get the consent of North America to the article yielding the right of search?   She has told us, in the most peremptory terms, that she will never assent to it; and it should be remembered that this confederacy must either be universally binding or it is of no avail.   It will avail us little that ninety-nine doors are closed, if one remains open.   To that one outlet the whole Slave Trade of Africa will rush.

* Class B. (Further Series), 1837, p. 30.

Does any one suppose that even in the space of half a century we shall have arrived at one universal combination of all countries for the suppression of the Slave Trade? And a delay of fifty years, at the present rate of the traffic, implies, at the very least, the slaughter of eleven millions of mankind.

But let us suppose this combination to have been effected, and that all nations consent to the four leading articles of the Spanish Treaty. When that is done, it will be unavailing.

In the first place, during the three years which have elapsed since the treaty with Spain, the Slave Trade has been carried on by the Spaniards, at least to as great an extent as formerly. On the 2d January, 1836, the Commissioners at Sierra Leone say, " There is nothing in the experience of the past year to show that the Slave Trade with Spain has, in any degree, diminished."*

The Commissioners at the Havana say, " Never has the Slave Trade at the Havana reached such a disgraceful pitch as during the year 1835."†   I

---

* Class A. 1835, p. 9.

† Ibid. p. 206. On the 19th January, 1839, Her Majesty's Commissioners thus addressed the Captain-General of Cuba : " We regret to feel it a duty incumbent upon us to call your Excellency's attention to the alarmingly increasing importation of Bozal negroes into this island ;" and on the 20th Feb. 1839, they reported to Lord Palmerston " that there continues every appearance of the trade being persevered in with the same vigour as during the past year." And on the 20th March following, they state that " there is every appearance of its being still further extended."—Class A. (Further Series), 1838-9, pp. 115, 119, 121.

could corroborate this statement, that there is no
diminution in the Spanish Slave Trade, by a variety
of letters.   One gentleman, upon whose sources of
information and accuracy I can entirely rely, says, in
a letter dated September, 1836, " The Slave Trade,
which was thought to be dead here some years ago,
has still a mighty being, and stalks over the island
in all its pristine audacity."   Another, of date
November, 1836, says, " Article First of the late
Treaty between England and Spain states, ' The
Slave Trade is hereby declared, on the part of Spain,
to be henceforward totally and finally abolished in
all parts of the world.'   In answer to this, we assert
that the Slave Trade carried on by the Spaniards is
more brisk than ever.   In December, 1836, a gentleman, detained a month at St. Jago de Cuba, witnessed the arrival of five slave cargoes from Africa."

But it may be said that this arises from the facility
with which the Portuguese flag is obtained, and that
when Portugal, and all other powers, shall have con-
sented to the Spanish Treaty, this mode of evasion
will have ceased.   It is perfectly true that the Portuguese flag is obtained with the greatest facility at
a very moderate price. At the Cape de Verd Islands,
at the River Cacheo, at St. Thomas's, at Prince's, and
at Angola, the Portuguese flag may be easily and
cheaply purchased.   But notwithstanding, we find
by the last parliamentary papers, that out of the
twenty-seven vessels condemned at Sierra Leone,
eight were under the Spanish flag; and of the

seventy-two vessels which left the port of Havana
for the coast of Africa, in 1837, no fewer than *nine-teen* at least were *Spanish*.* The slave-traders
surely did not think that the Spanish Treaty was a
death-blow to the trade, or they would not have neglected the precaution of purchasing, at a very easy
price, the protection afforded by the flag of Portugal.

They have their choice of the Spanish flag, attended
by all the dangers supposed to arise from the Spanish
Treaty, or the Portuguese flag, which is not liable
to these dangers; and, for the sake of saving a very
trivial sum, they prefer the former.†

* Class A. (Further Series), 1837, p. 68.

† The Commissioners at Sierra Leone, of date 12th Nov., 1838,
make the following observation :—" We have before alluded to
the practice adopted by Cuba vessels, of carrying both Portuguese
and Spanish papers, the former of which are made use of when
they are boarded and searched by Her Majesty's cruizers—and
with the latter they clear out from Havana, and again re-enter
that port in ballast."—Class A. (Further Series), 1838-9, p. 68.—
I observe in the same papers a curious description of the changes
of names and flags which take place in the trade. In Feb., 1833,
the French ship " Paquebot Bordelais" became the Spanish
" Europa;" under this name she made a number of voyages till Sept.,
1834, when she became the Spanish ship " Alerta," under which
name she sailed for Africa. In Feb., 1836, she returned, and, as
the " Europa," again sailed for Africa, returning as the Portuguese " Duquesa di Braganza" in January, 1837. She subsequently became the Spanish ship " Provisional," after which, being too old for the African trade, the plan of building a new vessel to navigate under her papers was formed, and with them the
American ship Venus became the Portuguese " Duquesa di Braganza."—Class B (Further Series), p. 32, 1839. See note, p. 43.
" The Venus."

But there is another mode of measuring the importance which the slave-traders attach to the Spanish Treaty. The Commissioners, in their Report of 1836, after stating that the first effect of the treaty was to arrest the Slave Trade, add, that this alarm soon wore away, and " now the only visible effect of the reported new treaty is an increased rate of premium out and home, with an augmented price of negroes."*

The Spanish Treaty has been for some time a topic of continual congratulation and complacency; and there are many who think that if we could but induce Portugal and other countries to follow the example of Spain, there would be an end of the Slave Trade. A case occurs in the papers presented to Parliament in 1838, which throws a strong light on the real efficacy of the Spanish Treaty; and, though I can give but a scanty outline of it here, it deserves particular attention. The Vencedora, a Spanish vessel, officered by Spaniards, having lately returned from a trading voyage to Africa, came into the port of Cadiz, bound for Porto Rico. At Cadiz she took in forty-nine passengers, and proceeded on her way. The passengers suffered considerable annoyance from the effluvia proceeding from the lower parts of the ship. By this, and by other circumstances, some vague suspicion seems to have been engendered. Leaving Porto Rico, the vessel proceeded towards Cuba; on her way thither

* Class A. 1835, p. 207.

she fell in with the Ringdove, Captain Nixon. The captain of the Vencedora denied that he had negroes on board ; but the mate of the Ringdove insisted on pursuing his search, and in the forepeak of the vessel, closed up from light or air, were found twenty-six negroes :* "most of them were young, from ten years old upwards."

They could not speak one word of Spanish, unless it be true, which the Spanish witnesses labour hard to prove, that one of them was once heard to use the word " Señor." From these circumstances, from the stench perceived by the passengers after leaving Cadiz ; from the fact of three iron coppers being found, and large quantities of rice and Indian corn having daily been dressed in them ; from the care taken to debar the passengers from all access to those parts of the ship where they were found ; and from the testimony, through an interpreter, of the negroes themselves, " who all declared, most solemnly, that they had never been in another vessel, and swore to it, after the manner of their country ;" from all these circumstances it is clear (however incredible the atrocity) that these wretches had been shipped at Congo, in Africa, had been carried across the Atlantic to Cadiz, again across the Atlantic to Porto Rico, and were, when taken, in the progress of a third voyage.

* They appeared to be of recent importation, had no other clothing than a piece of cloth tied round their loins, their heads were shaven, and some of them were in a sad state of emaciation. Class A. 1837, p. 40.

No record exists of the number originally shipped, nor of those who were so happy as to perish by the way, nor of the extent of misery undergone by those who endured a voyage from Africa to Europe, and from Europe to America, of not less than 6000 miles, pining in their narrow, loathsome, and sultry prison, for want of air, and light, and water. These particulars will never be known in this world; but who will deny that the English captain is justified in calling it a case of " utter barbarity ?" He might have added, of " utter perfidy." In a private letter, he says, — " The Vencedora took her wretched cargo round by Cadiz (can you conceive such barbarity ?), and there got armed with government authority as a packet, wearing the royal colours and pendant: they (the slavers) will be liberated, and I may be prosecuted." The fact of her having slaves on board must have been known to the custom-house authorities at Cadiz.

However, thanks to the Spanish Treaty, the ship is captured at last, and the Spanish authorities will be, of course, as eager as ourselves to punish the villain who has thus defied her decrees. Captain Nixon took his prize to the Havana, and she was tried before the Mixed Commission Court. The captain of the slaver set up the impudent defence— First, that these naked, filthy, shaven, emaciated creatures were " passengers," and, next, that they were " parcels of goods from Porto Rico."

The court, by the casting vote of the Spanish umpire, found this false and flimsy pretext valid, acquitted the slaver, restored the vessel, and condemned the innocent negroes to slavery, while Captain Nixon is exposed to heavy damages for doing his duty!* The captain of the Vencedora is triumphant, and, in a complaint which he made relating to certain articles which, as he alleges, are missing, closes the scene by a high-flown address to the court, on " the faith of treaties," " the sacred rights of property and national decorum," and " the outraged honour of the respected flag of England !"

Worse than all is the fact that this case has been taken as a precedent, and already another vessel, the Vigilante, has been liberated on the strength of this decision.

Had I fabricated a case to show the perfidy of the Spanish authorities, and the barefaced evasions which are sufficient, in Lord Palmerston's words, "to reduce the treaty to mere waste paper," I could scarcely have produced one so much to the purpose.†

* It appears that Captain Nixon was sentenced to pay 600l. for detaining the Vencedora.   Class A. 1838-9, p. 95.

† Her Majesty's judge at Havana, of date 2nd July, 1838, thus addresses Lord Palmerston :—" I have reason to believe that the system has been carried on to a very great extent of making Porto Rico a depôt for slaves, and thence smuggling them into the Havana, in smaller vessels ; and the Commissioners at Havana, of date 21st April, 1838, say that in this way " an extensive and increasing trade appears to be carried on, which, unless checked, may probably counteract all our efforts for the suppression of this unhappy traffic."   Class A. 1838-9, pp. 113—95.

I am compelled to go further. It may be pretended that it was only by accident that the slaver, while she remained at Cadiz, escaped the vigilance of the custom-house officers, and by a second fortunate accident that she obtained permission to bear the royal pendant; but can it also be ascribed to accident that the two persons selected by the Spanish Government as commissioner and arbitrator should have acted throughout as if their proper business was to defend the slave-trader, and defeat the treaty? It would seem that, while hardly any evidence is strong enough to convict a slaver, no pretext is too miserable for his defence. For example, the Vencedora is declared to be " wrongfully detained," while the General Laborde, " a well-known and fully-equipped slaver," is liberated " because the wife and children of the supercargo were on board."*

I observe, in a despatch from Her Majesty's judge to Lord Palmerston, of date 17th August, 1838, that he says, in speaking of the conduct of the Captain-general, " It is impossible to come to any other conclusion than that his Excellency is prepared to lend the shelter of his authority to the traffic as much as any of his predecessors;" and he alludes to the " fees and perquisites" received by the Spanish authorities as the real hindrance to the discontinuance of the trade.†

Upon the whole, I can arrive at no other conclu-

* Class A. 1837, p. 91.
† Class A. 1838-9, p. 119.

sion than that the Spanish Treaty, as interpreted by the Spanish judges, is an impudent fraud; and that those who shall be credulous enough to rely upon it for the full attainment of our object will be fatally deceived.

Thus, then, stands the argument : we shall never obtain the concurrence of all the powers to the provisions of the Spanish Treaty; and if we get it, we shall find it not worth having. But even assuming that those insurmountable obstacles have been overcome, and that the Spanish Treaty, improved and rendered more stringent, becomes the law of the civilised world : it will still appear that this treaty will not accomplish our object. Another step must be taken ; and the next step will be to make slave-trading PIRACY, punishable with death.

Once more, then, we shall have to tread the tedious round of negotiation. To say nothing of the difficulty we shall find in inducing Portugal to adopt the greater measure, when she has so long refused to take the minor step ; and nothing of the difficulty of persuading Brazil to advance, when she has exhibited unequivocal symptoms of a disposition to retreat; nor of the reluctance of Spain (who thinks she has conceded too much) to make still further concessions—to say nothing of all these, France stands in our way. She has declared that, by her constitution, it cannot be made piracy.

I am afraid that there is not the remotest probability of inducing all nations to concur in so strong a measure as that of stigmatising the Slave Trade as piracy.

But we will suppose all these difficulties removed; a victory, in imagination, has been obtained over the pride of North America, the cupidity of Portugal, the lawlessness of Texas, and the constitution of France. Let it be granted that the Spanish Treaty, with an article for piracy, has become universal. I maintain that the Slave Trade, even then, will not be put down. Three nations have already tried the experiment of declaring the Slave Trade to be piracy—Brazil, North America, and England. Brazilian subjects, from the time of passing the law, have been continually engaged in the Slave Trade; indeed we are informed that the whole population of certain districts are concerned in it, and *not one* has suffered under the law of piracy. In 1820, a law was passed by the legislature of North America, declaring that if any citizen of that country shall be engaged in the Slave Trade, " such citizen or person shall be adjudged a pirate, and on conviction thereof, before the Circuit Court of the United States, shall suffer death." It will not be denied that American citizens have been largely engaged in the traffic; but I have yet to learn that even one capital conviction has taken place during the eighteen years that have elapsed since the law was passed.*

---

* Major M'Gregor has stated, in the letter to which I have before referred, that a vessel, with 160 Africans on board, had been wrecked at the Bahamas; and he says, " This pretended Portu-

Great Britain furnishes a still more striking illustration of the inefficacy of such a law. For ten years the Slave Trade prevailed at the Mauritius, to use the words of Captain Moresby before the Committee of the House of Commons, " as plain as the sun at noonday." Many were taken in the very act, and yet no conviction, I believe, took place. With these examples before me, I am not so sanguine as some other gentlemen appear to be, as to the efficacy of a law declaring the Slave Trade piracy, even if it were universally adopted. I fear that such a law would be a dead letter, unless, at all events, we had the *bonâ fide* and cordial co-operation of the colonists.* Were we able to obtain this in our own dominions? Our naval officers acted with their usual energy, on the coast of the Mauritius. When General Hall was governor there, and when Mr. Edward Byam was the head of the police, everything possible was done to suppress the traffic, and to bring the criminals to justice. No persons could act with more meritorious fidelity (and, I grieve to say, poorly have they been

guese vessel was fitted out at Baltimore, United States, having been formerly a pilot-boat, called the Washington. The supercargo was an American citizen from Baltimore." See also the Report of the Commissioners, Class B. 1837, p. 125.

* How far we are from having this co-operation, appears from the following :—Lord Palmerston, of date 13th June, 1838, says to Sir G. Villiers, that " No reliance can be placed upon any of the subordinate authorities of the Spanish Government, either in the colonies, or even in Spain itself, for the due execution of the laws of Spain and of the treaties for suppression of the Slave Trade." Class B. 1839, p. 22.

rewarded by the Home Government): it became, however, but too evident that the law was unavailing. The populace would not betray the slave-trader, the agent of the police would not seize him; if captured by our officers, the prisons would not hold him, and the courts would not convict him. General Hall was obliged to resort to the strong expedient of sending offenders of this kind to England, for trial at the Old Bailey, on the ground that no conviction could be obtained on the island. It is clear, then, that the law making Slave Trade piracy will be unavailing, without you obtain the concurrence of the colonists in Cuba and Brazil; and who is so extravagant as to indulge the hope that this will ever be attained?

But now I will make a supposition, still more Utopian than any of the preceding. All nations shall have acceded to the Spanish Treaty, and that treaty shall be rendered more effective. They shall have linked to it the article of piracy; the whole shall have been clenched, by the cordial concurrence of the authorities at home, and the populace in the colonies. With all this, we shall be once more defeated and baffled by contraband trade.

The power which will overcome our efforts is the *extraordinary profit* of the slave-trader. It is, I believe, an axiom at the Custom-house, that no illicit trade can be suppressed, where the profits exceed 30 per cent.

I will prove that the profits of the slave-trader are nearly five times that amount. " Of the enor-

mous profits of the Slave Trade," says Commissioner
Macleay, " the most correct idea will be formed by
taking an example. The last vessel condemned by
the Mixed Commission was the Firm." He gives
the cost of—

		Dollars.
Her cargo	. .	28,000
Provisions, ammunition, wear and tear, &c.	.	10,600
Wages	. . .	13,400
Total expense	. .	52,000
Total product	. .	145,000*

There was a clear profit on the human cargo of
this vessel of 18,600*l*., or just 180 per cent. A
still more striking case is that of the Venus, whose
departure from Havana is thus noticed by the Commissioner, in his despatch of Aug. 22, 1838 :—" The
Venus is destined for Mozambique, and is arranged
to bring as many as 1,000 negroes, in which case, it
is said, she would clear to the speculators from
100,000 to 200,000 dollars, her cost price being
estimated at 50,000, and the expenses of cargo and
slaves at another 50,000 dollars." Her return is
thus noticed in a private letter, dated Havana, Jan.
24, 1839 :—" The Venus is at this moment in the
port, having landed upwards of 850 slaves on the
coast a few miles south of Havana—she was intended

* Parl. Paper, No. 381, p. 37.

to carry 1,000, but the approach of some cruisers determined her captain to start without his complement." My informant thus calculates the profits of the adventure :—"The price of slaves at Havana is stated to be 70*l.* per head for prime slaves; but supposing the cargo of the Venus did not entirely consist of prime slaves, and that the average value did not exceed 50*l.*,

850 slaves, at 50*l.* each		£42,500
Allowing for expenses of voyage .	£2,500	
Cost of 850 slaves on the coast at 4*l.* per hd.	3,400	
		5,900
Net profit		£36,600"

Will any one who knows the state of Cuba and Brazil pretend that this is not enough to shut the mouth of the informer, to arrest the arm of the police, to blind the eyes of the magistrates, and to open the doors of the prison?

Lord Howard de Walden, in a despatch to the Duke of Wellington, dated 26th February, 1835, speaks of a vessel just about to sail from that port (Lisbon), on a slave-trading voyage. It shows the kind of reliance which we are justified in placing on the professions of that country, pledged twenty years ago " to co-operate with His Britannic Majesty in the cause of humanity and justice," and " to extend the blessings of peaceful industry and innocent com-

merce to Africa;" when, in her own capital, under
the guns of her own forts, in the face of day, and
before the eyes of our ambassador, a vessel is permitted, without molestation, to embark in the Slave
Trade; but it also exhibits the prodigious gains of
the man-merchant.

Lord Howard de Walden says, " The subject of
her departure and destination have become quite notorious, and the sum expected to be cleared by
the parties concerned in the enterprise is put at
40,000l."*

Mr. Maclean (Governor at Cape Coast Castle), in
a letter addressed to me, in May, 1838, says, " A
prime slave on that part of the coast with which I

---

* Class B. 1836, p. 27. The Commisioners at Havana, of date
18th Sept., 1838, say to Lord Palmerston,—" The ' General Espar-
tero' has made, it is said, a remarkably successful voyage, so that
the owner has cleared by the speculation upwards of 70,000 dollars;" and of date Jan. 19, 1839, they say—" With regard to the
ship ' Venus,' otherwise ' Duquesa di Braganza,' we should state
that the original cost, we understand, was 30,000 dollars; and
that the fitting-out and expenses of every kind for the voyage,
including the value of the return cargo, was estimated at 60,000
more, say altogether 100,000 dollars. The number of negroes
brought back, as has been before stated, was 860, and they are
said to have been sold at 340 dollars per head, producing the
sum of nearly 300,000 dollars, of which, therefore, two-thirds
was net profit. So long as such returns can be effected, we fear
that no efforts whatever will be effectual in suppressing the traffic,
and certainly not while the dealers have only to meet such a system
of corruption as pervades every department of the government of
the island."—Class A. (Further Series,) 1838-9. p. 109.

have most knowledge, costs about 50 dollars in goods, or about from 25 to 30 dollars in money, including prime cost and charges: the same slave will sell in Cuba for 350 dollars readily; but from this large profit must be deducted freight, insurance, commission, cost of feeding during the middle passage, and incidental charges, which will reduce the net profit to, I should say, 200 dollars on each prime slave; and this must be still further reduced, to make up for casualties, to, perhaps, 150 dollars per head."

It is remarkable that this calculation by Mr. Maclean almost exactly corresponds with that stated by the Sierra Leone Commissioners, giving for the outlay of 100 dollars a return of 280 dollars.

Once more, then, I must declare my conviction that the Trade will never be suppressed by the system hitherto pursued.*   You will be defeated by its enormous gains. You may throw impediments in the way of these miscreants; you may augment their peril; you may reduce their profits; but enough, and more than enough, will remain to baffle all your efforts.

* Mr. Maclean, in a letter dated 16th October, 1838, says, "My neighbour (as I may call him), De Souza, at Whydah, still carries on an extensive Slave Trade; judging by the great number of vessels consigned to him, he must ship a vast number of slaves annually.   He declares, and with truth, that all the slave treaties signed during the last 25 years have never caused him to export one slave fewer than he would have done otherwise."

CHAPTER IV.

SUPERSTITIONS AND CRUELTIES OF THE AFRICANS.

THE vast amount of human suffering, and the waste
of human life, which I have described, form, after
all, but a part of the evil ; and there remains a still
more dreadful feature in the condition of Africa :—
the Slave Trade stands as a barrier, excluding everything which can soften, or enlighten, or civilize,
or elevate the people of that vast continent. It sup-
presses all other trade, creates endless insecurity,
kindles perpetual war, banishes commerce, knowledge, social improvement, and, above all, Christianity, from one quarter of the globe, and from a
hundred millions of mankind.

The Slave Trade is the great cause of the depopulation and degradation of Africa, not merely from
its keeping the people in a state of disorganization,
but from its poisoning the whole policy of the country. Direct discouragement is thrown upon agriculture. A slave-dealing chief, who neglects his
own plantation, will not suffer his subjects to acquire
wealth from independent sources, and the quantity
of land which any one is permitted to plant is
therefore narrowly limited. It appears to them to
be their present interest to encourage the slave
trader at the expense of the honest merchant, and

the latter is kept waiting for weeks, while a slaver is getting her cargo.

It is not very easy to make out an accurate account of the condition of Africa previously to the commerce in slaves, because Europeans had then so little intercourse with that country. Some proofs, however, exist, that it was in a more flourishing state than we find it to be. It is remarkable that the geographers Nubiensis in the 12th century, and Leo Africanus in the 16th,* state that, in their time, the people between the Senegal and Gambia never made war on each other, but employed themselves in keeping their herds, or in tilling the ground. When Sir J. Hawkins visited Africa in 1562—7, with intent to seize the people (a practice which had been strongly reprobated by Queen Elizabeth), he found the land well cultivated, bearing plenty of grain and fruit, and the towns "prettily" laid out.

Bosman, about 1700, writes that it was the early European settlers who first sowed dissensions among the natives of Africa, for the sake of purchasing their prisoners of war. Benezet quotes Wm. Smith, who was sent by the African Company, in 1726, to visit their settlements, and who stated, from the testimony of a factor who had lived ten years in the country, that the discerning natives accounted it their greatest unhappiness ever to have been visited by Europeans.

Dupuis, in his journey up to Coomassie, in 1819,

* Quoted by Benezet, p. 43.

gives the following description of the country then recently laid waste by the King of Ashantee :*— " From the Praa, southward, the progress of the sword down to the margin of the sea may be traced by mouldering ruins, desolated plantations, and osseous relics ; such are the traits of negro ferocity. The inhabitants, whether Assins or Fantees, whose youth and beauty exempted them from slaughter on the spot, were only reserved to grace a triumph in the metropolis of their conquerors, where they were again subject to a scrutiny, which finally awarded the destiny of sacrifice or bondage ; few or none being left behind to mourn over their slaughtered friends, or the catastrophe of their unhappy country."

Traces are yet to be seen of cultivation which has once existed. Thus Ashmun, after a voyage which he made in 1822, for 200 miles to the south-eastward from Cape Montserado, remarks,† — " One century ago a great part of this line of coast was populous, cleared of trees, and under cultivation : it is now covered with a dense and almost continuous forest. This is almost wholly a second growth, commonly distinguished from the original by the profusion of brambles and brushwood which abounds among the larger trees, and renders the woods entirely impervious, even to the natives, until opened by the bill-hook."

* Dupuis, " Journal of a Residence in Ashantee," p. 33.
† " Life of Ashmun," p. 141.

Speaking of the St. Paul's, he says,* " Along this beautiful river were formerly scattered, in Africa's better days, inumerable native hamlets ; and, until within the last 20 years, nearly the whole river-bord, for one or two miles back, was under that slight cultivation which obtains among the natives of this country. But the population has been wasted by the rage for trading in slaves, with which the constant presence of slaving vessels, and the introduction of foreign luxuries, has inspired them. The south bank of this river, and all the intervening country, and the Montserado, have been from this cause nearly desolated of inhabitants."

In a letter which I have recently received from Mr. Clarkson, he observes that the country of Biffeche on the Senegal, which was once well inhabited, was, in a few years, entirely depopulated by the Moorish slave-hunters; and Mr. Rendall, in his papers, draws a strong contrast between the state of a district enjoying security of person and property, and when under the terrors of a slave trade. He states that he was at St. Louis on the Senegal from 1813 to 1817. At that time the place was in the possession of the English, and the surrounding population were led to believe that the Slave Trade was irrevocably abolished : they, in consequence, betook themselves to cultivating the land, and every available piece of ground was under tillage. The people passed from one village to another without arms and without fear, and everything wore an air

* " Life of Ashmun," p. 233.

of contentment.   Mr. Rendall was there again after the place had been made over to France, "and then," he says, "the Slave Trade had revived in all its horrors; vessels were lying in the river to receive cargoes of human flesh; the country was laid waste, not a vestige of cultivation was to be seen, and no one dared to leave the limits of his village without the most ample means of protection."

One apology for the Slave Trade has been suggested: that if there were not a market for the sale of the victims they would be put to death.   I am, however, about to show that the countries in which the Slave Trade chiefly prevails are precisely those in which human sacrifices are carried to the greatest excess.

It is possible, indeed, that, on the first check to the Slave Trade, the barbarous chiefs might be tempted to kill the captives who were no longer saleable.   The possibility should be viewed, in order that the evil may be guarded against by stipulations in our treaties; but, in fact, it does not appear very likely that such a horrible consequence would ensue: it has not done so in some instances with which we are acquainted.   Mr. Butcher, the missionary, speaks, in 1811, of the captives being immediately sent to till the ground, on the occasion of the check put to the Slave Trade in the Rio Nunez;[*] and Mr. Macbrair says, that the chiefs along the Gambia are now regretting the slaves whom they have formerly sold, as they find that their

* Sixth Rep. Afr. Inst., App., p. 163.

labour would be a source of greater wealth than the price received for their persons.   But the most satisfactory proof that such murders are not inevitable, is the fact, that they did not ensue in the English settlements at the period of the abolition.   The natives around Sierra Leone made up their quarrels, and suspended their wars without outrage or bloodshed.*

There may be a danger of riveting the chains of domestic slavery, but there seems to be no great fear that, with reasonable precautions, any dreadful massacre should occur.

In the present state of things, human life and human suffering are very lightly regarded; and so great are the cruelties and abominations now perpetrated that even injudicious interference could hardly render the condition of Africa worse than it now is: —any change must be an improvement.   Laird tells us that the inhabitants of the delta of the Niger were so demoralized and degraded, that he could not have conceived such a people to exist, within a few miles of ports which British ships had frequented for a century.†   At Calebar, skulls were seen " kicked about in every direction."   Captain Fawckner, who was detained in Benin, in great distress in 1825, says, " near the palace of the King of Benin are several fetish places,‡ the depositories of the usual

* Rep. of Com. for Afr. Inst., p. 28.   † Laird, p. 277.

‡ The " fetish " is a word for any being or object supposed to possess supernatural power: It is applied therefore to the demons whom the Pagans worship, and to the charms with which they protect themselves against their power.

objects of worship:" " many unfortunate slaves are sacrificed in front of these temples."* After reading this account of the sufferings of our countryman, whose vessel being stranded upon that coast was plundered, the crew made prisoners, and their lives only spared by a singular succession of favourable omens, it is curious to read in an author two centuries earlier that the people of Benin " will not do injury to any, especially to strangers;"† and that they were " a gentle, loving people;" and to hear from Reynolds, that they found more sincere proofs of love and good will from the natives than from the Spaniards and Portuguese,‡ even though they had relieved the latter from the greatest misery such has been the change of 200 years !

At Dahomey, Mr. Giraud says, he was at the King's fête in 1836, when " about 5 or 600 of his subjects were sacrificed for his recreation. Some were decapitated, and others were precipitated from a lofty fortress, and transfixed on bayonets prepared to receive them; all this merely for amusement."§

The Ashantees, at the same time that they were vigorous slave-traders,‖ were notorious for their

* Fawckner, pp. 83, 84.   † Purchas's Africa, 1601.

‡ Benezet's Account of Africa, p. 59.

§ Colonization Herald, July, 1837.

‖ The Ashantee slave-traders are so numerous and notorious, that the people of Moronho, a town 16 or 17 days' journey from Coomassie, have no doors to their houses, but enter by a ladder human sacrifices and bloody rites. Messrs. Bowditch, Tedlie, and Hutchinson,* were employed on a mission to Coomassie, the capital of Ashantee, in 1817 : on their very first entrance into the city, while waiting in the street for leave to attend the King, Mr. Bowditch says, " Our attention was forced to a most inhuman spectacle, which they paraded before us for some minutes : it was a man whom they were tormenting previous to sacrifice. His hands were pinioned behind him, a knife was passed through his cheeks, to which his lips were noosed like the figure of 8 ; one ear was cut off and carried before him ; the other hung to his head by a small bit of skin ; there were several gashes in his back, and a knife was thrust under each shoulder-blade ; he was led with a cord passed through his nose, by men disfigured with immense caps of shaggy black skins, and drums beat before him."†

Many slaves are killed at their various " customs," (the rites practised on the death of individuals of any consideration :)‡ "the decease of a person is announced by a discharge of musketry proportioned to his rank,

through the roof, as some security against their assaults. Bowditch, p. 171.

* Whatever may have been the views of the few travellers who have visited Ashantee, and however our envoys may have differed with respect to the policy to be pursued towards it, they agree perfectly in describing it as the theatre of the most revolting horrors. Thus Mr. Dupuis entirely confirms the account of Mr. Bowditch as to the scenes continually occurring.

† Bowditch, p. 33.   ‡ Bowditch, p. 282.

or the wealth of his family.   In an instant you see
a crowd of slaves burst from the house and run
towards the bush, flattering themselves that the
hindmost, or those surprised in the house, will
furnish the human victims for sacrifice, if they
can but secrete themselves till the custom is over."
One or two slaves are then sacrificed at the door
of the house. A scene of this kind took place
at the death of the mother of one of the principal
chiefs, August 2nd, 1817, of which Mr. Bowditch
was an eye-witness, though it was considered by no
means a great custom.*   " We walked," he says, " to
Assafoo at twelve o'clock : the vultures were hovering
round two headless trunks scarcely cold." Then
came troops of women, uttering dismal lamentations.
" The crowd was overbearing; horns, drums, and
muskets, yells and screeches, invaded our hearing
with as many horrors as were crowded on our sight.
Now and then a victim was hurried by, generally at
full speed ; the uncouth dress, and the exulting countenances of those who surrounded them, likening
them to as many fiends." He describes many other
barbaric ceremonies ; finally, the drums announced
the sacrifice of the victims.†   " The executioners
wrangled and struggled for the office ; and the indifference with which the first poor creature looked
on, in the torture he was from the knife passed
through his cheeks, was remarkable. The right

* Bowditch, p. 283. † Hutchinson, in Bowditch's Travels, p. 287.

hand of the victim was then lopped off, he was thrown down, and his head was sawed rather than cut off; it was cruelly prolonged, I will not say wilfully. Twelve more were dragged forward, but we forced our way through the crowd and retired to our quarters. Other sacrifices, principally female, were made in the bush where the body was buried. It is usual to " wet the grave" with the blood of a freeman of respectability. All the retainers of the family being present, a slave from behind stuns one of these freemen with a violent blow, followed by a deep gash in the back part of the neck, and he is rolled in on the top of the body of the deceased, and the grave instantly filled up. A sort of carnival, varied by firing, singing, drinking, and dancing, was kept up in Assafoo for several days, the chiefs generally visiting it every evening.

On the death of a king, all the customs which have been made for the subjects who have died during his reign, must be simultaneously repeated by the families, (the human sacrifices as well as the carousals and pageantry,) to amplify that for the monarch : which is also solemnized, independently, at the same time, in every excess of extravagance and barbarity. The brothers, sons, and nephews of the king, affecting temporary insanity, burst forth with their muskets, and fire promiscuously amongst the crowd ; even a man of rank, if they meet him, is their victim : nor is their murder of him or any other, on such an occasion, visited or prevented ; the scene can hardly be imagined. The king's Ocras, who will be mentioned presently, are all murdered on his tomb, to the number of 100 or more; and women in abundance. I was assured by several, that the custom for Sai Quamine was repeated weekly for three months, and that 200 slaves were sacrificed, and 25 barrels of powder fired each time. But the custom for the king's mother, the regent of the kingdom during the invasion of Fantee, is the most celebrated. The king himself devoted 3000 victims, (upwards of 2000 of whom were Fantee prisoners,) and 25 barrels of powder. Five of the largest places furnished 100 victims, and 20 barrels of powder each; and most of the smaller towns 10 victims, and two barrels of powder each. These human sacrifices are frequent and ordinary, to water the graves of the kings.

Mr. Dupuis, who was at Coomassie a year or two later, gives a similar account of the bloody customs of Ashantee; he tells us that before the king set forth on his campaign against Gaman, he began by sacrificing 32 male, and 18 female victims, as an expiatory offering to his Gods, but the answers from the priests being deemed by the council as still devoid of inspiration, the king was induced to *make a custom* at the sepulchres of his ancestors, where many hundreds bled. On the conclusion of the war 2000 prisoners were slaughtered over the royal death stool, in honour of the shades of departed kings and heroes.

The king's own account was not exaggerated, for two respectable Moslems at Coomassie, in describing to Mr. Dupuis the scenes of the Gaman war, declared, that they had witnessed the massacre of 10,000 old men, women, and children, besides numbers of chieftains, who were put to death by tortures the most revolting to humanity.

It appeared that the king rather concealed his human sacrifices while Dupuis was in Coomasie, for two reasons; the one, that they concerned the mission, as the king had been imploring his idols to incline the heart of the great king of England towards him; the other, that it might not be reported that the sovereign of Ashantee delighted in spilling human blood; which, it was known, gave as much offence to white men as it did to Moslems.[*]

I subjoin another case of atrocity abridged likewise from Dupuis : " On the 13th the Adai custom was ushered in by the discharge of fire-arms, and the sound of many barbarous instruments. Numbers of victims were offered up to the gods, although secretly, in the palace and the houses of the chieftains. The city itself exhibited the most deplorable solitude, and the few who were courageous enough to appear in the streets, fled at the approach of a captain, and barricaded the doors of their huts, to avoid the danger of being shot or sacrificed." "The following day a similar train of horrors succeeded, and still I was left in suspense, for my own

* Dupuis, p. 140.

linguists and messengers were not hardy enough to knock at the royal gate. They dreaded, as they said, the fetish men, who guarded the avenue, and who alone were suffered to enjoy free ingress." From the Moslems he learned further that seventy men and women had been put to death the day previous in the palace only, beside those who were sacrificed in private houses or in the forest. Most of these unhappy beings were Gaman prisoners, who had been purposely reserved as an offering to the gods; the others were criminals or disobedient slaves.

I find another instance, not the less touching because more simple, and more easily conceived by the mind than these hecatombs, and not less clearly proving the actual co-existence of a keen pursuit of he " trade," with a remorseless waste of the lives of its objects.

" March 2nd, 1837.—I learned from the king," says the Rev. Mr, Fox, " that they brought 350 Foulahs from Foolokolong, besides 100 they killed. I asked him how many of these Foulahs were at Madina, (having myself seen a few in the town,) when he answered only twelve, and immediately called an interesting little Foulah boy of about six years of age, who came trembling and weeping as he approached. His father, I learned, was killed in the attack upon Foolokolong. I therefore ventured to ask his sable majesty to give the boy to me; but no, he said he could not, and why? Because, horrid to

relate, he had dedicated this innocent and unoffend-
ing child to a greegree, or rather to the devil; and
who will doubtless by some cruel means be put to
death, previous to the intended attack upon Kimmington, to ensure success! Mantamba, I am told, is rather
nervous in his language against Koi, because he
does not sacrifice one of his own children; and hesi-
tated not to say that it was because he did not do this,
that the attack upon Dunkaseen was not more successful. I would fain have rescued this poor little
fatherless boy from the unmerciful grasp of these
wild barbarians, by giving a handsome present for
his redemption; but even had I succeeded, another
would doubtless have immediately been substituted in
his stead."

After the account of the home practice of the
Ashantees, we cannot be surprised at the barbarities
they exercised upon the British prisoners who fell
into their hands during the war in which we were
engaged with them. After the battle in which Sir
Charles M'Carthy was unfortunately killed, Mr.
Williams, an officer who was taken prisoner, said,
that whenever the Ashantees beheaded a prisoner,
they made him sit on one side of the large war
drum, while they took off their victim's head on the
other.* Mr. Jones, a merchant and captain of the
militia, having received five wounds, was immediately sacrificed; this, however, would have happened to him, had he been an Ashantee; for any

* Major Rickett's Narrative of the Ashantee War, p. 84.

one who has received five wounds in an action, whether friend or foe, is devoted to the fetish. It is said that the Ashantee chiefs ate Sir Charles M'Carthy's heart,* that they might imbibe his valour; and that his dried flesh and bones were divided amongst them as charms to inspire courage.

In the Landers' narrative, instances of similar atrocity are to be met with. We are informed† that at Jenna it is the custom for two of the governor's wives to quit the world on the same day with himself; and that the governor of that place, himself of necessity goes down to the grave on the demise of his sovereign, the king of Yarriba.

Mr. Laird‡ speaks of the decease of an aged chief while he was at Fundah, who left 15 wives; and he tells us that on the night this man was to be buried, the king went to the women's apartment, and selected one, who was to be hung, in order to accompany her husband to the next world.

Of the other barbarous customs of Africa, the continual appeal to the ordeal of " red water," or poison, is one of the worst. This, too, also shows the very low rate at which human life is valued. At Iddah Mr. Oldfield§ saw a procession of the wives of the king's son, just deceased, who were proceeding to establish their innocence of his death

* Major Rickett's Narrative of the Ashantee War, p. 105.

† Lander, vol. i., p. 92, 93.

‡ Laird, vol. i., p. 225.

§ Oldfield, vol. ii., p. 178.

by drinking poison; and he says, that " out of sixty of these poor infatuated wretches, thirty-one died."

I shall close this gloomy catalogue of barbarities with an account, extracted from Lander,* of some of the atrocities perpetrated in Badagry. He says, "The murder of a slave is not considered even in the light of a misdemeanour among them. Badagry being a general mart for the sale of slaves to the European merchants, it not unfrequently happens that the market is overstocked with human beings; in which case their maintenance devolves on the government. Thieves and other offenders, together with the remnant of unpurchased slaves who are not drowned along with their companions in misfortune and misery, are reserved by them to be sacrificed to their gods; which horrid ceremony takes place at least once a month. Prisoners taken in war are also immolated, to appease the manes of the soldiers of Adoilee slain in battle; and of all atrocities, the manner in which these wretches are slain is the most barbarous. Each criminal being conducted to the fetish tree, a flask of rum is given him to drink; whilst he is in the act of swallowing it, a fellow steals imperceptibly behind him with a heavy club, inflicts a violent blow on the back of the head, and, as it often happens, dashes out his brains. The senseless being is then taken to the fetish hut, and a calabash or gourd having been previously got ready, the head is severed from the trunk with an axe, and the

* Lander, vol. ii., p. 249.

smoking blood gurgles into it. While this is in
hand, other wretches, furnished with knives, cut and
mangle the body in order to extract the heart entire
from the breast, which being done, although it be yet
warm and quivering with blood, it is presented to
the king first, and afterwards to his wives and
generals, who always attend at the celebration of
these sacrifices; and his majesty and suite making
an incision into it with their teeth, and partaking of
the foamy blood, which is likewise offered, the heart
is exhibited to the surrounding multitude. It is then
affixed to the head of a tall spear, and with the
calabash of blood, and headless body, paraded through
the town, followed by hundreds of spearmen, and
a dense crowd of people. Whoever may express
an inclination to bite the heart or drink the blood,
has it immediately presented to him for that purpose,
the multitude dancing and singing. What remains
of the heart is flung to the dogs, and the body, cut in
pieces, is stuck on the fetish tree, where it is left till
wholly devoured by birds of prey. Besides these
butcheries, they make a grand sacrifice once a year,
under their sacred fetish tree, growing in a wood,
a few miles from the city. These are offered
to their malevolent demon or spirit of evil, quartered,
and hung on the gigantic branches of the venerable
tree, and the skulls of the victims suffered to bleach
in the sun around the trunk of it. By accident, I
had an opportunity of seeing this much talked of tree,
a day or two only after one of the yearly sacrifices—

its enormous branches literally covered with fragments of human bodies, and its majestic trunk
surrounded by irregular heaps of hideous skulls,
which had been suffered to accumulate for many
years previously. Thousands of vultures which had
been scared away by our unwelcome intrusion, were
yet hovering round and over their disgusting food,
and now and then pouncing fearlessly down upon a
half devoured arm or leg. I stood as if fascinated to
the spot by the influence of a torpedo, and stupidly
gazed on the ghastly spectacle before me—the huge
branches of the fetish tree groaning under their
burden of human flesh and bones, and sluggishly
waving in consequence of the hasty retreat of the
birds of prey; the intense and almost insufferable
heat of a vertical sun; the intolerable odour of the
corrupt corpses; the heaps of human heads, many
of them apparently staring at me from hollows which
had once sparkled with living eyes; the awful still-
ness and solitude of the place, disturbed only at inter-
vals by the frightful screamings of voracious vultures,
as they flapped their sable wings almost in my face—
all tended to overpower me; my heart sickened within my bosom,—a dimness came over my eyes, an in-
expressible quivering agitated my whole frame—my
legs refused to support me; and turning my head, I
fell senseless into the arms of Jowdie my faithful
slave.*"

The perpetual witnessing of such revolting scenes

* Lander, pp. 260—268.

and the constant perpetration of such atrocious deeds, as have been detailed in the foregoing pages, keep the African population in a state of callous barbarity, which can only be effectually counteracted by Christian civilisation—to impart which to them, the recital of such horrors may well animate our desires, and quicken our endeavours. In the meantime, it appears our duty to protest against them in all our official transactions, and to make the Africans aware, that they can only obtain the advantages of a connexion with Europeans, by renouncing practices which outrage the feelings of civilised men. And, as a more extended intercourse is opening between us and them, now is the time to establish this principle. That many of the Africans have a regard for European opinions, and that they are already aware that their bloody rites are offensive to Christians, is, I think, fully demonstrated by several facts which have been stated in this chapter. For this reason it is that those of them who live on coasts frequented by our traders, have betaken to the practice of perpetrating their sanguinary orgies under the shades of night; for this reason did the king of Ashantee endeavour to hide some of his butcheries from the British Envoy, that " he might not have to report that the sovereign of Ashantee delighted in spilling human blood." It was for the same cause that a friendly chief who visited Sir Charles M'Carthy in the Ashantee war,* had hung pieces of tartan round his war drums, to hide

* Rickett's Ashantee War, p. 38.

the jaw-bones and skulls with which they were ornamented, "being fearful, from what he had heard of the character of his Excellency, that they should give offence ;" and that King Dinkera desisted from the murder he was about to commit on the occasion of his sister's death, on hearing that the British Government disapproved of such practices.

As this portion of my work tends to exhibit the state of Africa under a new and most melancholy aspect, I did not feel justified in omitting it ; but it was my intention and desire to make it as brief as possible. I find myself, however, under the necessity of extending it. I have received from the secretaries of the Wesleyan Missionary Society the following narrative, which I have somewhat abbreviated. It gives a picture, the accuracy of which no one will doubt, seeing the quarter from which it comes, of events which have occurred during the current year, in a town not more than 150 miles distant from the British settlement of Cape Coast Castle :—

Extracts from the Letters and Journal of the Rev. THOMAS B. FREEMAN, *Wesleyan Missionary, containing an account of his visit to Ashantee in* 1839.

REVEREND AND DEAR SIRS,

Ever since my arrival on this station, (Cape Coast Castle,) I had felt deeply anxious to visit

Coomassie. The tales of horror, wretchedness, and cruelty which I had often heard respecting the Ashantees wrought in my mind a constant restlessness to commence missionary operations among them.

Feb. 2.—At half-past 3 P.M. I reached the town of Mansue, and was very kindly received by the chief and his captains.

Before I retired to rest, Gabrea (the chief) sent me a present, consisting of a good sheep, some plantains, and pine apples. His mother also sent me some yams and plantains.

3rd, Sunday.—At 4 P.M. I preached the word of life to the chief and his captains, and many of the people.

Considering their ignorant condition, they behaved very well. I do not remember that I ever witnessed a more interesting scene than that which took place at the close of the sermon. The sublime truths concerning the mysterious plan of human redemption, made such an impression on the minds of the chief and his captains, that they could no longer contain themselves, but spreading abroad their hands, and lifting up their voices, they acknowledged the loving-kindness of God, and declared, before many of their people, that they would worship God; and I verily believe they would, if they could be watched over by a missionary or a teacher.

6th.—At 6¼ A. M. I started from Berracoe for the river Prah,* which I reached nine minutes

* Boosemprah of Bowditch

before 9 A. M. The river, the largest I have yet seen in Africa, with its thickly-wooded banks abounding in palm treees and mimosæ, presented a beautifully picturesque scene. When the river is at its greatest height, its depth may be about thirty or forty feet, and its breadth about ninety yards. Near the crossing place its bed is very rocky; as it was very low, I could see many large pieces of granite above the surface of the water. The river Prah forms the boundary between Fantee and the dominions of the king of Ashantee. On the Fantee side of the river is a small town called Prahshoo.

The whole of the Fantee country through which I passed, from within a mile or two of Cape Coast Castle up to the river Prah, a distance of about eighty-five miles, is covered with luxuriant vegetation, consisting of plantains, bananas, palms, bamboos, pines, many large forest trees, covered with climbers, "*Epiphitical Archidaceæ,*" and ferns.

Immediately before entering Quissah, I passed over a hill of considerable height. Its soil is very rich, consisting of a mixture of yellow loam and clay. A spring of the most delicious water I ever tasted, rises above half way up the hill, (from what I could judge,) and after tumbling down its rocky bed of granite, bubbles by the small town of Quissah. The Assin country, though consisting of a very rich and fertile soil, covered with luxuriant vegetation, presents one unbroken scene of desolation,*

* If this brief account of Fantee and Assin is compared with

except here and there a few huts occupied by
Ashantees, whom the king sends to take care of the
path.

9th.—This morning the chief informed me that
Corintchie, the chief of Fomunnah, had sent over
for him to converse with him respecting me. Shortly
afterwards, a messenger arrived from Corintchie,
requesting me to go over and visit him, which I
immediately prepared to do. When I entered the
town, Corintchie was sitting before the front of his
house under his large umbrella, waiting to receive
me, his captains and people occupying the ground
on his right and left. After the usual compliments
on meeting, he asked me what object I had in view
in wishing to pass up to Coomassie. I told him I
had nothing to do with trade or palavers, but was
come into the country to promote the best interests
of the king of Ashantee and his people, by directing
them in the way of peace and happiness through the
preaching of the gospel. He then said he should
like to hear the gospel in his town, before I proceeded any further into the country. I hereupon
proceeded to speak to him and all present on the
being of a God, and the nature of the Christian religion. They readily gave their assent to all I said,
and Corintchie requested me to pay them a visit on

that given by Bowditch, p. 23-4, it will be perceived that the
Fantee country is rapidly improving under the fostering care or
the local government of Cape Coast, while the Assin country
abandoned by its rightful owners, is in ruins.

the morrow, that they might hear more from me concerning the Christian religion.   On my remarking, that as I was a minister of the gospel, I could not prudently make them presents according to the usual custom, it being beneath the dignity of Christianity, which is so truly excellent in itself that it requires no recommendation except a consciousness of its value, he answered, " We do not desire any of the customary presents from you, but wish rather to become acquainted with Christianity."

There were about 500 persons present.

10th, Sunday.—At 3 p. m. I again went over to Fomunnah, to preach the word of life, followed by the chief of Quissah.

I had a goodly number of our people with me, who assisted in singing the praises of God.

At the conclusion of the sermon, Corintchie and his captains said it was a " good palaver."   On my telling them that I had not laid before them a thousandth part of the sublime truths contained in the Bible, they said they should like to hear more of them, and especially what " Yancumpon" (God) liked, and what he disliked; and seemed much pleased when I told them I should be happy to preach to them again whenever they pleased.

On the 12th, Mr. Freeman received a present from the king of nine ackies of gold dust, (£2, 5s.,) and he was invited to remove to Fomunnah.

19th, Tuesday.—Last night a sister of Corintchie died, after a long sickness. Her death was announced by the firing of muskets, and the mourners going about the streets. When an Ashantee of any description dies, several of the deceased's slaves are sacrificed. This horrible custom originates in some shadowy ideas of a future state of existence, and in a notion that those who depart hence stand in need of material food, clothing, &c., the same as in the present world; and, consequently, as a vast number of concubines, slaves, &c. are the chief marks of superiority among them here, so they will be in a future state. Accordingly, as I walked out early in the morning, I saw the mangled corpse of a poor female slave, who had been beheaded during the night, lying in the public street. It was partially covered with a common mat, (made from the stem of the plantain tree,) and as this covering is unusual, I concluded that it was thrown over to hide it from my view. In the course of the day I saw groups of natives dancing round this victim of superstitious cruelty, with all manner of frantic gestures, appearing to be in the very zenith of their happiness.

In the evening I was informed that, as Corintchie and his captains did not wish me to see any more headless trunks lying in the streets, they had not sacrificed any more persons during the day, but would most probably do so during the night. I am happy to say, however, that I could not ascertain that any more sacrifices had been made. That *only one* person was sacrificed, I believe resulted entirely from my being in the town.

27th.—I had a long conversation with some of the natives, on the subject of the general resurrection, and of the injury done to their country by human sacrifices. Many of the natives seem to have an utter dislike to this horrid custom, while others are sunk into such a state of apathy, that they are quite indifferent about it, though their lives, as well as those of others, are continually in danger.

28th.—I paid Corintchie a visit, and reasoned with him closely on the painful consequences of human sacrifices and customs for the dead. He readily acknowledged the evil, and expressed himself as ready to do away with it, if he were at full liberty to do so, but he " feared the king."

The only reason he could give for making customs for the dead, was that they felt very unhappy when they lost their relatives and friends, and were then very glad to have recourse to drunkenness, or anything which would drive gloomy thoughts from their minds for a season.* As he thus gave me a good opportunity of directing him to the only sure refuge for a troubled mind,—the consolations of true religion,—I told him that God alone was able to sustain the human mind under afflictions and bereavements. He seemed affected with what I said to him.

* While I was staying at Fomunnah I once reproved Corintchie for drunkenness, when he said that the king had checked him for it once, and since I also had done it, which made the second reproof he had received, he would endeavour to avoid it for the future.

March 2d.—To-day, another human victim was sacrificed, on account of the death of a person of rank in the town. As I was going out of the town, in the cool of the evening, I saw the poor creature lying on the ground. The head was severed from the body, and lying at a short distance from it. Several large turkey-buzzards were feasting on the wounds, and literally rolling the head in the dust. This unfortunate creature appeared to be about eighteen years of age, a strong healthy youth, who might in all probability have lived many years longer. As I returned into the town, I saw that they had dragged the body to a short distance, and thrown it into the ditch where the poor female was thrown the other day.

On my conversing with some of the natives, concerning the horrible nature of human sacrifices, they said they themselves did not like them, and wished that they could be done away. While the poor creature was lying in the public street, many of the people were looking on with the greatest indifference; indeed, they seem to be so familiar with these awful and bloody scenes, that they think no more of them, nay, they do not think so much of them, as they would of seeing a dead sheep, dog, or monkey.

17th.—In the afternoon I again conducted Divine service, and preached from Matt. xix. 17, " If thou wilt enter into life, keep the commandments." Corintchie and several of his captains were present, and appeared much excited during the sermon, but more especially during that part in which I explained to them the Ten Commandments. They often stopped me in my discourse, to ask questions ; among which was the following :—" Is the offering a human sacrifice, murder ?" I answered, " It is even so ; and you will henceforth be left without excuse, if you still persist in that horrible practice." After I had directed their attention to the excellence of the commandments, especially the temporal and spiritual blessings which the consecration of the Christian Sabbath is calculated to introduce among mankind, I proposed the following question :—" Who are the happiest persons ? those who conscientiously keep God's commandments, or those who wilfully break them ?" They answered, without hesitation, " Those who keep them." And I verily believe that this answer was given in sincerity, as they appeared deeply impressed with the solemnity of the discourse.

On Mr. Freeman's afterwards telling them that he feared the delay of the king, in sending for him, proceeded from suspicion, and " that it was his duty to turn aside, and carry the glad tidings of salvation to another nation, if he found them averse to receiving the truth," they seemed very much concerned, and said they felt no disposition to oppose the introduction of Christianity amongst them, and that they believed the king would also be glad to hear the truths of the gospel, and that he would wish me to stay a long time in Coomassie, after my arrival and first interview.

In the afternoon, I rambled through the thicket, to the summit of a distant hill, where one of the most splendid pieces of scenery I ever saw, burst upon my view. The bush on the summit being rather low, I had an opportunity of viewing the surrounding country, in some directions, for several miles. Down the sloping sides of the hill the splendid plantain-tree was luxuriating and waving its beautiful foliage. Then followed the delightful vale, winding to the right and left, studded with gigantic silk-cotton trees, acaciæ, mimosæ, with an endless variety of climbers.

28th, Thursday.—I travelled through a fine fertile country of diversified hill and dale, covered with luxuriant vegetation, and studded with immense silk-cotton, and other forest trees.

April 1, at 2 p.m. a messenger arrived from the king, requesting me to proceed as early as possible. I immediately dressed myself; and while so doing three other messengers arrived, each bearing a gold sword, requesting me to hasten forward. I then proceeded towards the town, preceded by the messengers, and some soldiers bearing arms. Having reached the outside of the town, we halted under a large tree, and there awaited another royal invitation.

In a short time his majesty's chief linguist (Apoko) came in a palanquin, shaded by an immense umbrella, and accompanied by messengers bearing canes nearly covered with gold, to take charge of my luggage, and see it safely lodged in the residence intended for me. All these things being properly arranged, another messenger arrived, accompanied by troops and men bearing large umbrellas, requesting me to proceed to the market-place. "The king's commandment" being "urgent," we pushed along with speed, preceded by a band of music. As soon as we arrived at the market-place, I got out of my little travelling chair, and walked through the midst of an immense concourse of persons, (a narrow path being kept clear for me,) paying my respects to the king, and his numerous chiefs and captains, who were seated on wooden chairs, richly decorated with brass and gold, under the shade of their splendid umbrellas, (some of them large enough to screen twelve or fourteen persons from the burning rays of the sun, and crowned with images of beasts covered with gold,) surrounded by their troops and numerous attendants. I occupied half an hour in walking slowly through the midst of this immense assembly, touching my hat and waving my hand, except before the king, in whose presence I, of course, stood for a moment uncovered. I then took my seat at a distance, accompanied by my people and several respectable Fantee traders, who are staying in the town, to receive the compliments of the king, &c., &c., according to their usual custom.

After I had taken my seat, the immense mass began to be in motion; many of the chiefs first passed me in succession, (several of them cordially shaking me by the hand,) accompanied by their numerous retinue. Then came the officers of the king's household; his treasurer, steward, &c., &c., attended by their people, some bearing on their heads massive pieces of silver-plate, others carrying in their hands gold swords and canes, native stools neatly carved, and almost covered with gold and silver, and tobacco-pipes richly decorated with the same precious materials. In this ostentatious display I also saw what was calculated to harrow up the strongest and most painful feelings;—the royal executioners bearing the blood-stained stools on which hundreds, and perhaps thousands, of human victims have been sacrificed by decapitation; and also the large death-drum, which is beaten at the moment when the fatal knife severs the head from the body, the very sound of which causes a thrill of horror.* This rude

* The language of this drum is known by the natives whenever they are within hearing; so that they are as well aware of the moment when a sacrifice is made as though they were on the very spot. While the king was making sacrifices, during the custom for his brother, I was in a distant part of the town, conversing with my interpreter, who, knowing the fatal meaning of the sound of the drum, said, "Hark! do you hear the drum? A sacrifice

instrument, connected with which are the most dreadful associations, was literally covered with dried clots of blood, and decorated with the jaw-bones and skulls of human victims.   Then followed the king, (Quacoe Dooah,) under the shade of three splendid umbrellas, the cloth of which was silk velvet, of different colours, supported by some of his numerous attendants.   The display of gold which I witnessed, as his majesty passed, was truly astonishing.   After the king followed other chiefs, and lastly the main body of the troops.

This immense procession occupied one hour and a half in passing before me.   There were several Moors in the procession, but they made by no means a conspicuous appearance.

While I was sitting to receive the compliments of some of the first chiefs who passed, his majesty made me a present of some palm wine.

I suppose the number of persons whom I saw collected together, exceeded 40,000, including a great number of females.   The wrists of some of the chiefs were so heavily laden with gold ornaments, that they rested their arms on the shoulders of some of their attendants,

The appearance of this procession was exceedingly grand and imposing.   The contrast between the people themselves and their large umbrellas (seventy in

has just been made, and the drum says, ' King, I have killed him.' "

number) of various colours, which they waved and jerked up and down in the air, together with the dark-green foliage of the large banyan trees, under and among which they passed, formed a scene of that novel and extraordinary character which I feel unable to describe.

This morning I received information that the king had lost one of his relations by death, and that in consequence thereof, four human victims were already sacrificed, and their mangled bodies lying in the streets. I therefore concluded that I should not have an opportunity of seeing the king for a day or two. Shortly afterwards, I saw Apoko, the chief linguist, and told him that I was aware that there was bloody work going on to-day, as I saw a number of large hawks and turkey-buzzards hovering over a certain spot where I judged these poor victims were lying. He said it was even so, and in consequence, I should not have an opportunity of seeing the king to-day, and, perhaps, not to-morrow. I told him that I did not like the being confined at one small place, in a low, unhealthy part of the town, and that I must walk out and take exercise, otherwise my health would suffer. I also told him that I was anxious to commence my journey home to the coast on Monday next. On hearing this, he went immediately to the king, and informed him of what I said; shortly after which he returned, accompanied by two messengers, (one of them bearing in his hand an immense gold sword, to which was fastened a golden decanter which would hold about a pint,) stating that his majesty begged of me not to go out into the town to-day, as he was making a custom for a departed relative; and he knew Europeans did not like to see human sacrifices: and, also, that he did not wish to keep me from seeing over his capital; that he was fully satisfied my object was to do good; and that he would see me as soon as the custom was over. I, of course, complied with his wishes, and made up my mind to wait patiently.

Throughout the day I heard the horrid sound of the *death-drum;* and was informed in the evening that twenty-five human victims had been sacrificed; some in the town, and some in the surrounding villages, the heads of those killed in the villages being brought into the town in baskets. I fear there will be more of this awful work to-morrow.

6th, Saturday.—This morning I again talked of walking out into the town, when Apoko informed me that more sacrifices would be made during the day and that I must not go out until to-morrow. I therefore remained in my quarters until the afternoon, when, on finding myself in rather a dangerous state for want of exercise, I insisted upon walking out at one end of the town for half an hour. In the evening I learned that several more human victims had been sacrificed during the day, but could not ascertain the exact number. The most accurate account I could obtain was that fifteen more had suffered, making a total of forty in two days.

While speaking to Apoko I did not fail to remind him that the law of God forbids this awful practice, and that they were under a great error in supposing that the persons sacrificed, would attend on the deceased relative of the king in a future state.

These poor victims were allowed to be naked and exposed in the street, until they began to swell like dead dogs, and such is the callous state of mind in which the people live, that many were going about among these putrefying bodies, smoking their pipes with astonishing indifference.

Having asked his Majesty to allow me to see the town to-day, he readily gave me liberty to go where ever I pleased. I therefore embraced the opportunity of looking over it, which occupied about one hour. The streets are longer, and more clean and uniform than any I have seen in any other native town, since my arrival in Africa. The breadth of some of them is at least thirty yards, and the average length from 300 to 600 yards. The town is situated on a bed of granite, fragments of which are strewed in abundance over the finest streets, the average size of them being about twenty inches cube. A row of splendid banyan trees, at a considerable distance from each other, occupies the centre of some of the largest streets, affording a most delightful shade

from the burning rays of the sun.   The streets differ
also in appearance from those of any other town
which I have seen in the interior, by the houses on
each side having open fronts.   The floor being raised
from two to three feet above the level of the ground,
the space between the ground and the level of the
floor, and in some houses, a foot or two above the
level of the floor, presents a front of carved work,
beautifully polished with red ochre.   In some the
carved work is continued up to the roof, and where
such is the case it is covered with white clay, which
has the appearance of a lime white-wash.   The roofs
are made chiefly with bamboo-poles, or sticks with
the bark stripped off, and thatched with palm-
leaves.

Behind each of these open fronts are a number of
small houses, or rather open sheds, in which the people
dwell, (the room open to the street being more of a public seat than a private room,) at an average number of
from thirty to forty to each open front.   These small
dwellings in the back ground, are in many cases entirely hidden from the observation of any one passing
along the streets, the only indication of them being a
small door on the left or right of the open front.
The houses are all built on the same plan, from that
of the king down to the lowest rank of captains:
and these are, with a few exceptions, the only persons who are allowed to build in any public situation.
The rocky bed, on which the town is built, is in

many parts very irregular, and some of the streets are so full of holes, occasioned by the heavy rains washing the earth out of the fissures of the rocks during the rainy season, that any one attempting to walk through them in the dark would place his neck in danger.

There is only one stone built house in the town, which stands on the royal premises, and is called the castle; all other buildings are of wood and swish, and by no means durable.

The market-place, is a large open space about three quarters of a mile in circumference. There is no regularity in its form, but it approaches nearest to that of a parallelogram. One side of it is a large *dell* surrounded by large trees and high grass,* into which they throw at last, the mangled bodies of sacrificed human victims. As I passed by this *dell*, I smelt a most intolerable stench, proceeding from the poor creatures who were thrown there on Saturday last. My feelings would not permit me to look into this horrid receptacle of the dead, but the very idea of it is dreadful.

There are no regularly built stalls in the market-place. Many articles of merchandise were placed on the ground, and others on little temporary railings, which might be put up or taken down in a few

---

* There is a kind of grass in the immediate neighbourhood of Coomassie, which grows to the height of twenty feet, the stalk of which is about three quarters of an inch in diameter.

moments. Among the commodities exposed for sale, I saw Manchester cloths, silk, muslins, roll tobacco from the interior, large cakes of a kind of pomatum, made from the fruit of a tree in the depth of the interior, and used by the Ashantees for anointing their bodies, to give a polish to their skins; native tobacco pipes of very neat manufacture, cakes of a kind of whiting, used by the natives for marking their bodies, kankie (native bread), yams, plantains, bananas, pines, ground nuts, fish, and the flesh of monkeys and elephants.

11th, Thursday.—Feeling better to day, I walked out into the town for air and exercise. As I passed the end of one of the streets I saw a group of persons surrounding a large Caboceers umbrella. A band of music was playing, and a human victim lying on the ground before them, exposed to public view; I turned from the disgusting and awful sight with painful feelings.

In the course of the day, I reminded Apoko of my anxiety to obtain an answer from his majesty, respecting the establishment of schools, &c. in Ashantee, who answered, " The king will speedily give you an answer; and we hope you will come to Coomassie again, and pay us another visit, as we shall be always glad to see you. The king believes that you wish to do him and the people good."

14th, Sunday.—At half-past 7 A. M. I conducted divine service at my quarters. I continued in anxious

expectation of a message from the king until about
11 o'clock, when I found, on inquiry, that Apoko
had not reminded his Majesty of seeing me to-day,
because he thought I would not like to transact any
kind of business on the Sabbath day. This idea was
the result of a previous conversation with Apoko,
during which I had explained to him the nature and
claims of the Christian Sabbath. I told him, that my
business with his majesty was of a purely religious
nature, and that I had therefore no objection to seeing him to-day.

In about two hours Apoko returned, accompanied
by a host of attendants, linguists, and messengers,
with a present from his Majesty, consisting of two
ounces and four ackies of gold dust (£9 currency)
and a slave for myself; also eight ackies (£2 currency)
for my interpreter and other attendants. He also
gave me the following message from the king :—

" His Majesty knows that you cannot stop longer
on account of the rains, and as the things which you
have mentioned to him require much consideration,
he cannot answer you in so short a time; but if you
will come up again, or send a messenger after the
rains are over, he will be prepared to answer you."

With this message I felt pleased, and said that I
would certainly either come up again, or send a messenger at the time mentioned. I then repaired to
his Majesty's residence to take my leave, and found
him seated in one of his apartments, surrounded by

an immense number of attendants : when he requested
me, with a courtesy which one could scarcely expect
from a person so circumstanced, to present his compliments to his Excellency, President Maclean, and
take a message to him.

Having taken my leave, I commenced my journey
at noon, preceded by an escort of troops.   After I
had proceeded a short distance along the street, Apoko
came to testify his affection by a hearty shaking of the
hand.

When I reached Franfrahaw, the troops left me,
and I stopped a few minutes to emancipate the slave
whom his Majesty had given me.   This poor fellow
is from the depths of the interior, and is now in the
prime of his days.

On my informing him that he was now become a
free man, he appeared overwhelmed with gratitude,
and almost fell to the earth before me in acknowledgment thereof.   He had not all the joy to himself,
however, for whilst I enjoyed the luxury of doing
good, many of my people looked on him with delight,
and our pleasure was heightened when he told us,
that he had been brought out twice for the purpose
of sacrifice, during the recent custom, and had been
twice put in irons and sent back alive : and that
when he was brought out this morning he expected
to be sacrificed in the course of the day.   Happy
change !—Instead of having his head cut off, and his
body thrown to the fowls of the air, he now finds him-

self in the enjoyment of liberty, safely proceeding with us far away from the scenes of his captivity.

Night closed in nearly an hour before I reached my resting place, but we kept our path through the forest without much difficulty, and reached Fomun-nah a quarter after seven o'clock, wet, weary, and hungry. I immediately repaired to Corintchie's residence. He seemed overjoyed to see me, gave me a hearty shaking with both hands, put his arms around my neck in transport, and made me a present of palm wine, and a mess of soup made with the flesh of the monkey. I then retired to my lodgings, and thankfully partook of Corintchie's monkey soup to satisfy the cravings of hunger, having little else to eat.

17th, Wednesday.—Early this morning, Corintchie came to my quarters, shook me cordially by the hand, and testified his delight at seeing me safely returned from Coomassie. On my telling him that I should want him to assist me in holding further intercourse with the king, by sending messengers, &c., and that perhaps I should return to Coomassie in the course of the next dry season, he said he would readily do anything which I requested of him.

22d.—Reached Mansue: Gabree, the chief, welcomed me back.

On my inquiring whether he would like a mission to be established at Mansue, he said " Yes," and he should feel very happy if he had a missionary residing with him. Gabree is one of the most respectable chiefs in Fantee.

Mansue, and the adjacent villages, contain a population of at least 10,000 souls, and is admirably situated for the establishment of a mission.

Mr. Freeman reached Cape Coast in health and safety, April 23rd. In his letter to the secretaries of the Wesleyan missions, he adds, " I have no doubt as to getting up to Ashantee for the future, with much less expense than has been incurred in my first visit. The king would not make so much ado the second time, as I am no longer a stranger. I also think, that even, with a stranger, he would not adopt the same course as he did with me, inasmuch as the novelty is over."

Such is the fearful state of a large population in the vicinity of a settlement which has belonged to Great Britain for more than a century ; but, also, such are the openings for missionaries. I know not whether the one or the other constitutes the stronger argument for efforts in that quarter for the spread of education and Christian truth. I shall recur to this subject when I speak of the " Elevation of the Native Mind," only observing that a serious responsibility will rest upon Christian England, if such an opening into Interior Africa be neglected."

GENERAL REVIEW.

My object in this part of the work has been to

furnish a description of Africa as it now is,—I shall conclude with a few observations.

Towards the end of the last century the cruelty and the carnage which raged in Africa were laid open. From the most generous motives, and at a mighty cost, we have attempted to arrest this evil; it is, however, but too evident, that, under the mode we have taken for the suppression of the Slave Trade, it has increased.

It has been proved, by documents which cannot be controverted, that, for every village fired, and every drove of human beings marched in former times, there are now double. For every cargo then at sea, two cargoes, or twice the numbers in one cargo, wedged together in a mass of living corruption, are now borne on the wave of the Atlantic. But, whilst the numbers who suffer have increased, there is no reason to believe that the sufferings of each have been abated, on the contrary, we know that in some particulars these have increased; so that the sum total of misery swells in both ways. Each individual has more to endure; and the number of individuals is twice what it was. The result, therefore, is, that aggravated suffering reaches multiplied numbers.

It is hardly necessary to remind the reader that the statement I have given of the enormities attendant on the supply of slaves to the New World must, from the nature of the case, be a very faint picture of the reality—a sample, and no more, of what is inflicted and endured in Africa. Our knowledge is very limited; but few travellers have visited Africa —the Slave Trade was not their object, and they had slender means of information beyond what their own eyes furnished ; yet, what do they disclose!

If Africa were penetrated in every direction by persons furnished with the means of obtaining full and correct information, and whose object was the delineation of the Slave Trade—if, not some isolated spots, but the whole country, were examined—if, instead of a few casual visitors, recording the events of to-day, but knowing nothing of what occurred yesterday, or shall take place to-morrow, we had everywhere those who could chronicle every slave-hunt, and its savage concomitants,—if we thus possessed the means of measuring the true breadth and depth of this trade in blood—is it not fair to suppose that a mass of horrors would be collected, in comparison with which all that has been hitherto related would be as nothing?

It should be borne in constant memory, difficult as it is to realise, that the facts I have narrated are not the afflictions of a narrow district, and of a few inhabitants ;—the scene is a quarter of the globe—a multitude of millions, its population;—that these facts are not gleaned from the records of former times, and preserved by historians as illustrations of the strange and prodigious wickedness of a darker age. They are the common occurrences of our own era— the "customs" which prevail at this very hour. Every day which we pass in security and peace at home, witnesses many a herd of wretches toiling over the wastes of Africa, to slavery or death; every night villages are roused from their sleep, to the alternatives of the sword, or the flames, or the manacle. At the time I am writing, there are at least *twenty thousand human beings* on the Atlantic, exposed to every variety of wretchedness. Well might Mr. Pitt say, "there is something in the horror of it which surpasses all the bounds of imagination."

I do not see how we can escape the conviction that such is the result of our efforts, unless by giving way to a vague and undefined hope, with no evidence to support it, that the facts I have collected, though true at the time, are no longer a fair exemplification of the existing state of things. In the most recent documents relating to the Slave Trade, I find no ground for any such consolatory surmise; on the contrary, I am driven by them to the sorrowful conviction, that the year, from September, 1837, to September, 1838, is distinguished beyond all preceding years for the extent of the trade, for the intensity of its miseries, and for the unusual havoc it makes on human life.

If I believed that the evil, terrible as it is, were also irremediable, I should be more than ready to bury this mass of distress, and this dark catalogue of crime, in mournful silence, and to spare others, and especially those who have sympathised with, and laboured for, the negro race, from sharing with me the pain of learning how wide of the truth are the expectations in which we have indulged. But I feel no such despondency; I firmly believe that Africa has within herself the means and the endowments which might enable her to shake off, and to emerge from, her load of misery, to the benefit of the whole civilised world, and to the unspeakable improvement of her own, now barbarous, population. This leads me to the second point, viz., the capabilities of Africa.

There are two questions which require to be decided before we can assume it possible to extinguish the Slave Trade. First, Has Africa that latent wealth, and those unexplored resources, which would, if they were fully developed, more than compensate for the loss of the traffic in man? Secondly, Is it possible so to call forth her capabilities, that her natives may perceive that the Slave Trade, far from being the source of their wealth, is the grand barrier to their prosperity, and that by its suppression they would be placed in the best position for obtaining all the commodities and luxuries which they are desirous to possess?

Beyond all doubt, she has within herself all that is needed for the widest range of commerce, and for the most plentiful supply of everything which conduces to the comfort and to the affluence of man. Her soil is eminently fertile—Ptolemy says it " is richer in the quality, and more wonderful in the quantity, of its productions, than Europe or Asia." Are its limits narrow? It stretches

from the borders of the Mediterranean to the Cape
of Good Hope, and from the Atlantic to the Indian
Ocean.   Are its productions such as we little want
or lightly value ?   The very commodities most in
request in the civilised world are the spontaneous growth of these uncultivated regions.   Is the
interior inaccessible ?   The noblest rivers flow
through it, and would furnish a cheap and easy
mode of conveyance for every article of legitimate
trade.   Is there a dearth of population, or is that
population averse to the pursuits of commerce ?
Drained of its inhabitants, as Africa has been, it
possesses an enormous population, and these eminently disposed to traffic.   Does it lie at so vast
a distance as to forbid the hope of continual intercourse ?   In sailing to India, we pass along its
western and eastern coasts.   In comparison with
China, it is in our neighbourhood.

Are not these circumstances sufficient to create
the hope that Africa is capable of being raised from
her present abject condition, and, while improving
her own state, of adding to the enjoyments and sti-
mulating the commerce of the civilised world ?

It is earnestly to be desired that all Christian
powers should unite in one great confederacy, for the
purpose of calling into action the dormant energies
of Africa ; but if this unanimity is not to be obtained,
there are abundant reasons to induce this nation, alone
if it must so be, to undertake the task.   Africa and
Great Britain stand in this relation toward each

other. Each possesses what the other requires, and each requires what the other possesses. Great Britain wants raw material, and a market for her manufactured goods. Africa wants manufactured goods, and a market for her raw material. Should it, however, appear that, in place of profit, loss were to be looked for, and obloquy instead of honour, I yet believe that there is that commiseration, and that conscience, in the public mind, which will induce this country to undertake, and, with the Divine blessing, enable her to succeed in crushing "the greatest practical evil that ever afflicted mankind."*

* Mr. Pitt.

PART II.

THE REMEDY.

The desert shall rejoice and blossom as the rose.—Isaiah xxxv. 1.

PREFACE

TO

THE REMEDY.

As the remedy I contemplate is now, for the first time, published, it is necessary to explain the reason why it has hitherto been withheld. In the spring of 1838, I stated to several members of the cabinet my views as to the suppression of the Slave Trade. I could not reasonably expect, that, in the extreme pressure of business during the sitting of Parliament, they would be able to find time to give it the consideration it required, I therefore prepared for the press and printed a few copies of my work—describing the horrors of the Slave Trade, and proposing a remedy, for the private use of the members of the administration, and placed these in their hands on the day that the session closed. At the latter end of the year (December 22), after various communications with Lords Glenelg and Palmerston, I was officially informed that the Government had resolved to embrace and to adopt the substance of the plan. A question then arose as to the propriety of printing the whole work. It was thought highly desirable that the public should be put in possession of the facts which showed the extent of the Slave Trade, and the waste of human life which accompanied it. But as a negociation had been commenced with Spain for the cession to Great Britain of the sovereignty of Fernando Po, it was not deemed advisable to give publicity to the intelligence I had obtained as to that island, and the importance I attached to its possession. It was therefore resolved that I should publish the first part, withholding the Remedy till the fate of the negociation was determined; in consequence of which my first volume was put into circulation in the commencement of the year 1839.

The negociation has not, I regret to say, been as yet brought to an issue; but it is in that state, that a definitive answer must speedily be received, and I am assured that there is no occasion for any further delay.

There is another point upon which I wish to make myself clearly intelligible. Some of my most valuable associates have given me a friendly intimation that they " hold themselves wholly distinct from any measure the Government may adopt with respect to the defence of the Colonies, or the suppression of the Slave Trade by armed force; and that they are not to be considered responsible for the recommendations that any member of our committee may make, in connexion with such measures." This is a protest against those passages in my Remedy in which I advise that our squadron may for the present be rendered more efficient, and that our settlements should be protected by the British Government. I entirely feel, that the gentlemen who have made the protest cannot be considered as parties to this recommendation. It was a suggestion of my own—it was offered to Government before they had seen it—and Government will take its own course upon the subject. In my book I propose two distinct courses; and I couple them together in the same work, because the arguments employed bear upon each of these separate questions. In other words, I apply to the Government to do one thing for the suppression of the Slave Trade, viz. to strengthen our squadron; and I apply to individuals to join me in measures having the same object, but of a character totally different. Such, for example, as an attempt to elevate the mind of the people of Africa, and to call forth the capabilities of her soil.

I have no wish to disguise my sentiments about armed force. I deprecate, as much as any man, resorting to violence and war. These are against the whole tenor of my views. It will be admitted, I think, that I have laboured hard in this book to show, that our great error has been, that we have depended far too much upon physical force. It is, however, the duty of our Government to see that the peace of our settlements be preserved. The natives whom we induce to engage in agriculture must not be exposed to the irruption of a savage banditti, instigated by some miscreant from Europe, whose vessel waits upon the shore for a human cargo. Nor must our runaway sailors repeat in Africa the atrocities which have been practised in New Zealand. Again and again the Foulah tribes said to the missionaries on the river Gambia, " Give us security, and we will gladly till the land and pasture the cattle in your neighbourhood." There were no means of thus protecting them, and hence an experiment, founded on admirable principles, failed. But when I ask for an effectual police force, I ask for that only. I do not desire the employment of such a military force as might be perverted into the means of war and conquest. I want only, that the man engaged in lawful and innocent employment in Africa, should have the same protection as an agricultural labourer or a mechanic receives in England; and that there, as well as here, the murderer and man-stealer may be arrested and punished.

It is possible that in these views I may be mistaken; and that the gentlemen to whom I allude
may wholly differ from me.   But there is no reason
because they do so, avowing their dissent, that they
should abstain from joining me in the task of delivering Africa from the Slave Trade by the means of
her own mind, and her own resources, developed and
cultivated.   In this object we heartily agree; and
for its accomplishment we may heartily unite.   I
number amongst my coadjutors very many of the
Society of Friends; but I prize too highly the disinterested and unflinching zeal with which that body
pursues the objects which it approves, to be content
to lose any individual of the number, especially
through a misapprehension; and it is for the purpose
of averting this, that I have thought it necessary to
enter into this explanation.

I have already described the state of Africa.   It
will on all hands be said that there are great, if not
invincible, difficulties to the application of a remedy.
This is but too true.   There is only one consideration
strong enough to prompt us to grapple with these
difficulties, namely, a just apprehension of her
miseries.   I pray my readers not to shrink from the
task of sedulously studying the facts collected in this
book.   In the case of Africa, I fear hardly anything

so much as the indulgence of excessive tenderness
of feeling. If the benevolent and religious portion
of the public choose to content themselves with the
general and superficial conviction, that there is no
doubt a great mass of misery in Africa, but refuse to
sift and scrutinize each circumstance of horror,
pleading the susceptibility of their nerves as an apology to themselves for shutting their eyes and closing
their ears to such revolting details; then the best
hope for Africa—perhaps the only hope—vanishes
away. That resolute, unflinching, untiring deter-
mination which is necessary, in order to surmount
the difficulties which lie in the way of her deliverance, requires not only that the understanding should
be convinced, but that the heart should be moved.
Our feelings will be far too tame for the occasion,
unless we can, in pity to Africa, summon courage
enough to face, and to study, the horrors of the Slave
Trade, and the abominations which there grow out of
a dark and bloody superstition.

INTRODUCTION.

Iᴛ has been no very difficult task to collect materials
for a description of the varied and intense miseries
with which Africa is afflicted.   Every person who
visits that country,—whether his motive be the pursuit of traffic or the gratification of curiosity, the prosecution of geographical science or of missionary
labour,—brings back a copious collection of details
calculated to excite pity, disgust, and horror.

Happy would it be if it were as easy to point out
the remedy, as to explore the disease.

To this task I now address myself, difficult though
it be, from various causes—from the magnitude of
the evil—from the vast and complicated interests involved—and from the comparative scantiness of our
information. For, while the miseries of Africa are such
as meet the eye of the most casual traveller,—while her
crimes and woes are such as no one can overlook ;—
the sources from whence we must hope for the remedy
lie much deeper and far more hidden from our view.
We know so little really of the interior of Africa,—
her geography, her history, her soil, climate, and productions,—so little of the true condition and capa-

bilities of her inhabitants, that (having collected all
the information within my reach) it is with very great
diffidence I venture to put forth what appear to me,
to be the principles which must rescue her, and the
steps which we, as a nation, and as individuals,
are called upon to take, to carry those principles into
operation.

In one respect I apprehend no liability to error.
With all confidence we may affirm, that nothing permanent will be effected, unless *we raise the native
mind.* It is possible to conceive such an application
of force, as shall blockade the whole coast, and sweep
away every slaver: but should that effort relax, the
trade in man would revive. Compulsion, so long as
it lasts, may restrain the act, but it will not eradicate
the motive. The African will not have ceased to
desire, and vehemently to crave, the spirits, the
ammunition, and the articles of finery and commerce
which Europe alone can supply : and these he can obtain by the Slave Trade, and by the Slave Trade only,
while he remains what he is. The pursuit of man,
therefore, is to him not a matter of choice and selection, but of necessity, and after any interval of constrained abstinence he will revert to it as the business
of his life.

But, when the African nations shall emerge from
their present state of darkness and debasement, they
will require no arguments from us, to convince them
of the monstrous impolicy of the Slave Trade. They
will not be content to see their remaining territories

a wilderness, themselves in penury, their villages exposed day after day to havoc and conflagration, their children kidnapped and slaughtered,—and all for the purpose of gaining a paltry supply of the most inferior and pernicious articles of Europe. They will perceive, that their effective strength may be applied to other, and more lucrative purposes : and as their intellect advances, it is not too much to hope that their morals will improve, and that they will awaken to the enormous wickedness, as well as folly, of this cruel system. " Europe, therefore," (to use the words of one of the most distinguished of African travellers,*) "will have done little for the Blacks, if the abolition of the Atlantic Slave Trade is not followed up by some wise and grand plan for the civilization of the continent. None presents a fairer prospect than the education of the sons of Africa in their own country, and by their own countrymen previously educated by Europeans."

We may assume, and with almost equal confidence, that Africa can never be delivered, till we have called forth the rich productiveness of her soil. She derives, it must be confessed, some pecuniary advantage from the Slave Trade : happily, however, it is the smallest possible amount of revenue, at the largest possible amount of cost. The strength of our case, and the foundation of our hope, lie in the assurance,—I am tempted rather to call it, the indisputable certainty,—that the soil will yield a far

* Burckhardt, p. 344.

more generous return. Grant that the chieftains sell every year 250,000 of the inhabitants, and that into their hands £4 per head is honestly paid. (This is not the fact, however, for they are often defrauded altogether, and are always cheated by receiving merchandise of the most inferior description.) But let us suppose that they get the value of one million of money: we have, from this sum, to deduct, first, the cost of maintaining their armies intended for the Slave Trade: then of the reprisals which are made upon themselves, and the consequent ravage of their land and destruction of their property: thirdly, the material items of arms, ammunition, and ardent spirits, which form one-third of the whole of the goods imported into Central Africa, and the greater part of which are consumed in their horrid slave-hunts :*—to say nothing of any indirect loss, such as millions of fertile acres being left a desert; —nothing of perils encountered and torments endured ;—making no other abatement than the three sources of direct and unavoidable expense which I have named,—the million will have melted away to a very slender sum. Call the clear profit, for argument's sake, £300,000 ;—and is £300,000 all that can be reaped from so extensive a portion of the

---

* I remember it was given in evidence before a Parliamentary Committee, that an African chief thus concisely stated his mercantile views :—" We want three things, viz. powder, ball, and brandy ; and we have three things to sell, viz. men, women, and children. "

globe, inferior to none other in native wealth? Her fisheries, separately taken, would yield more; or her mines, or her timber, or her drugs, her indigo, or her sugar, or her cotton.

I am then stedfast in my belief, that the capabilities of Africa would furnish full compensation to that country for the loss of the Slave Trade. It may sound visionary at the present time, but I expect that at some future, and not very distant day, it will appear, that for every pound she now receives from the export of her people, a hundred pounds' worth of produce, either for home consumption or foreign commerce, will be raised from the fertility of her soil.

It is something to know that there is a natural and an infallible remedy for the distractions of Africa, and that the remedy is within reach, were there but the sagacity to use it. It is another question, how we shall cause that remedy to be applied, and how we shall make manifest to the clouded perceptions of her people, the false economy of selling her effective strength, while her plains remain a desert, instead of employing that strength in transforming that desert into a fruitful and smiling land. Capabilities are nothing to the unreflecting mind of the savage : he wants something present and tangible.

How then shall we undeceive her chiefs, and convince them, that it is for their interest that the Slave Trade should cease? This we *must* do for Africa:

we must elevate the minds of her people, and call forth the capabilities of her soil.

Bearing in mind, that every effort we make must be intended, either directly or remotely, to effect one, or other, or both of these objects, I now proceed to a detail of the remedial measures which it seems necessary to adopt.

CHAPTER I.

PREPARATORY MEASURES.

The first thing to be done, is to throw all possible impediments in the way of the Slave Trade, and to make it both more precarious and less profitable than it is at present.

In order to do this, *our squadron must be rendered more efficient ;* and this it is supposed may be accomplished—

1st. By concentrating on the coast of Africa the whole force employed in this particular service. It has been our practice hitherto to distribute a few ships along the African coast, while others cruise near South America and the West Indies. The former, though they have failed in suppressing the trade, have at all events done something towards the annoyance of the trader. The latter, with equal zeal, and a much larger force, have done little or nothing towards this object. On the average of the last four years to which the accounts extend, viz., 1834-5-6 and 7, we have had on the West Indian and South American stations 42 vessels of war ; on the African station, 14. By the former there have been taken and adjudicated, in four years, 34 slavers ; by the smaller squadron, 97.

I am not so ignorant as to infer that the Admiralty were in error in this distribution of their disposable force. I well know that other objects than the suppression of the Slave Trade demanded attention : as little do I presume to cast any reflection upon the naval officers in command. But from these facts I conceive I am entitled to draw the conclusion, that, as far as the Slave Trade is concerned, little or no benefit has been derived from the force stationed in the neighbourhood of Cuba and Brazil.

2dly. The efficiency of our squadron may be improved by an actual increase of the force.

I am aware that some gentlemen, seeing that all our past naval efforts have failed, are in favour of withdrawing our whole force, and of relying exclusively on other means ; but it appears to me, that in order to try these other means with the most advantage, it is needful, for a time, to retain our force on the coast of Africa.

If at the moment when we are beginning to encourage agricultural industry, and to give an impulse to the minds of her people, our navy were to abandon the coast, there can be no doubt that it would be a signal to the chiefs of the country (still ignorant of the resources of their soil, and still supposing that the Slave Trade alone can supply them with the luxuries of Europe) to prosecute their horrid traffic with even more than their usual energy. They would avail themselves of the removal of the only check which they have hitherto felt, and at the very moment when our last ship departed from the coast, Africa would present a scene of conflagration, massacre, and convulsion, such as even Africa has never before witnessed.

Can it be imagined that agriculture could thrive or the voice of the teacher receive attention, or the arts of peace take root, at such a moment? Having persevered so long and so unprofitably in the attempt to suppress the traffic by force, it would be a poor mode of repairing our error, to dismiss that force just at the time when we most required tranquillity, and when anything likely to give a new impulse to the Slave Trade would be peculiarly unseasonable.

It would appear to be a wiser policy to augment our force, and thus to multiply the risks, while we reduce the profits of the trade. We should try, if it were only for a given period, the full effect of what can be done by our maritime strength : instead of doling out, year by year, a force inadequate to our object, we should at this juncture strike a telling blow, so that the African, while measuring the advantages of that system which we wish him to abandon, against that which we desire to see adopted, may feel in its greatest force the weight of those hazards and discouragements which the British navy can interpose.

3dly. We may increase the efficiency of our squadron by the employment of steamers as part of the proposed reinforcement. I am, it must be confessed, but ill qualified to offer an opinion on a matter which comes rather within the province of naval officers. I can only say, that amongst the many persons conversant with the coast of Africa, and with the Slave Trade, from whom I have sought information, I have not met with an individual who has not urged that steamers might be employed with great advantage. It is not only, that they would be able to explore rivers and harbours, which other vessels cannot enter, but that in latitudes where frequent calms prevail, they might often come up with slavers, which have hitherto escaped our cruisers. We know too well, that with his slaves safely on board, and his vessel fairly at sea, it is not often that the slave trader is captured. " Once outside in my trim vessel, you may catch me if you can,"* is, unhappily, something more than an empty vaunt. In the proposed employment of steamers, to search the mouths of rivers, one precaution is indispensable. They must be manned by persons who can bear the climate to which they will be exposed. Admiral Elliott, now commanding on this station, objects to exploring the rivers, on account of the loss of life which invariably follows among British seamen: he recommends the enlistment of black seamen for this service, and the purchase of small armed steamers to be employed exclusively in river navigation.

I may as well say here, once for all, that, in all our African undertakings, I look to the employment (except in a very few cases) of the negro and coloured race, and that I have reason to believe that

* Vide page 164.

well qualified agents of that description may be procured without difficulty.

I proceed now to the suggestion of a second preparatory measure.

Treaties should be formed with native powers in Africa—they receiving certain advantages, proportioned to the assistance they afford in the prosecution of our objects, and engaging on their side, to put down the Slave Trade. I do not mean to say, that this is all that ought to be contemplated in these treaties. To give facilities for commerce and agricultural settlements will be a subject of consideration hereafter. All I urge at this point of the argument, is, that we should do our utmost to obtain the cordial co-operation of the natives in the suppression of their detestable traffic.

I am aware that a formidable objection to this proposition will present itself to many of my readers. It will be said, that it is visionary to suppose that these barbarian chieftains can be induced, except by force of arms, to connect themselves with us,—to lend us their aid in extinguishing their only trade,—to enter into peaceable commerce with us; and, yet more, to admit us, as friends, into their dominions, and voluntarily to grant us such an extent of territory and of privileges, as shall enable us to plant settlements among them.

I trust, however, that in this case, we are to be guided, not by preconceived opinions, but by facts gathered from experience. The truth is, and on this my hopes are built, that the natives, so far from shunning intercourse with us, and rejecting our overtures for peace and commerce, have been, in almost every case, eager and importunate that we should settle among them. If further progress has not been made, it is ourselves who have been to blame. I find abundant instances in which they have declared their willingness and ability to suppress the Slave Trade, and in which they have offered to grant every facility for commerce, —to cede territory,—and, in not a few cases, to put themselves under our dominion. I find even treaties to this effect, formed between British officers and native chiefs. But I can seldom find that these invitations to amity and commerce have been encouraged, or that these treaties have been ratified by the Home Government.

I grant that this anxiety on the part of the negroes to hold communication with us, is one of the most unexpected, as it is one of the most encouraging features of the whole case. It would have been far from strange if the disposition of African potentates had been adverse to a connexion with us. They have had but little reason to think favourably of European intentions, or to feel any great reverence for those who bear the name of Christians. If they are otherwise than distrustful of us, it must arise from their drawing a distinction between the course we pursue in Africa, and that taken by other civilised nations; and from their having learnt by experience duly to appreciate the nature of our settlements at

Sierra Leone and elsewhere; or else from a deeper sense than we give them credit for, of their own forlorn and disastrous condition, and a conviction that they would be likely to improve it by intercourse with us. It may be, that they loathe their present evils further than we know, and, feeling impotent to rise out of their distresses by their own vigour, hope for deliverance through our instrumentality. But we must reason on facts as we find them; and I believe that they bear me out in stating, that there exists throughout the whole space, from Senegambia to Benin, a marked confidence in the British; and not only a readiness, but an anxiety, to have us for their neighbours, and to enter into amicable relations with us. I need not say how much depends upon the truth or fallacy of this statement. If it be true, many of the most formidable difficulties in our way are removed, and there will be, at least, an admitted possibility of a league between England and Africa,—for the suppression of the Slave Trade,—for the spread of commerce,—and for the development of those vast resources which are buried in the African soil. This, then, I shall endeavour to prove; but as there is an exception to this facility of intercourse, I will state it at once.

I suspect it will be very difficult to gain the concurrence of the chiefs on the coast : these, in the words of a gentleman who has spent many years in studying the geography of Africa, and the character of its inhabitants, are " a rabble of petty chiefs, the most ignorant and rude, and the greatest vagabonds on earth."

They have been rendered habitual drunkards by the spirits which Slave Ships supply. As slave-factors, they have been steeled against all compassion and all sympathy with human suffering; and no better influence has been exercised over them, than that derived from intercourse with the dregs of Europe. Besides, they obtain a two-fold advantage from the Slave Trade. The goods they obtain from Europeans give a considerable profit when sold to the natives, while the slaves, received by them in return for those goods, yield a profit still more considerable, when sold to the slave-captain.

We must then expect great opposition from the chiefs on the coast. It appears, indeed, from the journals of all travellers in Africa, that every impediment has been thrown in their way, in order to prevent their proceeding to the interior of the country. It is, however, some consolation to learn from recent travellers, that the power of these chiefs has been greatly exaggerated.

But whatever difficulties we may have to encounter with the chiefs on the coast, (and I confess that, viewing their character, and the insalubrity of the climate near the sea, and at the mouths of rivers, I apprehend that they will be far from light,) there is good reason to believe that we shall find a much better disposition on the part of the Sultans and sovereigns of the interior, to receive, to treat, and to trade with us. I shall endeavour to show, first, that with respect to the two most powerful potentates of Central Africa, the Sheikh of Bornou, and the Sultan of the Felatahs, there is some reason for supposing that we need not despair of their co-operation.

Major Denham, in speaking of the Slave Trade at Bornou, says :—" I think I may say, that neither the Sheikh himself, nor the Bornou people, carry on the traffic without feelings of disgust, which even habit cannot conquer. Of the existence of a foreign Slave Trade, or one which consigns these unfortunates to Christian masters, they are not generally aware at Bornou ; and so contrary to the tenets of his religion, (Mahometanism,) of which he is a strict observer, would be such a system of barter, that one may easily conclude the Sheikh of Bornou would be willing to assist, with all the power he possesses, in any plan which might have for its object the putting a final stop to a commerce of this nature.

" The eagerness with which all classes of people listened to our proposals for establishing a frequent communication by means of European merchants, and the protection promised by the Sheikh to such as should arrive within the sphere of his influence, particularly if they were English, excites an anxious hope that some measures will be adopted for directing the labours of a population of millions, to something more congenial to the humanity and the philanthropy of the age we live in, than the practice of a system of predatory warfare, which has chiefly for its object the procuring of slaves, as the readiest and most valuable property to trade with.

"Every probability is against such a barter being preferred by the African black. Let the words of the Sheikh himself, addressed to us, in the hearing of his people, speak the sentiments that have already found a place in his bosom :—'You say true, we are all sons of one father! You say, also, that the sons of Adam should not sell one another, and you know everything! God has given you all great talents, but what are we to do? The Arabs who come here will have nothing else but slaves: why don't you send us your merchants? You know us now, and let them bring their women with them, and live amongst us, and teach us what you talk to me about so often, to build houses, and boats, and make rockets.' "

He adds, "Wherever El Kenemy, the sultan of Bornou, has power, Europeans, and particularly Englishmen, will be hospitably and kindly received. Although harassed by the constant wars in which he has been engaged, yet has not the Sheikh been unmindful of the benefits which an extended commerce would confer upon his people, nor of the importance of improving their moral condition, by exciting a desire to acquire, by industry and trade, more permanent and certain advantages than are to be obtained by a system of plunder and destructive warfare. Arab or Moorish merchants, the only ones who have hitherto ventured amongst them, are encouraged and treated with great liberality.

"It was with feelings of the highest satisfaction that I listened to some of the most respectable of the merchants, when they declared, that were any other system of trading adopted, they would gladly embrace it, in preference to dealing in slaves."

Denham makes these observations in 1824; in 1830, Richard Lander says, he learnt that the Sheikh of Bornou had prohibited the carrying of slaves any farther to the westward (that is, towards the coast) than Wawa, a town on the borders of his empire; and it is not unworthy of notice, that when Lander was at this place a few years before, the chief of Wawa said to him, "Tell your countrymen that they have my permission to come here and build a town, and trade up and down the Quorra" (the Niger).

Captain Clapperton visited Bello, the powerful sultan of the Felatahs, in 1823, at Sackatoo. Their conversation often turned on the Slave Trade, which Clapperton urged the sultan to discontinue. Bello asked the captain, if the king of England would send him a consul, and a physician, to reside in Soudan, and merchants to trade with his people? Clapperton said he had no doubt his wishes would be gratified, provided he would suppress the Slave Trade. The Sultan replied, "I will give the king of England a place on the coast to build a town." On another occasion, he assured Clapperton that he was able to put an effectual stop to the Slave Trade; and expressed, with much earnestness of manner, his anxiety to enter into permanent relations of trade and friendship with England. At the close of Clapperton's visit, Bello gave him a letter to the king of England, to the same purport as the conversation which had taken place between them. These offers on the part of the Sultan of the Felatahs must be held to be of great importance. He is the chief of a warlike, enterprising people, who have extended their sway over many of the nations and tribes around them; and who, from the testimony of recent travellers, are actively employed in carrying on war with their neighbours to supply the demands of the Slave Trade. It appears that Captain Clapperton met with an ungracious reception from Sultan Bello, in his last visit to Sackatoo in 1826; but this is accounted for by the Sultan's having discovered that Clapperton was on his way to visit his rival, the Sheik of Bornou, with whom he was then at war, and by the jealousy of the Arab merchants and slave-dealers, who had carefully instilled into his mind, of suspicions as to the intentions of Great Britain. I am not aware that anything has been done to counteract this impression; but it would not be difficult to disabuse the mind of Bello, who would, no doubt, be induced by a few presents, to afford his countenance and protection to British trade, by which Houssa would be so greatly benefited.

I will now proceed to prove, that there likewise exists on the part of the chiefs of less powerful tribes a

disposition to enter into friendly relations with us. I
give a single illustration :—In a despatch from Acting
Governor Grant, dated Sierra Leone, 28th February,
1821, I find that " an application had been made to
Governor Macarthy by the king of the Foulahs, a very
powerful prince in the interior, expressing a desire to
have an officer sent up to Teemboo, the capital of
his territories; and having myself," he says, "received
a very friendly letter from the king, I was induced,
in conformity with Governor Macarthy's intentions,
to despatch Mr. O'Beirn, assistant-surgeon to the
forces, on that service. The influence of the Foulah
nation, extending from the branches of the Sierra
Leone River to the banks of the Niger, and communicating with the principal countries of the interior, renders a friendly connexion with that country
of much importance to our commercial interests;
and it is with much satisfaction I have to report the
good effect of Mr. O'Beirn's exertions; which are already felt here, in the increased supply of ivory, gold,
and cattle, brought by the Foulahs to our different
factories situate on this river. Mr. O'Beirn is merely
accompanied by a few people of colour to carry his
luggage and presents, the expense of which will be
trifling." He was received in the most friendly
manner possible at Teemboo, the capital of the
Foulah nation, by the king, Almami Abdool Kad-
dree.

The following is an extract from Mr. O'Beirn's
Journal :—" I never saw more joy and complacency

in any countenance, than his expressed, on my being
introduced to him, and I have seldom in my life
experienced such a kind and warm reception." The
chiefs were assembled to hear his explanation of the
objects of his mission : he explained to them the
great advantage they would derive from carrying on
a trade with the colony, and how much superior such
a trade would be to the traffic in slaves ; and told
them, what England had done to put an end to it, and
to give freedom to their countrymen.

"Almami replied, that he had for many years
wished for a communication to be opened between
Sierra Leone and his country, Foota Jalloo, and
that it should continue free and uninterrupted to the
latest day; adding, that it was not his fault, or it would
have been effected years before. He likewise remarked, with respect to what I had said of the Slave
Trade, it was his opinion that it would be given up
ere long ; that is, sending them for sale to the coast,
and that he was fully convinced he would be brought
to account in the next world for disposing of his
fellow-creatures in that way ; but hoped, at the same
time, God would accept the excuse of the impossibility
that formerly existed of procuring the necessaries of
life in such abundance, or resisting the inducements
held out, at that time, by the white people that came
to purchase them."

I do not wish to impose upon my readers the
monotonous task of travelling through a variety of
such treaties which these chieftains have made, or

have offered to make, with the British Government: these will be given in the Appendix;* and I apprehend that those who take the trouble of examining them will find, that there is no unwillingness on their part to grant any reasonable quantity of land,— any powers however extensive,—and any conditions for the suppression of the Slave Trade, that we may think proper to propose; and that all this may be obtained for the trifling consideration of a few dollars, or a few pieces of baft. I am ready to admit that little benefit has hitherto resulted from these negociations, but this does not arise from any faithlessness on the part of the natives in the fulfilment of their engagements; on the contrary, I may quote the unexceptionable authority of Mr. Bandinel, of the Foreign Office, for the fact, that "compacts for the suppression of the Slave Trade have been concluded with the chiefs of several native states, and that those treaties have been faithfully maintained by the native sovereigns." Mr. Rendall, late Governor of the Gambia, also says:—" With respect to the general conduct of the chiefs, I am not aware of our having any just cause to complain of a breach of confidence being committed in the treaties heretofore made with them, nor do I think there is any just cause to fear that they are now more likely to forfeit their words and honour, particularly in cases where their interests are studiously considered."

The reason why greater advantage has not been

* Vide Appendix A.

derived from co-operation with these powers, is, as
I have before intimated, that the British Government has discountenanced almost all efforts in that
direction. " It has never," says Mr. H. Macaulay,
Commissary Judge of Sierra Leone, in his evidence before the Aborigines Committee, in 1837,
"been the policy of our government from the first,
while it was in the hands of the company, nor since
it has been transferred to the crown, to extend our
territory in any way. Even when General Turner
and Sir Neil Campbell were governors in former
years, and acquired by treaty, and other just means,
territory in the neighbourhood, and paid for it, the
government ordered us to give it back. They would
not allow us to take possession of it and occupy it
as a British territory. And though, in my opinion,
it would be desirable to extend our territory as our
population increases so much, yet it has not been
done." To the question—" Do you think it would
be expedient or just to take possession of the territory of these people without their consent?" He
answers, " Certainly not; but we are such good
neighbours, and they have such perfect confidence in
us, that I think there would be no difficulty in acquiring territory by treaty." " Have you found any
difficulty in preserving relations of amity with the
surrounding natives?"—" None whatever."

It appears to me well worth while to adopt an
entirely new line of policy, and to establish, to the utmost extent possible, a confederacy with the chiefs,

from the Gambia on the West, to Begharmi on the East ; and from the Desert on the North, to the Gulf of Guinea on the South.

Thus, I have suggested two distinct kinds of preparatory measures.

1st. An augmentation of the naval force employed in the suppression of the Slave Trade, and the concentration of that force on the coast of Africa, thus forming a chain of vessels from Gambia to Angola.

2ndly. A corresponding chain of treaties with native powers in the interior, pledging them to act in concert with us; to suppress the Slave Trade in their own territory ; to prevent slaves from being carried through their dominions, and, at the same time, to afford all needful facility and protection for the transport of legitimate merchandise.   Thus, by creating obstacles which have not heretofore existed, in the conveyance of negroes to the coast, and by increasing the hazard of capture after embarkation, I cannot but anticipate that we shall greatly increase the costs and multiply the risks of the Slave Trade.

If I am asked, whether I expect thus to effect its total abolition, I answer distinctly, No :—such measures may reduce, or even suspend, but they cannot eradicate the evil.   If we succeed in establishing a blockade of the coast, together with a confederacy on shore, and proceed no further, it will still be doubtful, as it has been in our former operations, whether more of good or of evil will be effected ;— good, by the degree of restraint imposed on the traffic, or evil, by rendering what remains concealed and contraband ; and when I recur to the fearful aggravation of the sufferings of the slaves, which has already arisen from this cause, I am almost disposed to think that it were better to do nothing than to do only this.

I propose the two measures I have just named, not as a remedy, but as an expedient necessary for a time, in order that the real remedy may be applied in the most effectual manner. For a time, the dangers and difficulties of the slave-trader must be increased, in order that the demand for slaves on the coast may be reduced in the interval that must necessarily elapse before a total suppression can be effected. There was a time, during the last war, when our cruisers were so numerous in the African seas, that it was difficult for a slaver to escape; and it was then observed that the chiefs betook themselves to agriculture and trade.

The greater the impediments that are thrown in the way of obtaining supplies through the accustomed channels, the stronger becomes the inducement to procure them in another and better mode; and thus, the diminution of the Slave Trade will operate as an encouragement to industry, and a stimulus to commerce. And the evil being thus temporarily held in check, time and space, so to speak, will be given for the effectual operation of the remedy.

CHAPTER II.

COMMERCE AND CULTIVATION.

' It was not possible for me to behold the fertility of the soil, the vast herds of cattle, proper both for labour and food, and a variety of other circumstances favourable to colonization and agriculture, and reflect withal on the means which presented themselves of a vast inland navigation, without lamenting that a country so abundantly gifted and honoured by nature, should remain in its present savage and neglected state."—PARK.

" The commercial intercourse of Africa opens an inexhaustible source of wealth to the manufacturing interests of Great Britain—to all which the Slave Trade is a physical obstruction."—GUSTAVUS VASA. *Letter to Lord Hawkesbury.* 1788.

But what is the true remedy ? It cannot be too deeply engraven upon the minds of British statesmen, that it is beyond our power to rescue Africa, if the burthen is to fall wholly and permanently on ourselves. It is not the partial aid, lent by a distant nation, but the natural and healthy exercise of her own energies, which will ensure success. We cannot *create* a remedy ; but, if it be true that this remedy already exists, and that nothing is wanting but its right application—if Africa possesses within herself vast, though as yet undeveloped, resources,—we may be competent to achieve the much less onerous task of calling forth her powers, and enabling her to stand alone, relying upon the strength of her own native sinews. The work will be done, when her population shall be sufficiently enlightened to arrive at the conviction, (grounded on what their eyes see, and their hands handle,) that the wealth readily to be obtained from peaceful industry, surpasses the slender and precarious profits of rapine.

Our system hitherto has been to obtain the co-operation of European powers, while we have paid very little attention to what might be done in Africa itself, for the suppression of the Slave Trade. Our efforts in that direction have been few, faint, and limited to isolated spots, and those by no means well chosen. To me it appears that the converse of this policy would have offered greater probabilities of success; that, while no reasonable expectations can be entertained of overturning this gigantic evil through the agency and with the concurrence of the civilised world, there is a well-founded hope, amounting almost to a certainty, that this object may be attained through the medium and with the concurrence of Africa herself. If, instead of our expensive and fruitless negotiations with Portugal, we had been, during the last twenty years, engaged in extending our intercourse with the nations of Africa, unfolding to them the capabilities of her soil, and the inexhaustible store of wealth which human labour might derive from its cultivation, and convincing them that the Slave Trade alone debars them from enjoying a vastly more affluent supply of our valuable commodities, and if we had leagued ourselves with them to suppress that baneful traffic, which is their enemy even more than it is ours, there is reason to believe that Africa would not have been what Africa is, in spite of all our exertions,—one universal den of desolation, misery, and crime.

Why do I despair of winning the hearty co-operation of those European powers who now encourage or connive at the Slave Trade ? I answer, because we have no sufficient bribe to offer. The secret of their resistance is the 180 per cent. profit which attaches to the Slave Trade. This is a temptation which we cannot outbid. It has been, and it will be, the source of their persevering disregard of the claims of humanity, and of their contempt for the engagements, however solemn, which they have contracted with us.

But why do I entertain a confident persuasion that we may obtain the cordial concurrence of the African powers? Because the Slave Trade is not their gain, but their loss. It is their ruin, because it is capable of demonstration, that, but for the Slave Trade, the other trade of Africa would be increased fifty or a hundred-fold. Because central Africa now receives in exchange for all her exports, both of people and productions, less than half a million of imports, one-half of which may be goods of the worst description, and a third made up of arms and ammunition. What a wretched return is this, for the productions of so

vast, so fertile, so magnificent a territory! Take
the case of central Africa; the insignificance of our
trade with it is forcibly exhibited by contrasting the
whole return from thence, with some single article of
no great moment which enters Great Britain. The
feathers received at Liverpool from Ireland reach an
amount exceeding all the productions of central
Africa; the eggs from France and Ireland exceed
one-half of it; while the value of pigs from Ireland
into the port of Liverpool is three times as great as
the whole trade of Great Britain in the productions of
the soil of central Africa.* What an exhibition does
this give of the ruin which the Slave Trade entails
on Africa! Can it be doubted that, with the extinction of that blight, there would arise up a commerce
which would pour into Africa European articles of
a vastly superior quality, and to a vastly superior
amount?

If it be true that Africa would be enriched, and
that her population would enjoy, in multiplied abundance, those commodities, for the acquisition of which
she now incurs such intense misery, the one needful

* Eggs, total amount unknown, but into London,
　　　Liverpool, and Glasgow, from France and　　£.
　　　Ireland alone　.　.　.　.　.　275,000
　　Feathers from Ireland to Liverpool (Porter's
　　　" Progress of Nation," p. 83)　.　.　500,000
　　Pigs from Ireland to Liverpool (Porter, Ibid.)　1,488,555

　　Total imports, productions of the soil of Central
　　　Africa (Porter's Tables, Supplement, No. 5)　456,014

thing, in order to induce them to unite with us in repressing the Slave Trade, is, to convince them that they will gain by selling the productive labour of the people, instead of the people themselves.

My first object, then, is to show that Africa possesses within herself the means of obtaining, by fair trade, a greater quantity of our goods than she now receives from the Slave Trade; and, secondly, to point out how this truth may be made plain to the African nations. I have further to prove, that Great Britain, and other countries (for the argument applies as much to them as to us), have an interest in the question only inferior to that of Africa, and that if we cannot be persuaded to suppress the Slave Trade for the fear of God, or in pity to man, it ought to be done for the lucre of gain.

The importance of Africa, as a vast field of European commerce, though it has been frequently adverted to, and its advantages distinctly pointed out by those who have visited that part of the world, has not hitherto sufficiently engaged public attention, or led to any great practical results. It is, perhaps, not difficult to account for the apathy which has been manifested on this subject—Africa has a bad name; its climate is represented, and not altogether unjustly, as pestilential, and destructive of European life; its population as barbarous and ignorant, indolent and cruel—more addicted to predatory warfare than to the arts of peace; and its interior as totally inaccessible to European enterprise. With the exception of

a few spots, such as Sierra Leone, the Gambia, the
Senegal, &c., its immensely extended line of coast is
open to the ravages and demoralization of the Slave
Trade, and the devastating incursions of pirates. The
difficulties connected with the establishment of a legitimate commerce with Africa may be traced principally to these circumstances; and could they be removed, by the removal of their cause, the obstacles
arising from climate—the supposed character of its
people—and the difficulty of access to the interior,
would be easily overcome.

Legitimate commerce would put down the Slave
Trade, by demonstrating the superior value of man
as a labourer on the soil, to man as an object of
merchandise; and if conducted on wise and equitable principles, might be the precursor, or rather
the attendant, of civilisation, peace, and Christianity,
to the unenlightened, warlike, and heathen tribes who
now so fearfully prey on each other, to supply the
slave-markets of the New World. In this view of
the subject, the merchant, the philanthropist, the
patriot, and the Christian, may unite; and should
the Government of this country lend its powerful influence in organising a commercial system of just,
liberal, and comprehensive principles—guarding the
rights of the native on the one hand, and securing protection to the honest trader on the other,—a blow
would be struck at the nefarious traffic in human
beings, from which it could not recover; and the
richest blessings would be conferred on Africa, so

long desolated and degraded by its intercourse with the basest and most iniquitous part of mankind.

The present condition of Africa in relation to commerce is deplorable.

The whole amount of goods exported direct from Great Britain to all Africa is considerably within one million sterling.

In the year 1835, the declared value of British and Irish produce and manufactures exported to the whole of Africa was £917,726.

Central Africa possesses within itself everything from which commerce springs. No country in the world has nobler rivers, or more fertile soil ; and it contains a population of fifty millions.

This country, which ought to be amongst the chief of our customers, takes from us only to the value of £312,938 of our manufactures, £101,104* of which are made up of the value of arms and ammunition, and lead and shot.

I must request the reader to fix his attention on these facts; they present a dreadful picture of the moral prostration of Africa,—of the power of the Slave Trade in withering all healthy commerce,—of the atrocious means resorted to, in order to maintain and perpetuate its horrors,—and of the very slender sum which can be put down as expended in fair and honest trading.

The declared value of British and Irish produce

* Parliamentary Returns for 1837.

and manufactures, exported in 1837, was, according
to parliamentary returns—

To Asia	£4,639,736
America . . .	15,496,552
Australia . . .	921,568
Hayti . . .	171,050
Central Africa . .	312,938

Deducting from this last sum the value of arms,
ammunition, &c., the remnant of the annual trade of
this country, so favoured by nature, and endowed
with such capabilities for commerce, is but £211,834.

There is many a cotton spinner in Manchester
who manufactures much more; there are some
dealers in London whose yearly trade is ten times
that sum; and there is many a merchant in this
country who exports more than the amount of our
whole exports to Africa, arms and ammunition included.

The imports from Africa into this country, though
they have, undoubtedly, increased since the year
1820, are still extremely limited; and it is observable that they scarcely embrace any articles produced
from the cultivation of the soil.   Their estimated
value, in 1834, was £456,014* (exclusive of gold
dust, about £260,000); they consisted chiefly of
palm-oil, teak timber, gums, ivory, bees'-wax, &c.,

* See Porter's Tables.

all extremely valuable, and in great demand, but obtained at comparatively little labour and cost.

So small an amount of exports from a country so full of mineral and vegetable wealth, either shows the extreme ignorance and indolence of the people, or the total want of security both to person and property which exists in consequence of the Slave Trade. All the authorities which are accessible, clearly show that the latter is the true cause why the commerce between Africa and the civilised world is so trifling; and there is one remarkable fact which corroborates it, namely, that nearly all the legitimate trade with central Africa is effected through the medium of those stations which have been established by the British and French governments on its coasts, and in and around which the trade in slaves has either been greatly checked, or has totally disappeared.

But limited as the commerce of Africa is at present with the civilised world, and infamous as one part of that commerce has been, it is capable of being indefinitely increased, and of having a character impressed on it, alike honourable to all parties engaged in it. The advantages which would accrue to Africa, in the development of her resources, the civilisation of her people, and the destruction of one of the greatest evils which has ever afflicted or disgraced mankind,—not less than the benefits which would be secured to Europe in opening new marts for her produce and new fields for her commercial enterprise—would be incalculable.

What can we do to bring about this consummation ? *It is in our power to encourage her commerce ;—to improve the cultivation of her soil ;—and to raise the morals, and the mind of her inhabitants.* This is all that we can do ; but this done, the Slave Trade cannot continue.

The first question, then, to be considered is, in what way can we give an impulse to the *commerce* of Africa? I apprehend that, for this purpose, little more is necessary than to provide security, and convey a sense of security : without this, there can be no traffic : this alone, with such resources as Africa possesses, will cause legitimate commerce to spring up and thrive of itself; it wants no more than leave to grow. Nothing short of so monstrous an evil as the Slave Trade could have kept it down.

Its natural productions* and commercial re-

---

* PRODUCTIONS.—*Animals.*—Oxen, sheep, goats, pigs, &c., &c., Guinea fowls, common poultry, ducks, &c.

Grain.—Rice, Indian corn, Guinea corn, or millet, wheat, Dourah, &c.

Fruits.—Oranges, lemons, guavas, pines, citrons, limes, papaws, plantains, bananas, dates, &c., &c.

Roots.—Manioc, igname, batalee, yams, arrow-root, ginger, sweet potato, &c., &c.

Timber.—Teak, ebony, lignum vitæ, and forty or fifty other species of wood for all purposes.

Nuts.—Palm-nut, shea-nut, cocoa-nut, cola-nut, ground-nut, castor-nut, netta-nut, &c., &c.

Dyes.—Carmine. yellow various shades, blue, orange various shades, red, crimson, brown, &c.

Dye woods.—Cam-wood, bar-wood, &c., &c.

Gums.—Copal, Senegal, mastic, sudan, &c.

sources are inexhaustible. From the testimony of merchants whose enterprise has, for many years past, led them to embark capital in the African trade ; and from the evidence furnished by the journals of travellers into the interior of the country,* we gather

Drugs.—Aloes, cassia, senna, frankincense, &c.

Minerals.—Gold, iron, copper, emery, sal-ammoniac, nitre, &c.

Sugar-cane, coffee, cotton, indigo, tobacco, India rubber, beeswax, ostrich feathers and skins, ivory, &c.

Fish.—Of an immense variety, and in great abundance.

NOTE.—The above is a very imperfect list, but it may serve to show, at a glance, some of the riches of Africa. For all the statements relating to Africa, its capabilities and productions, I have specific authorities ; but it seems hardly necessary to quote them.

* I shall here mention some of the names of countries and kingdoms : —

Timbuctoo, the great emporium of trade in central Africa.

The powerful kingdom of *Gago*, 400 Arabic miles from Timbuctoo to the south-east, abounds with corn and cattle. *Guber*, to the east of Gago, abounds with cattle. *Cano*, once the famous Ghana, abounds with corn, rice, and cattle. *Cashna Agadez*, fields abound with rice, millet, and cotton. *Guangara*, south of this, a region greatly abounding in gold and aromatics. *Balia*, celebrated for its fine gold, four months' voyage to Timbuctoo. *Bournou*, its capital very large, and inhabitants great traders. The country very rich and fertile, and produces rice, beans, cotton, hemp, indigo in abundance, horses, buffaloes, and horned cattle, sheep, goats, camels, &c. *Yaoorie* produces abundance of rice. The country between *R. Formosa* and *Adra* affords the finest prospect in the world. Inland it is healthy, and the climate good. Trees uncommonly large and beautiful, cotton of the finest quality, amazingly plentiful, and indigo and other dye stuffs abundant. The *Jabboos* carry on great trade in grain between *Benin and Lagos. Boossa* is a large emporium for trade. The place where the people from the sea-coast meet the caravans from Barbary to exchange their merchandise. From Boossa to Darfur there are numerous powerful, fertile, cultivated, well-wooded, watered, populous, and industrious states. Benin, Bournou, Dar Saley, that Nature has scattered her bounties with the most lavish hand ; and that what is required to make them available to the noblest purposes is a legitimate commerce sustained by the government, and directed by honourable men.

In the animal kingdom I find that, in addition to the wild beasts which infest its forests, and occupy its swamps, and whose skins, &c., are valuable as an article of commerce, immense herds of cattle, incalculable in number, range its plains. Hides, therefore, to almost any amount, may be obtained ; and well-fed beef, of excellent quality and flavour, can be obtained at some of our settlements, at from 2d. to 3d. per lb. There are also in various districts immense flocks of sheep ; but as they are covered with

Darfur, Kashua, Houssa, Timbuctoo, Sego, Wassenah, and many others, are populous kingdoms, abounding in metals, minerals, fruits, grain, cattle, &c.

Attah, on the Niger, healthy, many natural advantages, will be a place of great importance, alluvial soil, &c. The places on the banks of the Niger are rich in sheep, goats, bullocks, &c.

Fundah, population 30,000 ; beautiful country.

Doma, population large and industrious.

Beeshle and Jacoba, places of great trade.

Rabba, population 40,000.

Toto, population immense.

Alorie (Feletah), vast herds and flocks.

Bumbum, thoroughfare for merchants, from Houssa, Borgoo, &c., to Gonga, vast quantity of land cultivated.

Gungo (Island), palm-trees in profusion.

Egga, two miles in length ; vast number of canoes. Egga to Bournou, said to be fifteen days' journey.

Tschadda, on its banks immense herds of elephants seen, from 50 to 400 at a time.

a very coarse wool, approaching to hair, and their
flesh is not very good on the coast, it may be said, that
though numerous, they are not valuable ; their skins,
however, might form an article for export. Goats
of a very fine and large kind are equally numerous, and sell at a lower price than sheep. Their
skins are valuable. Pigs can be obtained in any
numbers ; they are kept at several of the coast stations. Domestic poultry, the Guinea hen, common
fowls, ducks, &c., are literally swarming, especially
in the interior, and may be had for the most trifling
articles in barter both on the coast and inland. Fish
of all kinds visit the shores and rivers in immense
shoals, and are easily taken in great quantities during
the proper season.

The mineral kingdom has not yet been explored, but
enough is already known to show that the precious
metals abound, particularly gold. The gold-dust obtained from the beds of some rivers, and otherwise produced, is, comparatively, at present, a large branch of
the African trade. It is said that gold may be procured
in the kingdom of Bambouk, which is watered by the
Felema, flowing into the Senegal, and is therefore
easily attainable in any quantity. Martin says, (vol.
iv., p. 540,) the main depositories where this metal is
traced, as it were, to its source, are two mountains,
Na Takon and Semayla. In the former, gold is very
abundant, and is found united with earth, iron, or
emery. In the latter, the gold is imbedded in hard

sandstone. Numerous streams (he adds) flow from these districts, almost all of which flow over sands impregnated with gold. The natives, unskilled in mining operations, have penetrated to very little depth in these mountains. Park found the mines of the Konkadoo hills, which he visited, excessively rich, but very badly worked. (Chapter on gold, vol. i. pp. 454, 465, 524, and vol. ii. pp. 73, 76.) The gold which forms the staple commodity of the Gold Coast, is chiefly brought down from mountains of the interior. It is said that the whole soil yields gold-dust, and that small quantities are obtained even in the town of Cape Coast.* There are reported to be mines within twenty or thirty miles of the shore, but the natives are very jealous of allowing Europeans to see them.† Dupuis and Bowditch speak of the " solid lumps of rock gold" which ornament the persons of the cabooceers in the court of the king of Ashantee, at Coomassie.‡ Mrs. Lee (late Mrs. Bowditch) says, that the great men will frequently on state occasions, so load their wrists with these lumps, that they are obliged to support them on the head of a boy. The largest piece she saw at Cape Coast weighed 14 oz. and was very pure.§ Dupuis, on the authority of some Mohammedans, says that a great deal of gold comes from Gaman, and that it is the richest in

* Sierra Leone Report, 1830, p. 87. † Ib. p. 88.
‡ Dupuis' Ashantee, p. 74; Bowditch's Travels, p. 35.
§ " Stories of Strange Lands," p. 66.

Africa.* Gold is said to be discovered in a plain near Houssa; and another writer (Jackson) says— " The produce of Soudan, returned by the akkabuahs, consists principally in gold-dust, twisted gold rings of Wangara, gold rings made at Jinnie (which are invariably of pure gold, and some of them of exquisite workmanship) bars of gold,† &c." He also states that gold-dust is the circulating medium at Timbuctoo.‡

Iron is found in Western Africa. The ore from Sierra Leone is particularly rich, yielding seventy-nine per cent., according to Mr. M'Cormack, and said to be well adapted to making steel.§ The iron brought from Upper Senegal, by Mollien, was found to be of a very good quality. Berthier found it to resemble Catalonian.|| Iron is found also near Timbuctoo, and is manufactured by the Arabs.¶ The discovery of this important metal in Africa is of the utmost consequence to its future prosperity, and will greatly facilitate the accomplishment of the object contemplated. Early travellers relate that the mountains of Congo are almost all ferruginous, but that the natives have not been encouraged by Europeans to extract their own treasures. Copper is so abundant in Mayomba, that they gather from the surface of the ground enough for their purposes.** Sal ammoniac is found in abund-

---

* Dupuis, Ap. lvi.   † Jackson's Timbuctoo, p. 245, 246.
‡ Jackson's Timbuctoo, p. 251.   § Sierra Leone Report, 1830.
|| Mollien's Travels, Appendix.   ¶ Jackson's Timbuctoo, p. 24.
** Degrandpré, T. F., p. 38.

ance in Dagwumba, and is sold cheap in the Ash-antee market; nitre, emery, and trona, a species of alkali, are found on the border of the Desert.* I might greatly enlarge this list, from the writings of travellers who have already visited the country, but it will be long before its mineral wealth will be ade-quately known.

It is not, however, to the mineral treasures of Africa that we chiefly look; we regard the produc-tions of the soil as of infinitely more value, especially those which require industry and skill in their culture. We look to the forests, and the plains, and the valleys, and the rich alluvial deltas, which it would take centuries to exhaust of their fertility aud products.

Fifty miles to the leeward of the colony, of Sierra Leone is a vast extent of fertile ground, forming the delta of the Seeong Boom, Kitiam and Gallinas rivers. This ground may contain from 1,000 to 1,500 square miles of the richest alluvial soil, capable of growing all tropical produce. According to Mr. M'Cormack, this delta could grow rice enough for the supply of the whole West Indies.† At present it produces nothing but the finest description of slaves.‡

* Bowditch, p. 333.

† Sierra Leòne Report, No. 66, p. 64.

‡ There is another large delta, formed by the rivers Nunez, Rio Grande, and Rio Ponga. It is described as very extensive and fertile. The Isles de Loss command the mouths of these rivers. The Rio Nunez runs parallel with the Gambia.—*Mɔ. Laird.*

From Cape St. Paul to Cameroons, and from thence to Cape Lopez, extends the richest country that imagination can conceive. Within this space from forty to fifty rivers of all sizes discharge their waters into the ocean, forming vast flats of alluvial soil, to the extent of 180,000 square miles. From this ground at present the greatest amount of our imports from Western Africa is produced, and to it and the banks of the rivers that flow through it, do I look for the greatest and most certain increase of trade. It is a curious feature in the geography of Africa, that so many of its great navigable rivers converge upon this point (Laird). The extent to which the Slave Trade is carried on in the rivers alluded to is immense, and offers the greatest possible obstruction to the fair trader.

With few inconsiderable exceptions, the whole line of coast in Western Africa, accessible to trading vessels, presents immense tracts of land of the most fertile character, which only require the hand of industry and commercial enterprise to turn them into inexhaustible mines of wealth.

But it is not to the coast alone that the merchant may look for the results of his enterprise. The interior is represented as equally fertile with the coast; and it is the opinion of the most recent travellers, as well as of those who preceded them, that if the labourer were allowed to cultivate the soil in security, the list of productions would embrace all the marketable commodities imported from the East and West Indies.

Between Kacunda and Egga, both large towns on the Niger, the country is described as very fertile, and from Egga to Rabbah, where the river is 3,000 yards wide, the right bank is represented to consist of extensive tracts of cultivated land, with rich and beautiful plains stretching as far as the eye can reach (Laird). The country does not deteriorate as we ascend the river. We have the testimony of Park, corroborated by Denham and Clapperton, in support of this statement, and their remarks embrace both sides of the river. The country surrounding Cape Palmas, the Gambia, the Senegal, the Shary, the Congo, presents to the eye of the traveller unlimited tracts of the most fertile portion of the earth.

The woods of this continent are extremely valuable. Travellers enumerate not less than forty species of timber, which grow in vast abundance, and are easily obtained; such as mahogany, teak, ebony, lignum vitæ, rosewood, &c.

While Colonel Nicolls was stationed at Fernando Po, he gives this account of its timber, in a letter to Mr. Secretary Hay. I extract the passage as a specimen of the nature of African forests. He says that some of the trees are ten feet in diameter, and 120 feet in height.—" Twenty men have been for a period of eight days cutting down one tree of these dimensions, for the purpose of making a canoe: it

was quite straight, without a branch; the wood
white in colour, close in grain, and very hard. I
have no name for it, but it very much resembles the
lignum vitæ, except in colour. The canoe cut out
of it is five feet within the gunwales, forty feet long,
and carries about twenty tons safely, drawing but
eight inches water. We have also a very fine description of red wood, close-grained, strong, and good
for beams, sheathing, ribs, and deck-planking of the
heaviest vessels of war. We could send home stern-
posts and stems, in one piece, for the largest ships.
This wood seems to have a grain something between
mahogany and oak: when cut thin to mend boats,
it will not split in the sun, and when tapped or cut
down, exudes a tough resinous gum, is very lasting,
and not so heavy as teak or oak, takes a fine polish,
and I think it a very valuable wood. There is
another hard-wood tree of very large dimensions, the
wood strong and good, in colour brown and white-
streaked; it also exudes, when cut, a strong gum,
which I think would be valuable in commerce.
Another, which we call the mast-tree, from the circumstance of its being very tall and straight, is in
colour and grain like a white pine. We have,
besides the above-mentioned trees, many which are
smaller, but very useful, their wood being hard,
tough, and of beautifully variegated colours; some
are streaked brown and white, like a zebra, others of
black, deep red, and brown."

In a despatch, 1832, Colonel Nicolls further

states, that he has Commodore Hayes' authority for
saying, that there never was finer wood for the purposes of ship-building.*

Of dye-woods† there are also abundance, yielding

---

* Desp. p. 5; Colonial Records, 1832.

† Many beautiful kinds of wood have been discovered by accident amongst the billets of firewood, brought home in the slave-
ships to Liverpool.   Mr. Clarkson gives the following anecdote in
his " Impolicy of the Slave Trade."   After mentioning the tulip-
wood and others, found in this manner, he says:—" About the
same time in which this log was discovered (A. D. 1787), another
wood vessel, belonging to the same port, brought home the specimen of the bark of a tree, that produced a very valuable yellow
dye, and far beyond any other ever in use in this country.   The
virtues of it were discovered in the following manner:—A gentleman, resident upon the coast, ordered some wood to be cut down
to erect a hut.   While the people were felling it he was standing by : during the operation some juice flew from the bark of it,
and stained one of the ruffles of his shirt.   He thought that the
stain would have washed out, but, on wearing it again, found that
the yellow spot was much more bright and beautiful than before,
and that it gained in lustre every subsequent time of washing.
Pleased with the discovery, which he knew to be of so much importance to the manufacturers of Great Britain, and for which a
considerable premium had been offered, he sent home the bark
now mentioned as a specimen.   He is since unfortunately dead,
and little hopes are to be entertained of falling in with this
tree again, unless a similar accident should discover it, or a
change should take place in our commercial concerns with
Africa.   I shall now mention another valuable wood, which,
like all those that have been pointed out, was discovered
by accident in the same year.   Another wood vessel, belonging
to the same port, was discharging her cargo ; among the barwood
a small billet was discovered, the colour of which was so superior
to that of the rest, as to lead the observer to suspect, that it was
of a very different species, though it is clear that the natives,

carmine, crimson, red, brown, brilliant yellow, and the various shades from yellow to orange, and a fine blue. Of gums there are copal, Senegal mastic, and Sudan, or Turkey gum, to be obtained in large quantities; and there are forests near the Gambia where, hitherto, the gum has never been picked. Of nuts, which are beginning to form a new and important article of trade, there are the palm-nut, the shea-nut, the cola-nut, the ground-nut, the castor-nut, the nitta-nut, and the cocoa-nut. The palm-tree grows most luxuriantly, and incalculable quantities of its produce are allowed to rot on the ground for want of gathering; yet it is now the most important branch of our commerce with Africa, and may be increased to any extent. The oil expressed from its nut is used in the manufacture of soap and candles, and in lubricating machinery. The shea, or butter-nut,* is scarcely less

by cutting it of the same size and dimensions, and by bringing it on board at the same time, had, on account of its red colour, mistaken it for the other. One half of the billet was cut away in experiments. It was found to produce a colour that emulated the carmine, and was deemed to be so valuable in the dyeing trade, that an offer was immediately made of sixty guineas per ton for any quantity that could be procured. The other half has been since sent back to the coast, as a guide to collect more of the same sort, though it is a matter of doubt whether, under the circumstances that have been related, the same tree can be ascertained again."—p. 9.

* The butter is prepared by boiling, and besides the advantage of keeping a whole year without salt, it is " whiter, firmer, and, to my palate," says Park (vol. i. p. 302), " of a richer

valuable than the palm-nut. Some travellers inform
their readers that it is an excellent substitute for
butter, and can be appropriated to the same uses
with the palm-oil. It is a remarkable fact, in the
natural history of these trees, that immediately
where the one ceases to yield its fruit, the other
flourishes abundantly. The ground-nut* is becoming also a valuable article of commerce; and this
with the other nuts mentioned, yield a rich supply of
oil and oil-cake for the use of cattle. The value of
the castor-nut, as an article of medicine, needs not
be particularly adverted to. The roots which grow in
Africa require generally but little attention in their
cultivation; among others, there are the following:—The manioc, yams, sweet potatoes, arrow-

flavour than the best butter I ever tasted made of cow's milk."
The shea-tree, which produces it, is said to extend over a large
part of the continent, from Jaloof to Gaboon. "It has been ana-
lysed by the French chemist, M. Chevreuil, and found well adapted
for the manufacture of soap. Being inodorous and highly capable
of taking a perfume, it would be valuable for the finer sorts."—
Mrs. Lee, *Stories of Strange Lands*, p. 26.

* The *ground-nut* yields a pure golden-coloured oil, of a plea-
sant taste, and has been sold here at 56*l.* per ton. From 750 to
1000 tons are produced on the Gambia; but these nuts appear
plentiful along the whole coast, are often mentioned by Park, and
were noticed by Denham, as very abundant near the lake Tchad.
It grows in a soil too light and sandy for corn—its stalks afford
fodder for cattle—it sells at six shillings per gallon, and is as good
as sperm-oil. The *castor-nut* also grows wild in great abundance
on the banks of the Gambia, and elsewhere.

root, and ginger :* the two latter are exportable, and the former yield a large amount of healthful and nutritious food. Yams can be so improved by cultivation that, at Fernando Po, Captain Bullen says, many weigh from fifteen to twenty-five pounds, and in taste almost equal a potato. On one occasion he bought upwards of four tons for seventy-six iron hoops; and says, " The nourishment derived from them to my people was beyond belief."† The fruits are oranges, lemons, citrons, limes, pines, guavas, tamarinds, paw-paws, plantains and bananas. The paw-paw and plantain trees (says Ashmun) are a good example of the power of an uniformly-heated climate to accelerate vegetation. You may see in the gardens many of the former, not more than fifteen months from the seed, already fifteen inches round the stem, and fifteen feet high, with several pecks of ripening fruit. Clear your lands, plant your crops, keep the weeds down, and the most favourable climate in the world, alone, under the direction of a bountiful Providence, will do more for you than all your toil and care could accomplish in America."‡ Tamarinds are

* The ginger of Africa is particularly fine, and high flavoured; it yields about sixty for one; and the people only want instruction in the method of preparing it for European markets.—*Denham, Desp.,* 21*st May,* 1827; *Sierra Leone Report,* 1830, *No.* 57, p. 30.

† Captain Bullen's Desp., November, 1826.

‡ Ashmun's Life, Ap. p. 66.

exportable. Of grain, there is rice, Indian
corn, Guinea corn, or millet, &c. The quantities
of these can be raised to any extent, and be
limited only by demand.* The Rev. W. Fox, the
Missionary, says, in his MS. Journal, August 22,
1836—" This afternoon I visited Laming, a small
Mandingo town (above Macarthy's Island). I could
scarcely get into the town for the quantity of Indian
corn with which it is surrounded; upon a very
moderate calculation, and for a very small portion
of labour, which generally devolves upon the poor
women, [they reap upwards of two hundred fold."
I am informed that Madeira wholly depends on
the maize raised in Africa, and that the rice produced there, when properly dried and prepared, is
equal to that grown in South Carolina. Of drugs,
there are aloes† and cassia, senna, frankincense, car-
damums, and grains of paradise, or Malagetta pepper. Amongst the miscellaneous products, which

---

* " Nothing can be more delightful than a stroll along the
borders of the beautiful fields, winding occasionally along
almost impervious clusters of young palms, whose spreading
branches exclude every ray of the scorching sun, then opening
suddenly on an immense rice-field of the most delicate pea-green,
skirted by the beautiful broad-leaved plantain and banana, 'literally groaning under the immense masses of their golden fruit."
Dr. J. Hall, Governor of Liberia. *Missionary Register*, 1836,
p. 360.

† A new use of the aloe plant has been discovered in the
beautiful tissue and cordage manufactured from its fibres, by M.
Pavy, of Paris. The fibres of the palm and banana-trees are also
wrought by him into glossy stuffs.

are in great demand in this country, may be enumerated ivory, bees'-wax, caoutchouc, or Indian-rubber.
The former of these articles will, of course, suffer a
gradual diminution as the forests are cut down, the
swamps, drained, and the plains cultivated ; but of
the latter scarcely any diminution need be appre-
hended. The bees'-wax of Africa is in great
repute, and can be had in any quantity ; and the
great price freely given for Indian-rubber might be
a sufficient inducement to lead the African to pay
more attention to its collection. Of this Mr. Rankin says,* describing what he saw in an excursion
amongst the Timmanese,—" A large lump of Indian-rubber (caoutchouc) lay on the table, also the
produce of Tombo. This article, at present acquiring a high value amongst our importations, is
not there made an article of commerce, Like almost every other produce of the neighbourhood of
Sierra Leone, it is scarcely known to exist, or is
entirely neglected. It grows plentifully, and may
be easily obtained by making incisions into the tree,
from which it flows like cream, into calabashes tied
underneath ; it hardens within a few hours."

Mr. Elliot Cresson, examined before the American
Committee on the Foreign Slave Trade, February,
1839, stated, in answer to the question,—" What
will be the commercial and political advantages to
the United States, from an intercourse with the
colony of Liberia ?" " Among the valuable articles

* Rankin's Sierra Leone, vol. ii. p. 218.

of export, wax and spices are obtained in large quantities in our colony. The India-rubber tree grows wild in the neighbouring woods, and ostrich feathers have been exported largely. Hides could be obtained in any quantities; so could rosewood, lancewood, and palmwood, and live oak of the best quality. One merchant in Philadelphia last year imported from the colony a quantity of pea or ground nuts, from which he realised the profit of 12,000 dollars. Cotton, of a very good staple, is found there, and cultivated with great advantage, as there is no frost there. And the articles desired in return are those produced by American manufactures and agriculture."—*Colonization Herald,* March, 1839, p. 124.

Ashmun, who seems to have had a clear view of the interest of the Liberian settlers, writes to them thus :—" Suffer me to put down two or three remarks, of the truth and importance of which you cannot be too sensible. The first is, that the cultivation of your rich lands is the only way you will ever find out to independence, comfort, and wealth." "You may, if you please, if God gives you health, become as independent, comfortable, and happy as you ought to be in this world." "The flat lands around you, and particularly your farms, have as good a soil as can be met with in any country. They will produce two crops of corn, sweet potatoes, and several other vegetables, in a year. They will yield a larger crop than the best soils in America. And they will produce a number of very valuable articles, for which in the

United States, millions of money are every year paid away to foreigners. One acre of rich land, well tilled, will produce you three hundred dollars' worth of indigo. Half an acre may be made to grow half a ton of arrow-root. Four acres laid out in coffee-plants, will, after the third year, produce you a clear income of two or three hundred dollars. Half an acre of cotton-trees will clothe your whole family; and, except a little hoeing, your wife and children can perform the whole labour of cropping and manu-facturing it. One acre of canes will make you inde-pendent of all the world for the sugar you use in your family. One acre set with fruit-trees, and well at-tended, will furnish you the year round with more plantains, bananas, oranges, limes, guavas, papaws, and pine-apples, than you will ever gather. Nine months of the year, you may grow fresh vegetables every month, and some of you who have lowland plantations, may do so throughout the year." *

I must also quote the authority of Denis de Montfort, a Frenchman of science, who in a paper on the gold of the Coast of Guinea, inserted in the " Philosophical Magazine," thus writes:—" There exists no country in the world so susceptible of general cultivation as Africa : we know that certain districts are fertile in corn ; and grain of every kind grows there, intermixed with sugar-canes lately in-troduced, and which protect the grain from hail. The plants of India, Europe, America, and Australia

* Ashmun's Life, Ap., p. 64.

will flourish there in perpetual spring, and the animals of all climates can be easily naturalised. The negroes, whose respect for the whites is extreme, notwithstanding what they have suffered from them, will cheerfully give up their fields to be cultivated by them. Servants, and even slaves, will not be wanting, and this will be a true method of preventing these nations from massacring their prisoners of war, as the king of Dahomey does at the present moment. May our feeble voices on this subject reach the ear of royalty! *

It is almost impossible to turn to any book of African travels, without meeting with some incidental observations upon the fertility of the soil. I should have supposed that nothing of this kind would have occurred in the narrative of Captain Paddock; yet he says:—" On the south was seen a very extensive country, abounding with little enclosed cities, large fields of grain, and productive gardens. In short, though the climate here is dry as well as hot, such is the great fertility of the soil, that it is capable of producing abundantly all the necessaries and most of the luxuries of life. What might it be under the cultivation of a civilised, industrious, and skilful people!†

" We made choice of a wheat-field, which lay but a few hundred yards from us; and we had entered it but a few paces when we found ourselves completely hidden, even while standing erect. Although my mate was five feet eleven inches in height, and myself

* Annual Register, 1815, p. 542.　　† P. 289.

five feet ten, the heads of the wheat were above our own. This was the finest piece of wheat I ever saw; it was all well headed; and had we not gone among it, and took its measure, we should have known it was very tall, though we never could have told how tall." *

It is observed by Brown, in his botanical appendix to " Tuckey's Voyage " (pp. 342-3), that from the river Senegal, in about 16° north latitude, to the Congo, in upwards of 6° south latitude, there is a remarkable uniformity in the vegetation of Western Africa—a fact which gives us promise of extending to any amount, our commerce in such vegetable productions as have already obtained a sale in Europe or America. Thus a tree which characterises nearly the whole range of coast, is the Elais Guineensis, or oil-palm, one of the most valuable to commerce. This grows in the greatest abundance in the delta of the Niger. There " the palm-nut now rots on the ground unheeded and neglected," over an extent of surface equal to the whole of Ireland. (Laird, vol. ii. p. 362.)

The whole extent, too, of the Timmanee, and a great part of Koranko, through which Captain Laing passed in 1822, was absolutely bristled with palm-trees, which, at the time he went up the country (April and May), were bearing luxurious crops of nuts. " There is no known instance, or any apparent danger, of a failure on the part of all bountiful nature in supplying the fruit: on the contrary, it

* P. 181.

is the opinion of Captain Laing, that were the population double, and had they all the industry we could wish, they would not be able to reap the abundant harvest annually presented to them."*

The soil of Africa produces indigenously nearly all the useful plants which are common to other tropical countries, and some of them in greater perfection than they are to be found elsewhere.

There are some articles that require more notice :

Hemp grows wild on the Gambia, and only requires a better mode of preparation to make it a valuable article of import. The same may be said of tobacco. Indigo grows so freely in Africa, that, in some places, it is difficult to eradicate it. " Immense quantities of indigo, and other noxious weeds," spring up in the streets of Freetown.†

It is known to grow wild as far inland as the Tchad, and even with the rude preparation bestowed by the natives, gives a beautiful dye to their cloths.‡

Coffee is another indigenous shrub, which well repays cultivation. When Kizell, a Nova Scotian, first observed it near the Sherbro, he pulled up two or three plants, and showed them to the people, who said that they thought it was good for nothing, but to fence their plantations. It was all over the country, and in some places nothing else was to be

---

* Sierra Leone Gaz., Dec. 14, 1822.

† Despatch, Mr. Smart to Sir G. Murray, 1828; Sierra Leone Report, No. 57, p. 30.

‡ Denham's Travels, p. 246.

seen.* Even in a wild state it seems to repay the trouble of gathering, for the Commissioners at Sierra Leone, in their Annual Report, of date 1st January, 1838, inform us " that the Foulahs have been induced, by the fair traders of the river Nunez to bring down for sale to them a quantity of coffee, of a very superior quality, the produce of the forests of their own country." An extract of a letter, which they enclose, observes that " one great advantage of peaceful commerce with the natives is, that valuable productions of their country are brought to light by our research, sometimes to their astonishment." Thus, till within the last two years, this abundant growth of coffee was " left to be the food of monkeys," but is now a source of profit to the natives and to our own merchants. A small quantity has been cultivated, both at Sierra Leone and the Gold Coast; and Ashmun (Life, Ap., p. 78) states that, in Liberia, no crop is surer ; that African coffee frequently produces four pounds to the tree, and that the berries attain a size unknown elsewhere. I am happy to learn that above 10,000 lbs. of African coffee were imported into this country in 1837, that its quality was excellent, and that it fetched a good price.†

* Afr. Inst 6 Report, Ap.

† Mr. M'Queen says, that the old Arabian traveller Batouta, who nad visited China, states, that in the interior parts of Africa, along the Niger, which he visited, the tea-plant grew abundantly.— M'Queen's *Africa*, p. 218. Dr. M'Leod, describing the kingdom of Benin, says—" In the opinion of one of the latest governors

Sugar-canes grow spontaneously in several parts of Africa; and when cultivated, as they are in various places, for the sake of the juice, they become very large. The expense of the necessary machinery alone seems to have hitherto prevented the manufacture of sugar;*

I now come to the article which demands the largest share of our attention, viz. cotton; because it requires little capital, yields a steady return, is in vast demand in Europe, and grows naturally in the soil of Africa.

As this last is a point of vital importance, I think it necessary to furnish a portion of the evidence I have collected as to the luxuriant and spontaneous growth of cotton in Africa:—

Sir Fulk Grevell making, by order of Queen Elizabeth, a report to Sir Francis Walsingham on a memorial of certain merchant adventures:—" Sir, You demaunde of me the names of such kings as are absolute in the East, and either have warr or traffique wth the kinge of Spaigne."   *   *   *   *
" Then followeth kingdoms of Gaulata, *Tombuto*, and Melly; whereof the firste is poore, and hath smal traffique; *the seconde populous, and rich in*

we have had, on the establishment in this country (Mr. James), and one whose general knowledge of Africa is admitted to be considerable, the tea-tree flourishes spontaneously here."— M'Leod's *Voyage to Africa*, p. 18.

* A company has been established at Mourovia, with a small capital, for the experiment.—Col. Herald, November, 1837

corne and beasts, but wanteth salte, wch the *Portugal* supplieth; the last hath store of corne, flesh, and *cotten woll,* wch are *carried into Spaigne* in great abundance." Quoted by Mr. Bruce, from a M.S. in the State Paper Office—Annals of the East India Company, vol. i., p. 121.

Beaver says, " Of the vegetables that are wild, the sugar-cane, cotton-shrub, and indigo-plant, seem the most valuable: no country in the world is more amply enriched than this is with the chief productions of the animal and vegetable kingdoms."

Mr. Dalrymple, who was at Goree in 1779, states, " that there are three different kinds of cotton; that samples sent home were considered by English merchants superior to that from the West Indies. It grows spontaneously almost everywhere, though it is sometimes cultivated."*

Cotton, says Col. Denham, grows wild about Sierra Leone, of three kinds, white, brown, and pink; the first is excellent.† He also " found it wild on the Tschadda."‡

Clapperton, saw some " beautiful specimens" of the African looms in the interior.§

Park‖ observes, almost every slave can weave.

* Evid. Slave Trade Com., 1790, p. 297.
† Col. Denham, Rep. Sierra Leone, Sess. 1830, No. 57, p. 16.
‡ Denham's Travels, p. 317.
§ Clapperton, p. 5.
‖ Park, vol. i. p. 429.

Ashmun* says, it is believed that none of the varieties of the American cotton-shrub answers, in all respects, to the indigenous African tree. The cotton of this country is on all hands allowed to be of a good quality, and the mode of growing, curing, and manufacturing the article pursued in America may be adopted here, making due allowance for the much greater size and duration of the African tree.

Lander says, " From Badagry to Saccatoo, the cotton-plant, indigo, &c., are cultivated to a great extent."

Laird says, "The increase of trade from the interior would, I think, consist chiefly of palm-oil, raw cotton, shea-butter, rice, and bees'-wax. These articles would, I think, be indefinitely increased."

The Rev. John Pinney,† an American missionary, says, " The crops of coffee, pepper, and cotton exceed all that could be boasted of in the United States."

And the Rev. J. Seys‡ speaks of the " excellent cotton" of the St. Paul's River.

I might, if it were necessary, multiply these proofs almost indefinitely, by references to M'Queen, Burckhardt, De Caillé, Dupuis, Robertson, &c.

It has been my endeavour, throughout the whole of this work, to take nothing for granted, and to

* Ashmun's Life, App., p. 76.
† Coloniz. Soc. Rep., quoted in Miss. Reg. for 1836, p. 22.
‡ Ibid.

prove, as I proceeded, all that I stated. It cannot be necessary, however, to stop for the purpose of establishing the vast importance to Great Britain of an additional market for the purchase of raw cotton. In our cotton-trade, there are about twenty millions of fixed, and twenty millions of floating capital invested. The total yearly produce of the manufacture amounts to forty millions. One million five hundred thousand persons earn their bread by it.

Africa is capable of yielding this necessary article : it is as near to us as North America ; nearer than the Brazils ; two-thirds nearer to us than India. The vast tropical districts along the southern side of the Great Desert, the fine plains, and gently-rising country from the northern bank of the Rio de Formosa, and from the Niger to the base of the Kong mountains, are adapted to the culture and production of the finest cotton. This portion of Africa alone, so rich in soil, so easy of access, offers an independent and abundant supply of that article, the want of which impedes and oppresses our manufacturing prosperity. But if Africa, when delivered from that evil which withers her produce, and paralyzes her industry, can be made to supply us with the commodity which we so much need, she, in her turn, will be the customer of Europe to the same vast extent, for the manufactured goods which Europe produces. If it be true that intercourse with Africa, of an honest description, would be twice blessed,—a blessing to the nation who confers, and to the continent which receives, cultivation and commerce,—nothing can exceed the folly (except the wickedness) of a system, which annually sweeps off nearly half a million of the inhabitants of Africa, and consigns, by its inhuman butcheries, one of the fairest portions of the earth to the sterility of a wilderness.

But it may be said, that though the land might be made to produce cotton, centuries must elapse before it can be made to yield any quantity of that article. I do not pretend to say that this will be suddenly accomplished; but an anecdote which I heard stated to the Marquis of Normanby, by a gentleman whose mercantile knowledge would not be disputed by any one, may serve to forbid despair. He stated that the person who first imported from America a bale of cotton into this country was still alive, that the person to whom it was consigned in Liverpool was still alive, and that the custom-house officer at that place refused to admit it at the lower rate of duty, because, to his knowledge, no cotton could be grown in America; yet that country which could grow no cotton, now, besides supplying her own demand, and that of all other countries, sends annually to Great Britain a quantity valued at about £15,000,000 sterling.

I propose, then, that an effort shall be made to cultivate districts of Africa, selected for that purpose, in order that her inhabitants may be convinced of the capabilities of their soil, and witness what wonders may be accomplished by their own labour when set in motion by our capital, and guided by our skill.

There is no doubt that mercantile settlements would effect a considerable measure of good; but the good is distant, and will be effected by slow degrees, while the condition of Africa is such, that the delay of a single year carries with it a world of misery, and the certain destruction of a multitude of lives.

I confess that I think it would be well, on many grounds, if we could, to confine ourselves to the establishment of factories. I fear, however, that this limitation would retard, if not defeat, our objects.

We should touch Africa at a few prominent points, —at each of these, a mart might be established, and something might be done towards the education of the children of those who entered our service. But the evil is gigantic, and it requires gigantic efforts to arrest it. I believe,—and every word that I have read or heard on the subject confirms me in the impression,—that Africa has, within herself, resources, which, duly developed, would compensate for the gains of the Slave Trade, if these were twenty times as great as they are. But it must never be forgotten that these resources are nothing, unless they are fairly and fully called into action.

Factories on the coast may lead the natives to gather the spontaneous productions of nature. They may supply us with wood, with palm-oil, with skins, and with ivory; but beyond the money or the goods paid for these, and beyond occasional and very lax employment to the natives, Africa would gain little. No habits of settled industry will be inspired; no examples will be placed before those, the avenue to whose understanding is through the eyes; and who, however slow they may be to reason, are quick to perceive, and intelligent to imitate.

I have already said, that two things must be achieved, or we shall fail: the one is, to call forth and elevate the native mind; the other is, to provide a larger source of revenue than that derived from the trade in man.

By agriculture—both will be accomplished. The ransom for Africa will be found in her fertile soil; and the moral worth of her people will advance as they become better instructed, more secure, more industrious, and more wealthy. And then will be felt the influence of cultivated intellect on rude reason; the children will be taught by our schools; our very machinery, doing easily what is impossible to their unaided strength, will eloquently speak to others, and beget that allegiance of mind, which is uniformly yielded by the untutored, to beings of superior capacity. The ministers of the gospel, the best of civilizers, will, as gently as irresistibly, work out a change in the current of opinion, and effect the cheerful renunciation of bloody and licentious customs.

Such essential reforms as these cannot be expected from the mere establishment of factories on the coast.

Something, no doubt, will be gained by these, but not enough, to execute the task (of all tasks the most difficult) of giving an impulse to the slumbering energies of the people, and making productive the latent capabilities of the soil. In one word, Africa wants more than commerces—he wants cultivation.

If cultivation be required, it becomes at once desirable that we should afford to the natives the benefit of our experience and skill—our example and capital. Why should the African be left to work his way upwards, from his rude and unprofitable tillage, to that higher order of cultivation, which we have reached by the labours of successive generations? Our discoveries in tropical agriculture must work a great physical change. It is probable, that we might reclaim a waste district in half the time, and at half the expense, that it would cost the inhabitants.

But I look also, as I have already hinted, to the *moral* effect which will hence be produced. Those of old, who carried the spade and the plough into barbarous countries were ranked with the deities.

By our seeds, and our implements, and our skill in abridging labour and subduing difficulty, we shall place before the natives, in a form which they cannot mistake, the vast benefits they are likely to derive from intercourse with us; and they will speedily perceive, that it is their interest to protect those strangers who possess secrets, which can make their land produce so unexpected and rich a harvest.

It is quite clear that the present commercial

intercourse between this country and Africa is extremely limited ; that the chief obstacle to its extension is the prevalence of the Slave Trade,* and

* The imports of palm-oil have diminished during four late years, as may be seen by the following returns, viz. :—

				Cwts.
1834	.	.	.	269,907
1835	.	.	.	234,882
1836	.	.	.	236,195
1837	.	.	.	201,906

This diminution has arisen, not in consequence of a decrease in the demand for the article, but on account of the extension of the Slave Trade on the coast, and the increased difficulty of procuring a supply.

" The industry of the natives, in a great degree, is stifled by the Slave Trade; and, though a good deal of oil is prepared and sold, the English traders, loading at the mouth of the river, are often interrupted, and obliged to wait, to the loss of profit and the ruin of the crew's health, while a smuggling slaver takes all hands on the coast to complete her cargo."—*Laird.*

" When there is a demand for slaves the natives abandon every other employment ; and the consequence is, that the British vessels trading on the coast are lying idle for want of trade.

" In consequence of the great demand for slaves, the natives here and in the interior abandon cultivation, the trees go to destruction, and no young trees are planted.

" At one place in Africa where a very considerable quantity of palm-oil has been annually supplied to the ships of our merchants, the Spanish and Portuguese have latterly so much increased the Slave Trade, that the cultivation of the palm-trees, which was giving occupation to thousands, has not only become neglected, but the native chiefs have been incited to blind revenge against British influence, and have set fire to and destroyed 30,000 palm trees."—*Recent Letters from Africa.*

that it might be indefinitely increased under the fostering and protective care of the British government. The grounds on which this supposition rests are the number and situation of its navigable rivers; its rich alluvial deltas, and extensive and fertile plains; its immense forests; its wide range of natural productions; its swarming, active, and enterprising population; its contiguity to Europe, and the demand of its people for the manufactures of this country.

In speculating on African commerce, it should be borne in mind that we have to deal with nations who are not only ignorant and uncivilised, but corrupted and deteriorated by the Slave Trade, and by intercourse with the worst class of Europeans. There will, therefore, be difficulties and obstructions to overcome before a clear field for honest commerce can be obtained. In the present state of the people we can hardly look to obtain from them articles which depend on an extensive cultivation of the soil, so as to compete with the productions of civilised nations. It is probable that in commencing an extensive intercourse with Africa, there will be at first a considerable outlay of money without an immediate return; but from whatever source this may be obtained, it should be considered as a gift to Africa It will ultimately be repaid a thousand-fold.

The articles desired by the Africans in return for the produce of their country are too many to enumerate. Lists of them are given by almost every traveller. It may, therefore, suffice to observe, that many of them are the produce or manufactures of our island, or of our colonies ; and it is an important consideration, that we may obtain the treasures of this unexplored continent, by direct barter of our own commodities, and that, while we cheapen luxuries at home, we also increase the means of obtaining them, by giving increased employment to our productive classes.

The extension of a legitimate commerce, and with it the blessings of civilisation and Christianity, is worthy the most strenuous exertions of the philanthropist, whilst to the mercantile and general interests of the civilised world it is of the highest importance. Africa presents an almost boundless tract of country, teeming with inhabitants who admire, and are desirous of possessing our manufactures. There is no limit to the demand, except their want of articles to give us in return. They must be brought to avail themselves of their own resources.

Attempts, as we have seen, have already been made to form cotton plantations, and the article produced is found to be of a very useful and valuable description. Perseverance in these efforts is alone required to accomplish the object in view, and, when once accomplished, the importance to this country will be incalculable. The trade in palm-oil is capable of immense extension, and the article is every year becoming more important and in more extensive use. In exchange for these, and many other valuable articles, British manufactures would be taken, and

British ships find a profitable employment in the conveyance of them.

It so happens that a considerable proportion of the goods which best suit the taste of the natives of Africa, consists of fabrics to which power-looms cannot be applied with any advantage. Any extension, then, of the trade to Africa, will have this most important additional advantage, that it will cause a corresponding increase in the demand for the labour of a class of individuals who have lately been truly represented as suffering greater privations than any other set of workmen connected with the cotton trade.

But the first object of our intercourse with Africa should be, not so much to obtain a remunerating trade, as to repair in some measure the evil that the civilised world has inflicted on her, by conveying Christianity, instruction, and the useful arts to her children. The two objects will eventually, if carried on in a right manner, be found perfectly compatible; for it is reasonable to seek in legitimate commerce a direct antidote to the nefarious traffic which has so long desolated and degraded her. We have shown the vast variety and importance of the productions which Africa is capable of yielding : we have already proved that, notwithstanding the bounty of nature, the commerce of Africa is most insignificant. Truly may we say with Burke, " To deal and traffic—not in the labour of men, but in men themselves—is to devour the root, instead of enjoying the fruit of human diligence."

CHAPTER III.

FACILITIES FOR COMMERCIAL INTERCOURSE.

I HAVE thus stated what I conceive to be the gist of the whole question, viz., that the deliverance of Africa must spring, under the blessing of God, from herself, and I have also shown, I trust to the satisfaction of every reader, that she possesses abundant capabilities for the purpose. The next question that arises, is, how are these capabilities to be made available? how are we to obtain access to them? Great, no doubt, are the difficulties; yet, such are the discoveries of the last ten years, that we may now lay aside the impressions of an impenetrable continent, and of interminable wastes of sand, which have accompanied us from our childhood. We now know that a mighty river, which discharges itself into the Bight of Benin, by upwards of twenty mouths, is navigable, with little interruption, from thence nearly to its source, a distance of more than 2,600 miles. We also learn from the travellers who have navigated the Niger, that there are many tributary streams, some of which, especially the Tschadda, or Shaderbah, are equally navigable, and afford every facility for intercourse with the numerous nations and tribes who inhabit the countries in their vicinity.

Mungo Park, in his last journey (1805), embarked on the Niger at Bammakoo, about 500 miles from its source. In his narrative he says, " Having gained the summit of the ridge which separates the Niger from the remote branches of the Senegal, I went on a little before, and coming to the brow of the hill, *I once more saw the Niger* rolling its immense stream along the plain." And he tells us, it is larger " even here, than either the Senegal or the Gambia, and full an English mile over." When preparing for his subsequent embarkation on the Niger, he says, " the best wood for boat-building is near Kaukary, on a large navigable branch of the Niger." Park descended the river to Boussa, where most unhappily he was killed.

In 1830, Lander, who had accompanied the enterprising Clapperton in his last journey to Houssa, was sent out by the British Government to explore the Niger. He succeeded in reaching Boussa by a land route : there he embarked on the river, and after a voyage of about 560 miles, reached the Bight of Benin, and thus solved the interesting problem which had so long exercised the talents and ingenuity of modern geographers.

Messrs. Laird and Oldfield, by the aid of steam-vessels, went up the Niger from the Bight of Benin, in 1832 ; and their journals contain much valuable information as to that river, and its tributary, the Tschadda. The latter, at the point of confluence, is represented to be one mile and a half broad ; and the country on the banks of both rivers is described to be most fertile, very populous, and, wherever there is any security from the ravages of the Slave Trade, highly cultivated.

Mr. Oldfield ascended the Niger to the town of Rabbah, and he explored the Tschadda, for about 100 miles from its confluence with the Niger at Addacuddah.

They also describe several towns, Eboe, Iccory, Iddah, Egga, Rabbah, and Fundah, proving how great are the facilities for trade and commerce with the interior afforded by the river.

It is to be regretted that so little of the Tschadda has been explored. Mr. Oldfield was informed, that its course lay through the heart of Africa, and that there were many large towns on its banks; and Laird in mentioning this river, says, "By it, a communication would be opened with all the nations inhabiting the unknown countries between the Niger and the Nile."

Here, then, is one of the most magnificent rivers in the world, introducing us into the heart of Africa: at a central point, it opens a way by its eastern branch, to the kingdoms of Bornou, Kanem, and Begharmi; by its western, to Timbuctoo,—each of them bringing us into communication with multitudes of tribes, and unfolding to us the productions of a most extensive and fertile territory.

The problem is, how shall that stream be closed to the passage of slaves to the coast; while it is at the same time opened as a secure and accessible highway for legitimate commerce. The solution seems almost self-evident : we must obtain the positions which command the Niger ; and without doubt, the most important of these, is Fernando Po.

FERNANDO PO.

I have already adverted to the importance of this island, as being decidedly the best locality on the coast for the reception of liberated negroes ; and for aiding us in a great effort for the civilization of Africa. It is situated about 20 miles from the mainland, in the Bight of Biafra, and commands the mouths of those great streams which penetrate so deeply into central Africa, along the coast from the Rio Volta to the Gaboon. These rivers are about forty in number, and Fernando Po is at the distance of from 40 to 200 miles. The island is exceedingly fertile ; the soil is composed of a fine deep black and brick mould : it abounds in many species of large and fine timber, fit for ornamental or useful purposes ; and it is capable of producing, in the highest perfection, not only every article of tropical produce, but also many kinds of European fruits and vegetables : it is 24 miles in length, and 16 miles in breadth. It has three ranges of hills, running parallel to the north-east side ; the centre rising into a conical volcanic mountain, to the height of 10,000 feet above the level of the sea.

Mr. Laird thus describes its aspect :—" On my

return to Fernando Po I recovered rapidly, and was able to walk and ride about in a fortnight after my arrival. The splendid scenery that distinguishes this beautiful island is well known from former descriptions, and to persons coming from the low marshy shore of the main land has indescribable charms.

"The view from the galleries of the government-house on a clear moonlight night I never saw equalled, nor can I conceive it surpassed. To the north-east, the lofty peak of the Camaroons, rising to the immense height of 14,000 feet, throws its shadow halfway across the narrow strait that separates the island from the main land; while the numerous little promontories, and beautiful coves, that grace the shores of Goderich Bay, throw light and shadow so exquisitely upon the water, that one almost can imagine it a fairy land. On the west, the spectator looks down almost perpendicularly on the vessels in Clarence Cove, which is a natural basin, surrounded by cliffs of the most romantic shape, and a group of little islands, which nature seems to have thrown in, to give a finish to the scene.

"Looking inland, towards the island, the peak is seen, covered with wood to the summit, with its sides furrowed with deep ravines, and here and there a patch of cleared land, showing like a white spot in the moonlight."

We are also informed, that, from the elevation of 3,500 feet above the level of the sea, there is always found the climate of an European summer.

The shores are bold, and, with hardly an exception, free from those swamps on the coasts of the main land, around the mouths of the rivers, which generate the fatal malaria which proves so destructive to the health and life of Europeans. From all this Fernando Po is entirely free; while the land remains uncleared and uncultivated, diseases, the attendants of every tropical climate, will, to a considerable extent prevail, but never equal to what is witnessed on the alluvial, flooded, and swampy shores of the adjacent continent. When, however, the land shall be cleared and cultivated, the climate, we may reasonably expect, will become healthy and safe for Europeans: the same as the climate is found to be in the elevated parts of Jamaica, and in those West Indian islands which are cleared, cultivated, and drained, such as Barbadoes and St. Christopher's, to the latter of which Fernando Po bears in many points a very strong resemblance. The putrid malaria, generated on the alluvial plains and swamps, on the shores of the sea, and in the neighbourhood of large rivers in the torrid zone, never rises to any great height, probably not 400 feet above the level of the sea at any place; and, consequently, it is very obvious that Fernando Po would, when cleared of the wood, afford a healthy, as well as convenient location for any British force, or settlement, which it may be considered necessary or advisable to place upon it. The island, moreover, is free from hurricanes: there are several bays which afford most convenient access: two of these, North West Bay and Maidstone Bay, were carefully surveyed by Commodore Bullen in 1826. He describes the latter bay, as perfectly easy of access, and at once healthy and very airy, the westerly wind blowing directly across it at all times of day and night. He also says that there is good anchorage in all parts of the bay; that it abounds with fish and turtle; and that many streams of excellent water run into it. There are in this bay two very fine coves, where ships might lie and refit, as smooth as in a mill-pond, combined with the benefit of a beautiful and refreshing breeze. Commodore Bullen further says, that if a look-out be kept from the shore of this bay, scarcely a vessel could leave the Bonny, Calabars, Bimbia, and Camaroons rivers, without being observed time enough to give a signal to any vessel lying in the bay to intercept her; and he cites as an instance, the capture of a slaver, " Le Daniel," by his own vessel. This capture was effected within four hours after first seeing her, although his vessel was then lying at anchor in the bay. Commodore, now Sir Charles Bullen, strongly recommended that a settlement should be formed for liberated Africans in Maidstone Bay; but it appears that Clarence Cove was preferred. Of the latter place we are told, that it affords the finest shelter and anchorage for shipping; 500 sail may there ride in perfect safety and lie quite close to the shore. It also abounds with excellent spring water, as in fact the island generally does; the fine streams rushing from the mountains to the sea, in beautiful waterfalls and cascades, down its bold coasts. " You have not," said a gentleman, who had resided there nine years, and whose testimony may be relied upon, " an island, either in the North or South Atlantic, equal to Fernando Po for shipping : a vessel may anchor there all the year round in perfect safety."

Colonel Nichols computes the natives to amount to about 5,000 ; and he states that, if the island were cleared and cultivated, it could easily maintain a very large population. He found the natives friendly, inoffensive, and willing to work : he employed them in clearing the ground for the British settlement at Clarence Cove.

The Colonel speaks in high terms of the products and capabilities of the island. The yams were the finest he ever saw, and he introduced the cultivation of Indian corn with complete success; and Captain Beatty thinks that a profitable whale fishery might be established on the shores of Fernando Po.

Mr. Laird, in his remarks on our commerce with Africa, observes, " My proposal is, to make the government's head quarters at Fernando Po, which, from its geographical position, is the key to central Africa, and within a few miles of the great seats of our present commerce on the coast. It is also the only place upon the whole line of coast, on which hospitals and other conveniences could be erected, far above the reach of the coast fever, where invalids from the naval, military, and civil establishments, from all parts of the coast, might recruit their health in a pure and bracing atmosphere."*

Fernando Po therefore, in every way, and in a very remarkable manner, possesses those advantages of which we stand in need. Is it our object to capture the slave-trader? Here is an island adjacent to his chief resort, so situated as to command and control the whole Bights of Benin and Biafra. Or is it our object to encourage legitimate commerce? Fernando Po is at the outlet of that great stream which offers a highway into the heart of Africa. I confess, I look forward to the day, when Africa shall unfold her hidden treasures to the world; and as a primary means of enabling her to do so, this island is of incalculable value. Do we dread the climate? Here, and as I believe, almost here alone, on the western coast of Africa, has nature provided a position, which enjoys the benefit of perpetual sea-breezes, free from the noxious effluvia which load even these breezes as we advance inland on the continent; whilst its high land is above " the fatal fever level." Or is it our object, as far as possible, to reduce the sufferings, and spare the lives of the negroes, whom we, with the most generous intentions, rescue from the slave-trader? Under the present system, we consign these negroes in vast numbers to destruction, consequent on a five weeks' voyage to Sierra Leone, when they could be landed on the

* Laird, vol. ii. p. 391.

island of Fernando Po, within a few hours, or, at most, within a few days, after their capture ; while, if located on that island, they would afford material for the formation of what may be termed a normal school, for the introduction of agriculture, civilization, and Christianity into the interior of Africa.

To the reader who may be desirous of obtaining further information respecting this island, I strongly recommend the perusal of the abstract of a letter which I insert in the Appendix.*   It was written, as its date (Sept. 1835) proves, without reference to the plans which I now propose, and it did not come into my possession, till after the above description of the island had been prepared.   It will be seen, however, how remarkably it confirms the statements I have made on other authorities.

Next in importance to Fernando Po, is a settlement at the confluence of the Niger and the Tchadda.   It can hardly be doubted, I think, even by those who are most sceptical with regard to predictions of future commercial greatness, that this position will, hereafter, become the great internal citadel of Africa, and the great emporium of her commerce.   It commands the Niger, with all its tributary streams and branches in the interior, while Fernando Po exercises the same control over its numerous mouths.   With these two positions, and with our steamers plying between them, it is not too much to say, that this great river would

* *Vide* Appendix B.

be safe from the ravages of the pirate and the man-
hunter, and would be open to the capital and enterprise of the legitimate merchant. I must here avail
myself of a passage from a work published nearly
twenty years ago :—*

"The extent of country and population whose
improvements, labours, and wants would be dependent
upon, and stimulated to exertions by a settlement on
the Niger, is prodigious, and altogether unequalled.
The extent comprehends a country of nearly 40° of
longitude from west to east, and through the greater
part of this extent of 20° of latitude from north to
south, a space almost equal to Europe. Where the
confluence of the Tschadda with the Niger takes
place, is the spot to erect the capital of our great
African establishments. A city built there, under
the protecting wings of Great Britain, would ere long
become the capital of Africa. Fifty millions of
people, yea, even a greater number, would be depend-
ant on it.

*   *   *   *

"The rivers are the roads in the torrid zone.
Nature seems to have intended these as the great
help in introducing agriculture and commerce.

* The "View of Northern Central Africa" was published before
it was known that the Niger emptied itself into the Bight of Benin, and when the prevailing theories gave that river an opposite
direction. The author, Mr. M'Queen, is at least entitled to the
credit of having clearly pointed out its true course; all that he
then asserted has been verified by the expedition of Laird and
Oldfield.

" Wherever the continents are most extensive, there
we find the most magnificent rivers flowing through
them, opening up a communication from side to side.
What is still more remarkable, and becomes of great
utility, is, that these mighty currents flow against the
prevailing winds, thus rendering the navigation easy,
which would otherwise be extremely tedious and
difficult. The prevailing trade-winds blow right up
their streams. This is the case with the Niger, and
in a more particular manner during the time it
is in flood. For ten months in the year, but more
particularly from May till November, the prevailing
wind in the Bights of Benin and Biafra is from south-
west, thus blowing right up all the outlets of the
Niger. In the Congo, Tuckey found the breeze
generally blowing up the stream. It is needless to
point out, at length, the advantages which may be
derived from this wise regulation in the natural
world."

I have dwelt thus much on the Niger and the
settlements connected with it, because it clearly holds
the foremost place among the great inlets to Africa ;
but the number and situation of many other navigable rivers on the western coast of Africa have been
much remarked by those who have visited them, as
affording the noblest means for extending the commerce of this country to the millions who dwell on
their banks, or occupy the cities and towns in the
interior. Along the coast, commencing at the southern

point of the Bight of Biafra, and embracing the coast of Calabar, the Slave Coast, the Gold Coast, the Ivory Coast, the Grain Coast, the Pepper Coast, the coast of Sierra Leone, and thence northwards to the Senegal, there cannot be less than ninety or one hundred rivers, many of them navigable, and two of them rivalling in their volume of water and extent the splendid rivers of North America. It is reported that a French steam-vessel plies more than 700 miles up the Senegal, and that the Faleme, which flows into it eight leagues below Galam, is navigable in the rainy season for vessels of sixty tons burden. The Faleme runs through the golden land of Bambouk, whence the French traders obtain considerable quantities of that precious metal. The Gambia is a noble river. It is about eleven miles wide at its mouth, and about four opposite Bathurst. How far it extends into the interior is unknown; it is said, however, that it has been ascended for some hundred miles.* It is also asserted that from the upper part of this river the Senegal can be reached in three, and the Niger in four days.

In addition to the mighty rivers above referred to,

---

* In 1834, Captain Quin carried Governor Rendall up to Macarthy's Island, in the Britomart sloop of war. Craft of 50 or 60 tons can get up to Fattatenda, the resort of caravans for trade with British merchants. Commodore Owen terms the Gambia " a magnificent river." It was surveyed in 1826 by Lieutenant Owen, R.N., on which occasion he was accompanied by the Acting Governor Macaulay, as far as Macarthy's Island, 180 miles up the river.—*Owen*, ii.

it has been ascertained that, from Rio Lagos to the
river Elrei, no fewer than twenty streams enter the
ocean, several of surprising magnitude, and navigable for ships (M'Queen) ; and that all the
streams which fall into the sea from Rio Formosa
to Old Calabar inclusive, are connected together
by intermediate streams, at no great distance from
the sea.

The geographical position of Africa, and its contiguity to Europe claim for it especial attention. The
voyage from the port of London to the Senegal is generally accomplished in twenty-five days; to the Gambia
in twenty-eight or thirty days; to Sierra Leone, in
thirty to thirty-five days; to Cape Coast Castle, in
forty-two to forty-eight days; to Fernando Po, forty-
eight to fifty-three days; to the ports in the Bight of
Biafra, in fifty to fifty-five days; to the Zaire or Congo,
in fifty-five to sixty days, respectively. Vessels leaving Bristol or Liverpool for the same ports possess
an advantage, in point of time, of from five to eight
days. The voyage is attended with little danger,
provided common care be used. The homeward voyage is of course considerably longer than the outward,
in consequence of the vessels being obliged to take
what is commonly called, the western passage, having generally to go as far as 40° west longitude.
The difference in the length of the voyages, outward
and homeward, may be stated at from three to four
weeks.

The use of steam would, of course, greatly diminish

the length of the voyage, and facilitate the operations of the trader, until establishments could be formed to which the produce required might be conveyed by the natives.

The best season for visiting the African coast is the *dry* season, that is, from December to May. But it may be remarked that the line of coast from Cape Palmas to Cape St. Paul's is less subject to rains than the Windward Coast or the Bights, and may be visited at any season. The worst period of the year is from the middle of July to the middle of December.*

With regard to commerce, then, this portion of Africa would have fair play : her resources may prove greater, or less than we suppose ; but, whatever they be, the traffic arising from them will possess that first and indispensable requisite—security.

I do not, however, anticipate that this commerce will in the first instance be large. Africa is only capable of producing : as yet, she does not produce. When it is found that there is security for person and

---

* The chief causes of the sickness and mortality on board trading vessels may be ascribed, first, to climate ; second, to overwork, and especially exposure to the action of the sun while working ; and, third, to drunkenness. This last is the chief cause of mortality. One great means of preventing sickness would be, to make it imperative for all trading-vessels to employ a certain number of natives, as is done on board men-of-war.

Mr. Becroft (a merchant who resided for a number of years at Fernando Po) went up the Niger in the Quorra steam-boat, on a trading voyage, in 1836 ; his expedition lasted three months. He had with him a crew of forty persons, including five white men. Only one individual died, a white man, who was previously far gone in consumption.

property, and that products of industry find a ready market, and command a supply of European articles which the natives covet, an impulse will, no doubt, be given to internal cultivation. But it is greatly to be desired, that this impulse should be as strong, and operate as speedily, as possible. What we want is, to supplant the Slave Trade by another trade, which shall be more lucrative. We cannot expect that savage nations will be greatly influenced by the promise of prospective advantage. The rise of the legitimate trade ought, if we are to carry the good-will of the natives along with us, to follow as close as possible upon the downfall of the trade in man : there ought to be an immediate substitute for the gains which are to cease. In short, the natives must be assisted, and by every method in our power put in the way of producing those things which will bear a value in the market of the world. It is impossible that we can be in error in assuming that Africa, under cultivation, will make more from her exports than she now receives from the sale of her population.

There is no danger that the experiment will fail, if time enough is allowed for the full development of its results : but there is very considerable risk that the experiment while advancing to maturity will fail, from the impatience of a barbarous people, who are not in the habit of contemplating distant results, and who, finding themselves stripped of one species of customary trade, have not as-yet been remunerated by the acquisition of a better source of revenue. For this reason, I have already suggested that we should, for a time, subsidize the chiefs of Africa, whose assistance we require; and, for the same reason, I now propose that we should give all natural, and even some artificial stimulants to agricultural industry.

If at the moment when the African population find themselves in unaccustomed security, and feel, for the first time, a certainty of reaping what they sow; when they see their river, which has hitherto been worse than useless to the bulk of the people— (for it has brought on its waves only an armed banditti, and carried away from their smouldering villages only that banditti exulting in their captured prey)— transformed into the cheapest, the safest, and the most convenient highway between themselves, and the civilized world, and discover it to be the choicest blessing which nature has bestowed upon them; if at the moment when a market is brought to their doors, and foreign merchants are at hand, ready to exchange for their productions the alluring articles of European manufacture, of which, sparingly as they have hitherto tasted, they know the rare beauty, and surpassing usefulness,—if at this moment, when so many specific and powerful motives invite them to the diligent cultivation of their soil, they are visited by a band of agricultural instructors, who offer at once to put them in possession of that skill in husbandry which the rest of the world has acquired, and they are enabled to till their ground in security, and find opened to them a conveyance for its productions, and a market for their sale ; and if simultaneously with these advantages we furnish that practical knowledge, and those mechanical contrivances which the experience of ages, and the ingenuity of successive generations, have by slow degrees disclosed to ourselves—I cannot doubt that those combined benefits and discoveries will furnish an immediate, as well as an ample compensation for the loss of that wicked traffic, which, if it has afforded profit to the few, has exposed the great mass of the inhabitants to unutterable wretchedness.

CHAPTER IV.

RESULTS OF EXPERIENCE.

AFRICA, it is true, is in great measure untried
ground, yet there is some information to be derived
from the history of those colonies, few and imperfect
though they be, which have been attempted along her
coasts. There are also important hints to be found
in the recorded opinions (many of them drawn from
actual experiment) of those who are best acquainted
with the subject, whether government officers, travellers, or others. It may now be convenient to turn
our attention to the colonies which already belong
to us in Africa : in the history of them there is much
to confirm my views. I extract the following passage
from a paper written by Mr. Bandinel, dated Foreign
Office, March 30, 1839 :—

" So long ago as in 1792, the colony of Sierra
Leone was founded by benevolent individuals, for the
express purpose of inducing the natives to abandon
the traffic. The course taken was two-fold :—the
one, to educate the natives, with the view of teaching
them to give up the Slave Trade, on a religious principle ; the other, to substitute for that trade a more
legitimate commerce.

" The accounts, soon after the settlement was
formed, stated, that the natives crowded round the
colony both for education and for trade ; and that the

beneficial effect on them, in inducing them to quit Slave-trading, was instantaneous. That effect has been continued, and has extended, in the neighbour- hood of Sierra Leone, to a very considerable distance round the colony. Traders bring down the ivory, the gold-dust, and palm-oil, as usual. Of late years, a very important branch has been added to the legal trade, by the cutting of timber for the British navy; and the minds of the natives are thus effectually di- verted from the baneful occupation of the Slave Trade, to the pursuits of legitimate commerce."

I admit, that Sierra Leone has failed to realize all the expectations which were at one time indulged. It must, I fear, be confessed, that the situation was ill-chosen,—the north-west wind blows on it from the Bulloom shore, covered with mangrove-swamps, which generate the most destructive malaria. The district is small, by no means affording space for a fair experiment of our system. Nor is the land of the peninsula well suited for the growth of tropical productions; and there is wanting that, without which we can hardly expect to see commerce spring up and thrive in a barbarous country,—a river navigable far into the interior. Besides these natural difficulties, there have been some, arising from the system which we have adopted, or " rather," in the words of one of the strongest advocates in favour of Sierra Leone, " in the want of anything like system or preconcerted plan in the administration of its government . . . the whole of its administration, with the exception of its judicial system, was left to the chapter of accidents. No instructions were sent from home ; every governor was left to follow the suggestions of his own mind, both as regarded the disposal and treatment of the liberated Africans, and the general interests of the colony. . . . . . Every governor has been left to follow his own plans, however crude and undigested ; and no two succeeding governors have ever pursued the same course. This remark applies more particularly to the management of the liberated Africans."

I find this view confirmed in the third Resolution of the Report of the Select Committee on the State of Sierra Leone, 1830, which runs thus :—" It is the opinion of this Committee, that the progress of the liberated Africans in moral and industrious habits has been greatly retarded by the frequent change of system in their location and maintenance, and by the yearly influx of thousands of their rude and uncivilized countrymen."

This resolution notices another peculiarity in the case of Sierra Leone, which ought always to be borne in mind when it is brought forward as an instance of what may be done in African colonies. This peculiarity consists in the nature of its population, " a heterogeneous mass," but mainly composed of the surviving cargoes of captured slave-ships,—men who have undergone a great shock,—uprooted beings,—compelled colonists of a strange land. In addition to this original disadvantage, there have undoubtedly been great errors and omissions in the management of them. According to Colonel Denham, superintendant of that department, there has been " the want of instruction, capital, and example ;" yet he adds, " with the very little they have had of either, conveyed in a manner likely to benefit them generally, it is to me daily an increasing subject of astonishment, that the liberated Africans settled here have done so much for themselves as they have."

Sierra Leone has unquestionably laboured under very great disadvantages.*   But, with all its defects, if anything has anywhere been done for the benefit of Western Africa, it has been there. The only glimmer of civilization; the only attempt at legitimate commerce ; the only prosecution, however faint, of agriculture, are to be found at Sierra Leone, and at some of those settlements which I have just named. And there alone the Slave Trade has been in any degree arrested. We may regret, therefore, that the experiment was not tried under more favourable circumstances, on a more healthy spot, on a more

---

* I have compared various and conflicting accounts of Sierra Leone ; the Reports of the Company, and of the African Institution ; the able Reports of Colonel Denham on the Liberated Africans, and other Government Despatches ; the Statements of Mr. M'Queen, and the Reply of Mr. Kenneth Macaulay ; and the Evidence before both the Aborigines Committees, and that on the state of Sierra Leone, together with several private letters of authority ; and I believe my statements will all be found accurate, though my authorities are too voluminous, and too varied, to quote or extract at length.

fertile and suitable soil, on a larger scale, less exposed to the inroads of the slave-trader, and in the vicinity of one of the great arteries of Africa. Still, experience speaks strongly in its favour, because many thousands of human beings, taken from the holds of slave-ships, and placed there in the rudest state of barbarism, have made considerable advances in civilization,* because thousands of Negro children have re-

---

* Captain Ramsay told me that he had been particularly struck with the intelligent conversation and refined manners of a person in whose company he dined at Fernando Po, and whom he thought capable of filling almost any situation. Had it not been for his complexion, he would have supposed that he had been educated in England. This man was brought thither, not many years before, in the hold of a slave-ship. Mr. H. W. Macaulay, Commissary Judge at Sierra Leone, stated before a Parliamentary Committee, in 1837, that a large portion of these people, brought, as they have been, to the " colony in a savage state," landed, as he has seen many thousands of them, in a diseased and wretched condition, yet become civilized and useful members of society. He states, that these men form the militia : they serve not only as constables and attendants on the Courts of Justice, but also as jurymen ; and they discharge this duty so satisfactorily, that Mr. Macaulay further states, that, having himself had questions of large amount before them, he should at all times be willing to abide by their verdict. In speaking of the advancement to which these people have attained, he says : " There are many such instances of liberated Africans : one in particular, which I recollect, where a man, who not very long since was in the hold of a slave-ship, is acquiring at present an income of, I suppose, from 1,200l. to 1,500l. a-year. He has the government contracts for the supply of beef to the army and navy, and has had them for many years past, and he has always fulfilled his contracts to the satisfaction of

ceived and are receiving the rudiments of Christian education, and because a trade has there taken root, in itself inconsiderable enough, it is true, but yet, *one-third of the whole legitimate trade* of Central Africa. The very fact, that so large a proportion of African commerce has taken refuge, as it were, in a spot so inconvenient, while none is found on that mighty river which flows from the centre of Africa into the Atlantic, is in itself, to my apprehension, an unanswerable and authoritative proof, that, could the system of protection and instruction be tried on right principles, and upon a large scale, we need not despair of witnessing a great and glorious change in the condition of that continent.

Since the above remarks were written, I have received a letter from Mr. Ferguson, a gentleman of great intelligence and experience, who was originally sent out to Sierra Leone under the auspices of the African Institution, and is now, and has been for the last eight years, at the head of the medical department there. The document is so interesting, and so highly important, that I have ventured to quote it at considerable length; not, however, without having, in parts, curtailed the original paper, as it respects a few facts and statements of minor importance :—

" Having resided at Sierra Leone during a period of seventeen years, and had many opportunities of

the Government. He is living in a very excellent house; has every comfort about him; and has educated two of his children in England."

intercourse with the nations in the neighbourhood of that colony, my views of the practicability of the measures you contemplate have reference chiefly to the Windward Coast, and in a more especial manner to the colony of Sierra Leone, and to the nations immediately adjacent.

"Though the friends of Sierra Leone have long ceased to look for, or to expect any great advantage to the cause of African civilization from that quarter, I entertain a rather confident hope of being able to show that the cause is by no means so hopeless as it is generally supposed to be; but on the contrary, that it is precisely in that quarter, and in its neighbourhood, and at the present time, that the objects you contemplate are likely to be most speedily, and for some years at least, most extensively accomplished.

" Much money as well as much parental care and encouragement were lavished on the infant colony of Sierra Leone; but matters were so mismanaged in the outset of the undertaking, especially in the breach of faith with the Nova Scotian settlers, refusing to allot to them the quantities of land for which they had previously stipulated, that distrust and discontent, neglect of agriculture, and inveterate habits of idleness, became general.

" After a lapse of some years, an accession was made to the colony of numbers, but by no means of moral strength, in a body of Maroons, who were sent from Jamaica after the Maroon war. They had been for many years the only body of free blacks in

the island of Jamaica.   Indolent, and averse to
agriculture in their native land, their habits were by
no means changed by the transatlantic voyage, nor
have they, in fact, studied to acquire habits of industry
until this day.   Thus agriculture and the useful arts
received no aid whatever from such elements as the
Sierra Leone Company had as yet employed in
furtherance of their benevolent designs.

" The abolition of the Slave Trade by Great
Britain, and its subsequently declared illegality,
under certain circumstances, by the governments of
Spain and Portugal, and the consequent capture of
vessels taken in the prosecution of the illicit trade,
introduced, in the body of liberated Africans, a third
element in the population of the colony, and it is to
the working of that third element—what it has
already done, is doing, and what may be prospectively
and reasonably expected from it, that I desire especially to direct your attention.

" The condition of a body of captured slaves on
their arrival at Sierra Leone for liberation, is the
most miserable and wretched that can be conceived—
emaciated, squalid, sickly-looking, ill-fed, barbarous,
confined in inadequate space, compelled to breathe an
atmosphere hardly fit for the sustenance of animal
life—is it to be wondered, that, in such circumstances,
the faculties of the soul should be cramped and
benumbed by the cruelties inflicted upon the body?
It is nevertheless from among such people and their
descendants at Sierra Leone, their minds at length

elevated by a sense of personal freedom, and by the
temperate administration of just and equitable laws,
that you are to look for the first practical results of
your operations. It is not my intention to trace the
progress of the liberated Africans from the depths of
misery alluded to, until we find them, after the lapse
of fifteen or twenty years, independent and respectable members of society, but to give you some notion
of them as a class, and of the position in society
which they occupy at the present day.

" Those most recently arrived are to be found
occupying mud houses and small patches of ground
in the neighbourhood of one or other of the villages,
which are about twenty in number. The majority of
these remain in their location as agriculturists ; but
several go to reside in the neighbourhood of Freetown as labourers, farm servants, servants to carry
wood and water, grooms, house servants, &c. Others
cultivate vegetables, rear poultry and pigs, or offer
for sale a variety of edible substances. They are a
harmless and well disposed people ; there is no
poverty nor begging amongst them ; their habits are
frugal and industrious, and their anxiety to possess
money remarkable.

" Persons of a grade higher than those just described are to be found occupying frame houses, and
are mostly employed either in carrying on small
trades in the market, in buying and retailing the
cargoes of native canoes, in curing and drying fish,
or in working at various mechanical trades. Re-

spectable men of this grade meet with ready mercantile credits, amounting from £20 to £60; and the class is very numerous.

" Those who have advanced another step are found in frame houses, reared on a stone foundation, of from six to ten feet in height. These houses are very comfortable; a considerable quantity of furniture of European workmanship, and of books, chiefly of a religious character, is to be found in them, and an air of domestic comfort pervading the whole. Persons of this class are nearly altogether occupied in shopkeeping, and may be seen clubbing together in numbers from three to six, seven, or more, to purchase large lots or unbroken bales; and the scrupulous honesty with which the subdivision of the goods is afterwards made, cannot be evidenced more thoroughly than in this, that, common as such transactions are, they have never yet been known to become the subject of controversy or litigation. The principal streets of Freetown, as well as the approaches to the town, are lined on each side by an almost continuous range of booths and stalls, among which almost every article of merchandise is offered for sale. They are all in easy circumstances, and are invariably anxious to possess houses and lands of their own, especially in Old Freetown. Property of this description has of late years become much enhanced, and is still increasing in value, solely from their annually increasing numbers and prosperity.

" Persons of the highest grade of liberated Africans

occupy comfortable two-story stone houses, inclosed all round with spacious piazzas. These houses are their own property, and are built from the proceeds of their own industry. In several of them are to be seen mahogany chairs, tables, sofas, and four-post bedsteads, pier glasses, floor cloths, and other articles indicative of domestic comfort and accumulating wealth. They are almost wholly engaged in mercantile pursuits, and are to be found in neatly fitted-up shops on the ground-floor of their respective dwelling-houses. Many of them have realized considerable sums of money. Peter Newland, a liberated African, died a short time before I left the colony, and his estate realized, in houses, merchandise, and cash, upwards of £1,500. I am well acquainted with one of these individuals, whose name, shortly before my departure from the colony, stood on the debtor side of the books of one of the principal merchants for £1,900, to which sum it had been reduced from £3,000 during the preceding two months. Many of them at the present moment have their children being educated in England at their own expense.

" There is at Sierra Leone a very fine regiment of colonial militia, more than eight-tenths of which are liberated Africans. The amount of property which they have acquired is ample guarantee for their loyalty, should that ever be called in question. They turn out with great alacrity and cheerfulness on all occasions for periodical drill. They also serve on juries; and I have repeatedly heard the highest legal autho-

rity in the colony express his satisfaction with thei.
decisions.

" From the preceding details it may be inferred,
that a leading feature in the character of the liberated
Africans is their great love of money. But this,
though remarkable, is by no means of that sordid
nature which induces the miser to hoard up his wealth
for its own sake. On the contrary, their whole
surplus means are devoted to the increase of their
domestic comforts and the improvement of their outward appearance of respectability A comfortable
house is the first great object of their desire. For
this they are content to labour at any sort of work,
and turn themselves diligently and cheerfully to any
honest means of earning money. The working hours
are from six in the morning till four in the afternoon,
with one hour of interval for breakfast. Labour is
to be had in abundance at 4*d*. per diem. Very needy
persons may sometimes be found who will work for
3½*d*. A good overseer or headsman may be had at
5*d*. per diem, or 13*s*. per month.

" Of the liberated Africans as a body, it may with
great truth be said that there is not a more quiet,
inoffensive, and good humoured population on the
face of the earth. Of their religious spirit it is not
easy, from the very nature of the subject, to form a
decided opinion, but I know that their outward obser-
vance of the Sabbath-day is most exemplary. On
that day the passion for amusements is altogether laid
aside, and the whole body of the people are to be

found at one or other of the churches or chapels, which abound in the colony.

" It may be presumed, from what has been said of their love of gain, that in their habits and desires they are decidedly industrious. But, however successful, from the abundance of European example, they may have been in the application of their energies and industry to pursuits of a mercantile nature, it is to be regretted that no similar example in the department of agriculture has as yet been placed before them. Were such example afforded in the culture of such articles as would at all times meet with a ready purchaser, I am warranted in averring, with much confidence, that energies similar to those which (as we have already seen) have been so zealously and successfully directed to trade, would promptly, and with equal zeal, be found engaged in agriculture. In 1826 Mr. Clouston, a respectable merchant of Freetown, planted a small quantity of ginger by way of experiment, and having reported favourably of it, its culture was immediately taken up by a vast body of liberated Africans. Ignorance was, however, displayed at every step of their progress. They planted indiscriminately in sterile and in rich soils, so that the sample produced was a mixture of plump and meagre roots. By some the sample was dried previously to being offered for sale, by others not; by some it was carefully cleaned, which others neglected; so that the merchants became averse to purchase it, and the growers saw their hopes blighted. In 1829 their attention was turned to the culture of capsicum, by the sale of a lot at Freetown, which fetched 2*s*. 6*d*. per pound. It would have been difficult at that time to have collected two tons of pepper in the colony, but in the course of a very few years individual merchants were found exporting 100 and 150 tons per annum. The price however, fell to 4*d*. per pound; sales could not even then be effected; and the hopes of the cultivators were again disappointed. In 1833 their expectations were similarly raised and blighted by the encouragement held out for the manufacture of cassada starch. Instances might be multiplied, but I think those just noted are sufficient to show that the liberated Africans are not only willing but desirous that their attention should be directed to the culture of such articles as will afford them a certain return for their labour and industry; and that the position at which they have arrived in the social state is precisely that to which the labours of philanthropists may be applied satisfactorily to themselves, and with a certain prospect of advantage to that interesting people.

" Among other circumstances indicative of the improvement of their worldly means, and of their desire still further to avail themselves of European example, none stands more prominently forward than the system which they have lately commenced of sending their children to England for education. Thirty years ago a few liberated African boys were sent to England and educated at the expense of the

African Institution, with a view to their aid in working out the general objects of the Institution at Sierra Leone. These boys, on their return to the colony, with one exception, speedily fell back on the barbarous habits of their youth, and their public utility fell far short of the expectations of their patrons. We now, however, behold under different auspices the same class of persons considerably advanced in wealth and civilization, desiring European education for their children of their own accord, without advice or pecuniary aid from others, and moved thereto solely by a conviction of its intrinsic excellence. There are now, however, but few outlets for the employment of educated young men in the colony; and it appears clear that the quantity of talent of this description which will become available will in a short time far exceed the means of employment. The present is therefore precisely the time for the friends of African civilization to adopt such measures as may appear best calculated to secure the effectual co-operation of the new element which is about to be placed before them.

" Several articles of tropical agriculture have been from time to time tried at Sierra Leone on a small scale, and the experiments have been generally successful. The most decided, as well as the most carefully performed and most successful of these, was the introduction, a few years ago, by some of the gentlemen of the Church Missionary Society, of some of the seeds of the Sea-island cotton. I have stated above, that were examples in agriculture offered as liberally as they have been in trade, the former would be followed up by the liberated Africans with as much diligence and zeal as they have been found to have devoted to the latter. It would, however, be important, in conducting such an experiment, that their attention should, in the first instance, be directed to such articles as in their culture require the smallest outlay of money, the shortest time to bring them to maturity, and a sure sale whenever and in whatever quantity they may be brought to market.

" No article seems to afford these requisites with such a prospect of certainty as cotton; and a normal farm of 100 acres, for the culture of that article, in the south-eastern part of the colony, would, I am well assured, be followed within two years by a general rush of the whole agricultural population towards its production. The actual sight of a considerable quantity grown in the colony, offered for sale, and immediately purchased, would render any further experimental effort in regard to that article useless; except, indeed, in respect of the best kind of seed to be used, and the most approved mode of culture.

" But this is, perhaps, the smallest amount of benefit that would ensue. The natives of the countries in the immediate vicinity of Sierra Leone take a large quantity of British manufactures in return for African teak, the cutting and squaring of which is nearly altogether performed by slave labour. The

sort of traffic to which it has given rise, has, nevertheless, so clearly demonstrated to the native chiefs
how much more advantageous it is to work their
slaves than to sell them, that Slave Trading (I mean
the selling of slaves) in the countries adjacent to
Sierra Leone has nearly altogether ceased. In
some of these countries the timber is now obtained
with much more difficulty than formerly, owing to
the greater distance from the water-side at which
it has to be procured. Should this difficulty increase to such a length as to render the cutting of
timber no longer profitable, the hands left unem-
ployed in such a case would, in the culture of cotton, find ample means of profitable employment; and
by this means the continuance and permanence of
the first great step in African civilization would, to
the inhabitants of those countries, be secured. I fear
that these people are not yet so far removed from
the recollections of a flourishing Slave Trade as to
render its abandonment by them the result of sound
principle, or of a conviction of its cruelty. The continuance of the legitimate trade on which they have
already so successfully entered, may, however, in the
hands of another generation, establish its final abandonment on more reputable motives. Meantime, in
the cutting of timber, and in the growth of rice, we
have undoubted proofs of their industry, and of their
willingness, by bodily labour, to obtain what they may
require of European manufactures.

" I trust that in this sketch of the liberated

Africans, of the progress which they have already made, and of the efforts which they are still making, towards civilization, you will find not only sufficient encouragement to induce you to devote towards the colony of Sierra Leone a portion of your fostering care ; but also that you will perceive that the present is the time when instruction and encouragement, especially in the practice of agriculture, afford a fairer prospect of being crowned with success, than at any other period in the previous history or condition of the colony.

" I have a moral certainty that the advances which they have already made in knowledge and in wealth cannot possibly be arrested at the present stage, and that an impulse has been given to the onward course of improvement, the limit of which, in respect to them, is not yet in sight.　But however certain their future progress may be in the course on which they have so auspiciously entered, it is clear that that progress might be accelerated tenfold, were there, in well conducted examples, and in competent instruction, as it were a beacon held out to them, teaching them alike what to avoid and what to cling to, as well in the mode of culture, as in the article to be cultivated.

" There are places on the Windward Coast of Western Africa, other than Sierra Leone, which I think would repay any care that might be bestowed on them, in the way of agricultural instruction and example ; and, perhaps, none will be found better calculated for its application than the settlements on the river Gambia. The soil is rich, and more easily brought under culture than even that of Sierra Leone; ground nuts and corn are grown there; and cotton, also, in a considerable quantity, and of a texture which, as I have been informed by respectable merchants, equals much that is brought from the West Indies and South America, although their mode of preparing it is inferior. At the extensive Government farm near Bathurst, which is worked by liberated Africans, such quantities of ground nuts and corn are raised, as far more than pay all the expenses of management; and were example and the necessary instruction afforded, the culture of cotton might there be substituted with great advantage, and at no additional expense.

" Keeping steadily in sight your principle of substituting a harmless and profitable trade for one that is illegal and worse than profitless, I am also desirous of directing your attention to what has been going on during the last year or two in the Rio Nunez. This river, though now little spoken of, was in former years notorious for Slave Trading.

" At Kaikandy, the chief trading place, situated about 100 miles from the sea, and in the country of the Landemas, numerous factories, occupied by French and English traders, are established; to which Foulahs, Seracoolies, Bambarras, and people of other nations, resort in great numbers. I spent some time there in February last, and was assured

by the merchants that the Foulahs were gradually
weaning themselves from the Slave Trade, and that
they had of late years brought down a much larger
quantity of native produce than formerly; an assurance which was confirmed as well by the number of
English and French merchants established there in
the prosecution of legitimate commerce, as by the
single slave-trader, Señor Caravalho, a Portuguese.

" About three years ago, some of the Foulah
traders who resort to Kaikandy, brought down small
parcels of coffee, and offered them for sale. The
coffee was so eagerly purchased by the European
merchants, that the Foulahs immediately turned their
attention to the further supply of it. It appears that
there are vast forests of indigenous coffee in the Foulah
country, and of much finer quality than that of the
West Indies or South America. The Foulahs evince
great satisfaction in the possession of such an unexpected source of wealth, and the quantity supplied
has of course greatly increased; but, unfortunately,
this infant trade, at the very dawning of its existence,
is threatened with destruction; it being found that
the protective duty for British plantation was so high
as to prove tantamount to a total exclusion of the
Foulah coffee, the duty on the former being 6*d*., and
on the latter 1*s*. 3*d*., per pound. The merchants at
Kaikandy have, nevertheless, continued to purchase
the coffee, in whatever quantities it has been offered,

in the hope that the British Government may yet be disposed to relieve them of their difficulties.

"But the most grievous part of the disappointment is, that it would be difficult to devise any mode calculated more powerfully and effectually to disenthral the people from the desire of kidnapping and selling each other, than the admission of the Foulah coffee into the ports of Great Britain on terms similar to those of British plantation.

"You will perceive from this detail, that the Foulahs, without any extrinsic aid, have already done much in furthering the object you have at heart; that they want assistance; that the present is the time at which that assistance may most effectually be applied; and also the nature of the assistance required.

"The Foulahs are an intelligent people, and are very anxious to extend their commercial dealings with the British. They seem to have already perceived that it is more profitable for them to preserve the element of labour in their own country, than to deprive themselves of its assistance by selling each other to strangers; so that it may be said, without a metaphor, that in every hundred-weight of coffee which they collect and take to Kaikandy, at least one human being is preserved from slavery.

"An instance illustrative of their desire to preserve and extend their commercial relations with the British occurred a few months ago. A temporary

interruption was thrown in the way of both the export
and import trade of the river (Nunez), by certain
dissensions among the tributary chiefs, the continuance of which was likely to prove highly detrimental
to the interests of the British and other merchants
established at Kaikandy. Lieutenant Hill, of her
Majesty's brig Saracen, on being made acquainted
with the danger to which British property was exposed, very promptly set sail for the Rio Nunez for
its protection. On his arrival there, a grand palaver
was called, for the purposes of investigating the
causes of this disturbance, and of restoring tranquillity. The conference which ensued was presided over
by a Foulah chief, who appeared to be established at
Kaikandy in an official character, and to be clothed
with functions (as the event showed) of a nature more
full and extensive than those of a mere consul or
chargé d'affaires.

" It appeared by the majority of voices, and by an
almost unanimous concurrence of opinion, that the
cause and continuance of the disturbances were attri-
butable to the intrigues of a Mandingo named Boi
Modao.

" The Foulah chief addressed himself to Lieut.
Hill, in a speech explanatory of the great anxiety of
the Foulah king to maintain and to extend commercial intercourse with the British, and his determina-
tion to put down and remove any obstacle to its continuance that should arise ; and to satisfy Lieut. Hill

of the sincerity of his professions, he offered then and there to decapitate Boi Modao, and thus at once restore trade to its usual channels. Lieut. Hill, of course, declined a proof of sincerity so unequivocal and convincing.

" The conference was no sooner at an end than Boi Modao, with marks of great haste and much alarm, fled from that part of the country, and trade was carried on as usual."

We now proceed to the further consideration of the Gambia. " In the year 1814," says Mr. Bandinel, " a colony was formed at St. Mary's, on the river Gambia, by British settlers, who removed from the coasts of Senegal, when it was restored to the French. This colony has increased and flourished beyond all reasonable calculation, and is already more powerful and wealthy than any of those elder settlements of the British in Africa, which were formed for the purpose of promoting the Slave Trade.

" The beneficial effects of the settlement of St. Mary's, on all the tribes along the banks of the Gambia, are perhaps still more prominent than those which have taken place round Sierra Leone."

"The Gambia was formerly a great mart for slaves. The population along its banks are now eager for lawful commerce, in which alone they are now engaged. The trade is extended above 400 miles up the river; a new and lucrative branch has also been lately opened there in gum; and the only exception to the cheering picture occurs in the French establishment at Albreda, where still some slaves are said to be harboured, obtained from natives in the interior, and sent overland afterwards to Goree."

The Slave Trade is, however, so small and so declining at Albreda, that the exception may be almost said to prove the rule ; because it shows, that though an European establishment exists, ready to trade in slaves, it does not flourish against the rivalry of a legal commerce.

In the year 1833, a mission, in connexion with the Wesleyan Society, was established at Macarthy's Island on the Gambia, with the view of promoting the civilization of the neighbouring tribes of Foulahs through the medium of Christianity. To the missionaries connected with this establishment I am indebted for much valuable information respecting the present state of Western Africa. The Rev. R. M. Macbrair, in a M.S. statement with which he has favoured me, ascribes the abolition of the Slave Trade in the neighbourhood of the Gambia to two causes ; first, to the vicinity of the British colony, and its command over the river ; and, secondly, to the existence of a good market for the produce of the soil. The change effected by these circumstances Mr. Macbrair thus describes :—" Culture is more practised in the neighbourhood of the Gambia, where affairs are now comparatively peaceful. Before the abolition of the Slave Trade, there were considerable factories here; and one native merchant, now at St. Mary's, was sold no less than three times by another, who resides in the same place. One of the kings also, is said to have "seized and disposed of some of his subjects whenever he wanted a horse, a wife, or other purchasable commodity." But now that the slave-market is abolished, and the natives can find a ready market for the produce of their lands by means of the British merchants, the cultivation of the soil increases every year; and the Aborigines have been heard to say, that they now wish they had their slaves back again, because they could get more by their labours in husbandry, than they did by selling them to Europeans."

Mr. Finden, who has been a resident merchant on the Gambia for the last 17 years, says, in a letter to me, dated 4th May, 1838—"Prior to the formation of the settlement, the trade consisted almost wholly in slaves; and vessels, fitted out for the purpose, proceeded up the river about 300 miles. Since that period, I can state from correct information, and my own knowledge, that no slaves have been exported in any vessel from the Gambia; and in lieu of this horrible traffic, a valuable and legitimate commerce has been established there, which by encouragement might be considerably increased and rendered most valuable to the mother country.' "This," he thinks, "might be effected by extending protection, at least as high up the river as it is navigable in the dry season. I should consider

Fattatenda* and Kantally Coonda the most desirable spots. By this means, greater quantities of our exports could be thrown into the country, and trade drawn from a much greater distance, and we should thus be enabled, in a great measure, to check the slave-traders who pass these places on their way to the different leeward slave-depôts. An armed steam-vessel would be of great service, and would afford a protection to trading vessels and factories established on the banks of the river, which are at present rendered unsafe by the depredations committed by marauding chiefs."

These views are fully concurred in by the Rev. John Morgan, to whose zeal the Foulah mission partly owes its origin. He recommends the purchase of tracts of land adjoining the principal rivers which flow into the Atlantic, in which the natives might find security from the predatory incursions of the chiefs, and from the cupidity of the slave-trader; and he likewise suggests the employment of an armed steam-vessel attached to each settlement. He says, " I am convinced that thousands would flee to such places of refuge, as soon as they could be assured of protection, and thus a dense free population would

* A considerable trade is already carried on at the port of Fattatenda, beyond which merchant-vessels do not proceed. The Rev. W. Fox, who visited it in 1837, describes it as " the resort of caravans from the interior;" and consequently a considerable concourse of people is invariably attracted thither in the pursuit of commerce.

soon spring up, and agriculture and commerce would rapidly extend. These settlements might soon be rendered capable of defending themselves, and a great saving of European life would be immediately effected, as the interior of the country is far more salubrious than the coast."

Here I must again express my regret that the usefulness of our principal African settlements should have been impaired by an injudicious selection of localities, and by a too contracted scale of operations. The disadvantages with which they have had to contend are thus stated by Mr. Morgan:—" Being situated on the coast, those who most needed refuge could not reach them: secondly, they have ever been so small, that it was impossible for more than a small number to provide the means of subsistence on either of them: thirdly, in several cases, protection has not been offered to those who have fled to them." To these causes, I think, it may be attributed that our success has been so limited, and that so little has been done towards the accomplishment of our main object.

We find, however, in the immediate neighbourhood of the Gambia, where the influence of the British flag is felt, the Slave Trade has been suppressed, and comparative tranquillity and security have been established. But we do not proceed far into the interior, before we meet with the same scenes of violence and rapine as before. In many cases, the slaves who were formerly brought to the mouth of the river, are now transported over land to other parts of the coast ; the depredations of the powerful chiefs still continue and have hitherto rendered abortive the attempts which have been made by the missionaries to establish native settlements on the main land, without the aid of British protection. These circumstances confirm me in the opinion which I have formed, in common with those who are best acquainted with the subject, that our settlements, in order to be effective, must be fixed in the interior, where the Slave Trade originates, and where our experiments can be tried at a less costly sacrifice of human life.

I cannot conclude my notice of this colony, without adverting to the success which has attended the labours of the missionaries, from whom I have so largely quoted. By the latest official returns of the establishments at St. Mary's and Macarthy's Islands, it appears, that there are " 559 members in church fellowship, with congregations amounting to more than double that number." The Mandingo language, which is generally used in that part of Western Africa, has been reduced to grammatical form, and translations of the gospels have been made. In the schools, which are partly conducted by native teachers, 220 are instructed in the elements of a plain education ; and the missionaries state that they are encouraged to persevere in their labours, by the increasing desire manifested by the people to obtain instruction. An interesting feature in this missionary enterprise is the experiment which is about to be made of following up the preaching of the gospel by instruction in the arts and pursuits of civilized life. The site of a native village has been selected in Macarthy's island, and 600 acres of land have been allotted by the British government, on which some of the Christian natives are already receiving elementary instruction in agriculture.

THE GOLD COAST.

Our settlement on the Gold Coast is another illustration of the advantage of stations in Africa. In this case, there are two unquestionable facts, —1st, That the Slave Trade did prevail in the district of the Gold Coast. 2ndly, That it has been entirely suppressed, and that a considerahle and increasing trade has sprung up in its place. To any one familiar with the earlier period of the Slave Trade controversy, it will not be necessary to say, that it was perpetually referred to, as the district which furnished by far the greater part of the slaves taken to the British colonies. We not only established forts there for the express purpose of encouraging that trade, but there seems to have been no difficulty in obtaining from parliament munificent grants for their maintenance—30,000l. was the annual sum thus applied.

" These establishments," says the governor of the colony, " constituted the great emporium whence the British West India colonies were supplied with slaves. Such being the case, and considering also

the vast number of slaves which were annually exported in order to meet the demands of so extensive a
market, we are fully warranted in affirming, that in
no part of Africa was the Slave Trade more firmly
rooted, or more systematically carried on, than in
these settlements."

What is now termed legitimate commerce was, previously to the passing of the Abolition Act, but little
thought of, and only attended to, so far as it was aux-
iliary to the grand object—the acquisition of slaves
" Daily accustomed to witness scenes of the most cold-
blooded cruelty, the inhabitants became utterly callous
to human suffering; each petty chieftain oppressed
and plundered his weaker neighbours, to be in his turn
plundered and oppressed by one stronger and more
powerful than himself. In no portion of Africa, in
short, was the demoralising, the brutalising influence
of the Slave Trade more fearfully displayed, than in
those extensive tracts of country which now form, or
are adjoining to, our settlements on the Gold Coast."

But, happily, this state of things no longer
exists. Within a few short years so complete a revolution has been effected, that, in the expressive
words of Governor M'Lean, " *from Apollonia to
Accra, not a single slave has been exported since
the year* 1830."

It becomes, then, highly interesting to ascertain
how, and by what means, the Slave Trade has been
eradicated from a portion of Africa, comprehending a
space which Governor M'Lean rates at 4000 square

miles inland, and a line of coast 180 miles in extent,
—where it had been planted, protected, fostered, and
munificently encouraged for centuries.

This great object has not been accomplished by our
naval squadrons. Her Majesty's cruisers have certainly been in the habit of visiting the settlement,
but only for the purpose of procuring supplies, and of
affording, if called upon, aid to the local authorities.
No cruiser (says the Governor) has ever, at least for
many years, been stationed off the Gold Coast for
the purpose of intercepting slaves.

This revolution has been effected by the very
agency which I desire to see tried on other parts of
the coast, and on a greater scale,—by the establishment
of a station, which, while it multiplies the difficulties and dangers of the slave-trader, will afford protection to the native in the cultivation of the soil, by
giving security to the trader, and opening a market
for the sale of the productions he rears. Crops have
been grown, and articles produced, and labour bestowed, because he who sowed knew that he should
reap, and he who laboured was no longer exposed to
the probability of seeing his acquisitions rifled, and
himself hunted after, by the marauders whom his prosperity had attracted.

It is not to be denied that there were great difficulties in the outset. The trade in man has its attractions
—it combines the hazard of the chase, with the name
and the profits of merchandize. It affords a field for the
exercise of skill—for the display of courage—for the

employment of stratagem—for the gratification of revenge. It calls forth all those martial passions, in which savages, and others than savages, conceive that all glory resides. To some, no doubt, it yielded wealth : a successful sally—a fortunate adventure—a sudden and daring surprise—rendered a profit larger than a month's labour would produce. It was, moreover, the inveterate custom of the country. The inhabitants knew the art of kidnapping, and knew no other art : there seemed to them no other way by which they could obtain those supplies of foreign manufacture and produce, which long habit had rendered necessaries of life.

These difficulties stood in the way of the effectual abolition of the Slave Trade : they were only to be overcome by proving to the natives experimentally that it was their interest to suppress it; in other words, that they would gain by the sale of their productions a larger amount of those foreign luxuries which they craved, than by the sale of man. It was therefore necessary to create some other species of traffic, whereby the native could procure his wonted supplies. This end could not have been effected without the aid of resident merchants and a local government : the one, to afford a perpetual and ready supply of the articles which the African required, and to urge him to provide the goods which would be taken in exchange ; the other, to protect legitimate commerce, and to redress, and, if needful, to punish the exportation of slaves.

The experiment has been successful. The difficulties and perils which, after the Abolition law, attached to the Slave Trade, called into existence various articles of commerce previously unknown. The soil, which formerly did not yield sufficient for the sustenance of the inhabitants, now exports a very large amount of corn to Madeira; and the natives, as we are expressly told by the governor, are better supplied with European and other merchandize than formerly, when it was the chief mart for slaves.

It does not diminish my satisfaction to know that this result was brought about by slow degrees. For many years after the Slave Trade was abolished by law, the conflict between lawful and unlawful trade continued. It was not likely that the natives would be weaned in a moment from the customs of their forefathers, or by anything short of a succession of experiments. But innocent commerce has at length fairly won the victory, and the last case which occurred is thus described. I quote it, because the narrative proves that prior to 1830, our influence had checked the Slave Trade; and because it incidentally shows, in an official form, the customary horrors of the traffic, which, as far as the Gold Coast extends, we have been so happy as to repress.

" In the month of January, 1830, the king of Apollonia, an ally, though not a dependent on the British government, despatched messengers to Cape Coast Castle, to intimate that a Spanish slaver had anchored off Apollonia fort, the captain of which asserted, that he had obtained the president's leave to purchase a cargo of slaves, and had already landed goods for that purpose; that he (the king of Apollonia) wished to ascertain whether there was any truth in the Spanish captain's assertion, as he should certainly furnish him with no slaves, without the full consent and permission of the president. The president, in reply to this message, highly commended the conduct of the king of Apollonia, as a reward for which he sent him a handsome present, at the same time strictly prohibiting him from exporting, or permitting to be exported, a single slave, and explaining to him the British laws on that subject.

"In the mean time, the king had contrived, by fair promises, to get into his possession the whole of the Spanish cargo of goods; and when his messengers returned from Cape Coast Castle, he flatly refused to deliver a single slave, or return the cargo. The Spanish captain managed, however, to get on board his vessel several of the king's family, and intimated to him, that, unless the slaves contracted for were furnished immediately, he would certainly carry them (the king's hostages) off the coast; whereupon the king, mustering his more immediate attendants and adherents, sallied out into the town, in the night time, and seizing all without distinction whom he could find, sent them, to the number of 360, on board

in irons, at daybreak, receiving in return the persons detained as hostages.

" Here were 360 free people, living in their own
houses, in perfect peace and apparent security, seized
without the shadow of pretext, by a rapacious and
remorseless tyrant, whom they had been taught to
look up to as their father and protector.   One of
them, a Mulatto girl, about sixteen or seventeen years
of age, was afterwards redeemed, and she described
the consternation and horror of the poor people,
when they found themselves ironed in the slaver's
hold."

In a letter which I received from Governor
M'Lean, dated 28th September, 1838, he again ad-
verts to the formerly disordered state of the colony,
which he thus contrasts with its present condition :—
" In 1830, all communication with Ashantee, and
through it with the interior, had been entirely stopped
for 10 years previously ; and the only trade done
was for what gold and ivory could be procured in the
districts adjoining the coast.   The whole country
was one scene of oppression, cruelty, and disorder ;
so much so, that a trader dared not go twenty miles
into the ' bush.'   At present our communication with
the interior is as free and safe as between England
and Scotland; single messengers can, and do, travel
from one end of the country to the other with perfect
safety; and no man can oppress another with impunity."   Such is the important change which a local

government, with but limited resources at its command, has been enabled to effect throughout this extensive territory, in the short period of eight years, and principally by means of a strict and impartial administration of justice. The natives, long used to the most cruel tyranny, warmly appreciate their present mild and equal system of government, and rely, with perfect confidence, upon the integrity of their rulers. The consequence is, the trade of the Gold Coast already repays more than twenty-fold the sum granted by Parliament for the support of the local establishment.* Its exports to Great Britain amount to 160,000l. per annum, forming one-fifth of the whole commerce of Africa; although the country is by no means so fertile as many other parts of that continent, and has not the advantage of navigable rivers.

It is also gratifying to find that, through the labours of the Wesleyan missionaries, Christianity is making considerable progress in this part of Africa. The Rev. T. B. Freeman, in a letter to the parent Society, dated 10th October, 1838, after describing in animated terms, the prosperous state of the mission, and the field which is now open for Christian enterprise, communicates the following interesting intelligence :—" I have received information, *viâ* Fernando Po, that several liberated Africans in the Island of Jamaica, who are members of our Society in the Kingston circuit, and who are natives of Cape

* United Service Journal, March, 1838.

Coast, Annamaboe, and Accra, and other places along the western coast of Africa which are under the British flag, are very anxious to return to their native land. But they are afraid of being again torn away from their homes, and exposed to all the horrors of slavery ; and, secondly, of being deprived of those Christian privileges which they now enjoy. Please to inform them that their fears are groundless ; that their persons and property will here be perfectly safe, and that several hundreds of their countrymen have embraced the truths of Christianity. They can also have employment as soon as they arrive here."

A striking contrast to the state of the Gold Coast is presented by the town of Wydah, situated on the Bight of Benin. This place is the residence of the notorious De Sousa, the slave-broker of the king of Dahomey, and it enjoys very little, if any, legitimate trade. The captain of a merchant-ship states, that he has seen there 28 slave vessels under Spanish and Brazilian colours. "These vessels," he observes, " would carry, on an average, 350 or 400 slaves each. On returning, ten months after, I have seen several of these vessels in the same roadstead, having in the interim completed a slavery voyage to Brazil and back."

To these portions of Africa, in particular, Great Britain owes a heavy debt of justice, for the many years of misery which she inflicted upon them by making them the seats of the Slave Trade ; a debt, which she can only hope to repay, by carrying out the salutary measures which have proved so successful in the case of the Gold Coast. But as the injury was not limited to these localities only, so her redress should not terminate there: in order that her compensation may be ample, and her remedy efficient, they must be applied nearer the sources of the evil.

Our efforts, as far as they have gone, have been successful, and although our principal object has not been attained by them, we have proved what may be effected, by granting our protection, by encouraging commerce and agriculture, and by diffusing the blessings of Christianity. By adopting a similar policy in positions more favourable, and in connexion with the other measures which I propose, I am led to believe we shall effectually check the Slave Trade, and produce a revolution in Africa, still more signal than that which has been already experienced in our present settlements.

It appears, then, that these three cases, Sierra Leone, Gambia, and the Gold Coast, as far as they go, illustrate and strengthen my views. When the errors which have been committed in their management shall be rectified,—when education and Christian instruction shall prevail, and when an effective impulse shall have been given to commerce and agriculture, we, seeing what has already been done, may reasonably hope that a salutary change will be effected in this unhappy continent.

A further confirmation of this hope is derived from the recorded observations of gentlemen, worthy of all confidence, who have collected their opinions on the spot,

Governor Macarthy, in addressing the merchants of St. Mary's on the Gambia in a visit he paid them in 1818, used the following words:—" I consider the extension of an honourable trade in Africa as benefiting a considerable portion of the human race. I anticipate with delight the period when, in lieu of the horrid traffic in human life, British trade and industry will spread, and the Christian religion prevailing over Africa, the inhabitants of this vast continent will, by their emancipation from moral and physical slavery, rank among civilized nations." *

General Turner, governor of Sierra Leone, appears to have been a man of vigorous and enlarged mind : had he lived, he would probably have done much for the suppression of the Slave Trade. His reports are the more interesting to me, because I find that his views, as to the mode of accomplishing that object, closely correspond with those which I have adopted. He appears to think that the abolition is to be effected by means of treaties with the native powers; by engaging them to lend their assistance ; by thus rooting out the Slave-trader from his usual field of exertion; and by the employment of steamers on the coast: above all, by the influence of legitimate commerce.

* Nineteenth Report of Church Missionary Society.

*Extracts from Despatches from Major-General
Turner, late Governor of Sierra Leone.*

Dated 20*th July*, 1825.

" The great increase of the Slave Trade in this
neighbourhood, together with the inadequacy of the
ships of war on the station, have caused me to turn
my attention seriously to the evil, as well as to the
remedy for it ; and whilst I admit the evil to exist
to a shameful extent, I am happy to say, that I will
undertake, at little or no expense, without the aid of
the navy, without compromising the government,
and without risk of failure, to complete in six months
such arrangements as will prevent any vessel, of any
nation, carrying away a cargo of slaves from Western
Africa ; and I pledge myself that the completion of
these measures will produce to Africa more peace and
good order, more industry, prosperity, and morality,
—and to England, a larger and better field for the
exercise of her benevolence.

*   *   *   *

" England should prevent the *collection of these
unhappy victims,* and bestow her care upon nations
with knowledge to appreciate, and character to retain
the advantage of an intercourse with her : that there
are such nations within our reach, and that they are
anxious to open a communication with us, is within
my knowledge ; and that I will accomplish all these
objects without much expense, if approved of, I pledge
myself.   If there should be any doubt, I should beg
that those who know me best may be referred to, whe-

ther I am likely to engage in wild, visionary schemes. Should such measures be approved of, all I want from England are two small steam-boats.

" These two boats, in addition to the one already ordered for the general work of this extended command, will be enough to occupy and maintain our sovereignty over the various rivers from Senegal to the Gold Coast—a sovereignty which I will procure from the natives, if approved of, at a small expense; and I will establish and maintain the British flag on them, which will cause them to be considered British waters, and give us the power to exclude all nations from them."

Dated 18*th October*, 1825.

" On approaching the Sherbro, I caused the king and chiefs of the maritime districts engaged in the war, to be assembled; and as they had already applied to me for protection against their enemies, I informed them that the only condition upon which I would grant them effectual security would be the giving up for ever the Slave Trade, making over to me for the King of England the sovereignty of their territories, acknowledging the laws of England, laying down their arms in the present war, and agreeing never to undertake any other without the consent of the government of Sierra Leone for the time being. They immediately agreed to these terms, and a treaty was accordingly signed and ratified, in presence of all the people.

*   *   *   *

" By this treaty, upwards of 100 miles of sea-coast

are added to this colony ; a circumstance which, in this
particular case, will tend greatly to increase its trade
and general prosperity.

* * * *

" As regards the Slave Trade the district now
ceded has, for many years back, been the theatre of
its most active operations in this or perhaps any
other part of the coast ; and the best information that
I can collect warrants my stating the number annually exported at not less than 15,000, all of whom
will in future be employed in cultivating the soil,
preparing and collecting articles of export, and improving their own condition.

* * * *

" The other parties engaged in the war, and who
are an inland people, I sent a messenger to, to desire
that they would no longer carry on the war, as I had
taken the country under my protection ; they expressed their willingness for peace, and some of the
principal men among them came down and begged to
be *taken under our protection*, which was done.   I
could not remain long enough in the Sherbro to receive the more distant ones ; but I make no doubt I
shall be able to bring about a general peace throughout these countries, and cause the kings and chiefs to
turn their attention to more humane and profitable
pursuits.

* * * *

" The affairs of this colony (Sierra Leone) are
taking a much wider range, and the valuable pro-

ducts of the interior are finding their way here in much larger proportion than formerly, and the influx of strangers from very distant nations is very great. The name and character of the colony are spreading rapidly, as is proved by the *repeated messengers sent to me from the rulers of distant nations,* and *the eagerness with which they seek our friendship and alliance.* Our influence and authority ·with the smaller states immediately around are getting greater, and the beneficial results very visible. * * * *
" The most powerful of them, the king of the Mandingoes, has placed himself under our orders."

Dated 1st November, 1825.

" I have just received from chiefs to the northward of this colony, an offer to give us the sovereignty of their country, and to abolish for ever the Slave Trade, receiving, in return, our protection and the benefits of a free trade with us."

Dated 20th December, 1825.

Reports the success of his expedition up the rivers Rokell and Port Logo, which, by their junction, form the river and harbour of Sierra Leone. The Rokell is the direct route to the countries round the source of the Niger.

* * * *

Having overcome the difficulties which had called for his active interference, General Turner entered into a Convention with the people, the substance of which I give in his own words :—
"The Convention, in the first place, puts an effec-

tive stop to all slave-trading, to internal wars, a
scourge more baneful to Africa than the Slave Trade
itself, and gives security and stability to persons and
property : it causes the chiefs and others to become
industrious, in order to procure, either by cultivation
or trade, those articles of luxury which they formerly acquired by the sale of slaves or plunder in
war; it will lead to civilization, morality, and a
desire of education and useful knowledge, by showing the advantage which educated men will have in
trade over uneducated ones; and the becoming provinces of this government will create a strong desire
to learn our language and religion.

"To us it will have the effect of greatly extending the sphere of our mercantile transactions, by
enabling agents and travellers to pass through the
country in security, of extending and improving our
geographical knowledge, of obtaining correct information of the power, wealth, and resources of each
nation, and thereby forming, in the course of time,
a large outlet for our manufactured goods, and of
receiving, in return, valuable raw materials, and of
spreading throughout distant nations impressions of
our wealth, influence, and greatness.   These facts
are already beginning to be felt, and the surrounding
countries generally, (with the exception of a few
factious chiefs who live by plundering travellers,)
aware of the advantage of being connected with
Sierra Leone, are petitioning this Government to
interfere to put an end to their wars, and to take

them under its protection. Your Lordship will observe, *that the public are put to no expense for the accomplishment of these objects ;* that there is no increase of our military establishments required.

*   *   *   *

" I would submit that a small yearly salary should be given to each native chief placed in charge of these provinces or districts, from 50*l.* to 100*l.* per year."

I have given these extracts at considerable length, because they are highly valuable, as showing, on the testimony of a person who had great experience, that the true way to suppress the Slave Trade, and to extricate Africa from its present abyss of misery, is to be found in friendly intercourse with the natives; in the encouragement of their legitimate trade ; in the cultivation of the soil, and in alliances with them for the suppression of the Slave traffic. Acting upon this system, he says, " I have little doubt but I shall have the honour, ere long, to announce to your Lordship the total abolition of the Slave Trade for 1000 miles around me, and a tenfold increase to the trade of this colony."

I may be permitted to relate the melancholy, but to me highly interesting termination of the career of this officer. In the early part of the spring of 1826, he proceeded to the Sherbro country, for the purpose of consolidating those arrangements for the abolition of the Slave Trade which he had entered into with the king and the native chiefs. On his

arrival at the Sherbro, he discovered, that the great
slave-traders, who had retired from that district on
the signing of the convention, prohibiting the exportation of slaves, had joined with those of the Gallinas,
and had come to the resolution of establishing the
Slave Trade by force, even in the districts where it
had been voluntarily given up by the native chiefs,
and were then assembled in force up the Boom river,
seizing our people, and putting at defiance our power
and our rights.

Upon this band of miscreants he made a successful attack, and he concludes his despatch on the 2nd
of March, 1826, by saying : " After carrying away
the guns and stores, and destroying by fire the town
and neighbourhood, we embarked, and got safely to
the shipping in the Sherbro on the 23rd, after destroying the two principal strongholds, with eight
smaller towns, where these wretches kept their
victims in chains, until the ships were ready to receive
them ; and I sincerely trust that this lesson will teach
the deluded of this country not to put further faith
in the vain boastings of these wicked people, who,
by administering to the worst passions of the ignorant and unfortunate inhabitants, *not only depopu-
late and turn into deserts the most fertile plains
which I have ever seen*, but so blunt their feelings,
and brutalize their natures, that, for a few bottles of
rum and heads of tobacco, the parent is found, without remorse, casting away his offspring ; each village
is engaged against the other, for the purpose of

making prisoners; and men, like beasts of prey, are ever on the watch to seize their neighbours and their fellow-men."

I received an account of this expedition from a gentleman who joined it as a volunteer. He spoke of the conduct of General Turner with admiration. Not content with heading the attack, and commanding the boats in the descent, he took with his own hands the soundings of every part of the river, and underwent more physical toil than the lowest of the crew. He paid the greatest attention to the health of all his party, and administered medicine to them upon the slightest symptom of incipient fever. The only point of which he was regardless was his own health; and to this imprudence he fell a victim. One of his officers ventured to remonstrate with him on the subject, and told him that he saw he was indisposed. The General replied, that nothing could touch his iron constitution; that he never had taken a dose of physic, and never would. On his arrival at Sierra Leone, he wrote with his own hands the despatch dated March 2nd, from which I have already made quotations. On the 3rd of March he begins a short letter to Lord Bathurst thus :—" I lament exceedingly that an attack of fever got up the Boom river should prevent my having the honour of submitting to your Lordship observations upon the bearings which the circumstances detailed in my despatch of the 2nd inst. have upon the state of this unhappy country, and the prospects which they hold out, for a great revolution in the affairs of the inhabitants." After adverting, in three lines to the expedition, he says :—" Although the bar of the Gallinas river is an extremely difficult and hazardous undertaking, I think that, by blockading them, and making a strong party there, I shall completely break up the Slave Trade, and stop for ever, from those shores, the export of near 30,000 slaves annually, substituting agriculture, security of person and property, industry, civilization, and knowledge of the Christian religion. At all events, if my health is restored, I will do my best."

According to my informant, he found the General at his desk, quite insensible, with his pen still in his hand, and this letter before him. It is well worth notice that, in his last words, he should have dwelt upon the extinction of the Slave Trade, by the substitution of agriculture, security of person and property, industry, civilization, and knowledge of the Christian religion.

The effect of General Turner's measures are thus described by his successor, in a despatch, dated 2nd of July, 1826 :—

" The measures adopted by General Turner have secured peace, safety, and tranquillity to a large extent of country, have destroyed an annual export of at least 15,000 slaves, and have prevented all the wretchedness, misery, and bloodshed which would otherwise have attended the making of these slaves.

*   *   *   *

" More real service has been performed by him towards the abolition of the Slave Trade, and that, too, permanently, *should his measures be followed up*, than by all the other means employed by His Majesty's Government for that purpose."

I cannot express how deeply I deplore that twelve years should have elapsed, in which little or nothing has been done by the Government in furtherance of views so sound, so enlightened, and so promising.

Colonel Nicholls, who was Governor of Fernando Po, during our occupation of that island, and who has had, perhaps, as much knowledge, derived from experience, as any man, of the nature of the Slave Trade, and of the most effectual modes of preventing it, in a memorial to Government in 1830, thus describes his general view :—

" There is one means, and I am persuaded but one effectual means, of destroying the Slave Trade, which is, by introducing a liberal and well-regulated system of commerce on the coast of Africa. At present, the African is led to depend principally on the slave-dealers for his supplies of manufactured articles, of which he is so fond, and stands so much in need. The individuals engaged in this traffic are persons of the most infamous and unprincipled description : they come in their ships to the mouths of the different unexplored rivers, where they land a quantity of trade goods of the worst kind, and leaving their supercargoes to exchange them with the chiefs for slaves, return to the sea whilst their cargoes are collecting, where, as pirates, they rob our merchant-ships, murder their crews, and, when glutted with plunder, return to the coast to ship their victims, for whom they pay about 7*l.* or 8*l.* a-piece, and sell them for 70*l.*, 80*l.*, or 100*l.* each. In conducting the barter for these poor creatures with the chiefs, the slavers are frequently guilty of every sort of violence and injustice. Of this the chiefs are well aware, and submit to it only because they have no redress. Were it put in their power to procure better manufactured goods from merchants who would have some regard to justice and fair dealing in their transactions with them, they would eagerly give them the preference, particularly if they were protected from the resentment of the slave-dealers.

" I will give, as nearly as I can recollect, the substance of a conversation which passed between one of the native chiefs and myself on this subject. I began by asking him how he could act so unwisely as to sell his countrymen for 7*l.* or 8*l.*, when he might render them so much more profitable to him, by making them labour? The chief mused awhile, and then said, ' If you will show me how this is to be done, I will take your advice.' I asked him how much palm-oil a man could collect during the season? ' From one to two tuns,' was his answer. I then inquired, how a man could be employed when it was not the palm-oil season? ' In cutting down and squaring wood, gathering elephants' teeth, tending

cattle, and cultivating rice, corn, and yams,' was the
reply.   I then said to him, ' Suppose a man collects
a tun and a half of palm-oil in a season ; that, according to its present value, will amount to 11*l.* or 12*l.* ;
and suppose he picks up one elephant's tooth, the
value of which is about 2*s.* per lb., the weight frequently fifty pounds ; but reckon it at one-half that
weight, that will be 2*l.* 10*s.* more.   The value of
these two articles alone will be nearly double what
his price brings you, if you sell him; and this he would
bring you every year, allowing him all the other kinds
of his labour for his own maintenance.   Upon this
simple calculation, the truth of which cannot be denied, what a loser you are by selling him.   Besides,
you get goods inferior, both in quality and quantity,
to those you could procure by exchanging the produce
of this man's labour with British merchants.'   The
chief acknowledged I was right ; but said that, when
I was gone, the slavers would come, and if he did not
get slaves for them, they would burn his town, and
perhaps take away himself and his family, in place of
the slaves they expected him to collect for them ; but
that if this could be prevented, he would sell no more
slaves.   I then told him, if he promised this, I would
come to his assistance, in case the slavers committed
any violence against him, and put the miscreants in
his power : that I should advise him to assemble his
head-men, and try and punish the delinquents by his
own law, and I thought they would not trouble him
again.   I assured him, that he and his countrymen

were considered by us as much better men than these slavers, and that we would protect them if they would trade fairly with us in other produce than slaves.

" This chief drove off the first slaver that came, as I directed him : he is now carrying on a thriving trade, and his people are more civil and kind to us than any I have yet seen.   I feel convinced that' I could influence all the chiefs along the coast in the same manner ; but, to be able to effect this, it would be necessary to have the means of moving from one place to another, with a degree of celerity that a steam-vessel alone could give us.   This would be requisite, both to enable us to keep our promise of protecting the chiefs from the slavers, and also for the purpose of going up the rivers, which are at present unknown to us, with the least possible risk of health, or loss of time.

" Steam-boats would also be of incalculable use to commerce, by towing ships over bars and agitated currents, whilst, as a means of catching the slave-ships, and protecting the coast from the depredations of their crews, three steamers would effect more than the expensive squadron now maintained there. These three vessels should carry four heavy guns each, be of as light a draught of water as possible, and be manned with fifty white * and fifty black men each : they would not cost one-half as much as one large frigate, one corvette, and two gun-brigs, whilst they

* Colonel Nicholls now thinks that a much smaller number of white sailors would be sufficient.

would be an infinitely more efficient means of attaining the end proposed by the use of them. I pledge myself to put an end to the whole of our expense, and totally to suppress the Slave Trade in two years. But if this plan be not adopted, we may go on paying over and over again for the liberated Africans to the end of time, without performing anything beneficial in their behalf."

Mr. Rendall, who was Governor of the Gambia, (where he died,) it appears, contemplated, some years ago, a plan for the suppression of the Slave Trade; and had made some progress in a letter intended to be addressed to the Duke of Wellington. I extract a few passages from it, which will serve to show, that experience conducted him to the same conclusion as that which has been arrived at by the authorities I have already cited. In the introduction, he says—" Of all the measures calculated to insure the prosperity of Africa, none promises so well as the encouragement of its legitimate commerce and agriculture." He recommends the immediate clearance and cultivation of a district, " which would at once embrace two of the most important objects; viz., the improvement in salubrity, and the production of such articles of export as would render the colony valuable to the mother country." " Give," he says, " an impulse to industry by establishing model plantations ; let moral and religious education go hand in hand; and thus most firmly do I believe that the great and benevolent objects of the real friends of

Africa will be most securely attained."—" Government," he adds, " must begin, by showing to the
natives the practicability and profit of cultivation."
But he is convinced that the outlay thus required
would be speedily and abundantly repaid. He
speaks of cotton, coffee, indigo, and ginger as being
the produce that would thrive the best.

I now insert some extracts, bearing on the same
points, which I find in Mr. M'Queen's '" View of
Northern Central Africa :"—

"There is no efficient way to arrest the progress of
this deep-rooted evil, but to teach the negroes useful
knowledge, and the arts of civilized life. Left to
themselves, the negroes will never effectually accomplish this. It must be done by a mighty power, who
will take them under its protection,—a power sufficiently bold, enlightened, and just, to burst asunder
the chains of that grovelling superstition which en-
thrals and debases their minds, and that, with the
voice of authority, can unite the present jarring elements which exist in Africa, and direct them to
honourable and useful pursuits. Till the native
princes are taught that they may be rich without
selling men,—and till Africa is shown that it is in
the labour and industry of her population, and in the
cultivation of her soil, that true wealth consists,—
and till that population see a power, which can protect them from such degrading bondage, there can
be no security for liberty or property in Africa ;

and, consequently, no wish or hope for improvement amongst her population.

*   *   *   *

"It is in Africa that this evil must be rooted out,— by African hands and African exertions chiefly that it can be destroyed. It is a waste of time and a waste of means, an aggravation of the disorder, to keep lopping off the smaller branches of a malignant, a vigorous, and reproductive plant, while the root and stem remain uninjured, carefully supplied with nourishment, and beyond our reach. Half the sums we have expended in this manner would have rooted up slavery for ever. Only teach them, and show them that we will give them more for their produce than for the hand that rears it, and the work is done. All other methods and means will prove ineffectual.

*   *   *   *

"The change contemplated in Africa could not be wrought in a day. But were we once firmly established, in a commanding attitude on the Niger, and an end put to the two great scourges of Africa, Superstition and an external Slave Trade, the progress of improvement would be rapid, and the advantages great.

*   *   *   *

"Nothing can be done,—nothing ever will be done, to alter their present indolent and inactive mode of life, till justice and general security are spread throughout these extensive regions. It would be

vain to expect industry or exertion on their parts, in
order to procure the comforts and the luxuries of life,
when no one can call anything he may possess his
own, or where the superior wealth which he does
possess serves only to mark him out as the prey of
the unfeeling robber or sovereign despot."

The opinions also of travellers, who have visited
different parts of Africa at different times, are very
similar, both as to the capabilities of Africa, and as to
the opposite effects produced by the antagonist systems of the Slave Trade and legitimate commerce;
and they concur in declaring that the encouragement of the one ever tends to the destruction of the
other.   This truth was admitted even by Golberry,
who was so far from being carried away by the phan-
toms of philanthropy,—that he owns he felt some
difficulty in checking the expression of his " just
indignation" against the " cruel theories" of those
pretended philosophers, who imposed on the vulgar
by decrying the Slave Trade.

" I have also observed," says Golberry, " that this
surface of Africa (all the country between Cape
Blanco and Cape Palmas), is at least 374,400 square
leagues, which is more than a fifth of the total
superficies of this large continent; and that, if we
should one day be enabled to traverse freely and habitually this extensive space, not only Europe would
discover new sources of wealth, and new objects for
industry, but that, by a natural and inevitable consequence, the whole of Africa would soon be enlight-

ened, and everything which yet remains ambiguous
in the centre of this continent would be laid open to
investigation.

"There is reason to presume that more active
relations, together with agricultural and mercantile
establishments, and wholesome institutions, whose
object should be the instruction and civilization of
the negroes, would, in the course of fifteen years,
augment these products from thirty to more than
sixty millions ;* and if, during this period, England
and France act in unison—if the Governments of
the two first nations in the world were to proceed,
with emulation, in pursuit of the same object, then,
far from the Slave Trade being augmented, it would
soon diminish to one half, and it would quickly be
abolished by a natural consequence; the inexhaustible fertility of a soil which the natives would learn
to cultivate, and which has hitherto remained, in a
manner of speaking, abandoned to nature, would
administer to the wants and enjoyments of Europe;
the African would become civilized; and the ardent
wishes of a rational philosophy would speedily be
accomplished."

Robertson speaks to the same effect :—"If Africa
is to be made subservient to the views of Europe,
let her have an interest in her own labour, and
that interest will be the strongest and best security for her friendship. Show her the advantages

* Francs.

of industry, and will she deviate so far from the
usual motives which actuate mankind, as not to cultivate such a connexion, in order to improve her
own condition ?   There is but one system for us,
which can secure her friendship, and her social intercourse, and that is, an equitable use of our and
her rights."

Park's testimony is similar :—" It cannot, however, admit of a doubt that all the rich and valuable productions, both of the East and West
Indies might easily be naturalized, and brought
to the utmost perfection, in the tropical parts of
this immense continent.   Nothing is wanting to
this end but example, to enlighten the minds of
the natives ; and instruction, to enable them to direct their industry to proper objects.   It was not
possible for me to behold the wonderful fertility of
the soil, the vast herds of cattle, proper both for
labour and food, and a variety of other circumstances favourable to colonization and agriculture,
and reflect, withal, on the means which presented
themselves of a vast inland navigation, without lamenting that a country, so abundantly gifted and
favoured by nature, should remain in its present
savage and neglected state.   Much more did I lament
that a people, of manners and disposition so gentle
and benevolent, should either be left, as they now are,
immersed in the gross and uncomfortable blindness
of pagan superstition, or permitted to become converts to a system of bigotry and fanaticism which,

without enlightening the mind, often debases the heart."

Mr. Laird, discussing the best mode of establishing trade, and of civilizing Africa, proposes establishing a chain of British posts up the Niger, and across to the Gambia : he proposes six or seven stations, and says : — "There are two ways in which this might be done with comparative economy : the one, by merely establishing a trading post; the other, by acquiring a small territory and importing West Indian and American free negroes, who would bring with them the knowledge they have acquired in the cultivation of sugar and other tropical produce, and would form, in fact, agricultural schools for the benefit of the surrounding population."

" By the Niger, the whole of Western Africa would be embraced ; by the Sharry (which I have no doubt will be found navigable to the meridian of 25° east longitude) a communication would be opened with all the nations inhabiting the unknown countries between the Niger and the Nile. British influence and enterprise would thereby penetrate into the remotest recesses of the country; one hundred millions of people would be brought into direct contact with the civilized world ; new and boundless markets would be opened to our manufactures; a continent teeming with inexhaustible fertility would yield her riches to our traders; not merely a nation, but hundreds of nations, would be awakened from the lethargy of centuries, and become useful and active members of the great commonwealth of mankind ; and every British station would become a centre from whence religion and commerce would radiate their influence over the surrounding country.   Who can calculate the effect that would be produced, if such a plan were followed out, and Africa, freed from her chains, moral and physical, allowed to develope her energies in peace and security ?   No parallel can be drawn, no comparison can be instituted,· between Africa enslaved, and Africa free and unfettered."

Lander confirms these views :—" It is more than probable, as we have now ascertained, that a water communication may be carried on with so extensive a part of the interior of Africa, that a considerable trade will be opened with the country through which we have passed.   The natives only require to know what is wanted from them, and to be shown what they will have in return, and much produce that is now lost, from neglect, will be turned to a considerable account.   The countries situated on the banks of the Niger will become frequented from all the adjacent parts, and this magnificent stream will assume an appearance it has never yet displayed."

Major Gray, summing up the means for bringing the Africans to a state of civilization, and relieving the people from the tyranny of their chiefs, says,— " It has occurred to me there are no means more available, and, I may add, more speedily practicable, than the enlargement of our intercourse with the people, and the encouragement and protection of the internal commerce of Africa. By this, we can improve them in the way of example ; by the other, we can benefit them and ourselves in the way of interchange of commodity : our habits and our manners will gain upon them in time, and our skill tend to stimulate and encourage theirs."

" By increasing their commerce, we also obtain another happy consummation, we give them employment, and we consequently, to a certain extent, secure them from the incessant meddling of their maraboos. We could congregate them in greater numbers together, and therefore the more readily instruct them ; and I may venture to add, that if a fair trial of zeal were used in such a delightful employment, within a very few years they would prove themselves not unfitted for the enjoyment of liberal institutions."

"That there are powers of mind in the African, it were quite idle to dispute ; that the productions of the country are capable of being beneficially employed must, I think, be equally incontestable to any one who has carefully perused the preceding pages ; and, to act with honesty, we should not allow both, or either, to lie for ever dormant."

" The European governments," says Burckhardt, " who have settlements on the coasts of Africa, may contribute to it by commerce, and by the introduction among the negroes of arts and industry."

Capt. W. Allen, R.N.,* in a letter addressed to me August, 1839, observes:—"I have read your 'Remedy' with great interest and attention, the more so, as I find embodied in it all the ideas I had formed on the same subject, deduced from observations written on the spot."

There is no species of argument which carries with it a greater force of conviction to my mind, than the concurrence of a variety of persons, who, being competent to judge, and having opportunities of forming a sound judgment, examine a given object with very different purposes, from very different points of view, yet arrive, without concert, or previous communication, at the same conclusion. In the case before us, we collect the unpublished despatches, letters, and journals of the several Governors of Sierra Leone, Fernando Po, the Gambia, and the Gold Coast. These documents were written at different times, with no view to publication, and there was no connection between the officers who wrote them. Differing on many points, they harmonise exactly on those which affect my case. Each speaks of the exuberant fertility of the soil; each laments the desolation which, in spite of nature, prevails; and each looks to the cultivation of those fertile lands, and to the growth of legitimate commerce, as the remedy to the distractions of Africa, and the horrors of the Slave Trade. For example, it appears that General Turner at

* Captain W. Allen was employed by the Admiralty to ascend the Niger in Laird and Oldfield's expedition.

Sierra Leone, and Colonel Nicolls of Fernando Po, had in view much such a plan as I have suggested, when they spoke in their despatches of putting an end to the Slave Trade in two or three years. This unconscious union between themselves is not all. The views of these gentlemen correspond with those which I find in the private journals of the Missionaries, who have gathered their experience, and formed their opinion, while labouring among the native tribes of the Gambia. That which is the opinion of these soldiers and of these teachers of religion turns out to be the opinion of the most distinguished travellers and of intelligent traders. Captain Becroft, who traded on the Western Coast, and Captain Raymond, who did the same on the Eastern, tell me,—that trade, springing from the cultivation of the soil, will, and that nothing else will, abolish the Slave Trade.

This uniformity of opinion between governors and missionaries, travellers and traders, stops not here. Mr. M'Queen and Mr. Clarkson,* who have spent their lives in studying Africa, but not in the same school, here cease to differ. Mr. Clarkson thus concludes a long letter to me, dated November 20th, 1838 (after having noticed and approved each suggestion I had made, particularly the purchase of a large tract of country, for the establishment of pattern farms, and the selection of Fernando Po) : — " Upon the whole, it is my opinion that, if Govern-

* For Mr. Clarkson's judgment on the views and principles stated in this book, see Appendix D.

ment would make the settlements which you have pointed out; if they were to substitute steamers in the place of sailing ships; if they were, by annual presents, to work upon the native chiefs; if they were to buy the land upon which their settlements would be built, and introduce pattern farms for the cultivation of cotton, indigo, rice, or whatever other tropical production they might think fit, they might as certainly count upon the abolition of the Slave Trade, even in a short time, as upon any unknown event, which men might expect to be produced, from right reasoning, or by going the right way to work, in order to produce it.   As far as our knowledge of Africa, and African manners, customs, and dispositions goes, a better plan could not be devised—no other plan, in short, could answer. Had this plan been followed from the first, it would have done wonders for Africa by this time, and it would do much for us now : in two years from the trial of it it would become doubtful, whether it was worth while to carry on the Slave Trade ; and in five years I have no doubt that it would be generally, though, perhaps, not totally, abandoned.   Depend upon it, there is no way of civilizing and christianizing Africa, which all good men must look to, but this." " Teach them," says Mr. M'Queen, " that we will give them more for their produce, than for the hand that rears it, and the work is done. All other methods and means will prove ineffectual."

Other illustrations of this coincidence might be quoted. The Society of Friends, anxious to benefit

Africa, could devise no better means, than the establishment of a school and a farm in the neighbourhood of St. Mary's. The experiment failed, or it seemed to fail, owing to the death of the agent whom they had sent; but it was with no small pleasure that I found, in the papers of the brother of a deceased governor of the colony, this evidence that their labours were not entirely lost. After stating that the Society had formerly established a school and a farm on a point of land forming Cape St. Mary's, " as eligible a spot for such an undertaking as could be found in the country," he goes on to say, "The natives of the neighbourhood must have observed, with some degree of attention, the mode adopted by these settlers in their agricultural pursuits. Indeed, it must be inferred that many of them assisted on the works of the farm, as at this date (viz. 14 years after) they conduct matters in a more neat and satisfactory manner than is to be observed in other parts of the country. Their grounds are well cleaned and enclosed; vegetation, of one kind or another, appears to be kept up during the year ; the quality of their articles is superior to their neighbours; and altogether there is a superiority among these people, a neatness about their persons and villages, that pleases the eye, particularly as these things do not exist in other parts of the country. The old chief of the district loses no opportunity of making the most particular inquiries after his friends the Quakers, and of expressing his regret that such good people should not have remained amongst them, as their kindness will ever live in the memory of the inhabitants. The chief and his sons are worthy good folks, and much attached to the English. The seeds which Mr. W. Allen and other gentlemen have sent to the Gambia have been of infinite service, in improving the quality of the cotton and rice."*

I hardly know anything more encouraging than the facts which have thus unexpectedly come to light. Here an effort has been made, exactly in conformity with the views which I am endeavouring to urge, but it was soon abandoned; yet the effect of that imperfect experiment is still visible in the improvement of the face of the country, and in the manifest distinction between that district which had been thus befriended, and the desolate regions which surround it.

The fact, too, that these simple people retain a lively and grateful recollection of their benefactors, and cease not to pant for their return, proves that in the minds of the people, as well as in the quality of the soil, there are materials on which we may work. When so much was effected by a slight effort, what may we not expect to be accomplished, when the same merciful measures shall be adopted permanently, and upon a large scale?

One further coincidence, and not the least remarkable, remains to be stated. I gave a description on a former occasion† of a slave-hunt, or gazzua,

* Rendall.　　　† Page 91 of this edition.

which was perpetrated in the dominions, and by the permission of the Pasha of Egypt. Some strong representations of the impolicy and atrocity of such proceedings were made to him by some of our countrymen, particularly by Dr. Bowring.* And I have now to describe the influence which these have exercised over his conduct.† From a manuscript which purports to be an official account of the journey of his Highness to Soudan, of the views in which it originated, and of the policy which was adopted with regard to the natives, I extract the following particulars. In the autumn of 1838 the Pasha's attention was turned to his savage territory of Soudan, and he resolved to take measures for the abolition of the Slave Trade, and to introduce a reformation in the customs, commerce, and agriculture of the inhabitants: for this purpose he repaired thither in person, accompanied by his usual attendants, and several scientific persons, collected not only from his own country, but from the continent of Europe. He embarked in a steam-boat, October 15th, 1838. In passing the cataracts, he had to endure some hard-

* Vide Appendix E., p. 564, for an extract from a letter from Sir. W. H. Pearson to Mr. Buxton, junior, containing an account of that gentleman's visit on board a slave-ship on the Nile.

† The consul at Alexandria, of date 5th May, 1838, narrates a conversation which he had had with Mahommed Ali, in which the pasha said that he would not permit his officers in the interior to seize slaves: and he adds that the pasha himself does not now purchase any more slaves for his own use or service.—Class D., 1838-9, p. 14.

ships, and was exposed to considerable danger. After passing the first cataract, he had to remain during a night without provisions or attendance : in the attempt to pass the second, the boat in which he was seated was dashed violently on the rocks, and it was with difficulty that he effected his escape, while the vessel was carried away by the current. On the eleventh of November, the cataract of Annek was reached : it appears from the narrative, that this was the first attempt that was ever made to pass it : from Dongola, he went across the desert to Kartoum, the capital of Sennaar, on the confluence of the Blue and the White Nile ; he proceeded along the Blue Nile, and there was joined by some pupils of the schools of language and mineralogy. At Fazoglo, hearing of depredations, committed, according to custom, by a tribe of mountaineers on their more feeble neighbours, he despatched a force against them, under the command of a superior officer, who returned with 540 prisoners. His Highness had them brought before him, and spoke to them at great length on the odiousness and barbarity of stealing and selling their fellow-creatures ; then, wishing to join example to precept, he permitted them to depart, after having distributed to every one ten days' provisions and given dresses to five of the chiefs. Learning that some prisoners had been taken at Kordofan, he ordered them to be dismissed, with permission to return home, or to establish themselves as cultivators on the banks of the White Nile, issuing at the same time a manifesto, declaring that slave-hunting was strictly forbidden; and that if any quarrels should arise between neighbouring tribes, their differences were to be brought before the Governor-general, who was commissioned to decide them. At length he arrived at the mouth of Fazangoro, where, after inspecting the gold mines, he laid the foundations of a town, which is to be called by his own name, Mohammed Ali, and to contain houses for fifteen hundred families. The chiefs of the country showed their readiness to co-operate with him, by offering a much larger force for the working of the mines : this however he declined. We are expressly told, that he pays his workmen wages, and provides them with dresses adapted to the climate : also, that he granted land to Arab agriculturists for the formation of model farms, supplied them with the necessary implements and animals, and declared them to be exempt from taxes for five years. The land of Sennaar is extremely fertile ; it readily returns sixty for one ; the dourah grows quickly and produces very rich ears ; animals and wood abound ; cotton succeeds wonderfully, almost without cost, and it produces more wool than that of Egypt, which is cultivated at a great expense. Hitherto, however, cultivation has been entirely neglected. The Pasha collected round him a great number of the sheikhs, made them presents, and addressed them in a speech, remarkable not only for its good sense, but for the quarter from whence it was delivered. " The people of other parts of the world were formerly savages; they have had instructors, and, by labour and perseverance, they have civilized themselves; you have heads and hands like them; do as they have done: you also will raise yourselves to the rank of men; you will acquire great riches, and will taste enjoyments of which you can at present, from your profound ignorance, form no conception. Nothing is wanting for this purpose: you have a great quantity of land, cattle, and wood: your population is numerous, the men strong, and the women fruitful. Up to the present time you have had no guide: you have one now :—it is I !—I will lead you to civilization and happiness. The world is divided into five great parts; that which you occupy is called Africa: in every country, except this, the value of labour is understood, and a taste for good and useful things prevails; men devote themselves with ardour to commerce, which produces wealth, pleasure, and glory —words, which you cannot even comprehend. Egypt itself is not an extensive country; yet, thanks to labour and the industry of its inhabitants, it is rich, and will become more so: distant provinces are acquainted with it; and the territory of Sennaar, which is twenty times larger than Egypt, produces almost nothing, because its inhabitants remain as idle as if they were without life. Understand well that labour produces all things; and that without labour nothing can be had."

His Highness then explained to them, in detail, the advantages of agriculture and commerce. His auditors, astonished at what they heard, begged him earnestly to take them into Egypt, that they might be instructed in those arts. " It would be better," replied his Highness, " that you should send your children there ; they will learn more easily, because they are younger, and will remain longer useful to these countries, when they return to them. I will place them in my colleges ; they will learn there all that is useful and ornamental. Be not uneasy about their welfare, they shall be my adopted children ; and, when they are sufficiently instructed in the sciences, I will send them back to be happiness to you, and to these countries, and a glory to you."

The sheikhs very willingly accepted the offer :— every one wished to send his children into Egypt ; the most powerful among them, named Abd-el-Kadir, having no son, asked the favour for his nephew. His Highness then urgently recommended Ahmed Pasha to labour for the welfare and civilization of these people ; and, for the purpose of encouragement, announced, that he should himself return next year, in order to judge the progress that might be made, and incite them to fresh exertions.

The Viceroy departed the next morning, and returned to Fazoglo on the 1st of February, when he renewed his exhortations to the sheikhs of that dis trict ; and proceeded to Kartoum, where he was delighted to find the good effects of his late visit, in some land being already in full cultivation. From thence he visited, in like manner, the White Nile, and, on returning to Kartoum, he set on foot the building of a Christian church. Before leaving the place, he proclaimed the freedom of trade in indigo, which the provinces of Dongola and Berber produce in considerable quantities, and ordered the governor to supply implements, and everything necessary, for the development of its cultivation. After which, he embarked with his suite, leaving M. Lambert, with the charge of making two reports,—the one, upon a projected railroad, in that part of the desert which separates Abu-Muhammed from Kurusku; the other, on the formation of a canal between the White River and Kordofan, destined to furnish water for the irrigation of the land, and to facilitate the carriage of the iron-ore of the mines.

The cataracts were repassed on his return ; and, on the 14th of March, the cannon of the citadel of Cairo announced to Egypt the arrival of the Viceroy, after an absence of five months and four days.

Having freely, in another place, commented upon the conduct of the Pasha, in permitting the continuance of the gazzua, and in allowing his officers to reimburse themselves, for any arrears of their pay, with the human booty which they might seize, we are bound to do justice to the course which he has now pursued, and to acknowledge that the zeal and energy which he has displayed, in acting upon his new opinions, furnish an example, which any civilized and Christian nation may do itself honour by following. It must be confessed, there were great

impediments in his way : it was not likely that he, a
follower of Mahomet, whose religion justifies the enslavement of the infidel, should have shared our abhorrence of all that pertains to the trade in man : he
must have had to surmount many strong and deep-
seated prejudices in his own bosom, and must have
exposed himself to public reproach, if not danger,
before he resolved to set his face against a system so
long established, and so lucrative.   It was an act
of great vigour in a prince, seventy years of age,
threatened by a formidable enemy, and holding his
authority in some considerable measure, by his own
personal presence and influence, to undertake a journey, of more than five months' duration, through a
country so rarely visited, exposing himself to consi--
derable perils and fatigue, and the expense of conveying with him a large body of well-qualified
assistants.   It is greatly to the credit of his understanding to have seen so distinctly that a greater
amount of wealth may be drawn from the cultivation
of the soil, than from the chase and capture of the
inhabitants.   The language which he uses to the
native chiefs proves that he well comprehends the
principles by which a degree of civilization may be
spread among savage tribes, and valuable products
reared from their rich but untilled lands.   But the
point which deserves most notice is, that, from the
moment he was convinced, he acted, at once and
boldly.   In a very short period, he has executed a
voyage of discovery ; he has selected an excellent posi-

tion for a town, and commenced building it.   He has
entered upon a system of hiring labour and paying
wages (in itself, I am afraid, an innovation); he has
laboured to convince the native chiefs that it is better
to sell their productions than their subjects: he
has made some provision for the education of their
children; he has relinquished taxes, and established
free trade in articles which have hitherto been subject to a monopoly; he has given orders for the formation of a canal and a railroad; and he is employed in
opening through the cataracts a way sufficiently wide
for the passage of boats of large dimensions: moreover, and it confirms one of my most important anti-
cipations, he has found better cotton in Soudan than
that which is grown by himself in Egypt: in short, if
I may judge by his actions, as represented in the narrative which is put forth under his authority, there is
no more thorough-going advocate of the policy which
I am labouring to recommend to the British nation
than the personage whom, but a few months ago, I
had to point out to public indignation as the patron
of the horrible gazzua.   It must, however, be borne
in memory that we have only seen the BEGINNING of
a new system.   The character of the Pasha will be
judged, not by what he has hitherto attempted, but by
the fidelity with which he shall adhere to the principles he has professed, and by the sagacity with which
he shall carry into execution the wise and benevolent
design which seems to reflect so much credit upon him.

I have thus shown that many persons, whose

veracity we have no reason to doubt, whose experience furnishes the best means of forming a correct
judgment, and who cannot be suspected of acting in
concert, arrive at precisely the same conclusions. The
argument deducible from this coincidence of opinion
enforced itself on me with peculiar effect. I possessed neither the practical experience which belongs
to a traveller, a trader, or the governor of a colony,
nor the intimate acquaintance with native mind acquired by the missionary; nor that deep knowledge
of all that has been written concerning Africa, in
which Mr. Clarkson and Mr. M'Queen excel. Yet in
ignorance of almost all the opinions to which I have
now referred, I had, by a process, and from documents, quite distinct, arrived at the same result. I
attentively examined the papers on the Slave Trade,
annually presented to Parliament : they demonstrated
the unwavering sincerity of the Government, by
whatever party administered, and the generous compassion of the nation: at the same time, they forced
upon me an undoubting conviction, that the evil
could never be eradicated by this mode of correction.
Ready to abandon all further effort, in despair of
being able to effect any practical good, and from an
abhorrence of the task of afflicting myself and others
by a recital of evils, which I could not cure, and of
horrors, which every effort seemed to aggravate, I cast
my eyes, in every direction, in order to discover if there
yet existed any effectual remedy. It then occurred to
me, that Africa, after all, obtains a very inconsider-

able revenue from the Slave Trade; while the outlay, so to speak,—the desolation, the slaughter, the bloody and diabolical superstition, and the human suffering from all these,—are indeed prodigious: the net profit to Africa (whatever it may be to the civilized ruffians who instigate the trade) is mise rably scanty. " Thou sellest thy people for nought; and dost not increase thy wealth by their price." There was something hopeful in the fact that the interests of Africa were not involved in the continuance of the Slave Trade. It gave birth to the inquiry, Is it not possible for us to undersell the slave-dealer, and to drive him out of the market, by offering more for the productions of the soil than he ever gave for the bodies of the inhabitants?

This opened a new field of investigation. I eagerly turned to every book of travels which might furnish an insight into the capabilities of that quarter of the globe. There was anything but a dearth of materials: I found evidence, sufficient to fill volumes, that Africa, though now a wilderness, may rank with any portion of the world in natural resources and in the power of production. Travellers, whatever may be the scarcity of other topics, never fail to speak of the exuberance of the soil on the one hand, and the misery of its inhabitants on the other. These two subjects occupy three-fourths of the pages of those who have visited Africa. It is sufficient here to say that I rose from that part of the investigation, in possession of incontrovertible proof that nature had

provided an abundance of all things which consti-
tute agricultural wealth. The question then arises,
Are there hands to till the earth? Africa, notwithstanding the annual and terrible drain of its inhabitants, teems with population : but for the Slave Trade,
there is no reason to doubt that it would be as
densely peopled as any part of the globe. Can
labour be obtained there as cheaply as in Brazil,
Cuba, or the Carolinas? We have some light on
this subject. We know that a slave fetches, in
Interior Africa, about 3*l.*; in Brazil, at least 70*l.* ;
when seasoned, as an African is in his own country,
100*l.* Africa, then, has this great advantage over America, that it can be cultivated at one-twentieth of the
expense. Why, then, should the inhabitants be torn
from Africa, when her native labourers upon her
native land might hold successful competition with
any Slave State? The soil being equal, a labourer
in Africa will raise as much produce as the same
labourer transported to America, but at less expense; for you can hire ten labourers in the former
at the price that one costs in the latter. Hence I
infer, that the labour and produce of Africa, if fairly
called forth, would rival the labour employed, and
the produce raised in America, throughout the
markets of the civilized world.

Besides all this, the labourers stolen in Africa are
not, in fact, carried to America. What the one
loses, the other does not gain. Africa loses three
labourers; America obtains but one: in no species

of merchandise is there such waste of the *raw* material, as in the merchandise of man.   In what other
trade do two-thirds of the goods perish, in order that
one-third may reach the market ?

Apart, then, from all considerations of humanity
and Christian principle, and narrowing the question
to a mere calculation of pecuniary profit, it would
appear a strange kind of economy to carry away
the population from their native fields, which need
nothing but those hands for their cultivation, in order
to plant them in diminished numbers, at a prodigious
expense, in another hemisphere, and on land not
more productive.

But would these men be willing to work for
wages ?. I did not require to be taught that men will
work, not only as well but ten times better, for reward,
than they were ever made to do by the lash : proof,
however, of this truth presented itself.   As I shall
have to enlarge upon that subject before I close this
book, I will only say here, that of all the fictions
ever invented by interested parties to quiet their
own consciences, or delude the world, there is none
so gross as the doctrine, that less labour is to be won
by wages, than can be extorted by the whip.

Thus, then, the study of the writings of travellers
proved to me that Africa possessed all the separate
elements necessary for vast production and extensive
commerce ; but these materials, were, if I may so express myself, asunder : the hands, both able and willing to labour, had never been brought to bear upon

the land, so capable of yielding a grateful return. It was not till after I had come to the conclusion that all that was wanting for the deliverance of Africa was that agriculture, commerce, and instruction should have a *fair trial*, that I discovered that those views were not confined to myself, and that others had arrived, by practical experience, at the same result which I had learnt from the facts; and from reasoning upon them; and I was very well pleased to renounce any little credit which might attach to the discovery, in exchange for the solid encouragement and satisfaction of finding that what was with me but theory, was with them the fruit of experience. I cannot but remember that a poet, who possessed the faculty of combining the closest reasoning with the most flowing verse, saw, and availed himself of this species of argument for the defence of Christianity :—

> " Whence, but from Heaven, could men unskill'd in arts,
>   In several ages born, of several parts,
>   Weave such agreeing truths ; or how, or why,
>   Should all conspire to cheat us with a lie ?"

CHAPTER V.

PRINCIPLES.

" True faith, true policy, united run."—POPE.

" If you plant where savages be, do not only entertain them with trifles and gingles, but use them *justly* and *graciously*, with sufficient guard nevertheless."—LORD BACON.

" The greatest advantage a Government can possess is to be the one trustworthy Government in the midst of Governments which nobody can trust.'—EDINBURGH REVIEW, Jan. 1840.—*Life of Clive*, p. 330.

IT appears to me a matter of such peculiar moment that we should distinctly settle and declare the PRINCIPLES on which our whole intercourse with Africa, whether economic or benevolent, whether directed exclusively to her benefit, or mingled (as I think it may most fairly be) with a view to our own, shall be founded, and by which it shall be regulated, that I venture, though at the risk of being tedious, to devote a separate chapter to the consideration of them. The principles, then, which I trust to see adopted by our country, are these,—

Free Trade.

Free Labour.

FREE TRADE.

Nothing, I apprehend, could be more unfortunate to the continent we wish to befriend, or more discreditable to ourselves, than that Great Britain should give any colour to the suspicion of being actuated by mercenary motives; an apology would thus be afforded to every other nation for any attempt it might make to thwart our purpose. We know, from the Duke of Wellington's despatches, that the powers on the continent were absolutely incredulous as to the purity of the motives which prompted us, at the congress of Aix la Chapelle, to urge, *beyond everything else*, the extinction of the Slave Trade.

In a letter to Mr. Wilberforce, dated Paris, 15th Sept., 1814, the Duke of Wellington says, " It is not believed that we are in earnest about it, or have abolished the trade on the score of its inhumanity. It is thought to have been a commercial speculation; and that, having abolished the trade ourselves, with a view to prevent the undue increase of colonial produce in our stores, of which we could not dispose, we now want to prevent other nations from cultivating their colonies to the utmost of their power."

And again, in another letter to the Right Honourable J. C. Villiers :—

Paris, 31*st August*, 1814.

" The efforts of Great Britain to put an end to it (the Slave Trade) are not attributed to good motives, but to commercial jealousy, and a desire to keep the monopoly of colonial produce in our own hands."

The grant of twenty millions may have done something to quench these narrow jealousies, but still, the nations of the continent will be slow to believe that we are entirely disinterested. It should, then, be made manifest to the world, by some signal act, that the moving spring is humanity ; that if England makes settlements on the African coast, it is only for the more effectual attainment of her great object ; and that she is not allured by the hopes either of gain or conquest, or by the advantages, national or individual, political or commercial, which may, and I doubt not, will follow the undertaking. Such a demonstration would be given, if, with the declaration, that it is resolved to abolish the Slave Trade, and, that in this cause we are ready, if requisite, to exert all our powers, Great Britain, should couple an official pledge that she will not claim for herself a single benefit, which shall not be shared by every nation uniting with her in the extinction of the Slave Trade ; and especially

First,—That no exclusive privilege in favour of British subjects shall ever be allowed to exist.

Secondly,—That no *custom-house* shall ever be established at Fernando Po.

Thirdly,—That no distinction shall be made there, *whether in peace or in war,* between our own subjects and those of any such foreign power, as to the rights they shall possess, or the terms on which they shall enjoy them. In short, that we purchase Fernando Po, and will hold it for no other purpose than the benefit of Africa. I am well aware that these may appear startling propositions ; I am, how-

ever, supported in them by high authorities : the suggestion as to the custom-house was made to me by
Mr. Porter, of the Board of Trade; and that respecting neutrality in peace or in war, originated with the
learned Judge of the British Vice-Admiralty Courts.
Supported by his authority, I may venture to say
that, though a novel, it would be a noble characteristic
of our colony. As it is intended for different ends, so
it would be ruled by different principles, from any
colony which has ever been undertaken : it would
have the distinction of being the neutral ground of the
world, elevated above the mutual injuries of war;
where, for the prosecution of a good and a vast object,
the subjects and the fleets of all nations may meet
in amity, and where there shall reign a perpetual
truce.

Let us look to the tendency of the proposition,
that no custom-house shall be established at Fernando
Po, or at the post to be formed at the junction of the
Niger and the Tchadda : we might then hope that
the history of these stations would be a counterpart
to that of Singapore, which is described as having
been, in 1819, "an insignificant fishing-village, and
a haunt of pirates," but now stands as an eloquent
eulogy on the views of its founder, Sir Stamford
Raffles, proving what may be effected, and in how
short a time, for our own profit and for the improvement of the uncivilized world, "by the union of native
industry and British enterprise," when uncurbed by
restrictions on trade.

I now turn to the second great principle, viz.,— Free Labour.

It may be thought by some almost superfluous that this should be urged, considering that there is an Act of Parliament, which declares that " Slavery shall be, and is hereby utterly and for ever abolished *in all the* colonies, possessions, and plantations of Great Britain." But if ever there were a case in which this great law should be strictly and strenuously enforced, and in which it is at the same time peculiarly liable to be neglected or evaded, it is in the case of any possessions we may obtain in Africa. It is necessary to be wise in time, and never to suffer this baneful weed to take root there. Let us remember what it has cost us to extirpate it from our old colonies. It is remarkable that among the whole phalanx of antagonists to the abolition of West India Slavery, there was never one who was not, by his own account, an ardent lover of freedom. Slavery, in the abstract, was universally acknowledged to be detestable; and they were in the habit of pathetically deploring their cruel fate, and of upbraiding the mother-country, which had originally planted this curse among them; but property had entwined itself around the disastrous institution, and we had to contend with a fearful array of securities, marriage settlements, and vested interests of all kinds. Again, bondage, it was said, had seared the intellect, and

withered all that was noble in the bosoms of its victims. To have begun such an unrighteous system
was an error, only less than that of suddenly eradicat-
ing it, and of clothing with the attributes of freemen,
those whose very nature had been changed and defiled
by servitude.

I firmly believe that much of all this was uttered
in perfect sincerity; and yet, I feel the most serious
apprehensions lest these wholesome convictions should
evaporate before the temptations of a country, where
land of the richest fertility is to be had for 1*d.* per
acre, and labourers are to be purchased for 4*l.* per head.
We know, not only that the Portuguese are turning
their attention to plantations in the neighbourhood of
Loango, but that they have been bold enough to ask
us to guarantee to them their property, that is their
slaves, in these parts. This, together with certain
ominous expressions which I have heard, convinces
me that my apprehensions are not altogether chimerical; and I am not sure that we shall not once more
hear the antique argument, that Negroes, " from the
brutishness of their nature," are incapable of being
induced to work by any stimulus but the lash: at all
events, we shall be assured, that if we attempt to establish Free Labour, we shall assail the prejudices of
the African chiefs in the tenderest points. If we do
not take care, at the outset, to render the holding of
slaves by British subjects in Africa highly penal, and
perilous in the last degree, we shall see British capital
again embarked, and vested interest acquired in hu-

man flesh. We shall, in spite of the warning we
have had, commit a second time, the monstrous error,
to say nothing of the crime, of tolerating slavery.
A second time the slave-master will accuse us of
being at least accomplices in his guilt; and once
more we shall have to buy off opposition by an extravagant grant of money.

The suggestion, then, that I make is that we shall
lay it down, as a primary and sacred principle, that
any man who enters any territory that we may
acquire in Africa, is from that moment " Free, and
discharged of all manner of slavery," and that Great
Britain pledges herself to defend him from all,
civilized or savage, who may attempt to recapture
him. That one resolution will do much to give us
labourers,—to obtain for us the affections of the population,—to induce them to imitate and adopt our
customs,—and to settle down to the pursuits of peaceful industry and productive agriculture.

No more daring attempt was ever made to form a
settlement in Africa than that undertaken by Captain
Beaver, near the close of the last century. His object
was to establish a colony on the island of Bulama.
Notwithstanding the errors into which he fell, and
which proved fatal to his expedition, yet was it
highly creditable to him, that at a time when the
abolition of the Slave Trade had made but little way
in the public mind, and when the extinction of slavery
was not thought of, he should have perceived, and
applied principles so wise and so humane as those we

find scattered in his interesting volume. His Narrative proves two points,—first, that the natives of Africa may be led to prefer legitimate commerce to slave-dealing. Secondly, that they were very willing to labour for wages.

The chief dissimilarity which first struck the Africans, in the conduct of this and that of other European settlements, was their refusal to purchase slaves.

" This they could not account for ; neither were they altogether pleased with it at first; for, when negotiating with Niobana for the purchase of the Biafara territory, he said, that ' It was very hard that we would not buy his slaves !' Having made him comprehend that our intention was rather to cultivate the earth than to trade ; but that we should, notwithstanding, at all times, trade with him for wax, ivory, clothes, &c.,—in short, that we would buy everything which he had to sell, except only slaves, whom he could always dispose of as he had been accustomed to do heretofore—he appeared satisfied ; although he could not comprehend why we would not purchase the one, nor why we cultivated the other."

By their steadiness in this point, they got the character of being the first white men the natives had ever heard of " who could not do bad." And " from no circumstance," says Captain Beaver, " did we derive so much benefit, as from our not dealing in slaves."

The natives not long after found out that these new colonists not only refused to purchase slaves,

but that no man in their settlement was permitted to
be considered in the light of a slave. The two first
who came to Captain Beaver were full of suspicion ;
they remained with him a little more than three
weeks, and then signified their desire to depart at
the time when their help was most needed. Captain
Beaver wisely did not even ask them to remain, but
paid them their wages, and dismissed them with presents. Their report induced others to take service,
and he never after wanted grumetas : in one year, he
employed nearly two hundred of them. The Africans of these parts always, he says, go armed, and
never voluntarily place themselves in the power of
even a friendly tribe ; but when they had once ascertained that these English colonists neither bought
nor sold slaves ; that every man was paid for the full
value of his labour, and suffered to depart whenever
he chose, " They came to me unarmed," says Captain Beaver, " and remained for weeks and months
at a time on the island, without the least suspicion of
my ever intending them evil." And this, though he
was occasionally obliged to inflict punishment on
individuals of their number for disorderly conduct.
" Thus," he says, " by the negative merit of treating
these people with common integrity, was I not only
able to acquire their confidence, and, by their labour,
to do almost all that was done upon the island, but
also to overturn one of their strongest prejudices
against us, and to convert their well-grounded
suspicion of fraud and deceit in all Europeans, into

esteem and respect for the character of a white man."

I cannot dismiss the work of Captain Beaver, without expressing my satisfaction in finding, that he, like others whom I have named, gathers from his experience on the coast of Africa that the Slave Trade is to be overthrown by fair dealing, and by the wealth which is to be raised from the soil. " One great motive of the Africans in making slaves, indeed I may say the only one, is to procure European goods; slaves are the money, the circulating medium, with which African commerce is carried on : they have no other. If, therefore, we could substitute another, and at the same time that other be more certain and more abundant, the great object in trading in slaves will be done away. *This may be done by the produce of the earth.* " Let the native chiefs be once convinced that the labour of a free native in cultivating the earth may produce him more European goods in one year than he could have purchased if he had sold him for a slave, and he will no longer seek to make slaves to procure European commodities, but will cultivate the earth for that purpose." And this is the testimony which he bears to African industry, and to the facility of procuring labour:—

" I know that those who choose always to see the African character in its worst light will probably say that they never will be induced voluntarily to labour; and that I betray a total ignorance of it, in supposing that they can ever be brought to cultivate the earth for wages. That assertion may be made; but my answer is, ' Put it to the test.' And I moreover say that, as far as my little knowledge of the Africans will enable me to judge, I have no doubt of their readily cultivating the earth for hire, whenever Europeans will take the trouble so to employ them. I never saw men work harder, more willingly, or regularly, generally speaking, than those free natives whom I employed upon the island of Bulama. What induced them to do so? Their desire of European commodities in my possession, of which they knew that they would have the value of one bar at the end of a week, or four at the end of a month. Some of them remained at labour for months ere they left me; others, after having left me, returned: they knew that the labour was constant, but they also knew that their reward was certain. I think, therefore, that as far as my experience goes, I am warranted in saying that the Africans are not averse to labour, unless those in the neighbourhood of Bulama are unlike the rest of their species. So much as to the question of labour.''*

If I have quoted at unusual length from Captain Beaver's work, it is because here is testimony upon which no shade of suspicion can rest. This work was published before a word had been uttered upon the controversy, as to free and slave labour; and it comes from a gentleman who took nothing upon the

* Beaver's African Memoranda, p. 385.

authority of others, but formed his opinions from his own personal experience in Africa.

I shall subjoin in the Appendix further proof, on the authority of General Turner, Colonel Denham, and Major Ricketts, who also spoke from what they saw at Sierra Leone, as to the disposition of Africans to work for wages.*

The Rev. W. Fox, missionary at M'Carthy's Island, whom I have already quoted, says, " The Eastern Negroes, ... come here and hire themselves as labourers for several months, and, with the articles they receive in payment, barter them again on their way home for more than their actual value on this island." In the journal of the same gentleman, just received, under date of April, 1838, he writes thus : " I have to-day paid off all the labourers who had been employed on the mission-ground, and have hired about eighty more, with three overseers ; *many others applied for work*, and I should have felt a pleasure in engaging them, but that I wished to keep the expenses within moderate bounds."

It thus appears that free labour is to be obtained in Africa, even under present circumstances, if we will but pay the price for it, and that there is no necessity at all for that system of coerced labour, which no necessity could justify. I am aware that I have trespassed on the patience of many of my readers, who require no arguments against slavery ; but I have already expressed, and continue to feel, if there be

* Vide Appendix C.

danger anywhere in the plan for the cultivation of
Africa, it lies in this point. And I wish the question of slavery to be definitively settled, and our principles to be resolved on, in such a way as shall render
it impossible for us to retract them, before a single
step is taken, or a shilling of property invested in the
attempt to grow sugar and cotton in Africa.

I shall here introduce the consideration of two
other points, which though they cannot precisely be
classed as principles, yet are nearly akin to them, and
deserve our very serious attention.

The proposal of a settlement in Africa, necessarily
recalls to mind our vast empire in India ; and, surely,
no sober-minded statesman would desire to see renewed, in another quarter of the globe, the career
we have run in the East.

I entirely disclaim any disposition to erect a new
empire in Africa. Remembering what has now been
disclosed, of the affliction of that quarter of the globe,
and of the horrors and abominations which every spot
exhibits, and every hour produces, it would be the
extreme of selfish cruelty to let a question so momentous be decided with an eye to our own petty interests ;
but there is another view of the case,—it would also
be the most extreme folly to allow ourselves to swerve
one iota from its right decision, by any such indirect
and short-sighted considerations.

What is the value to Great Britain of the sovereignty of a few hundred square miles in Benin, or
Eboe, as compared with that of bringing forward

into the market of the world millions of customers, who may be taught to grow the raw material which we require, and who require the manufactured commodities which we produce? The one is a trivial and insignificant matter; the other is a subject worthy the most anxious solicitude of the most accomplished statesmen.

It appears to me, however, that the danger of our indulging any thirst for dominion is rather plausible than real. In the first place, the climate there forbids the employment of European armies, if armies indeed formed any part of my plan, which they do not. I look forward to the employment, almost exclusively, of the African race. A few Europeans may be required in some leading departments; but the great body of our agents must have African blood in their veins, and of course to the entire exclusion of our troops.

2dly. In Asia, there was accumulated treasure to tempt our cupidity: in Africa, there is none. Asia was left to the government of a company: the African establishments will, of course, be regularly subjected to parliamentary supervision. Our encroachments upon Asia were made at a time, when little general attention was bestowed, or sympathy felt, for the sufferings and wrongs of a remote people. Now, attention is awake on such topics. India stands as a beacon to warn us against extended dominion; and if there were not, as I believe there are, better principles among our statesmen, there would be a check to rapacity, and a shield for the weak, in the wakeful commiseration of the public.

I may add, that, were the danger as great as some imagine, it would have disclosed itself ere this.   The French have had for some time a settlement on the Senegal; the Danes on the Rio Volta; the Dutch on the Gold Coast; the Portuguese at Loango; the Americans at Cape Mesurado, and the English at Sierra Leone, in the Gambia, and on the Gold Coast; and I know not that there has been upon the part of any of these a desire manifested to raise an empire in Central Africa.   Certainly, there has been none on the part of the British : on the contrary, I think there is some reason to complain that our government has been too slow, at least for the welfare of Africa, in accepting territory which has been voluntarily offered to us, and in confirming the treaties which have been made by our officers.   We have been in possession of Sierra Leone not very far short of half a century ; and I am not aware that it can be alleged that any injury has been thereby inflicted upon the natives.

Lastly. There is this consideration, and to me it seems conclusive :—Granting that the danger to African liberty is as imminent as I consider it to be slight, still the state of the country is such, that, change as it may, it cannot change for the worse.

The other point to which I would call attention is, the encouragement which may be afforded to the infant cultivation of Africa, by promoting the admission and use of its productions.   I shall not advert to the assistance which we may fairly expect from the Legislature in this respect, when the subject is brought under its consideration in all its important bearings; with the example of France and the United States before them, I cannot doubt that Government will introduce such measures as a liberal and enlightened policy will dictate. But individuals have it in their power to contribute largely to the encouragement of African produce, by a preference that will cost them little. Let them recollect that for centuries we were mainly instrumental in checking cultivation in Africa: we ransacked the whole continent in order to procure labourers for the West Indies. Is it, then, too much to ask, now when we are endeavouring to raise her from the gulf of wretchedness into which we have contributed to plunge her, that while she is struggling with enormous difficulties, we should force her industry and excite her to unfold her capabilities by anxiously encouraging the consumption of her produce?

CHAPTER VI.

ELEVATION OF NATIVE MIND.

***

"Wisdom is a defence, and money is a defence; but the excellency of knowledge is, that Wisdom giveth Life to them that have it."—Ecclesiastes, vii. 12.

" That peace and happiness, truth and justice, religion and piety, may be
established among them for all generations."—Liturgy.

***

I NOW come to the point which I deliberately consider to be beyond all others momentous in the question before us. I lay great stress upon African commerce, *more* upon the cultivation of soil, but *most*
of all upon the elevation of the native mind.

This is a wide subject; it embraces the consideration of some difficult questions. They resolve themselves into these: 1st. Are the Africans able and
willing to learn? 2d. *What*, and *how shall we teach*
them?

It is true that the inhabitants of Africa are in the
very depths of ignorance and superstition; but, still,
there are amongst them redeeming symptoms, however slight, sufficient to prove that the fault is not in
their nature, but in their condition; and to teach us,
that when we shall have put down that prodigious evil
which forbids all hope of their improvement, it is abundantly possible that the millions of Africa may assume

their place among civilized and Christian nations; and that a region, whose rank luxuriance now poisons the atmosphere, may be brought under subjection to the plough, may yield a wealthy harvest to its occupants, and open a new world, as exciting to our skill, capital, and enterprise, as was America on its first discovery. In these views it is a satisfaction to me that I can lean upon an authority so stable as that of Mr. Pitt. Mr. Wilberforce, writing to Mr. Stephen in 1817, says: "Reflection renders me more and more confident that we shall, or, at least, that they who live a few years will, see the beginnings of great reforms in the West Indies, as well as *opening prospects of civilization in Africa.* In the latter instance I must say, even to you, that Pitt's death has been an irreparable loss to us. He had truly grand views on the topic of our moral and humane debt to Africa." *

And there is a speech on record, of which Mr. Sheridan said at the time, " If Mr. Pitt were always thus to speak, the opposition could not survive a fortnight;" and of which Mr. Fox said 15 years afterwards, that it was "the most powerful eloquence that ever adorned those walls; a speech not of vague and showy ornament, but of solid and irresistible argument;" in that speech Mr. Pitt said, "Some of us may live to see a reverse of that picture, from which we now turn our eyes with shame and regret; we may live to behold the natives of Africa engaged in the calm occupations of industry, and in the pursuit of a just and legitimate commerce; we may behold the beams

* Wilberforce's Life, vol. iv. p. 306.

of science and philosophy breaking in upon their land, which, at some happier period, in still later times, may blaze with full lustre, and, joining their influence to that of PURE RELIGION, may illuminate and invigorate the most distant extremities of that immense continent."

In the first part of this work I have given a description of the deadly superstition which prevails in Africa, and of the effect it produces. The reader is requested to carry a sense of this most miserable state of things along with him, while we are considering what can be done towards the moral, intellectual, and religious improvement of the people.

Preliminary to this, I beg to call attention to certain indications,—faint, no doubt,—but, considering the difficulties and impediments to improvement in Africa, encouraging indications,—of a capability for better things ;

And also, to show that there are facilities for giving instruction to the inhabitants, which hold out the hope that our labours, if we shall be induced to make them, will not be in vain.

Hence an argument for a mighty effort towards the moral and intellectual improvement of Africa, may be successfully derived.

Before I proceed to these indications of capability, I must premise that a just judgment cannot be formed of the Africans without reference to the circumstances in which they are placed. Things which would be no proof at all of intelligence in an European, who had been taught the truths of religion, and been under the influence of a certain measure of refinement and civilization, denote positive intellect in an African savage from his birth, imbibing the grossest superstition, and bereaved of motives to action by his insecurity.

What Allowance then should be made in favour of the Negro?

When we find that at this period of the world there are nations not very remote from the centre of civilization, who have as yet learned the use of no agricultural implement but the hoe, and who, eager for wealth, have not energy enough to till their land, or work their mines, or in any way to avail themselves of the prodigal bounty of nature, we are apt to rush to the obvious but fallacious conclusion, that they are not men in the ordinary sense of the term, but beings of a stunted intellect, and of a degraded order.

This false conception has been the cause of infinite suffering to the negro race. During the whole controversy on the subject of slavery, it was the great defence and apology of the planters; it constituted their whole case. They triumphantly pointed at the idleness of the negro, and extracted from it a justification of the *necessary* severity with which he was treated. The error has not as yet been dissipated; many benevolent persons, judging of the African under his present aspect, despair of his improvement.

It will serve better than a thousand arguments to dispel this idea of inferiority in the African, and to induce us to make large allowances for him, notwithstanding his existing debasement, if I produce before my readers individuals of European extraction, of a race which amongst Europeans is supposed to stand in the highest rank for energy and intelligence, who have been, in the space of a few months, corrupted and debased by oppression. When Englishmen are masters, and Africans their slaves, we charge them with sloth, deception, thievishness; and we rate them as another and an inferior order in the family of man. I am going to reverse the picture, and to show that when Africans are masters and Englishmen their slaves, they reckon us a poor, pitiful, degraded race of mortals; inveterate thieves, and proverbial liars; too lazy to work, too stupid to learn, too base to be credited; hardly sensible of the obligation of an oath; and fit only to be hewers of wood and drawers of water to the true believers, to whom God, in answer to their prayers, has been pleased to send them.

> " It may from many a blunder free us,
> To see ourselves as others see us."

Such, as I shall show, is the reproach in each case; and in each case I doubt not that it is just. Let Slavery be imposed on man of whatever race, that man is found a poor, tame, degenerate creature. The black, being a slave, thieves; so does the white. He lies; so does the white. The black will not do a

stroke of work, except under the terror of the lash;
just so the white. The fact, in both cases, is true;
and the fallacy lies, not in an erroneous opinion of
the demerits of the slave, but in this—that each
forms his estimate on a being corrupted by oppression. He forgets that it is natural that the man
reared in slavery should be tainted with slavish vices;
that, denied access to knowledge, it is natural he
should be ignorant; that, wanting a motive, he necessarily wants perseverance.

Before we can pronounce a man, or a race of men,
desperately wicked, and incorrigibly idle, they must
have their fair chances as men—we must give them
a motive for their exertions. We must associate
with the fatigues we call for, a sense of personal
advantage to spring from them; we must awaken
whatever there may be of native vigour sleeping in
their bosoms, and we must release them from the
trammels which incumber their progress, if we desire
to see them advance with rapidity.

One corroboration of this doctrine is to be found
in the history of Adams, who was wrecked upon the
coast of Africa, made a slave to the inhabitants, and
was carried to Timbuctoo. Adams was a British
sailor, and our consul at Mogadore thus describes
him at the termination of his captivity:—" *Like
most other Christians, after a long captivity and
severe treatment among the Arabs, he appeared, at
his first arrival, exceedingly stupid and insensible.*"*

* Adams's Residence at Timbuctoo. Introd. p. 24.

But a still more forcible illustration of the truth of this theory is to be found in the very interesting narrative of the loss of the Oswego, on the coast of Africa, and the enslavement of Captain Paddock and his crew. He was a man on whose statement every reliance could be placed. De Witt Clinton, governor of New York, thus writes to him, October 1817,— " I have been urged by several respectable gentlemen, who, together with myself, repose the utmost confidence in your candour and veracity, and who have been a long time acquainted with the respectability of your standing in society, to solicit from you a statement of your sufferings and adventures." In compliance with this application, the narrative was published.

Captain Paddock was a Quaker, high in repute with the Society of Friends, by whom no man will be respected who is not strictly veracious. He himself gives proof of the effect which slavery had upon his own morals. He furnishes an elaborate description of his various modes of robbing and deceiving his master. He steals his corn, his tobacco, his fruit, his boat. He makes no scruple of telling falsehoods out of number to his master, and of purloining everything he could lay his hands on.

Of this, the following will serve as an illustration : —" I was soon after called away to furnish tobacco for a few who were smoking under the shade of the walls. When they had done, my second mate, who was as fond of tobacco as myself, suggested a query as to the propriety of robbing the pouch of a little.

We did so, and divided the spoil among such of our company as were tobacco-chewers. Not long after, some new company having come, I was again called upon to bring the pouch; and the fellow, on opening it, charged me with stealing from it. Against that charge I defended myself as well as I could. For some time I was unwilling to make the hazardous attempt again; but at last, while the Arabs were all lying asleep under the shade, I proposed to my second mate that we two should go off together to some distance, where we might have an opportunity of taking some out in such a manner as not to be suspected.

*　　*　　*　　*　　*

" We sat down in the finest piece of wheat I ever saw, and commenced the business that we went upon, taking particular notice of the turns of the string and knot of the pouch, in which, when we had unrolled it, we found two little sticks, laid in such a manner as to detect me in my next attempt upon it, and doubtless for that purpose. Having opened the tobacco, we took out as much of it as we durst, and replaced the little sticks as exactly as possible, when we rolled it up again, putting round it the string just as we found it, and hurried out of the field." *

The Africans having discovered that their captives were exceedingly idle, resorted to exactly our own methods of procuring (what was formerly so much dwelt upon in this country) " steady labour in the sun." They beat them, they starved them; they said to them, " If you will not work, neither shall

* Loss of the Oswego, p. 181.

you eat;" and even threatened to shoot them for
their indolence. Captain Paddock says, " Early in
the morning of the 27th, the sickles that the Arabs
brought with them were made ready, and all of us
were ordered out to work." This he refused, for
which he received their curses and threats, but determined not to heed them. "This controversy lasted
an hour, and they got my men into the field at last.
Some of them could handle a sickle as well as the
Arabs themselves; and I told one of them (the man
that I was fearful would be of the most service to
our enslavers) to cut his own fingers, as if by accident. They all understood my meaning, and it was
not long after my men had been dragged into the
field before I found they were doing very well;
I mean *well* for our own purposes. Some by accident, and some intentionally, perhaps, cut their
fingers and hands with their sickles, and made loud
complaints; while others, who were gathering up
the grain for binding, did it in such a wasteful
manner, that their work was a real loss to the owner.
Upon this the Arabs took away the sickles from those
that had been reaping, and set them to haul the
grain up by the roots. They did so, but laid it in
the worst form that was possible. By managing
things in this way, they beat the Ishmaelites, and
got the victory."*

Their masters, finding that all their efforts to overcome the indolence of their Christian slaves were
ineffectual, directed their vengeance against Pad-

* Loss of the Oswego, p. 157 to 159.

dock, saying, "If Rias works, his men will, for he is
the head devil among them."

It is curious to remark that the opinions the Africans entertained of us bore a strong resemblance to
the doctrine, now I trust obsolete, but not long ago
in full vogue amongst ourselves, of the inferiority of
the African race. All who took an interest in the
question of negro emancipation must remember the
deep prejudice which was felt by the white population of the West Indies against any approach towards
social intercourse with those who had black blood in
their veins. I have heard of a clergyman who was
persecuted for admitting persons of colour to the
Sacrament at the same time with the whites; of a
gentleman who was banished from society for the
crime of permitting his own coloured daughters to
ride with him in his carriage through the public
streets; and upon the occasion of two gentlemen of
colour being admitted under the gallery of the House
of Commons when their own case was under discussion, I heard a member of Parliament express in a
very animated speech his disgust at the insult thus
offered to the representatives of the people : " He had
hoped never to have seen the day when the laws of
decency and of nature might thus be trampled on."
We are not the only persons who have insisted on this
aristocracy of complexion. Paddock and others have
recorded that " swinish-looking dogs and white-
skinned devils were the appellations which were fami-
liarly applied to them by Africans." " The Arabs
were well received here ; but we were more ridiculed

than ever we had been, receiving an abundance of
the vile epithets so common to these people, who had
ever viewed us as a *poor degraded set of beings,*
scarcely fit to live in the world. The old man
(Ahomed) was seated opposite the gate at the time.
He spoke to me, and bade me sit down; I sat down,
but, happening to sit near him, he ordered me away
to a greater distance, saying, he did not allow a Christian dog to be so near him; I obeyed, and moved
off a little. The women were foremost in inso-
lence and abuse; but their children were not far
behind them."*   " They frequently spoke of us, but
in such a manner as often to remind me of the old
adage, ' Listeners seldom hear any good of themselves.' That saying was verified here completely.
The heads of their discourse concerning us were,†

* Loss of the Oswego, page 208.

† About the same estimate of negroes was at one time entertained by British subjects.   " An Act for the Security of the
Subject" was passed in Bermuda in 1730.   A passage of it runs
thus :—" Whereas, they (negroes, Indians, mulattos) being, for
brutishness of their nature, no otherwise valued or esteemed
amongst us than as our goods and chattels, or other personal
estates; be it therefore enacted, that if any person or persons
whatsoever, within these islands, being owner or possessor of any
negroes, Indians, mulattos, or other slaves, shall, in the deserved
correction or punishment of his, her, or their slave or slaves, for
crimes or offences by them committed or supposed to be committed,
accidentally happen to kill any such slave or slaves, the aforesaid
owner or possessor shall not be liable to any imprisonment, arraign-
ment, or subject to any penalty or forfeiture whatsoever; but if
any person or persons whatsoever shall *maliciously and wilfully*
kill and destroy any slave or slaves, then the aforesaid person or

that we were a poor, miserable, degraded race of mortals, doomed to the everlasting punishment of hell fire after death, and, in this life, fit only for the company of dogs; that our country was so wretchedly poor that we were always looking out abroad for sustenance, and ourselves so base as to go to the coast of Guinea for slaves to cultivate our land, being not only too lazy to cultivate it ourselves, but too stupid to learn how to do it; and finally, that if all Christians were to be obliged to live at home, their race would soon be extinct;" and "an old man swore that we were not worthy of a mouthful of bread."* " They think that there are no' people in the world so active and brave as themselves, nor any so well informed; and they proudly say that they are at war with all the world, and fear nobody." †

Upon one occasion, the Arab appears to have had the best of the argument. " Ahomed made some inquiries of me respecting the manufactories of my own country, which I answered as well as I could; and I took the liberty to tell him how much better he would be treated than we had been, if by any accident he should be thrown on our shores; that, in such an event, instead of being held in bondage, and sold from tribe to tribe, our sultan would have him conducted back to his native country in safety. He heard me out, and then warmly retorted upon me as follows:—' You say, if I were in your country, your

persons shall forfeit and pay unto our Sovereign Lord the King the full sum of ten pounds current money."

* Loss of the Oswego, p. 148.　　　　　† Ibid. 144.

people would treat me better than I treat you. There
is no truth in you. If I were there, I should be
doomed to perpetual slavery, and be put to the hardest
labour in tilling your ground. You are too lazy to
work yourselves in your fields, and therefore send
your ships to the negro coast, and, in exchange for
the useless trinkets with which you cheat the poor
negroes, you take away ship-loads of them to your
country, from which never one returns; and had your
own ship escaped our shore, you yourself would now
be taking the poor negroes to everlasting slavery.'

"Although the purpose of my voyage had been
very different from what Ahomed suspected, yet I felt
the sting of this reproach in a manner that I can
never forget."

Upon another occasion, Ahomed drew no very
flattering comparison between the conduct of Christians and that of the followers of the Prophet. " The
negroes are men that you Christian dogs have taken
from the Guinea country, a climate that suits them
best. You are *worse than Arabs,* who enslave you
only when it is God's will to send you to our coast.
Never, I must confess, did I feel a reproach more
sensibly."*

The distinction made by the Arab between the
conduct of Mussulmans and Christians, was as just as
it was ingenious. Their creed permits the disciples
of the true Prophet to enslave the heretics; whereas,
our purer faith says, " Whatsoever ye would that
men should do to you, do ye even so to them;" and

* Loss of the Oswego, p. 112.

abounds in noble passages, denouncing God's wrath against the oppressor, and particularly that oppressor who is a man-stealer, and " who taketh his neighbour's labour without wages, and giveth him nought for his work."

We remember the time when a negro slave who absconded was convicted and punished as a thief. He had run away with his master's chattels, *i. e.* his own body. The Arab seems to have adopted a somewhat similar train of reasoning. " After a few minutes' silence," says Captain Paddock, " Ahomed accosted me in the following manner :—' *There is no confidence to be placed in Christians;* for whenever they come ashore on our coast, they bury their money in the sand, as you yourself have done, to prevent it from falling into the hands of the true believers. *It is our property.* We pray earnestly to the Almighty God to send Christians ashore here : he hears our prayers, and often sends us good ships ; and if you did as you ought to do, we should have the benefit of them."*

It is very curious that, in the course of their journey, they fell in with a tribe of African abolitionists and Mahommedan quakers. At one town their reception was different to what it had usually been. " I inquired," said Paddock, " who they were. He replied, ' They belong to a sect called *Foulah*. They will not mix with the other inhabitants, but choose to live altogether by themselves ; and are so stupid, that if the Emperor of Morocco should march

* Loss of the Oswego, p. 190.

an army to cut off the whole race, they would not defend themselves, but would die like fools, as they are.'
I asked him if they used fire-arms. ' No,' said he,
' they make no use of them ; and if God was pleased
to send a Christian ship ashore near them, they would
neither seize upon the goods nor the men, nor would
they buy a slave of any kind.' I asked him if they
were numerous ; and he answered, ' No, they are not
numerous ; but the dwellings you see on the sides of
the hills yonder are theirs, and in many other places
they are to be found ; and wherever they are, they
always keep together by themselves.' Finally, I
asked him if they were Mahometans. ' Yes,' he
answered, ' they are, or else we would destroy them ;
but they are poor ignorant dogs, and little better
than the Christians.' "*

I should feel myself called upon to apologise to my
readers for these lengthened quotations, were it not
important to show that Europeans and Christians
are not proof against that moral poison which belongs
to oppression. Let a man, European, American, or
African, imbibe that taint, and its virulence will be
manifest in the stupidity of his understanding, in the
deadness of his moral sense ; it will be visible to the
eye of the most careless observer, even in the external
features and carriage of its victim. Reduced to the condition of a slave, he will droop and relax, and become
good for nothing, or next to nothing. We see that
a race fortified by early association, by the resources
of intellect and education, and by the elevating prin-

* Loss of the Oswego, p. 199.

ciples of Christianity, placed in precisely the same circumstances as the African, exhibits precisely the same degree of degeneracy. And can we wonder that they who have so long been the victims of every species of cruelty, should not as yet have put forth those generous qualities and that higher order of intellect which will not grow, except in a genial atmosphere, and on a favouring soil? Does not this rescue the African from the supposed stigma of inferiority?

Franklin defines a slave to be " an animal who eats as much, and works as little, as possible." The black, the brown, the red, the white races of men, are alike indolent when they want a motive for exertion. " Ye be idle, ye be idle," was the reproach of Pharaoh to his Israelitish bondsmen; " ye be idle, ye be idle," says the master to the slave in all nations and in all ages.

> " 'T is liberty alone that gives the flow'r
> Of fleeting life its lustre and perfume,
> And we are *weeds* without it.

I now proceed to the enumeration of the symptoms which lead me to hope that in due time the African races may be excited to industry, ingenuity, and perseverance.

I admit that on the coast there is a belt of slave-trading chiefs, who, at present, find it more profitable to supply the slave-markets than to conduct a legitimate commerce. Little business can be done when there are any slavers at their stations,—indeed, the fair traders are always compelled to wait until the human cargoes are completed. These chiefs not only obstruct the fair trader on the coast, but as much as possible prevent his access to the interior. Insecurity, demoralisation, and degradation are the results; but as we recede from the coast, and ascend the rivers, comparative civilisation is found, industry becomes apparent, and no inconsiderable skill in many useful arts is conspicuous. All travellers have observed the superior cultivation, and comparatively dense population of the inland regions. Laird, in ascending the Niger, writes, " Both banks of the river are thickly studded with towns and villages; I could count seven from the place where we lay aground; and between Eboe and the confluence of the rivers, there cannot be less than 40, one generally occurring every two or three miles. The principal towns are Attah and Addakudda; and averaging the inhabitants at 1,000, will, I think, very nearly give the population of the banks.   *   *   *   The general character of the people is much superior to that of the swampy country between them and the coast. They are shrewd, intelligent, and quick in their perception, milder in their disposition, and more peaceable in their habits." Oldfield says (vol. i. p. 163,) that, from the great number of towns they passed, he is inclined to suppose that the population must be very dense indeed. And (vol. ii. p. 17,) " no sooner does the traveller approach one town, than he discovers three or four, and sometimes five others." Park speaks (vol. ii. p. 80,) of the " hills cultivated to the very summit, and the surplus grain employed in purchasing luxuries from native traders."

Laing speaks (p. 156) with delight of " the extensive meadows, clothed in verdure, and the fields from which the springing rice and ground-nuts were sending forth their green shoots, not inferior in beauty and health to the corn-fields of England, interspersed here and there with a patch of ground studded with palm-trees." Tuckey reports (p. 342) a similar improvement in the face of the country at some distance up the Congo, where he found towns and villages following each other in rapid succession. Ashmun, writing from Liberia, says, " An excursion of some of our people into the country, to the distance of about 140 miles, has led to a discovery of the populousness and comparative civilisation of this district of Africa, never till within a few months even conjectured by myself. We are situated within 50 leagues of a country, in which a highly improved agriculture prevails; where the horse is a common domestic animal, where extensive tracts of land are cleared and enclosed, where every article absolutely necessary to comfortable life is produced by the skill and industry of the inhabitants; where the Arabic is used as a written language in the ordinary commerce of life; where regular and abundant markets and fairs are kept; and where a degree of intelligence and practical refinement distinguishes the inhabitants, little compatible with the personal qualities attached, in the current notions of the age, to the people of Guinea." *

The wants of the people in Africa must not, any more than their industry and enterprise, be judged of

* From Miss. Regr. for 1828, p. 335.

by what is observable on the coast. The Moors, who have preceded us in the interior, have imparted more knowledge of commercial transactions than we may suppose. Captain Clapperton told Mr. Hamilton that he could have negotiated a bill on the Treasury of London at Soccatoo. The Moors have introduced the use of the Arabic in mercantile affairs; and that language is nearly as useful in Africa, as the French language is in Europe. In 1812, Mr. Willis, formerly British Consul for Senegambia, stated his belief that in the warehouses of Timbuctoo were accumulated the manufactures of India and Europe, and that the immense population of the banks of the Niger are thence supplied. A Moorish merchant reported to Mr. Jackson, that between Mushgrelia and Houssa there were more boats employed on the river than between Rosetta and Cairo ; and that the fields of that country were enclosed and irrigated by canals and water-wheels,*—a demonstrative proof of the activity, industry, and civilisation of the people.

" Thirty years' experience," says an African mer-chant (Mr. Johnston), " of the natives, derived from living amongst them for the whole of that period, leaves a strong impression on my mind that, with due encouragement, they would readily be led to the cultivation of the soil, which I think in most places capable of growing anything." Mr. Laird, in a letter to me, observes,—" As to the character of the inhabit-ants, I can only state that, if there is one characteristic

* Jackson's Timbuctoo, pp. 24, 38, and 427.

that distinguishes an African from other uncivilised people, it is his love of, and eagerness for, traffic : men, women, and children trade in all directions. They have regular market-places where they bring the produce of their fields, their manufactures, their ivory, and everything they can sell. * * * At the Iccory-Market I have seen upwards of one hundred large canoes, each holding from ten to forty men, all trading peaceably together. I was informed by the natives that it was considered neutral ground, and that the towns at war with one another, attended the same market amicably." The industrious inhabitants of the Grain Coast supply Sierra Leone, and Liberia with the greatest portion of their food.

One of the sub-agents of the Slave Trading Company, which I have already noticed, thus writes to his principal from the town of Gotto, about ten leagues up the river Benin, of date 20th June, 1837 : " I was astonished to see so large a market the day I arrived. The town is large and eligible ; there were at least 4000 persons at market with all sorts of commodities for sale."

Of their capabilities of improvement we may judge from the rude efforts of negroes transported from North America, or liberated from slave-ships at Sierra Leone. What these men have wanted, as Colonel Denham remarks, is " instruction, example, and capital;" and he adds, " that, with the small amount of either that they have received, it is a sub-

* Class A, 1838-9, p. 64.

ject of astonishment to him that they have done what they have."—(Despatch, 21st May, 1829.) They supply the market of Freetown with plenty of fruit and vegetables, such as yams, cassada, Indian corn, ground-nuts, pine-apples, sugar-canes, &c., &c.

Nearly the same account may be given of the exuberant fertility of the eastern as of the western coast, and of the lucrative character of the commerce which might be there carried on were it not for the destructive Slave Trade. I have been informed by the captain of a merchant-vessel who was long on the eastern coast, that before the Slave Trade absorbed the whole attention of the people, two merchant-ships used to be annually despatched from Lisbon, which for the most paltry outfit, brought home return cargoes of from 40,000*l*. to 60,000*l*.*

Other testimonies might be added to show that the African is not wanting in those qualities which accompany civilisation, and he only requires that a right direction should given to his industry and intelligence, to qualify him for intercourse with the more refined European.

* The gentleman who furnished this information, mentions the following articles of commerce on the eastern coast of Africa :— Gold, silver, copper, iron, ivory, horns, tallow, hides, skins, tortoiseshell, ostrich-feathers, pearls, ambergris, amber, gums and various drugs, palm-oil, cocoa-nut oil, black whale-oil, spermoil, bees'-wax in great abundance, coffee, tobacco, indigo, corn, rice, &c. A most profitable trade might also be carried on in cowries, which abound on the coast, where he has purchased them at 4*d.* a-bushel; on the western coast they are the current coin, and are told out by the hundred. All these articles find a ready market at Ceylon, Bombay, and Calcutta.

The eagerness with which the Timmanees entered into the laborious and fatiguing work of cutting, squaring, and floating to the trading stations the immense bodies of heavy teak timber exported from Sierra Leone, is a convincing proof of their readiness to engage in any employment where they can get a reward, however small, for their labour. It is well known that during the time the timber trade was in activity, several native towns were formed on the banks of the river, and many natives came from a distance up the country to engage in it. Timber was cut at the termination of the largest creeks at Port Logo, and even so far as Rokou, and floated down to Tombo, Bance Island, and Tasso. (Laing, p. 77.)*

I have lately seen a portion of the Journal of the Rev. W. Fox, written at Macarthy's Island, in which, of date September 3, 1836, he mentions having given away a considerable number of Arabic Scriptures to Mandingoes, and to Serrawoollies, or Tiloboonkoes, as they are here more generally termed; which literally means Eastern people, as they come from the neighbourhood of, and beyond, Bondou, and are strict Mahommetans. They come here and hire themselves

---

* " Twenty years ago," says Laird (vol. ii. p. 363), " African timber was unknown in the English market. There are now from 13,000 to 15,000 loads annually imported. In 1832 Mr. Forster, in a letter to Lord Goderich, stated the importation as high as ' from 15,000 to 20,000 loads, giving employment to 20,000 tons of shipping annually.' From 3,000 to 4,000 loads of red teak-wood are exported annually from the Gambia," and the mahogany from that river is now much used for furniture.

as labourers for several months, and with the articles they receive in payment barter them again on their way home for more than their actual value on this island.

The Kroomen who inhabit Cape Palmas are a most extraordinary race of men. They neither sell nor allow themselves to be made slaves. These men leave their homes young, and work on board the trading vessels on the coast, or at Sierra Leone. Their attachment to their country is great, nor will they engage themselves for more than three years. " To my mind," says Mr. Laird, in the letter to me which I have before quoted, " these men appear destined by Providence to be the means of enabling Europeans to penetrate into the remotest parts of Africa by water. They are patient, enduring, faithful, easily kept in order, and brave to rashness when led by white men. Any number may be got at wages from two to four dollars per month."

We thus find that little difficulty exists in procuring either labourers or seamen in Africa.

To those disposed to make the necessary allowances, it is something to know that it has been remarked by many travellers, that the Africans are by no means devoid of aptitude and ingenuity in imitating European manufactures. Thus, at the island of Tombo Mr. Rankin* saw the lock of a rifle which had been so well repaired by a Foulah, who had never seen any but the fractured one, that strict examination was necessary to discover what part had been

* Rankin, vol. i. p. 130.

replaced. In Benin they make muskets, procuring only the locks from Europe; and at the market of Jennè, De Caillie observed gunpowder, of an inferior kind indeed to ours, but of home manufacture. In most parts of Africa the natives have some notion of working metals.* They are acquainted with many dyes, and make much use of indigo. Colonel Denham† says that the dark blue of the tobes (or tunic) worn in Bornou cannot be excelled in any part of the world; and Kano is famed for its indigo establishments. I am told that they are also acquainted with a plant which produces a more brilliant blue than the indigo. From other vegetable substances they obtain other colours; thus Wadstrom stated to the Committee of 1790,‡ that the whole army of the king of Damel was clothed in cloth of native manufacture, dyed orange and brown. They also give a red or black dye to their leather; for the tanning of which they use several kinds of bark.§

In the year 1818 Mr. Clarkson had a conference, on the subject of the Slave Trade, with the Emperor Alexander at Aix-la-Chapelle. I have before me a private letter which he wrote to J. J. Gurney, Esq., describing the interview. He states that he exhibited articles in leather, in iron, in gold, in cotton cloth, mats, &c. " Having gone over all

---

* The Rev. Mr. Fox has recently presented me with two gold rings of excellent workmanship, manufactured by a native of the Gambia.

† Clapperton, p. 60.

‡ Abbrev. Evid. vol. iii. p. 10.

§ Rankin, vol. i. p. 132. Clapperton, p. 61, 62.

the articles, the Emperor desired me to inform him
whether he was to understand that these articles were
made by the Africans in their own country, that is,
in their own native villages; or after they had arrived
in America, where they would have an opportunity
of seeing European manufactures. I replied, that
such articles might be found in every African village,
both on the coast and in the interior; and that they
were samples of their own ingenuity, without any
connection with Europeans. ' Then,' said the Emperor, ' you have given me a new idea of the state of
these poor people. I was not aware that they were
so far advanced in society. The works you have
shown me are not the works of brutes, but of men
endued with rational and intellectual powers, and
capable of being brought to as high a degree of pro-
ficiency as other men. Africa ought to be allowed
to have a fair chance of raising her character in the
scale of the civilised world.' I replied that it was
the cruel traffic which had prevented her from rising
to a level with other countries, and that it was really
astonishing to me that the natives had, under its im-
peding influence, arrived at the perfection which displayed itself in the specimens he had just seen. The
Emperor replied that it was equally astonishing to
him, for that wherever the trade existed, a man could
have no stimulus to labour; being subject every hour
to be taken away for a slave, he could not tell whether
he should enjoy the fruits of it; he was sure upon
this principle that no man in Africa would sow more
corn than was sufficient for his own consumption;

and so the same principle would prove an obstacle to any extraordinary cultivation of the works of art."

The natives have some turn both for husbandry and gardening. In the more settled parts of the interior more pains are taken with cultivation, and even the slaves are said to work better than those on the coast. One of the best specimens of African agriculture is given by De Caillie, as observed by him at Kimba, on the road between Kankan and Jennè:—

" I walked about in the neighbourhood of our habitation, and was delighted with the good cultivation; the natives raise little mounds of earth in which they plant their pistachios and yams; and these mounds are arranged with some taste, all of the same height, and in rows. Rice and millet are sown in trenches; as soon as the rainy season commences, they put in the seed around their habitations, and when the maize is in flower they plant cotton between the rows. The maize is ripe very early, and they then fill it up to make room for the other crop. If they do not plant cotton, they turn up the ground after the maize is got in, and transplant the millet into it, a practice which I never observed in Kankan. I was surprised to find these good people so laborious and careful; on every side in the country I saw men and women weeding the fields. They grow two crops in the year on the same land; I have seen rice in ear, and other rice by its side scarcely above the ground."*

Agriculture is obviously one of the first arts to

* De Caillie's Travels, vol. i. p. 293, 294.

which we ought to direct their attention, not merely
as furnishing the surest ground for our future commercial intercourse, but as tending to bring the people
into a condition of life most favourable for the reception and spread of Christianity.   When Mr. Read
set forth to convert the Bushmen on the frontier of
Cape colony, he is reported to have said, " We take a
plough with us; but let it be remembered, that in
Africa the Bible and the plough go together."   And
in the same spirit should I desire that our operations
might be carried on.   At present, indeed, trade (the
barter of such articles as the country spontaneously
produces, and which may suffice for the limited demand
Africa has hitherto known,) is likely to be more to
their taste than an occupation requiring regular
labour ; still the cultivation which has arisen in many
places on the stoppage of the Slave Trade, the ground-
nuts grown for sale on the Gambia, the corn raised
for exportation on the Gold Coast, the cutting of
timber at Sierra Leone, and the preparation of palm-
oil at the mouths of the Niger, prove that these people
may be led to adopt new methods of earning wealth
by honest industry.   In fact I think it is evident that,
as Sir R. Mends wrote in 1823 to the Admiralty,
" wherever the traffic in slaves has been checked, the
natives have shown a fair and reasonable desire for
cultivating the productions of their country."*

* It is impossible not to observe with regret how little these
" desires " have met with encouragement from Europeans.   Captain Arabin, in describing the fertile banks of the river Cassa-
manza, where the Portuguese have factories, thus refers to the

The negro's aptitude for letters has, as we may well suppose, been still less exercised than his manual skill; but we have proof, I think, that as a race, they are by no means deficient. On this point I may quote the words of an accurate observer, a Quaker lady,* who devoted much of her life to the promotion of African education, and at last sacrificed it in the cause.

" If my heart might speak from what my eye has seen, I would say I am fully convinced that it is not any inferiority in the African mind, or natural capacity, that has kept them in so depressed a state in the scale of society, but the lack of those advantages which are, in the usual order of Providence, made use of as instruments for the advancement and improvement of human beings. Those disadvantages which they, in common with other uncivilised natives, have suffered, have with them been cruelly increased, by that oppression, which, wherever exercised, has a natural ten-

inhabitants, who, though now hardly to be distinguished from the aboriginal negroes, yet are partly descended from the first settlers. " They have remarkably fine cotton and indigo, and manufacture from them cloth of a dye and texture highly esteemed in Africa, and susceptible of much greater improvement; but the Portuguese, neglecting these advantages and capabilities of a people who have a mixture of their own blood in their veins, direct their attention almost wholly to the traffic in slaves, and sell indiscriminately these ingenious artificers, with their wives and children, whenever they can catch them."—" State of the Slave Trade," in the *Amulet*, 1832, p. 218.

* Hannah Kilham, who made three voyages to Africa for the sake of acquainting herself with the native languages; she reduced to writing the Wolof or Jaloof, in which she printed reading lessons.

dency to fetter, to depress, and to blunt the powers
of the mind ; and it is very unfair, and a great aggravation of the cruelty, to reflect on the victims of it, as
wanting ability for any other station than that which
they have been suffered to fill. I do not think that
even here [Sierra Leone] Africans have had a fair
trial of what they might be, had they the same advantages in education, and circumstances connected with
education, which Europeans have been favoured with,
yet their intelligent countenances, and the ability they
show when rightly instructed, evince certainly no
deficiency in the natural powers of the mind ; they
come here, as to a foreign land, the language of
which is quite strange and unknown to them, they are
taught in this strange language, (those of them who
have school instruction,) from lists of detached words,
spelling lessons, many of which they never hear but
in those lessons, and their meaning therefore remains
unknown."*

"It seems very evident from what we hear, that
civilisation is prevented, or has been prevented, along
the coast, by the prevalence of the horrid traffic in
men ; and the interior, north of the line, is much more
civilised than near the coast. The interior of the
south appears to be little known. I wish the sceptical as to African capacity could have seen a Foulah
man, of striking and intelligent countenance, who was
here the other day, and have heard his melodious
reading of Arabic manuscripts. I am informed, both
here and in the Gambia, that the Mahomedans of

* Letter from H. Kilham to W. Allen, 1824.

Western Africa are the most orderly and well conducted part of the African population. Their zeal
in the promotion of Arabic schools should stimulate
Europeans of higher profession. If persons be suit-
ably introduced, so as that their designs are fully
known, I believe intercourse, where only good is
intended, would, in most places, be made more easy
than some are willing to believe." *

FACILITIES FOR GIVING INSTRUCTION.

There is no more encouraging feature than the
readiness which has been generally observed on the
part of the negroes, to obtain for their children, and
sometimes for themselves, the advantages of education. Their love of acquiring knowledge, especially
that of languages, is thus spoken of by Mr. Laird.

" The eagerness with which the Africans thirst
after knowledge, is a very striking feature in their
character; on the coast great numbers have learned
to read writing from the captains of merchant vessels."†
He mentions that the late Duke Ephraim, chief of
Old Calabar, though he could not read a newspaper,
yet considered it essential to have a supply of books.
" The schools at Sierra Leone and Cape Coast have
done most, if not all, the good that has been done. I
know an instance now of a captured slave, resident
at Fernando Po, who sent his son to England for
education. All the chiefs would gladly pay for the

* Appendix to Second Report of African Instruction Society,
p. 11.

† Laird, vol. ii. p. 395.

board and education of their children. In the interior, in every village where Mahommedanism is professed, the children crowd to learn to mutter Arabic prayers and scraps of the Koran."

Liberia presents the example of a black community managing their own affairs on civilised principles. There, besides the governor, there is scarcely a white man in authority. They have two public libraries, a press, and the journal of the colony, "The Liberian Herald," is edited by a negro, the son of a slave of Virginia, and frequently contains able dissertations written by men of the same race.

Mr. Ashmun found the natives bordering on the American Colony of Liberia very desirous of putting their children under his care. He writes in a Report, 1825 :—" No man of the least consideration in the country, will desist from his importunities until at least one of his sons is fixed in some settler's family.*

At this time many of the natives reside in the colony, and are gradually adopting the habits of civilised life. Many came thither for the express purpose of obtaining a Christian education, for which purpose, also, many of the native kings continue to send their sons. Missionaries of various denominations have penetrated into the neighbouring states, and all have sent cheering accounts of their success and prospects.†

* Life of Ashmun, p. 271.

† Address of Judge Payne to the Vermont Colonisation Society, 1838.

Two Wesleyan ministers, Messrs. Dove and Badger, visited the " Plantains," an island on the mouth of the 'Sherbro', in April, 1839.

Mr. Dove says, " The island has a beautiful appearance, and the cattle on it look as fine as any I ever saw in my native land. The island, though small, belongs to King Calker, who treated us with great kindness. We took up our abode in the royal apartments, and the next day we dined with his Majesty. He is certainly a sensible man, and seems to be quite free from the vile and superstitious customs practised throughout the ' Sherbro' country; he possesses a pretty good knowledge of English, and expressed a wish to have a missionary to live with him; we had the high gratification of seeing him reading an English Bible. His brother, also, is a sincere inquirer after truth: having received some instruction when young, and living in Freetown, he now instructs both children and adults, and when we witnessed the result of this king's brother's labour, we could not but rejoice. He has translated several portions of the sacred Scriptures, catechisms, and some of our excellent hymns, into the ' Sherbro' language : he wishes me, if possible, to get them printed for the use of the heathen around him."

Besides this eagerness on the part of the African tribes to obtain intellectual and useful instruction, there is also a most encouraging willingness to receive, and listen to, the teachers of Christianity. Indeed, I am not aware of any instance of Christian

teachers having been repelled, when their object has
been fairly understood, except, indeed, by the notorious influence of European Slave Traders.   These
miscreants obliged the church missionaries to leave
some of their stations; an event deeply to be regretted, as they had established some excellent
schools on the Rio Pongas˙: one of their scholars
was Simeon Wilhelm, who died in England in 1817,
and was well known as a young man of remarkable
promise.*

Within the last three years Mr. Fox has visited
the chiefs of Woolli, Bondou, Barra, and Nyani, and
obtained from all, Pagan and Mahomedan, invitations
for missionaries.   The following is the account he
gives of an interview with Saada, the Almamy of
Bondou.

On Saturday, April 28, 1838, Mr. Fox reached
Boollibanny, the capital of the Mahomedan state of
Bondou, and on the following day had an interview
with Saada, who was encamped six miles from the
city, and was about to start on a marauding expedition.   On being introduced, Mr. Fox immediately
stated the object of his journey, adding that he had
visited the kingdoms of Barra, Nyani, and Woolli, and
that those kings were favourable to his design; and
giving, at the Almamy's request, a brief summary of
the doctrines and precepts of Christianity.   The
Almamy replied, that all that had been said was very
good ; and that Mr. Fox might look at the Bondou

* See the Life of Wilhelm, by the Rev. Mr. Bickersteth.

ground, and inform him when he had fixed upon a place; but that he and his people must still follow Mahomet.

" This being ended," Mr. Fox continues, " I told him I had one request to make; namely, that he would abandon the war he had in contemplation. In reply to my request, the Almamy asked, Why I did not wish him to go to war? I answered, From the misery that must of necessity follow; but especially because of the Divine command given to Moses, ' Thou shalt do no murder.' Shortly after this, I shook hands with this powerful chief, and we returned to our lodgings at Boollibanny.

" About an hour afterwards, to my surprise and that of others, the Almamy and his war-tribe came galloping home."

Mr. Freeman's visit to Ashantee has been already noticed. On this occasion his converts gave proof of the effect of the gospel which he had preached to them. No nation could have been more barbarously treated by another, than the Fantees by the Ashantees; who had exercised their power in the most ferocious manner, not only slaying them by thousands in the field, and destroying their villages, but putting hundreds of them to death by torture. It has been only British protection that has preserved the weaker race; yet no sooner did the ill-used Fantees hear of Mr. Freeman's views than they entered fully into them, and became, as he says, " not only willing, but anxious for him to go up to Coomassie." Such a salutary feeling has religion wrought in them, that they are now making a voluntary subscription to send the gospel to their blood-thirsty enemies.

We have also seen the results of Mr. Freeman's evpedition ; the impression made upon his mind was thus stated by himself after his return. " I am happy to inform you, that through the mercy of the God of missions, I have surmounted every difficulty, and returned fully satisfied that even the sanguinary Ashantees are ready to receive the gospel, and that, as soon as the committee can send a good supply of missionaries to this station, we shall, by the blessing of God, establish a mission among that people." *

In their last report, the Church Missionary Society state that they also hope soon to be able to extend their operations from Sierra Leone into the interior, that some preliminary excursions had been made by the missionaries, and that *the reception they met with from the people was encouraging*.

AGENTS TO BE OBTAINED.

We have already seen the desirableness of educating and civilising the inhabitants of Africa ; and a number of facts have been brought to light, tending to show, that there is at least as great a readiness on their part to receive instruction, as on ours to communicate it; the question now remains—Who are to be the instructors ? The climate is generally viewed as unfavourable to Europeans, and this being

* Wesleyan Missionary Notices, November, 1839, p. 166.

the case, I have great satisfaction in finding, that from among the liberated Africans in our West Indian Colonies, we are likely to be furnished with a number of persons, in whom are united the desirable qualifications of fitness for the climate, competency to act as teachers, and willingness to enter upon the work.

An important feature of the present time is this, that the exertions of the missionaries in the West Indies are beginning to tell on their converts in the missionary spirit which they have imparted. There is a feeling in the hearts of our emancipated negroes towards the land of their origin, which seems to have arisen spontaneously in various congregations.

Last December, in the hope that openings might ere long occur for the employment of native agents, I addressed, through the Rev. Mr. Trew, a circular to the heads of missionary societies, inquiring whether trustworthy persons could be found for various departments of our operations. Before answers could be received, the Rev. Mr. Dyer, the secretary of the Baptist Missionary Society, transmitted to me an inquiry on their part in the following letter to the committee at home, from the minister of one of their congregations in Jamaica.

Montego Bay, Jan. 21*st*, 1839.

" We beg to press upon your attention a subject of vast importance, and shall feel thankful if, at the very earliest opportunity, you will bring it before the

members of the committee, with our earnest request
that they will take it into their prayerful and serious
consideration, and without delay adopt measures to
realise the desires of many thousands of their fellow
Christians in this island.   The subject is, a mission
to the interior of Western Africa; the land from
which the beloved people of our charge, or their
forefathers, were stolen, and which is at present
without the light of the gospel, and suffering under
accumulated wrongs.   We, their ministers, feel on
this subject an intense interest, while in *their* hearts
the strongest emotions are excited for the perishing
land of their fathers.   The conversion of Africa to
God is the theme of their conversation and their
prayers, and the object of their most ardent desires.
For this they are willing to toil, and devote the fruits
of their labour, while some are anxious to go themselves, and proclaim to their kindred the love of
Christ in dying for their salvation.   In short, a feeling prevails among the members of our churches, to
check which would be to injure their piety, and we
believe would grieve that Divine Spirit, by whose
gracious influences those feelings have been excited.

" There being no direct communication between
this island and Africa, and few sources of information
respecting that country being opened to us, we are at
a loss to fix upon any plan to carry our desires into
effect, and are therefore desirous that the committee
should give it all the consideration it demands, and as
early as possible communicate their sentiments to us."

The following letter to myself, from a highly respectable gentleman, is of a somewhat similar character:—

Kingston, Jamaica, May 1st, 1839.

" It is very remarkable that before being acquainted with the movements in England, *we* had been acting in some measure practically on your principle. Three or four months ago a large meeting, consisting of betwixt 2000 and 3000 persons, was held in this city, for the purpose of considering the best means of Christianising Africa, by such Christian agency as we could collect in this island. I was president of that meeting, and on my return home, what was my surprise to find upon my table Mr. Trew's circular, inquiring to what extent a Christian commercial agency for operations in Africa, could be procured here! . . . . . We have had since another meeting, when a society was organised for the Evangelisation of Africa, by means of native agency. The object has excited the deepest interest in the black population, and I have no doubt be shall we able to make a commencement at least. Your plan is much more extensive. I think you may rely on securing from the West Indies an agency of negro and coloured persons, efficient for establishments either civil or commercial, as might be thought advisable. A good *common* education is generally within the reach of all classes now. . . . . . The negro is naturally a very susceptible creature, perhaps naturally the most favourably disposed of any of the human family, to receive and avail himself of the advantages which may be put in his way; but by some fatality, unaccountable on any principle, save that ' the time to favour it had not come,' the tribe has remained an outcast, and the country a waste.

" One poor African, named James Keats, left this country a few months ago, really on a pilgrimage to his native land, that he might carry the gospel there. We are anxious to hear of him. He had reached Sierra Leone, and had, I believe, embarked in Her Majesty's ship Rattlesnake for the Congo river, which he intends to ascend."

I have also received a letter from the Rev. John Beecham, stating that a number of agents might be obtained from among the Wesleyan negroes in the West Indies, who are already qualified for the work " to a good extent," and who, by the necessary training, might prove valuable auxiliaries to the cause.

The Rev. Mr. Holberton, Rector of St. John's, has also stated his views on the subject, in a letter to the Rev. Mr. Trew, dated Antigua, March 6, 1839, of which the following is an extract:—

" The subject of your circular has long occupied my mind; and now that it has come, soliciting inquiry on the point, I cannot help laying before you what seems to me a very feasible, and comparatively inexpensive mode of proceeding in this deeply interesting work. Instead of having a college erected in one of the islands for the reception of native black and coloured youths of promise, I would respectfully recommend that an agent be sent to *this* island, and there gather about him a band of black and coloured youths, to be trained and educated expressly for the employments proposed in your letter, more especially as missionaries. *Nothing is better than an infant school as the first training place for the future missionary*, as he is there likely to be moulded into a pains-taking, persevering, simple-minded man.

" From persons so employed and approved, your agent might make a selection. Such as he made choice of should be trained by him, and domesticated with him for a time; and when the necessary measure of fitness was apparent, should be sent for one year to the Church Missionary Society's college in England. And when you forward them from England, send as their superintendent, one of our-selves, a minister who shall direct their energies aright, bear with their weaknesses, and keep united heart and mind in the great work on which they had been sent out. I do not see how you can move a step in this great undertaking without sending out an agent of decided piety, sound judgment, and com-petent ability, to instruct and direct those who are to be committed to his charge; but let him be *no sectarian*.

" On the whole, then, you will see that I do not hold the scheme which you state in your letter to be at all a visionary one; but am sanguine enough to hope, that if you proceed on the plan I have ventured to recommend, you will attain to the desired end by a very speedy, and sure and safe way. I rejoice in the prospect of such an undertaking. It will be the most righteous compensation that could be made to Africa for all the wrongs England, through former years, took part with other nations in doing to her. Of a truth how beautiful will be to her, the feet of the sons of those who were cruelly torn from her soil in years past, returning to her shores again with the everlasting gospel in their hands, and their mouths opened to declare unto her what God hath wrought."

The Rev. John Clark, baptist missionary in Jamaica, stated to me, in a letter dated September 16, 1839, " that the case of Africa was exciting deep sympathy amongst the members of his congregation." He also named several negroes, already qualified to some extent, who were willing and even anxious to enter immediately upon the work; and stated his full conviction that an ample number of native agents might, after suitable education, be available from the island of Jamaica, for the important purposes of African instruction.

Advances already made.

To this it must be added that some advances have already been made. The Church Missionary Society have a normal school for the education of teachers

at Sierra Leone; by the last statement it appears
that sixteen are now in the course of education, under
the effective instruction of the Rev. G. A. Kissling,
who speaks favourably of his scholars.   By a summary, issued May, 1839, it appears that there are
5098 of all ages under the care of this society; and
the report of this year states, "with thankfulness to
Almighty God, the steady progress of this first
established of the society's missions."

The Report of the Wesleyan mission for this year
has the following paragraph, p. 68:—" The state of the
work at the West African stations is very gratifying,
and the openings for more extended usefulness are
most inviting.   At Sierra Leone nearly 2000 persons are united together in religious fellowship, and
the schools are prosperous.   The stations at the
Gambia are increasing in importance.   At Macarthy's
island the committee for the civilisation department
are exerting themselves for the benefit of the converted natives.   The kingdoms of Woolli and Bondou, which the enterprising spirit of Mr. Fox has
explored, and other places, are open to the missionaries.   At Cape Coast, the rapid spread of the
gospel calls for the most grateful acknowledgments
to Almighty God, who has crowned the labours
of his servants with signal success.   And in the
midst of the discouragements resulting from the painful visitations of disease and death, which these missions from time to time experience, it is an alleviating
consideration that a native agency is rising up, by

which the work may at no distant period be prosecuted, without so large a sacrifice of life and health on the part of European missionaries."

The Wesleyans have declared their intention to establish a college on Macarthy's island for the education of children of natives of the higher classes, in connexion with the experimental farm. One benevolent individual, Dr. Lindoe, has engaged to give £1000 to this institution.

The Church Missionaries have prepared, and with the help of the Bible Society, printed, translations of the gospel of St. Matthew in the Bullom, Mandingo, and Susoo languages, in which they have also printed grammars, or lesson-books, as well as in the Eyo or Aku,* and the Sherbro. The American missionaries have published elementary books in the Greybo and Bassa languages. I have before mentioned the Wolof lessons of Hannah Kilham. The Rev. R. M. Macbrair, of the Wesleyan Society, has published a complete grammar of the Mandingo. Another Wesleyan missionary, the Rev. W. Archbell, has published a grammar of the Sechuana language of South Africa, which has been also critically investigated by the French missionary, M. Casalis, and is supposed to be the key to the dialect prevailing from the Congo to Delagoa bay.

---

* It is worthy of remark that the Aku language has been found to be understood by the great majority of the captured negroes. Mr. Ferguson is my authority for this: from this circumstance important facilities are likely to arise.

I am not amongst the number of those who derive encouragement from the vicinity of the Mahomedans. I must confess that I apprehend a more stubborn resistance to the diffusion of knowledge, especially that which is the best and the most civilising, from the followers of the Prophet, than from the simple and docile, though barbarous, tribes of Central Africa. Mahomedanism also gives the sanction of religion to the Slave Trade, and even enjoins it as a mode of converting the heathen. That people are " Kaffering, and do not say their prayers, the dogs!" is sufficient reason for the true believers making war upon them,* and carrying them into slavery. Their prejudices are so deeply rooted, that some missionaries do not hesitate to say they would rather deal with Pagans than with Mahomedans.

Yet even with these there is some encouragement; to a certain extent they go along with us. There are points in the Mahomedan faith which we may turn to account in attempting to introduce better instruction. The Mussulmans of the west do not regard Christians with the same horror as those of the east; they seem to be favourably impressed by finding that we acknowledge much of their own sacred history ; and with them, the names of Abraham and Moses serve to recommend our holy books.

We may make common cause also with them in Africa, in our common abhorrence of the bloody rites and sacrifices of the Pagans. Thus Mr. Hutchison

* Denham, p. 149.

writes from Coomassie :—" This place now presents the singular spectacle of a Christian and a Mahomedan agreeing in two particulars—rejecting fetishes, and absenting themselves from human sacrifices and other abominations. The rest of the people, of whatever country they may be, when the king's horns announce anything of the kind, strive who will get there first, to enjoy the agonies of the victims !"

Hitherto education has been entirely in the hands of the Mahomedans ; and in fact, the Arabic is, to a considerable extent, the common language of Central Africa.

The travels of the Mahomedans have to a certain degree enlarged their minds. They are the leaders of most of the caravans, and some travel merely for pleasure. Mr. Fox mentions seeing at Macarthy's Island, a Moor who had come across the continent from Medina, and was much interested on being shown on a map the places he had passed through. " When questioned as to the object he had in view in coming so far, his answer was, he merely came for 'take walk'—' he wished to see the Gambia, Senegal, &c.' " Mr. Fox gave him the New Testament in Arabic, which he read with tolerable ease.

It becomes evident, therefore, that our way is not totally blocked up, but that there are many circumstances which will tend to facilitate our efforts for disseminating knowledge and religion among those who are the objects of our sympathy. And the encouragement and stimulus to exertion which we derive from these, ought to be in proportion to the

magnitude of the enterprise we contemplate, and of
the results we expect will follow. The elevation of
the native mind, as it is the only compensation
we can offer for the injuries we have inflicted on
Africa, so it is the truest, the cheapest, and the
shortest road to the downfall of the Slave Trade, and
of those frightful superstitions which it has tended to
preserve.

In what way, then, can this advance of mind be
most effectually and speedily attained? I answer in
the words of Mr. Burke, when speaking on a kindred
subject,* " I confess I trust more, according to the
sound principles of those who have at any time
ameliorated the state of mankind, to the effect and influence of religion, than to all the rest of the regulations put together." The Gospel ever has been, and
ever must be, the grand civiliser of mankind. Happily for Africa, a mass of evidence is to be found corroborative of this assertion, in the Report of the Committee of the House of Commons in the sessions 1833
and 1834, on the Aborigines Question, appointed to
consider, amongst other things, " what measures
ought to be adopted to promote the spread of civilisation among the Aborigines of our colonies, and to lead
them to the peaceful and voluntary reception of the
Christian religion." A main branch of that inquiry
was, " Whether the experience of the several missionary societies led to the belief that it would be
advisable to begin with civilisation in order to intro-

* Burke's Works, vol. ix. p. 287 : Letter to Dundas on Civilisation of Negroes in the Two Hemispheres.

duce Christianity, or with Christianity in order to
lead to civilisation." It is a striking fact, that the
representatives of the missionary bodies who were
examined on that occasion, without any previous concert between themselves on the subject of the inquiry,
arrived at precisely the same conclusion, namely,
" That there is no means so effectual, under the divine
blessing, to benefit man for 'the life that now is,' as
well as ' that which is to come,' as Christianity."

In proof of this, Mr. Coates, secretary of the
Church Missionary Society, observes to the committee :

" I find the preceptive part of Christianity tends to
make man peaceable, honest, sober, industrious, and
orderly. These, in my opinion, are the very elements
of civilisation, in the moral sense of it.

" The impression of its great principles on the
heart tends directly to make him humble, self-denying,
philanthropic, beneficent, apart from the consideration
of those effects which may be deemed more strictly of
a religious or theological kind. I see in it, therefore, an arrangement and process by which the human
mind is to be operated upon in a more powerful manner
than by any other agency that can be imagined.

" If I look at the world when, at the rise of Christianity, it found Rome in the zenith of her power
and glory, in the highest state of civilisation, as civilisation could exist in a heathen land, at that period,
among other practices, that of selling their prisoners
of war into slavery, prevailed. I find, too, in their
gladiatorial games, man opposed to man in mortal

conflict.   And this not an accidental occurrence, or a scene exhibited in private, but habitually at their theatres, and to the most polished and distinguished of the whole population.   What do I find at the expiration of a few ages?   Christianity gains the ascendancy, and these things are extinct.

" I would only attempt further to illustrate this bearing of the subject from three or four facts of a recent date.   At a recent period, suttees prevailed throughout our possessions in India—they are now prohibited : and this was effected by the expression of Christian opinion and feeling in this country.   I look back on the enormous evils of the Slave Trade. The Slave Trade is suppressed, and suppressed unquestionably by the force of Christianity in this country.   I come to a still more recent period, and see slavery abolished throughout all the British colonies, and that at the cost of £20,000,000 of public money ; the result most unquestionably of the state of Christian principle and feeling.

" I now take up the question under a different aspect—I mean as it is illustrated by the effects of modern Protestant missions.   I notice more particularly those of the Church Missionary Society.

" Mr. George Clarke, a catechist, who has been twelve years in New Zealand, thus writes :—' Here are a number of poor cannibals collected from the different tribes around us, whose fathers were so rude, so savage, that for ten years the first missionaries lived among them, often expecting to be devoured by them.   A few years ago, they were ignorant of every principle of religion; had glutted in human blood, and gloried in it; but now there is not an individual among them who is not in some degree acquainted with the truths of the Christian religion. Not six years ago they commenced with the very rudiments of learning; now many of them can read and write their own language with propriety, and are completely masters of the first rules of arithmetic. But very few years ago a chisel made out of stone was their only tool; now they have not only got our tools, but are learning to use them.'

" Mr. R. Davis thus writes from the same mission: —' During the last quarter my time was principally occupied in preparing agricultural implements, and in attending to my natives employed about different work—carpentering, sowing, fencing, taking up the potato crop, and clearing land for the plough.' "

We next turn our attention to the testimony of another labourer in the Christian field, who no less strongly supports the preceding statements.

The Rev. John Beecham, of the Wesleyan Missionary Society, after expressing similar opinions to those delivered by Mr. Coates, as to the sole efficacy of Christianity in establishing and promoting refinement and civilisation, with their attendant comforts, and very clearly illustrating his idea by a reference to ancient history, proceeds further to support his sentiments by referring to the testimony of Kahkewaquonaby,* a chief of the Chippeway Indians, whose

* The literal meaning of Kahkewaquonaby is " Sacred," or

name has been subsequently changed into Peter Jones. This tribe, notwithstanding their rejection of the offers of Government made to induce them to renounce their roving course of life, afterwards embraced the gospel when preached to them, and devoted themselves to the pursuits of civilized life.

Mr. Jones thus writes :—" The improvements which the Christian Indians have made, have been the astonishment of all who knew them in their pagan state. The change for the better has not only extended to their hearts and feelings, but also to their personal appearance, and their domestic and social condition. About ten years ago this people had no houses, no fields, no horses, no cattle. Each person could carry upon his back all that he possessed, without being much burthened. They are now occupying about forty comfortable houses, most of which are built of hewn logs, and a few of frame, and are generally one and a half story high, and about twenty-four feet long and eighteen feet wide, with stone or brick chimneys ; two or three rooms in each house. Their furniture consists of tables, chairs, bedsteads, straw mattresses, few feather beds, window curtains, boxes, and trunks for their wearing apparel, small shelves fastened against the wall for their books, closets for their cooking utensils, cupboards for their plates, knives and forks ; some have clocks and watches.

" Eagle's feathers ;" the chief being of the Eagle tribe. He was baptised by the name of Peter, and assumed the name of ·Jones from his sponsor.

They have no carpets, but a few have mats laid on their floors. This tribe owns a saw-mill, a workshop, a blacksmith's shop, and a warehouse, the property of the whole community. They have about 200 acres of land under cultivation, on which they grow wheat, Indian corn, potatoes, &c. In their gardens they raise vegetables of various kinds, and a few have planted fruit trees. They have a number of oxen, cows, horses, and pigs; a few barns and stables; a few wagons and sleighs; and all sorts of farming implements.

"The gospel has of a truth now proved the 'savour of life unto life,' among our poor degraded women. The *men* now make the houses, plant the fields, provide the fuel and provisions for the house; the business of the women is to manage the household affairs. The females eat with the men at the same table. You will be glad to hear that they are not insensible to the great things the gospel has done for them. I have often heard them expressing their thanks to the Great Spirit for sending them missionaries to tell them the words of eternal life, which have been the means of delivering them from a state of misery and degradation."

The testimony of the Rev. William Ellis, secretary of the London Missionary Society, is to the same effect. "True civilization and Christianity," he observes, "are inseparable; the former has never been found but as a fruit of the latter." And he proceeds to show with much force and perspicuity, the inefficiency of a mere demi-civilization to penetrate to the root of human evil, and to lead to comfort and to Christianity.

In the report of the London Missionary Society for 1835, a comprehensive view is taken of the effects produced by its labours in the South Sea Islands, and which may serve as an illustration of the benign and salutary influences of Christian truth, when per-severingly pressed upon the acceptance of the most barbarous people.   The report observes,—" Forty years ago, when this society was formed, the islands of the South Seas had been discovered, explored, and abandoned, as presenting no objects worthy of fur-ther regard.   Their inhabitants were sunk still lower in wretchedness by intercourse with foreigners, and left a prey to the merciless idolatry that was fast sweeping them from the face of the earth.   To them the attention of our venerable fathers in this cause was first directed, and a mission was auspiciously commenced.   Idolatry was subverted, infant murder and human sacrifices ceased, education was promoted, converts flocked around the missionaries, churches were gathered, missionary societies formed, and teachers sent forth,   Now, the people, fast rising in the scale of nations, have, as fruits of the Divine blessing on missionary perseverance, a written lan-guage, a free press, a representative government, courts of justice, written laws, useful arts, and im-proved resources.   Commercial enterprise is pro-moting industry and wealth, and a measure of domestic comfort, unknown to their ancestors, now pervades their dwellings. A nation has been born at once, and surrounding nations have been blessed through their mercy."

Testimonies of this kind might be multiplied to a great extent. The annals of missionary proceedings teem with information of the most conclusive character, whilst the newly converted heathen themselves, ever ready to testify to the blessings they are thus brought to enjoy, are heard to exclaim, " But for our teachers, our grass on the hills, our fences and houses, would have been fire ashes long ago; and we should have been upon the mountains squeezing moss for a drop of water, eating raw roots, and smothering the cries of our children by filling their mouths with dirt, grass, or cloth." "We were all blind till the bird flew across the great expanse with the good seeds in its mouth, and planted them among us. We now gather the fruit, and have continual harvest."

No less striking is the evidence of Andrew Stoffell, a converted Hottentot, before the Aborigines Committee. He is asked, " Have the character and condition of the Hottentots been improved since the missionaries came among them, and in what respects?" He replies, "The young people can now read and write, and we all wear clothes; many of us have learned trades, and we are altogether better men. We have ploughing, wagon-makers, and shoemakers, and other tradesmen, amongst us. We can make all those things, except a watch and a coach. The missionaries have done much good, and they have tamed the Hottentots."

The testimony of Mr. Elisha Bates, who was a member of the Society of Friends, before the same Committee, furnishes the most convincing evidence of the efficacy of Christianity in promoting the improvement of the temporal condition of savage nations, even where other means had failed. He observes, speaking of the Indians of the United States, "Within the last few years we have had occasion to review the whole course of our proceedings, and we have come to the conclusion, from a deliberate view of the past, that we erred in the plan which was originally adopted, in making civilization the first object ; for we cannot count on a single individual that we have brought to the full adoption of Christianity." Having been further asked, "Do your Society now regret that they did not begin with Christianity, in order to lead the way to other advantages ; and if you had to recommence the same undertaking, would you now begin with Christianity ?" he emphatically replied, "Decidedly we should, from a full conviction that the attempt to civilize without Christianity has failed ; and that the plan now adopted is to make Christian instruction the primary object."

From these facts, gathered from different sources, the inference does not appear by any means doubtful, that whatever methods may be attempted for amelio-

rating the condition of untutored man, THIS alone can
penetrate to the root of the evil, can teach him to love
and to befriend his neighbour, and cause him to act
as a *candidate* for a higher and holier state of
being.

The hope, therefore, of effecting Africa's civilization, and of inducing her tribes to relinquish the
trade in man, is, without this assistance, utterly vain.
This mighty lever, when properly applied, can alone
overturn the iniquitous systems which prevail
throughout that continent.   Let missionaries and
schoolmasters, the plough and the spade, go together,
and agriculture will flourish; the avenues to legitimate commerce will be opened; confidence between
man and man will be inspired; whilst civilization
will advance as the natural effect, and Christianity
operate as the proximate cause of this happy change.

If, indeed, it be true that such effects will follow
in the train of religion, and that Christianity alone
can effect such changes and produce such blessings,
then must we pause before we take a single step
without it.   The cause of Africa involves interests far
too great, and results far too stupendous to be trifled
with.   The destinies of unborn millions, as well as
of the millions who now exist, are at stake in the
project; and the question is one of life or of death,
of comfort and happiness, or of unutterable misery.

I believe that Christianity will meet the necessities
of the case, and will prove a specific remedy for the
moral evils of Africa.

My next proposition consequently is, that it is our duty to apply this remedy if we can.

One part of our national debt to Africa has already been acknowledged by the emancipation of our colonial slaves. There remains yet, however, a larger debt uncancelled,—that of restitution to Africa itself. We shall have much difficulty in ascertaining the amount of this obligation. Had we the means of discovering the total number of the sufferers whose miseries we have caused, or could we form the faintest idea of the nature and extent of the woes which are justly chargeable upon us as a nation, the duty of making reparation to Africa would be obvious.

Next to the debt which we ourselves owe, I can form no conception of a stronger argument in favour of carrying thither civilization and Christianity, than the existence of the Slave Trade itself, as it is found at this day, attended, on the one hand, by desolation; on the other, by a blind and devouring superstition; and in all directions encircled by ferocity and carnage, by torture, by terror, by all the evils through which man can be afflicted; and this variety of woes ending in the annual sacrifice of 500,000 human beings.

I repeat, that a stronger proof we cannot have, that it is the duty of the people of this empire to take up the cause upon Christian grounds, as a measure of atonement for the injuries we have done to her, as the only means now within our power of making restitution to her still degraded population; and as the most successful implement for uprooting from its very foundations that gigantic and accursed tree, which for ages has nourished beneath its shadow lamentation, and mourning, and woe.

Let but the people of this Christian country take up this cause *as a duty*, nationally and religiously, and no difficulties, however great, can, with the Divine blessing, hinder its success.

Nationally and religiously, the duty is plain. We have been put in trust with Christianity,—we have been the depositaries of a pure and holy faith, which inculcates the most expanded benevolence, and yet have not only neglected, as a nation, to confer upon Africa any real benefit, but have inflicted upon it a positive evil. Covetousness has dimmed our moral perceptions of duty, and paralysed our efforts, during many generations; and now that the nation has awakened from its lethargy, it is high time to act up to the principles of our religion.

Africa still lies in her blood. She wants our missionaries, our schoolmasters, our bibles, all the machinery we possess, for ameliorating her wretched condition. Shall we, with a remedy that may safely be applied, neglect to heal her wounds ? Shall we, on whom the lamp of life shines, refuse to disperse her darkness ?

" If there be any consolation in Christ, if any comfort of love, if any fellowship of the spirit, if any bowels of mercies,"* we must awake to the duty, amidst every difficulty, of freely and liberally distri-

* 1 Cor. vi. 9.

buting to others those rich and abundant blessings which have been entrusted to us.

I dwell no longer on the point of duty, but proceed to prove that *we can* apply the remedy.

I have dwelt the longer on the facilities which exist for the instruction of the natives, in order to show that the attempt to raise negro intellect, and to impart moral culture and religious instruction, is not of that forlorn character which many suppose. The facts I have stated are, I apprehend, sufficient to show that there is, amongst the Africans, a capability of receiving instruction; that there are agents within our reach, well calculated to assist in conferring it; that there is, in many parts at least, a thirst for education, and a readiness to accept the services of missionaries; and that, although the steps already taken have been very few, there has been some little advance. Other circumstances render the project of sending instructors more feasible at the present than at any former time. They will be carried to their destination by water. British steamers will be upon the Niger to protect them (at the only time that missionaries want protection) on their first settlement among the natives. Missionaries find less difficulty than any other class of persons, perhaps, in winning the confidence of native tribes. The secret of their success, is, the spirit of fair dealing, and the manifestation of upright and benevolent intentions, which they carry with them. These speak to all men, but especially to the uncivilised, in a language which they accurately comprehend, and to which they freely respond. It would seem, then, that the difficulties, considered a few years ago insurmountable, in the way of an attempt to diffuse intellectual, moral, and religious knowledge amongst millions of the human race, plunged in the very depths of ignorant superstition, have been in a great measure removed. Hence it is evident, that the question is not so much as to our power, but as to our willingness, to provide the means of conferring the inestimable benefits of intellectual advancement and true religion.

Having arrived at this point, it will naturally be asked, what scheme of instruction do I propose? I answer, I hardly dare to propose any scheme. Would that there were that charity among the Christians of the happier quarters of the world, which would induce them to lay aside their minor differences, in order to make a combined effort, of the most determined and strenuous character, to pour instruction upon Africa! But if this unity be too much and too good to be expected, we may at least hope that every department of the Christian church will separately press forward into that vast field which will, I trust, speedily be opened, and where there is room enough and need enough, physically and morally, for all.*

* I have no fear that missionaries to Africa will be wanting from our own country; but it gives me satisfaction to find the following passage in the South African Commercial Advertiser:—
" It will be agreeable to all who can comprehend the grandeur of

I may, however, recommend—

Firstly. That in every settlement formed on the views here laid down, the religious, moral, and industrial education of the natives should be considered an essential and fundamental object, claiming the early and careful attention of the founders of such settlement.

Secondly. That missionary societies should, by mutual agreement, subdivide and apportion the parts of this common field, so that each section of the Christian church may have undisturbed possession of its own sphere of labour.

Thirdly. That immediate arrangements should be made by each for normal schools,* intended to rear

this opening prospect, to learn that the people of the United States of America have determined to unite with the discoverers and regenerators of Africa. In a private letter, addressed to a gentleman of this colony, which we have just seen, the writer, one of the heads of a college in New Jersey, announces the deep interest which this subject has already excited in that country; and he inquires, with an anxiety approaching to impatience, as to the course their first missionaries should take, and the regions in which they are likely to be most useful. Thirty students in that college, he says, will be ready to start in a few months. At present their views are chiefly directed to Central Africa. It is not improbable, therefore, that they may follow the course of the newly-opened Niger."

* I am happy to say that this suggestion is by no means a novel one. In 1835, the Moravians contemplated a plan for establishing an institution in Jamaica, " for training native missionaries and teachers for needy Africa." The Rev. Hugh Stowell has recently proposed " an institution akin to Bishop's College, in the East

not only native teachers of religion, but native arti-
zans, mechanics, and agriculturists, well instructed
for the purpose, and themselves converts to Christianity.

Fourthly. That the African Civilization Society
now being instituted shall befriend and protect all who
are engaged in disseminating the truths of Christianity.

My object will be attained if two things are
effected,—if a spirit of harmony shall reign amongst
all who devote themselves to the benefit of Africa,—
and if, wherever channels of commerce are opened,
or agricultural locations made, there shall be put in
operation at the same moment a system of instruction
which shall raise up and send forth teachers of all
that Africa requires to learn.

Indies, where those of the liberated Africans and of their teeming
offspring who should give promise of distinguished piety and
talent might be educated as future missionaries to the land of
their forefathers." He goes on to say that, " without the services
of converted natives, humanly speaking, very extended success
cannot be anticipated. If, in other countries, this principle holds
good, how much more in the case of Africa. There the fatality
of the climate to European constitutions, the untamed savageness
of the interior tribes, and the multiplicity of their motley dialects,
present next to insuperable barriers to other than aboriginal
agency."

CHAPTER VII.

SPECIFIC STEPS TO BE TAKEN.

I HAVE sufficiently explained what my object is. *It is the deliverance of Africa, by calling forth her own resources.* We contemplate that her population, instead of being sold into Foreign Slavery, and of perishing by tens of thousands in the process of transportation, shall be employed in the tillage, and in the commerce, which may be found at home.

In order to do this, we must

    1st. Impede and discourage the Slave Traffic.

    2ndly. Establish and encourage legitimate commerce.

    3rdly. Promote and teach agriculture.

    4thly. Impart moral and religious instruction.

To accomplish the *first*, we must

    Increase and concentrate our squadron, and make treaties with the chiefs of the coast, the rivers, and the interior.

To accomplish the *second*, we must

    Obtain commanding positions; settle factories; and send out trading-ships.

To accomplish the *third*, we must

    Set on foot an agricultural company.

    Obtain, by treaty, lands for cultivation, with so much power as may be necessary to keep the slave-trader at a distance.

The territory we obtain should be freely offered to us, without any kind of constraint.

It should be in the vicinity of some navigable river.

The climate should be, for Africa, healthy.

The soil should be capable of growing tropical productions.

Its limits should be extensive.

To accomplish the *fourth,* we must

Support the benevolent association now established.

Besides these special purposes, there is one general object, which must be carefully provided for, viz. : that the agents employed in Africa, whether on their own account, or in connection with an association at home ; whether engaged in commerce, cultivation, or instruction, may be *sufficiently protected.*

Of the work to be done, a part belongs to the Government, and a part must be executed by individuals.

The Government should

Take on itself the whole duty and expense of preserving the peace, and of affording the necessary protection, to new British settlements in Africa.

Increase and concentrate our naval force.

Obtain Fernando Po, and such other commanding positions as may be found necessary.

Prepare, — instruct, — and send out embassies, with all practicable dispatch, (or authorize their African governors,) to form treaties, including either, or all, of the following points, viz. :—Prevention of Slave-traffic ;—arrangements for legitimate trade or cultivation,—with such privileges and powers as may be necessary for their well-doing ; and with grants of land for cultivation.

The part which devolves on individuals interested in the fate of Africa is,—

1st. Strenuously to assist the benevolent association already mentioned, the objects of which are—to assist individuals or societies who may engage themselves in the task of educating the population of Africa ;—to promote by every means in its power,—direct and indirect,—its civilization, cultivation, and commerce ; to obtain and circulate statistical, geographical, and all other information concerning that country, especially availing itself of the opportunity shortly to be presented of doing so, by appointing agents to accompany the expedition, which it is intended to send out in the ensuing autumn ; and, lastly, to keep alive the interest of the people of England on the subject.

2ndly. To form an agricultural company, which shall, hereafter, send out persons well acquainted with tropical climates and productions; to form settlements, guided by such arrangements and treaties as the Government may have made; to commence pattern farms and establish factories, well supplied with European goods; in a word, to use all the means that experience may point out, for a profitable and successful employment of British skill and capital in the African continent. *No Slavery, no monopoly, forbearance towards the natives, and utter enmity towards Slave Trade and Slavery in all their forms,* must be the fundamental principles of such a company; and an honest adherence to these will, in my full belief, insure its prosperity and profit.

I have proposed two associations, a Benevolent Society, which shall watch over and befriend the interests of Africa, and a Company, which shall cultivate her soil.   In one sense they are entirely separate; the object of the one is, charity,—of the other, gain.   As they are distinct in their principle, so, I think, they ought to be kept entirely separate in the prosecution of their details.   Yet, it is impossible that they should not subserve and benefit each other. It is impossible to spread education, scientific knowledge, and the civilizing influence of Christianity, without communicating that to the population, which will most materially contribute to the advance of commerce and agriculture: on the other hand, there is no better way of advancing the moral and physical condition of the people, than by the introduction of

our skill, and the sagacious and successful employment of our capital amongst them.*

To the question which has already been repeatedly
put to me, by those who have been moved to compassion by the sorrows of Africa, *What shall we. do ?*
my answer is,—Join the African Institution, which
we are endeavouring to revive ; and join the African
Agricultural Association, which we are about to establish.

* Statements and proposals of a more definite nature respecting these two associations will, I trust, be laid before the public at
no distant day.   In the mean time, it may be well to observe, in
answer to the inquiry in what manner it is proposed to work land
in Africa, that it is intended that those employed as superintend-
ents should be, as far as possible, of negro extraction, but that
none should be sent but men of moral and religious character.
That such are to be had I have, I trust, shown in the Chapter on
the Elevation of Native Mind (page 491).

But in what species of agriculture is it proposed to employ
them ?   In the first instance, perhaps, in the cultivation of cotton ;
on the facilities for which I have dwelt at some length (page 332) ;
but as we become better acquainted with Africa, we shall know
how to turn its cultivation to the best advantage, and of course we
shall grow those articles which will find the readiest and most
profitable market in the civilized world.

CONCLUSION.

I CANNOT close this work, without suggesting some considerations, which, in the review I have taken of the whole subject, have forcibly impressed themselves on my own mind. Great as is the undertaking, there are, at the present time, many concurrent and favourable circumstances, which have not previously existed.

England is at peace. Since the abolition of the Slave Trade by Great Britain, it is not too much to say, that there has been, both at home and amongst many of the nations of the continent, an increase of a benevolent and enlightened spirit. Our sincerity with regard to the Slave Trade has been established, by sacrifices which admit of no misconstruction. The principles involved in that great measure have been carried out by the abolition of slavery, and by the willingness of the nation to pay the price of that most costly act of duty. Thus, then, we are in a condition (our own hands being clean) to ask the co-operation of France, Russia, the United States, and other great powers; and we have a right to demand from Spain, Portugal, and Brazil that they should no longer delay the execution of their engagements.

Again, there are certain circumstances, which render Africa far more accessible than at any former period. We now know the course of the Niger, and an entrance into the centre of Africa is opened, by means of this noble river. We have now got, in *steam*, a power which enables us to traverse it; to pass rapidly through the unhealthy parts of it; to ascend it against the current; in short, to command its navigation.

Beyond, and besides all these, there is another circumstance lately brought into existence which may supply us with the necessary agents capable of enduring the African climate. I wish not, with too sanguine an eye, to anticipate the course of events, but I cannot help believing, as I have elsewhere stated, that in the present condition of the negro race in our West Indian colonies lies one of the best hopes of Africa. They are rising, under the influence of freedom, education, and religion, to a rank, which will fit them to be messengers of peace to the land from which their fathers were torn; and already, though the time has been so short, various, distinct, and unconcerted symptoms have appeared, proving that " it pitieth them to see her in the dust."

At the moment, then, that a highway is discovered into the heart of Africa, and that a new power is placed in our hands enabling us to command its navigation, and that agents present themselves qualified by physical constitution to endure the climate, and by intellectual cultivation to carry with them the seeds of true improvement; at that moment, we learn the utter fallacy and inutility of the system for the suppression of the Slave Trade which we have hitherto been pursuing.

But there is another consideration, though quite of a different order, which bears strongly upon this point. New markets for the sale of our manufactured articles are urgently required, at a time when we are excluded from some of our accustomed channels of sale.

Nor is the supply of the raw material less important; new fields for its growth ought to be opened, in proportion to the increasing consumption of the world. I firmly believe that, if commercial countries consulted only their true interests, without reference to motives of a higher character, they would make the most resolute and persevering attempts to raise up Africa—not to divide her broad territory amongst them, nor to enslave her people, but in order to elevate her into something like an equality with themselves, for their reciprocal benefit.

But I am well aware that it is a case in which we must act under circumstances of considerable discouragement; and especially that of our great ignorance with regard to the real internal condition of Africa, both physical and moral.

Upon any other subject, the dimness of our knowledge would supply an unanswerable reason for pausing; but the state of Africa admits no delay. The complicated horrors which are crowded into the space of a single month, furnish sufficient reasons for all possible dispatch, and for adventuring on measures, which, under other circumstances, would be premature and probably rash. Better to fall into a thousand errors in the detail, and to incur the expense and mortification of the miscarriages they will cause, than to sit still, and leave Africa to her woeful fate.

If nothing be done, Africa will be at the end of 50 or 100 years what she now is, and we shall still be as ill-informed, as we now are, of the readiest means for her relief. But if we grapple with the evil, we shall either find ourselves in the right road, or grope our way to it; and the very mistakes we now make will serve to direct us aright hereafter.

I am not so sanguine as to suppose that we can at once, by a single effort, solve the problem which lies before us. The deliverance of Africa will put our patience and perseverance to no ordinary trial. We must deliberately make up our minds to large and long-continued expense, to persevering labours, and to severe disappointments. I wish not in any degree to conceal from myself, or from others, these truths.

But the question is,—Shall such an experiment be made? There are two mighty arguments which should prompt us to such an undertaking: the intense miseries of Africa, and the peculiar blessings which have been showered upon this country by the mercy of Divine Providence. With regard to the first, I need not again plunge into the sickening details of the horrors which accompany this bloody trade, and of the sanguinary rites, which there bear the name of religion. Whether we look to the vast space which is there made a theatre of public misery, or calculate how many deeds of cruelty and carnage must be perpetrated every day in the year, in order to make up the surprising total of human distress, which, by indisputable documents, we know to be realized, there is enough to awaken the deepest pity, and to arouse the most energetic resolution.'

Turning to the second consideration, we cannot fail to see how signally this nation has been preserved, and led forward to an extent of power and prosperity, beyond what almost any other nation has been permitted to reach. "It is not to be doubted that this country has been invested with wealth and power, with arts and knowledge, with the sway of distant lands, and the mastery of the restless waters, for some great and important purpose in the government of the world. Can we suppose otherwise than that it is our office to carry civilization and humanity, peace and good government, and, above all, the knowledge of the true God, to the uttermost end of the earth?" *

Since that passage was written, Great Britain has refuted the idle, yet once the all but universal doctrine, that confusion, havoc, and bloodshed must follow the extinction of slavery. And with this doctrine of universal convulsion has also fallen the

---

* The Rev. Mr. Whewell's Sermon before the Trinity Board.

allegation, that negroes will not work, except under
the impulse of the whip. It is confessed by every
authority, that wages have charmed away what used
to be called "the natural and incurable indolence of
the African." I do not say a single word here upon
the controverted question, whether the negroes demand excessive remuneration. We may assume, for
the sake of argument, that they are exorbitant. This
may be a fault, though, under all the circumstances,
not an unnatural or surprising one ; but this does not
touch my assertion, grounded upon all the papers which
have been produced to Parliament, that, when satisfied with the rate of wages, they do labour indus-
triously, and execute more work, in better style, and
in less time, than when they were slaves. There
never was a greater delusion, than that negroes
could not be induced to work for money.

A nobler achievement now invites us. I believe
that Great Britain can, if she will, under the favour
of the Almighty, confer a blessing on the human race.
It may be that at her bidding a thousand nations now
steeped in wretchedness, in brutal ignorance, in devouring superstition, possessing but the one trade, and
that one the foulest evil that ever blighted public prosperity, or poisoned domestic peace, shall, under British tuition, emerge from their debasement, enjoy a
long line of blessings—education, agriculture, commerce, peace, industry, and the wealth that springs
from it; and, far above all, shall willingly receive that
religion which, while it confers innumerable tempo-

ral blessings, opens the way to an eternal futurity of happiness.

I have already confessed that I am not experienced or skilful in matters which touch the commercial part of the question. I tread this ground with diffidence. I say no more, than that it appears to me that the soil in Africa being rich, and the people being found upon it, it is not advisable to carry them to a distance. It is possible, however, that some fallacy, unsuspected by me, may lurk under my theory, if theory of mine it can be called; but when I come to humanity, justice, and the duties of Christian men, I stand upon a rock. It may be, or it may not, that while we act under the impulse of charity to the most afflicted of mankind, we are also obeying the dictates of the most far-sighted policy, and the most refined ambition. It may prove, or it may not, that while we are leading Africa to grow at home, cheaper sugar than Brazil, and cheaper cotton than the United States, we are renovating the very sinews of our national strength. Be this as it may, without doubt it is the duty of Great Britain to employ the influence and the strength which God has given her, in raising Africa from the dust, and enabling her, out of her own resources, to beat down Slavery and the Slave Trade.

I am aware that it is quite a different question whether the means I propose are practicable, and likely to be crowned with success. It belongs to the nation to consider whether the suggestions now

offered, and the policy which I have ventured to recommend, are likely to eradicate that mighty evil
which desolates Africa, degrades Europe, and afflicts
humanity. If it shall appear that my views are not
chimerical,—that they have some grounds of reason in
themselves, and are fortified by a great mass of evidence of a practical nature,—and if it shall appear
that, whether we look to the great interests of humanity, or consult the prosperity and honour of the British empire, it is our duty to proceed, undeterred by
difficulty, peril, or expense,—then I trust that steps
will be taken boldly and rapidly, for the accomplishment of the object.

But if it shall appear that this, and every other
plan is likely to be futile, or, if the Government shall
not feel itself justified in braving the difficulties and
expense which will be required, then must I express
my painful conviction, that it would be better for the
interests of humanity that we should withdraw altogether from the struggle;—better to let the planters
of America satiate themselves with their victims,
than to interpose our efforts, unavailing in reducing
the magnitude of the evil, while they exasperate the
miseries which belong to it,—better to do nothing than
to go on, year after year, at great cost, adding to the
disasters, and inflaming the wounds of Africa. But I
cannot contemplate such a result,—I must hope better
things.

The case is now fairly laid before the nation. It
belongs to no individual, to no party,—it is a distinct

and isolated question. My desire has been to lay it upon the national conscience of Great Britain. There I must leave it; having fully stated what I believe to be the only remedy, and the best means of applying that remedy.

I find, in the sacred writings, a faithful picture of sorrows,—such as those with which Africa is now afflicted; but I find also annexed to that description a prophetic promise, which we must fervently desire to see realised to miserable Africa:—

" Thus saith the Lord of Hosts,—Before these days there was no hire for man, nor any hire for beast: neither was there any peace to him that went out, or came in, because of the affliction : for I set all men, every one against his neighbour.

" But now I will not be unto the residue of this people as in the former days, saith the Lord of Hosts.

" For the seed shall be prosperous ; the vine shall give her fruit, and the ground shall give her increase, and the Heavens shall give their dews: and I will cause the remnant of this people to possess all these things."

APPENDIX A.

On Facilities of making Treaties.

THE following instances may prove the disposition of the native chiefs to form connexions with us :—

Sir Charles MacCarthy, in giving an account of the negotiations for taking possession of the Isles de Loss, states, that the treaty " was made with great facility, without drunkenness or bribery *." In 1826 the king of Barra ceded to Great Britain, by treaty, a tract of land on the northern shore of the Gambia, 36 miles in length, by one in breadth, for 400 Spanish dollars yearly ; all slave-trading to be finally prohibited. In 1827 the king of Combo guaranteed to the British crown rights nearly amounting to sovereignty over his dominions, extending about 30 miles along the southern bank of the river, and 10 miles along the coast, and from 10 to 15 miles in breadth, with the prohibition of the Slave Trade, for an annual payment of 100 dollars.

Treaties with the king of Bulola and Biafra, made by Sir Neil Campbell, cede the sovereignty of those districts, and a right on the part of Great Britain to establish forts or factories, with clauses for the abolition of the Slave Trade. From the Pongas and Nunez rivers, little or no produce,

---

* Mr. Hutton, acting governor at the Gambia, effected an arrangement with the chief of Contalacunda, which being deemed a place of importance by our merchants, he did not consider 50 dollars annually (about 10*l.*) ill bestowed in securing its chief's friendship.

except slaves, is exported. In 1827, Sir N. Campbell saw the chiefs of these rivers, and obtained " the cession of the most commanding points up the mouth of each." Mr. Hutton states, in 1829, that he made a treaty with the king of Woolli at Fattatenda, and obtained the full sovereignty of that town, with stipulations in favour of our commerce, for the payment in merchandise of 200 dollars annually. He also made a treaty with the king of Bondou, and observes, " The object of 300 or 400 dollars is trifling, compared with the advantage that would result from such a connexion with both these kings, whose influence extends not only through the whole of Bondou and Woolli, but also to the adjoining countries of Shendrum and Tanda, celebrated for gold, gum, &c." Though we have not availed ourselves of these openings,—though the payments to the chiefs were soon suspended,—some benefit seems to have been derived from these engagements. Rev. T. W. Fox, a Wesleyan missionary, as appears from his journal in my possession, paid a visit to Woolli in 1837, and urged upon the king the benefits of Christianity: " He," says Mr. Fox, " listened attentively, appeared pleased, and said that was what he wanted; and if I would come and sit down on his ground, he would give me as much land as I wished, and his own children to be educated." I replied, " That if I sent a missionary, I hoped he would protect him, and not allow anybody to trouble him;" Koy (the king) answered, " that he *belonged* to white man, and that if *Tobaba fodey* (the white priest) came to sit down in his kingdom, nobody should, or would, trouble him." He also said, " he hoped God would preserve me; the object I had in view was very good."

The king of Bondou, also, whom Mr. Fox likewise visited in 1838, offered to give him ground for a settlement, and said, " They were all glad to see him, and they loved him

very much, because he was a good man." It is something
in the present disastrous condition of Africa, that there is
a good feeling towards the British, and no rooted indisposi-
tion to listen to their agents.

In 1827, the king and head men of Brekama solicited
Sir N. Campbell to take them under British protection:
they stipulated to renounce the Slave Trade, and to enter
into no wars, in return for British alliance, "and four pieces
of baft annually."

Governor Rendall gives a list of 19 kings or chiefs, on
the northern and 20 on the southern, bank of the Gambia,
with whom we have some intercourse or connexion. The
total sum annually divided amongst these, for rents and pro-
pitiatory presents, reaches only 300l. This liberality is
not without its effect. Governor Rendall reports 75l. spent
in presents to chiefs and head men, on both banks of the
river, between Bathurst and Woolli, and says, " This expenditure has not been in vain, as I have received intelligence that the war in Carbo, which has lasted 12 years, is
finally settled, both parties having taken my advice, and
called in umpires to decide their difference: the paths
through Carbo and Footah-Jallow will now be open to the
river, by which a great influx of trade must take place."
Besides the tribes lying immediately on the Gambia, Governor Rendall says, that " messengers are often received at
Bathurst from the kings of Boaul and Cayor, to the northward of Bondou; Cassan, and Kaarta-Bambarra, to the
eastward; and the Almanez of Footah-Jallow, to the south-
east." I am aware that no definite ideas can be derived
from this catalogue of barbarous chiefs: we have, however,
evidence sufficient to show that the soil is fertile, and suited
to tropical productions; that the forests are full of mahogany and valuable woods, and that the country yields gold:
hence we may justly infer, that from a territory so extensive,

for which nature has done so much, there is a capability of large cultivation, and of considerable commerce. The Commissioners of Inquiry sent out to that country in 1827, report thus,—" When the magnitude of the river Gambia, and the various countries through which it takes its course are duly considered, it will probably be concluded that, with capital and enterprise, its trade may be increased to a considerable extent ;" they add, and I entirely unite with them in the opinion, " Great as the advantages, in this point of view, which it presents, they can never be completely available, without the establishment of a more intimate and friendly intercourse with the natives of the country." Following the coast, we come to the Portuguese settlements of Cacheo and Bissao; and then to a belt of Slave-dealing states, extending to the Congo, and blocking out legitimate commerce from the interior. Here, however, we have some claims, of which we have not availed ourselves. The fine little island of Bulama, in the estuary of the Rio Grande, belongs to Great Britain: it is unoccupied ; and, in 1826, Governor Macaulay recommended that liberated Africans should be located there. I find, in Captain Beaver's " African Memoranda," the following report of the cession of this island to us :—" The original purchase of the island of Bulama, made by Captain Beaver in 1792, was effected without any difficulty; though, on the first arrival of the English, they had offended the natives by cutting wood without permission, and in the quarrel which ensued, some lives had been lost." When Captain Beaver entered into a palaver with the two kings of Canabac, touching the purchase of their hunting island of Bulama, one of them, while he attributed the affray to our taking the liberty to help ourselves, without any leave from the native authorities, expressed his desire to treat with us amicably on fair terms. He said, " He was sorry for what had happened, but that then they neither knew who we were, nor what were our intentions : we were strangers, and we took their land." Being, however, convinced of the pacific and just dispositions of the English, and of the great reciprocal benefits that were likely to result from an European colony established in their neighbourhood, they readily made over the sovereignty and possession of the said island to the king of Great Britain, for 473 bars of goods (about 78*l.* 16*s.* 8*d.*)

Two chiefs on the mainland afterwards put in a claim for a part of the price ; and Captain Beaver, having ascertained that "there was some justice in these people's claims," wisely satisfied them, and bought their concurrence in the cession of the island, together with a still larger tract on the mainland, for goods, the cost price of which he estimated at 25*l.* 13*s.* 1*d.* There were some further charges for European agency in these transactions.*

Captain Beaver, at all events, did not apprehend that there was any difficulty in his time in obtaining any extent of territory on reasonable terms : for he proposes to the Government, that they should purchase between the Gambia and the Rio Grande a tract of 18,000,000 of acres, which, in his opinion, might be bought for 5000*l.*, or less.

* See the copy of these treaties in Johansen's "Account of Bulama and the Bulam Association," pp. 28, 29.

APPENDIX B.

Vide Page 34.

Abstract of a Letter written in 1835, *relative to Fernando Po.*

THIS island belongs to Spain, and was formerly called " Formosa," or the beautiful island, a designation it well deserves. It has three ranges of hills running parallel with the north-east side of it, the centre one rising into a mountain of about 10,000 feet in height. After some negotiation between the governments of England and Spain, it was agreed in 1827, that the former might place an establishment on the island for the purpose of locating upon it such negroes as might be captured, and emancipated, under the Slave Trade Abolition Treaties, and a governor was sent from hence, and various buildings were erected; but some difficulties arising, in consequence of the Spanish Crown refusing to transfer the sovereignty of the island, it was abandoned, after the outlay of a considerable sum. This termination of the negotiation is most deeply to be lamented, as the island, in the hands of Great Britain, would prove a most important and valuable possession as regards her commerce; but it would be still more important to the civilization of Africa, forming, as it does, the key to the centre of that vast continent, and in this view, to the philanthropist, its occupation by the British Crown would be invaluable, as the prepossession of the natives on the opposite coast (from which it is distant only a few miles) in favour of the English, over all other nations, is very remarkable : but to any maritime trading nation, it would prove a valuable acquisition. The Americans have already shown a desire for opening a trade with it, and in 1834 one or two vessels were engaged in whaling there.

On the northern end of the island there is a very fine bay, where the different points of land form an inner and outer anchorage, and where from 400 to 500 vessels might ride in all the months of the year in complete security. The facilities for discharging and taking on board their cargoes are also very great, as they may lie in three or four fathoms of water within 40 or 50 feet of the shore, the depth increasing greatly at every additional few feet : it is remarkable, too, that these seas are not visited by the hurricanes so prevalent on other parts of the coast, and that even the tornadoes are less violent than elsewhere. These advantages, joined to its immediate vicinity to the great rivers which penetrate to the heart of Africa, render it unnecessary to say a word to enforce the desirableness of its becoming an English possession. At the period when the island was abandoned a town had been laid out at the head of the bay, a considerable number of houses had been built, and a good drainage cut through each street. The population, then amounting to about 700 persons, were in a flourishing condition, being constantly employed in cutting timber, building, and cultivation, and the town was bidding fair to become one of the most—perhaps the most—important on the coast. The native population, in its immediate vicinity, was estimated at between 500 and 600 persons, whose ready submission to the English government gave every facility to the progressive improvement of the new colony : they looked up to the whites, and readily received instruction in the schools which were established, and they attended church with great regularity and decency on the Sundays—on which days they came into the town in great numbers.

The island produces, in rich abundance, palm-oil, cocoas,

plantains, and yams; and it is covered with a vast variety
of trees, many of them of the most useful qualities: there
are whole forests of palms, and many different kinds of
trees which would be valuable for cabinet work; but, in
a commercial point of view, the most important amongst
its timber trees, and in which it also abounds, is that which
is peculiarly adapted for ship-building, and which may be procured of almost all lengths. Several ships, both belonging
to the government and to merchants, have been repaired
with it at the island, and many cargoes have been imported
into England, and used in the king's and merchants' yards.
The palm-tree is invaluable to the negroes, who use palm-
wine as a beverage. The soil is so rich, that no limits can be
assigned to its productiveness: it is capable of producing
almost every luxury in the vegetable world for the use of
man and beast.

Much has been urged in favour of, and also against, the
climate of this island; but when the timber, with which it
abounds, is felled,—and this, if the island were occupied by
the British, would be constantly progressing, as it is, as has
been already stated, of a very valuable kind,—there can
scarcely be a doubt that it would become, ere very long, the
Madeira of the western coast: as almost any degree of temperature may be obtained on the different ranges of its mountains; and the vegetables of the temperate as well as of the
tropical climates, flourish in its soil, which is extremely fertile.
The water, too, is pure and abundant; game is plentiful, and
its coasts swarm with fish. It is a fact well established,
that, in plains in tropical climates where fever exists at a
temperature of from 80° to 90°, it is not found on the neighbouring mountains, where at noon the thermometer does not
range higher than from 70° to 75°.

Extract of a Letter from another Gentleman, dated Clarence, Fernando Po, May, 1835.

" We anticipate with much anxiety the (we trust not very far distant) period, when this establishment will be again resumed by our government : for, on investigation into the real state of the colony, it must necessarily take place, and then prejudices will surely give way, and truth prevail over the false representations, through which, one of the most beautiful and profitable spots in Africa has been so injudiciously abandoned.   Indeed, I can, in addition to its beauty and great utility to British trade in Western Africa, safely say, that, in point of salubrity, if not more so, it is at all events equal to any other British settlement on the coast.

" Since ——'s departure, we have drawn up our militia, and designated it ' The Clarence Militia Corps,' and I feel great pleasure in stating, that, considering the short period the men have been under arms, and their natural awkwardness at first, I should not be ashamed to welcome the Commander-in-chief with a captain's guard, whenever Admiral Campbell will deign to honour us with a visit.

" Our little town of Clarence has also undergone some alterations and improvements ; the town, which formerly laid scattered in the midst of a forest of plantains and bananas, has been brought in nearer to the cove, and properly laid out ; the streets are made broad, and cut each other at right angles, on either side of which are the houses and allotments, of equal dimensions : so, that in what street soever you may be, instead of the suffocating atmosphere that formerly assailed one, you now enjoy a cool and refreshing current of air, which must certainly be conducive to health, and justify our anticipating even healthy wet seasons.

" While we go on thus improving among ourselves, I do not despair of working a complete revolution in the manners and habits of the aborigines, who are rapidly becoming inhabitants among us, and are already beginning to adopt our customs; assume a more active and industrious character; and supply us with much greater quantities of palm-oil than formerly."

APPENDIX C.

Copy of a Despatch from General Turner to Earl Bathurst.

Dated Sierra Leone, January 25th, 1826.

" It is found that, under this system of putting them (the liberated Africans) to easy and regular labour such as they have been used to, on their landing from slave-ships, they become very orderly good labourers; but in the cases where they have been located in the villages, and have received gratuitous maintenance, they can, with difficulty, be induced to give a day's labour for good wages.

" It would but lead to disappointment to imagine that a large mass of poor ignorant people, without capital, skill, or industry, could be brought to maintain themselves, and to raise articles of export, without the assistance of labour-wages. Could such a system succeed even in England, the poor rates might soon be abolished."

General Turner further says, that if men of colour who understand the cultivation of cotton and coffee, were brought from the West Indies, to superintend such plantations as would not fail under such facilities to be formed by capitalists, he is satisfied much would be done in a few years for the improvement of the country.*

* Parliamentary Papers, Sierra Leone, p. 7, Session 1830, No. 57.

Copy of a Despatch from Lieutenant-Colonel Denham,* General Superintendent of the Liberated African Department.

Dated Sierra Leone, May 21st, 1827.

" What this colony, or rather the liberated Africans, have felt the most want of is, instruction, capital, and example: with the very little they have had of either, conveyed in a manner likely to benefit them generally, it is to me, daily, an increasing subject of astonishment, that the liberated Africans settled here have done so much for themselves as they have.

" I have not observed any disinclination for voluntary labour: it appears to be a system perfectly understood and practised by the liberated Africans here; and strengthens with their strength, as they become more sensible of the sweets of labour, by enjoying the profits of it, and the comforts those profits enable them to purchase: indeed, to the many hundreds of liberated Africans that have been employed as labourers on the different Government works, as well as on the buildings erected by private individuals, during the last few years, may in some measure be attributed the comparatively small number of agricultural labourers in the villages.

" Labourers' wages have varied from 1s. to 6d. per day: yet has there never been a deficiency of liberated Africans, who were willing to labour for hire. On the Naval Stores, now erecting by contract on King Tom's Point, are nearly 200 liberated African labourers, who work well and steadily, at 20s. per month, one-half paid in money, and the remainder in goods taken from the stores of the merchants who have the contract.

" The period of labour also forms a longer portion of the day here than even in the South of Europe, where for se-

---

* The celebrated African traveller, and eventually Governor of Sierra Leone.

veral hours, when the sun has most power, a general cessation of labour, or indeed employment, takes place. Labourers in this colony work from six in the morning till five
in the afternoon, constantly, with the exception of the hour
from nine till ten, which they are allowed for breakfast.

" Husbandry and practical agriculture should be encouraged by every possible means ; but yet I am inclined to
think the kind of labour in which so many of the liberated
Africans have been and still are employed, has been upon
the whole beneficial to them : they must acquire intelligence,
habits of regularity, and steady labour, with much general
knowledge, by being employed with artificers, and watch-
ing the progress of the public buildings from the foundatio
to the roof,—the roof, to the finished whole,—as in the case
of the extensive Barracks, and a very handsome building
intended for the Naval stores, which are both nearly completed.

" They are already sensible of the rewards of industry,
by being in possession of the profits ; and the advantage of
property is becoming daily an increased object of interest.

" An anxious desire to obtain and enjoy the luxuries of
life is apparent in every village, from the oldest settler to
the liberated African of yesterday. European articles of
dress are the first objects of their desire, and for the means
of acquiring these both sexes will cheerfully labour; and a
gradual improvement has taken place in their dwellings, as
they become possessed of the necessary means for that purpose. Of the practicability of introducing free labour
amongst the liberated Africans settled here, I have not the
slightest doubt, nor do I believe they would work half as
well in any other way, unless the greatest cruelty should be
exercised towards them.

" My opinion on this subject is formed from facts, collected
during an actual residence in each of the settlements of

liberated Africans, of from one to three weeks, and I shall
merely state those facts, as I consider them better than any
reasoning. The number of frame-houses with stone foundations, and also stone houses, has increased in all the villages,
particularly the mountain ones of Gloucester and Regent.
Three sold during the last three years at Wellington. There
are seven stone houses nearly finished, all begun during the
last two years. The owners of these habitations, which cost
them from 100 to 200 dollars, have all acquired the means
of so permanently establishing themselves, by *free labour*
and industry : they were all, with the exception of a few discharged soldiers from the Fourth West India Regiment,
landed from the ships here after capture, and merely given
a lot of ground and rations for a time : they became masons,
carpenters, coopers, smiths, and farmers.

" The markets at Freetown are supplied with fruit and
vegetables, almost exclusively, by the mountain villages; and
from 80 to 100 men, women, boys, and girls, are to be seen
daily on the hill leading to Gloucester town, with the produce of their farms and gardens. This is also entirely the reward of their own industry and perseverance, for not the
least instruction on this important branch of labour have they
ever received."*

Major Ricketts in a despatch, dated June 30th, 1829,
speaking of the produce raised by the liberated Africans,
says :—

" The value of these articles may be estimated by the
well-known fact, that a labouring man can go into the market and purchase as much food for a penny-halfpenny as
will suffice for two meals. Some of the persons supplying the
market are known to travel from Waterloo and Hastings,
the former being 22, and the latter 16 miles from Freetown,
carrying their produce in baskets on their heads. This kind

* Papers relative to Sierra Leone, September, 1830, No. 57, p. 15—17.

of industry clearly manifests the desire the liberated Africans have to labour voluntarily, to enable them, by honest means, to become possessed of those luxuries, which they see their more wealthy brethren enjoying."*

APPENDIX D.

Playford Hall, 17th *July,* 1839.

My Dear Friend,

Having read your little book, bearing the name of " The Remedy," I congratulate you on having at last discovered a way, which if followed up in all its parts, would most certainly lead to the abolition of that execrable traffic called the Slave Trade.

Two of the measures which you hold forth to accomplish this object, are the employment of steamers in conjunction with sailing vessels, and the annexation of the island of Fernando Po to our foreign possessions. Simple and insignificant as the means may at first sight appear, they will be decisive in their consequences, and fully answer the end as far as the capture and destruction of slave-vessels are concerned. Steamers, it is obvious, will come up with these, at times and seasons, when our best sailing ships cannot touch them, and Fernando Po is a station, in the *sight of which eight-tenths* of the existing slaves must pass to be carried on. Commodore Bullen, whom you have quoted, says, " that if a look-out be kept from the shore of this bay, (in Fernando Po) scarcely a vessel could leave the Bonny, Calabars, Bimbia, and Camaroon rivers, without being observed time enough to signalize to any vessel lying in the bay to intercept her;" and he cites as an instance the capture of a slaver Le Daniel by his own vessel. This capture

* Papers relative to Sierra Leone, September, 1830, No. 57, p. 39.

was effected within four hours after first seeing her, although his vessel was then lying at anchor in the bay. Taking in these three happy circumstances together, the employment of steamers, the vicinity of Fernando Po to the coast, and that the island commands a sight of eight-tenths of the Slave Trade now carried on, I cannot doubt that *ten* vessels would be captured where *one* was taken before. I verily believe that our cruisers would make such havoc among the slave vessels in three months, that when the news of what they had done should reach Cuba, Brazil, &c., the insurance there would be raised to a frightful amount, and merchants begin to query, whether it would be advisable to send any more adventures to that part of the coast. So far for the first three months; but after this, other vessels would be on their way to the Niger, ignorant of what had happened, and would share the same fate. Here a fresh report of captures would be communicated to the people of Brazils, Cuba, &c., and what effect would this produce there? No insurance at any rate! No heart to venture again in this trade! And here I cannot help stating the benefit that Fernando Po would be to the slaves who should be captured on these occasions: instead of being carried to Sierra Leone, as heretofore, many of them in a diseased state, a voyage of five or six weeks, during which a prodigious loss of life has occurred, they would be landed there in health in three or four days, some of them in a few hours, where they would be liberated, and set to work, and earn their own maintenance immediately. I have been writing hitherto under the supposition that we are at liberty to take vessels of this description bearing the Portuguese flag. It is said that a treaty is on foot for that purpose with Portugal, but if that should fail, existing treaties would bear us out in the capture of such vessels.

But supposing these two measures should be successful,

as you think they would be, in putting an end to the Slave Trade, what do you recommend next? You recommend that a *new trade* should be proposed to the natives in exchange for that of the Slave Trade, in the productions of their soil; that is, by means of agriculture, by which their wants, and more than their usual wants, would be supplied, so that when the new trade should come fairly into play, they would find, practically find, that it was more than a compensation for the old; and that the rise of this new trade should immediately follow the downfall of the Slave Trade. But how is this new trade to be brought about? You answer by *treaties* with the native chiefs; by *subsidies* to some of them, which, though they would be important, would be of trifling amount; by *purchasing land*, which, though extensive, would be attended with little cost; by *introducing settlements* among them, by which their industry would be directed to the proper objects of cultivation, and that cultivation improved by our skill; by which their youth would be educated, their manners and habits civilized, and the gospel be widely spread among them.

There is no doubt that if all these things could be accomplished, not only the Slave Trade would be abolished, but the natives would never wish to return to it. Now you have shown by historical proofs that *all these things have been already done* in many instances in different parts of Africa, and that the results have been highly favourable, and this, without any particular pains being taken, except at Sierra Leone; in fact, without any but ordinary stimulus being given, the natives being left to their own will and pleasure, and without any other incitement than the protection which a settlement in this vicinity afforded them, and a simple declaration, " that they should be paid for their labour." What would be the case then, were a great company established in England, whose constant object would be to excite their energies by the prospect of a suitable reward, and by instructing them how to earn it?

Let us now see what these historical proofs are (and I shall quote from them very briefly) on which you place so much reliance. Sierra Leone offers itself for consideration first. You say that " the accounts, soon after the settlement was formed there, stated that the natives crowded round the colony, both for education and for trade, and that the beneficial effect upon them in inducing them to quit slave trading, was *instantaneous*. That effect *has been continued,* and has *extended* in the neighbourhood of Sierra Leone to a very considerable distance round the colony. Traders bring down ivory, gold-dust, and palm oil as usual. Of late years a very *important branch has been added to the legal trade* for the cutting of timber for the British Navy, &c. &c.

The river Gambia presents itself next. " In the year 1814," says Mr. Bandinel, "a colony was formed at St. Mary's on this river. This colony has increased and flourished beyond all reasonable calculation, and is already *more powerful and wealthy* than any of those older settlements of the British in Africa, which were formed for the purpose of promoting the Slave Trade."—" The beneficial effects of this settlement at St. Mary's on all the tribes along the banks of the Gambia, are perhaps still more prominent than those which have taken place round Sierra Leone."

In the year 1833, a mission in connexion with the Wesleyan Society was established at Mac Carthy's island. " Before the abolition of the Slave Trade," says the Rev. Mr. Macbriar, " there were considerable factories here, but now that the slave market is abolished, and the natives can find a ready market for the produce of their lands by means of the British merchants, the *cultivation of the soil increases every year;* and the aborigines have been heard to say, that they now wish they had their slaves back again, because they could get more by their labour than they did by selling them to Europeans."

Let us add another of your proofs. The Rev. J. Morgan, to whom the Foulah mission in the same river partly owes its origin, recommends the purchase of tracts of land adjoining the principal rivers. He says, " that thousands would flee to such places of refuge as soon as they could be assured of protection, and thus a dense free population would soon spring up, and commerce would rapidly extend." I myself am connected by subscription with a settlement in this river, and the accounts from thence, which I see yearly, are full of the *anxious desire* manifested by the natives on the banks of it, to be under our protection, and to cultivate their lands in peace, and to be civilized and christianized.

We come now to the Gold Coast. In no part of Africa, says the Governor, M'Lean, was the Slave Trade more firmly rooted, or more systematically carried on than in these settlements." " But a great change has taken place since its abolition. The soil, which formerly did not yield sufficient for the sustenance of the inhabitants, *now affords to export* a very large amount of corn to *Madeira*," " besides *greatly increased quantities* of gold-dust and ivory." " The exports to Great Britain amount to £160,000 per annum." Formerly " the whole country was one scene of oppression, cruelty, and disorder, so that a trader dared not go twenty miles into the bush. At present our communication with the interior is as *free and safe* as between England and Scotland." Add to this the statement, that " several hundreds of the natives, through the labours of the Wesleyan missionaries, have embraced the truths of Christianity."

Having now made a few quotations from what you have advanced relative to our *own colonies* on the continent of Africa, let us quote from what you have said relative to other parts of the same continent which are not in our possession. The first of these which presents itself in the order of location upon that coast, is the country in the neighbourhood of the Senegal. The natives having had reason to suppose that it was the intention of the British Government, when they took possession of this river, to abolish the Slave Trade as far as their new dominions extended, were filled with joy. "Seeing no probability of any further Slave Trade," says Mr. Rendall, who was a resident of St. Louis, in the Senegal, from 1813 to 1817, "they bethought themselves to *turn their attention to agriculture*, and all *disposable tracts of land* were in consequence *to be found in a state of cultivation*. The inhabitants passed from one village to another *without fear* or *protective weapons*, and contentment seemed to reign not only in the countenances, but in the humble huts of the inhabitants." This account of Mr. Rendall is very short. It is a pity that he did not dwell more largely, as he might have done, on the *extraordinary industry*, which this belief of the abolition excited; on the great quantity of land put in cultivation for miles along the banks of the Senegal, and on the markets which the people had opened for themselves. I had an account of these particulars, as they occurred, from persons at Fort St. Louis, myself, an had occasion afterwards to transmit them to the Congress at Aix-la-Chapelle, where I understood they were received and read.

The next place in order of location is the Island of Bulama, situated opposite to the country of Biafra, and not far from the great rivers Rio Grande and Nunez. Here Captain Beaver, at the close of the last century, attempted to form a colony. Two of the natives of the opposite continent soon crossed over to him, and though he told them "*he could have no dealing in slaves*," yet their report induced others to take *service with him*, and he never afterwards wanted grumettas or labourers. In one year he employed nearly two hundred of them. He never saw men work harder, more willingly, or regularly, generally speaking, than they did. And what induced them, says Captain Beaver, to do so? "Their desire of European commodities in my possession, of which they knew they would have the value of one bar at the end of the week, or four at the end of a month. Some of them remained at labour for months ere they left me. Others, after having left me, returned. They knew that the labour was constant, but they also knew that their reward was certain." To this account I may just add, that I knew Captain Beaver personally, and that I have heard these and other important statements from his own lips. He was a captain in the royal navy; and in private life he was most estimable, and a man of high moral character.

The last place in the same order, but some hundreds of miles further down the coast, which you quote, is the river Niger. Unfortunately the gentlemen you mention have not been resident in the interior of this country, and therefore can only speak of what they saw and heard while navigating this immense river. By this river, says Mr. Laird, one hundred millions of people would be brought into direct contact with the civilized world, new and boundless markets would be opened to our manufacturers, a continent teeming with inexhaustible fertility would yield her riches to our traders; not merely a nation, but hundreds of nations, would be awakened from the lethargy of centuries, and become useful and active members of the great commonwealth of mankind." And what says Mr. Lander of the disposition of this vast population of the countries through which this river goes? "The natives," he says, "only require to *know what is wanted from them,* and to be *shown what they will have in return,* and much produce that is now lost from neglect, will be returned to a considerable amount." But the most important evidence which you have cited for this part of the country is Colonel Nicholls. He tells us, that from his long experience in these and other parts of Africa, " there is one means, and he is persuaded but one effectual means, of destroying the Slave Trade, which is by introducing a liberal and well regulated system of commerce on the coast of Africa." He then gives us the substance of a conversation with one of the native chiefs on this subject, in which he convinced him of the folly of trading in the bodies of the inhabitants in comparison with trading in the productions of the soil, so that this chief gave up the Slave Trade : and says, " I feel convinced that I could *influence all the chiefs along the coast in the same manner :* but to be able to effect this, it would be necessary to have the means of moving with a degree of celerity that a steam-vessel alone would give us."—" Steam-boats would also be of incalculable use to commerce, by towing ships over bars and agitated currents, whilst, as a means of catching the Slave-ships, and protecting the coast from the depredations of their crews, *three steamers would effect more than the expensive squadron now maintained there.* I pledge myself to put an end to the whole of our expense, and *totally to suppress the Slave Trade*, in two years." O, how I wish that Colonel Nicholls could be sent again to Africa for this purpose! He is the only man alive to effect it. I know him well. His whole heart and soul are in the project. Besides, he has an intimate knowledge of these seas and harbours, of Fernando Po, and what it can do towards the abolition of the Slave Trade ; of the mouth of the Niger, and the great rivers falling into it ; of some of the native chiefs personally, and of the manners, customs, disposition, and temper in general of the inhabitants of these parts.

But why should I go further into "The Remedy" you propose ? It would be a waste of words. It has already appeared probable, nay, more than probable, that if steamers were employed, and Fernando Po added to our possessions, the capture of the vessels concerned in the hateful traffic would be comparatively easy; that treaties might be made with the African chiefs, and several of them subsidized in our interest; and that the energies of the natives on that vast continent might be called forth in a *new trade*, in the productions of their soil, (which of itself would sap the foundation of the Slave Trade,) and that thousands and tens of thousands of these natives might be engaged in it. Again, you have projected a large commercial and agricultural company, which should take off their produce, and supply their wants. What can you *devise*, and what can you *desire* more, to put down the Slave Trade and to civilize Africa? I hope then that you will not be so diffident as you appear to be relative to the success of your measures : if they do not succeed, none will. I have studied the subject for more than half a century, and give it as my opinion that yours is the only plan that will answer. I cannot doubt that the Government would readily promote your views, if they were only persuaded that it was probable that the abolition of the Slave Trade would follow, and that a great part of the country, the moral and religious part of it, would be grateful, very grateful, to them for so doing. And now, my dear Friend, having read your little work twice over, and having formed my conclusions upon it, and finding these in unison with your own, I thought that you would be pleased with them; and thanking you, as every abolitionist must do, for the great labour you must have undergone in preparing your present plan, I remain, with great regard,

Your sincere and affectionate Friend,

THOMAS CLARKSON.

APPENDIX E.

Sir,

I mention how my time has been chiefly occupied as an apology for my abbreviated account of the matter you are inquiring about; however, thus much I can state and verify. When I was travelling between Der, the capital of Nubia and Epsambool, I met a slave ship descending the Nile, and as I wished to see what was going on in the vessel, I went on board to purchase some ostrich feathers. This was in March last, I cannot tell the exact date, as my journals are in Paris. There were probably 20 or 25 slaves, of ages between 10 and 16. There was one man about 30 chained to the bifurcated end of a long pole; his neck was enclosed by the two branches, and a chain from one end to the other secured him even from a movement of his head. The other end of the pole was locked to the floor of the hold of the vessel. It appears that this man had attempted to escape. I actually *saw* but this one vessel, but my interpreter told me that several slave vessels had passed us in the night.

I was in the slave market in Cairo; I saw many slaves, male and female, on sale; being an European, I was not permitted to see the white slaves, nor do I know that there were any on sale at that time. The black slaves I had free access to; and I was *told* that there were some white ones in the rooms.

I am, Sir, your obedient Servant,

WM. HYDE PEARSON.

APPENDIX F.

Copy of a Letter from the Right Honouroble Lord John Russell to the Lords Commissioners of Her Majesty's Treasury. (Laid on the table of the House of Commons, 8th February, 1840.)

Downing Street,

MY LORDS, 26th December, 1839.

THE state of the foreign Slave Trade has for some time past engaged much of the attention of Her Majesty's Confidential Advisers. In whatever light this traffic is viewed, it must be regarded as an evil of incalculable magnitude; the injuries it inflicts on the lawful commerce of this country, the constant expense incurred in the employment of ships of war for the suppression of it, and the annual sacrifice of so many valuable lives in this service, however deeply to be lamented, are not the most disastrous results of this system. The honour of the British Crown is compromised by the habitual evasion of the treaties subsisting between Her Majesty and foreign powers for the abolition of the Slave Trade, and the calamities which, in defiance of religion, humanity, and justice, are inflicted on a large proportion of the African continent, are such as cannot be contemplated without the deepest and most lively concern. The Houses of Lords and Commons have, in their addresses to the Crown, expressed, in the most energetic terms, the indignation with which Parliament regards the continuance of the trade in African slaves, and their anxious desire that every practicable method should be taken for the extinction of this great social evil.

To estimate the actual extent of the foreign Slave Trade, is, from the nature of the case, an attempt of extreme difficulty; nor can anything more than a general approximation to the truth be made. But after the most attentive examination which it has been in my power to make, of official documents, and especially of the correspondence communicated to Parliament from the department of Her Majesty's Principal Secretary of State for Foreign Affairs, I find it impossible to avoid the conclusion, that the average number of slaves introduced into foreign states or colonies in America and the West Indies, from the western coast of Africa, annually exceeds 100,000. In this estimate a very large deduction is made for the exaggerations which are more or less inseparable from all statements on a subject so well calculated to excite the feelings of every impartial and disinterested witness. But making this deduction, the number of slaves actually landed in the importing countries affords but a very imperfect indication of the real extent of the calamities which this traffic inflicts on its victims. No record exists of the multitudes who perish in the overland journey to the African coast, or in the passage across the Atlantic, or of the still greater number who fall a sacrifice to the warfare, pillage, and cruelties by which the Slave Trade is fed. Unhappily, however, no fact can be more certain, than that such an importation as I have mentioned, presupposes and involves a waste of human life, and a sum of human misery, proceeding from year to year, without respite or intermission, to such an extent as to render the subject the most painful of any which, in the survey of the condition of mankind, it is possible to contemplate.

The preceding statement unavoidably suggests the inquiry, why the costly efforts in which Great Britain has so long been engaged for repressing the foreign Slave Trade have proved thus ineffectual? Without pausing to enumerate the many concurrent causes of failure, it may be sufficient to say that such is the difference between the price at which a slave is bought on the coast of Africa and the price for which he is sold in Brazil or Cuba, that the importer receives back his purchase-money tenfold on the safe arrival of his vessel at the port of destination. It is more than probable that the general profits of the trade, if accurately calculated, would fall exceedingly below this estimate, as indeed it is certain that in many cases it is carried on at a ruinous loss. But your Lordships are well aware, how powerful and constant an impulse may be given to any species of illegal traffic, however hazardous, when they who engage in it are allured by the hope of very large and quick returns, if their good fortunes could enable them to escape the penalties of the law. It may therefore be readily understood how effective is such a stimulus, when, as in the case in question, the law itself is regarded with general disfavour in the society to which the violator of it belongs, and is reluctantly executed by the government of that society. We must add to this exciting motive the security which is derived from insurances, and insurance companies, which are carried on to a great extent, and combined powerful interests. Under such circumstances, to repress the foreign Slave Trade by a marine guard would scarcely be possible, if the whole British navy could be employed for that purpose. It is an evil which can never be adequately encountered by any system of mere prohibition and penalties.

Her Majesty's confidential advisers are therefore compelled to admit the conviction that it is indispensable to enter upon some new preventive system, calculated to arrest the foreign Slave Trade in its source, by counteracting the principles by which it is now sustained. Although it may be impossible to check the cupidity of those who purchase slaves for exportation from Africa, it may yet be possible to force on those, by whom they are sold, the persuasion that they are engaged in a traffic, opposed to their own interests when correctly understood.

With this view it is proposed to establish new commercial relations with those African chiefs or powers within whose dominions the internal Slave Trade of Africa is carried on, and the external Slave Trade supplied with its victims. To this end the Queen has directed Her Ministers, to negotiate conventions or agreements with those chiefs and powers, the basis of which conventions would be, first, the abandonment and absolute prohibition of the Slave Trade; and, secondly, the admission for consumption in this country, on favourable terms, of goods the produce or manufacture of the territories subject to them. Of those chiefs, the most considerable rule over the countries adjacent to the Niger and its great tributary streams. It is therefore proposed to dispatch an expedition which would ascend that river by steam-boats, as far as the points at which it receives the confluence of some of the principal rivers falling into it from the eastward. At these, or at any other stations which may be found more favourable for the promotion of a legitimate commerce, it is proposed to establish British Factories, in the hope that the natives may be taught that there are methods of employing the population more profitable to those to whom they are subject, than that of converting them into slaves, and selling them for exportation to the slave traders.

In this communication it would be out of place, and indeed impracticable, to enter upon a full detail of the plan itself; of the ulterior measures to which it may lead, or of the reasons which induce Her Majesty's Government to believe that it may eventually lead to the substitution of an innocent and profitable commerce, for that traffic by which the continent of Africa has so long been desolated. For my immedia'e purpose it will be sufficient to say, that having maturely weighed these questions, and with a full perception of the difficulties which may attend this under-taking, the Ministers of the Crown are yet convinced that it affords the best, if not the only prospect of accomplishing the great object so earnestly desired by the Queen, by her Parliament, and her people.

Having instituted a careful inquiry as to the best and most economical method of conducting the proposed expe-dition, I find from the enclosed communication from the Lords Commissioners of the Admiralty, that it will be ne-cessary to build three iron steam-vessels for this service, and that the first cost of those vessels, including provisions and stores for six months, will amount to 35,000*l.* It fur-ther appears that the annual charge of paying and victual-ling the officers and men will be 10,546*l.* The salaries of the conductors of the expedition, and of their chaplain and surgeon, will probably amount to 4,000*l.* In addition to this expenditure, Presents must be purchased for the chiefs, and tents, mathematical instruments, with some other articles of a similar kind, will be indispensable for the use of the persons who are to be engaged in this service, when at a distance from their vessels. I have some time since given directions for the completion of this additional estimate, but with those directions it has not hitherto been found prac-ticable to comply. The charge for this branch of the pro-posed service will not be very considerable.

I have to convey to your Lordships my recommendation that in the estimates to be laid before the House of Com-mons for the services of the year 1840, the sums be in-

cluded which are necessary to provide for the expenses of
the proposed expedition to the Niger, on the scale already
mentioned, under the several heads of expenditure.

I have, &c.

(Signed)   J. RUSSELL.

INDEX.

A.

ABOLITIONISTS, African, 470

Abu-Muhammed, projected railroad from, to Kurusku, 433

Adamastos, a slave vessel that lost 304 out of 800 slaves on her voyage, 162

Adams, an Englishman enslaved at Timbuctoo, 462

Addah Cuddah, an African town destroyed in a slave hunt, 85

Addahkuddah, a town on the Niger, 472

Advances already made in introducing education and religion, 498

Africa, her early condition unknown, but more flourishing than in modern times, 227; engaged in agricultural pursuits in the twelfth and sixteenth centuries, 227; evidence of Sir J. Hawkins in 1562, 227; of Bosman in 1700, of W. Smith in 1726, description of the country by recent travellers, 228, 472, 473; of the interior, 474; inhabitants in a demoralised state, 231, 290; the knowledge we possess very limited, 269, 277; reason to suppose that her condition is far worse than it has been ascertained to be, 269; her capabilities, 271, 280, 307, 459, 476; disposition to trade, 272, 476; much confidence in the British, 289; favourable disposition of chiefs in the interior, 290; importance of, as a field of European commerce, 305; her productions, 310 to 337; willingness of the people to labour, 328; her geographical position, 357

African statistics, 307, 311; population, 472

African timber, extent to which it is imported, 478

African trade contrasted with other trades to show its present insignificance, 304, 307; its value in introducing civilisation and Christianity, 306; imports increased since 1820, 308; articles calculated for, enumerated, 310 to 329; might be largely extended in cotton, 335; at present checked by the slave trade, 340, 472; the import trade into Africa capable of vast extension, 341, 343, 377; facilities for commercial intercourse, 344; security necessary, 358; principles on which all trade with Africa should be conducted, 441

Agents, in all cases, should be negroes or coloured, 286, 454; to be obtained among the liberated Africans, 492; also from Jamaica, 494; from Antigua, 495; from Wesleyan negroes in the West Indies, generally, 495

Aglae, a slave vessel, description of her stowage of her slaves, 136

C.

O.

P.

Ricketts, Major, on the disposition to work for wages, Appendix C.
Riley, his information, 65 ; his account of the conveyance of slaves to the coast, 103
Rio da Plata, a slave vessel whose cargo was pirated after landing, 190
Rio da Prata, slave vessel, 38; her tonnage in relation to her licensed cargo, 39
Rio de Janeiro, slave importations, 17, 22, 24, 39, 49, 51; its imports of British manufactures for slave trading cargoes, 54
Rio Nunez, formerly notorious for slave trading, but now the site of many factories, 380
Rio Pongas, its schools, 489
Rio Volta, Danish settlement at, 454
Ritchie, his estimate of slave trade in Mourzouk, 65
Ritter, the geographer, his description of slave caravans, 65
Robertson, Mr., his suggestions for rendering Africa a source of profit to Europe, 418
Rodeur, a slave vessel, dreadful sufferings of her cargo from ophthalmia, 137
Rokel, an African town, destroyed in a slave hunt, 85
Rokell, a river, the direct route to the sources of the Niger, 404
Rokou, place where timber is cut, 477
Rosanna, an American slave vessel, 41
Ruppell, Dr., respecting the slaves captured by the Pasha of Egypt, 67; respecting the mortality consequent on their capture, 109

S.

Sackatoo, capital of the Felatahs, 63, 294; cotton planted to a great extent, 334; bills on England negotiable, 474
St. Jago, 31
Saint Joachim, a slave vessel, horrible state of her cargo, 136
Saint Leon, a slave vessel, lost by the ophthalmia of her cargo and crew, 139
St. Mary's, a settlement on the Gambia, its flourishing state, 384
St. Paul de Loanda, its slave exports, 50, 51
San José Hallaxa, a slave vessel, on board which the slaves died from starvation, 147
Schools described, 389 ; desire manifested for learning, 389 ; for agriculture at M'Carthy's Island, 390 ; native aptitude for learning described by Hannah Kilham, 484 ; on the Rio Pongas, 489 ; normal school at Sierra Leone, 498 ; college about to be established on M'Carthy's Island, 499 ; establishment of normal schools recommended, 517